Also by John Warfield Simpson

Visions of Paradise: Glimpses of Our Landscape's Legacy

Yearning for the Land: A Search for the Importance of Place

DAM!

"Looking up Hetch Hetchy Valley from Surprise Point"

Photograph by Isaiah West Taber, from *Sierra Club Bulletin,* vol VI, no. 4, plate XLVI, January 1908. Kolana Rock frames the right-hand (south) side of the view, with Tueeulala Fall (foreground) and Wapama Falls (background) opposite. The Tuolumne River meanders across the valley floor. Courtesy of the Sierra Club

DAM!

Water, Power, Politics, and Preservation

in Hetch Hetchy and Yosemite National Park

John Warfield Simpson

All rights reserved. Published in the United States by Pantheon Books,
a division of Random House, Inc., New York, and in Canada by
Random House of Canada Limited, Toronto.

Grateful acknowledgment is made to the University of California Press for permission
to reprint excerpts from *Visions of Paradise: Glimpses of Our Landscape's Legacy*
by John Warfield Simpson. Copyright © 1999 by John Warfield Simpson.
Reprinted by permission of the University of California Press.

Pantheon Books and colophon are registered trademarks of Random House, Inc.

Library of Congress Cataloging-in-Publication Data
Simpson, John W. (John Warfield)
Dam! : water, power, politics, and preservation in Hetch Hetchy and
Yosemite National Park / John Warfield Simpson.
p. cm.
Includes bibliographical references and index.
ISBN 0-375-42231-5
1. Water-supply—California—San Francisco Bay Area—History.
2. Water resources development—Political aspects—California—
San Francisco Bay Area. 3. Hetch Hetchy Reservoir (Calif.)—History.
4. Environmentalism—United States. I. Title.
TD225.S25S715 2005
363.6'1'0979447—dc22   2004065016

www.pantheonbooks.com

Book design by Iris Weinstein

Printed in the United States of America

First Edition

2 4 6 8 9 7 5 3 1

To Marie

Ever since the business of nation-making began, it has been the unwritten law of conquest that people who are too lazy, too indolent, or too parsimonious to defend their heritages will lose them to the hosts that know how to fight and to finance campaigns.

—December 9, 1913, *New York Times* editorial written in response to congressional approval of the Raker Act, which granted the City of San Francisco the right to dam the Hetch Hetchy Valley in Yosemite National Park

CONTENTS

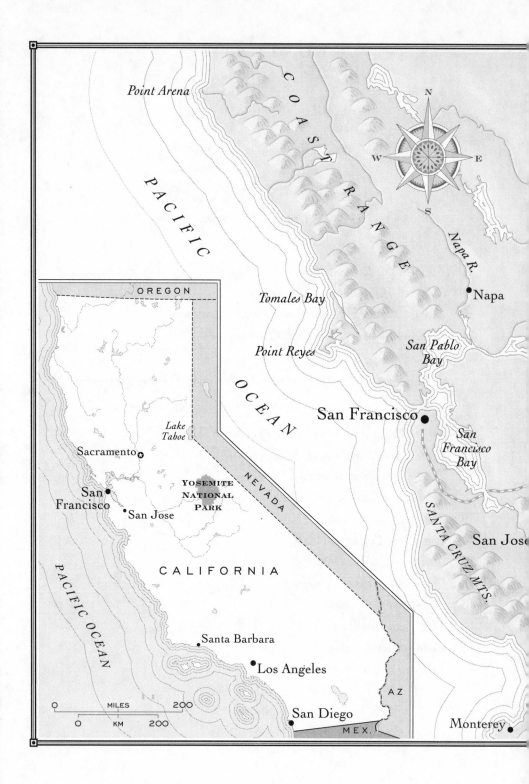

Point Arena

C O A S T

R A N G E

PACIFIC

N

W   E

S

Napa R.

Napa

Tomales Bay

San Pablo
Bay

Point Reyes

O C E A N

San Francisco

San
Francisco
Bay

Lake
Tahoe

Sacramento

NEVADA

SANTA CRUZ MTS.

San
Francisco

YOSEMITE
NATIONAL
PARK

San Jose

San Jose

OREGON

C A L I F O R N I A

PACIFIC OCEAN

Santa Barbara

Los Angeles

A Z

O   MILES   200

San Diego

O   KM   200

M E X.

Monterey

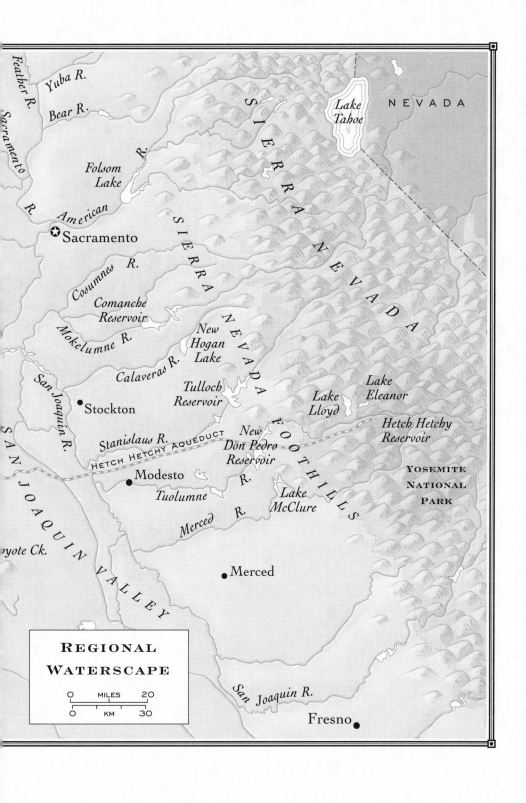

Feather R.

Yuba R.

Bear R.

Sacramento R.

Lake Tahoe

NEVADA

Folsom Lake

American R.

SIERRA

NEVADA

SIERRA

⊛ Sacramento

Cosumnes R.

Comanche Reservoir

Mokelumne R.

New Hogan Lake

Calaveras R.

Tulloch Reservoir

SIERRA NEVADA FOOTHILLS

Lake Lloyd

Lake Eleanor

Hetch Hetchy Reservoir

San Joaquin R.

• Stockton

Stanislaus R.

HETCH HETCHY AQUEDUCT

New Don Pedro Reservoir

• Modesto

Tuolumne R.

Lake McClure

R.

YOSEMITE NATIONAL PARK

SAN JOAQUIN VALLEY

Merced R.

Coyote Ck.

• Merced

San Joaquin R.

Fresno •

PREFACE

The Grand Canyon, Yellowstone, and Yosemite: no words or images can fully capture the sublime wonder of these transcendent places. That's why our predecessors thankfully protected their spectacular scenery from the ravages of resource development and commercial exploitation. What value would you place on their preservation?

Can you imagine damming the Grand Canyon or the wondrous valleys at the heart of Yellowstone and Yosemite? Proponents could argue that we need the water for irrigation or urban expansion, the hydroelectricity for our homes and businesses, and boating for recreation more than we need the undisturbed scenery. Without these necessities economic growth and development might be stifled. They could claim that no other options exist to obtain these necessities, at least less expensive options. They might even say the scenery would be improved by substituting a shimmering reservoir for the valley floor. And they could contend that the development of these commodities constitutes the highest and best use of our natural resources, better serving the basic needs of society—the utilitarian philosophy of the greatest good to the greatest number of people. Practical. Democratic. Progressive. Would their arguments prevail? Debates like these over our use of the public domain are common today. But dam the Grand Canyon, Yellowstone, or Yosemite? Where should we draw the line between resource development and wilderness protection? Surely we wouldn't sacrifice one of these treasures, would we?

But we did. The Yosemite Valley once had a sister—the Hetch Hetchy Valley—just twenty-five miles or so to the north, with towering gray granite walls carved by the same glacial processes that carved its sibling and waterfalls cascading over fifteen hundred feet to a narrow valley floor through which the Tuolumne River meandered. The Yosemite Valley *had* a sister, until, in the 1920s, Hetch Hetchy was dammed, and the valley was buried beneath several hundred feet of water.

"Imagine yourself in Hetch Hetchy on a sunny day in June," wrote John Muir in the early 1900s, "standing waist-deep in grass and flowers (as I have often stood), while the great pines sway dreamily with scarcely perceptible motion." He called the valley "a grand landscape garden, one of Nature's rarest and most precious mountain temples. As in Yosemite, the sublime rocks of its walls seem to glow with life, whether leaning back in repose or standing erect in thoughtful attitudes, giving welcome to storms and calms alike, their brows in the sky, their feet set in groves and gay flowers, while birds, bees, and butterflies help the river and waterfalls to stir all the air into music—things frail and fleeting and types of permanence meeting here and blending, just as they do in Yosemite, to draw her lovers into close and confiding communion."

To Muir and the directors of the Sierra Club, Hetch Hetchy was "a beautiful landscape park diversified by magnificent groves, gardens, and flowery meadows in charming combinations especially adapted for pleasure-seeking." They considered the valley to be "a counterpart to Yosemite; and a great and wonderful feature of the park, next to Yosemite in beauty, grandeur, and importance." Others agreed. The famous geologist Josiah Whitney—after whom nearby Mt. Whitney was named—called the Hetch Hetchy Valley "almost an exact counterpart of the Yosemite Valley [although] not on quite as grand a scale as that valley. But if there were no Yosemite," he continued, "the Hetch Hetchy would be fairly entitled to a worldwide fame." No more. Hetch Hetchy's fame now derives not from what it is, but from how and why we changed what it once was.

John Muir thought the dam would defile one of our most rare natural wonders, writing in 1912, "These Temple destroyers, devotees of ravaging commercialism, seem to have a perfect contempt for Nature, and instead of lifting their eyes to the God of the Mountains, lift them to the Almighty Dollar. Dam Hetch Hetchy! As well dam for water-tanks the people's cathedrals and churches, for no holier temple has ever been consecrated by the heart of man." As the leading advocate for the preservation of America's rapidly dwindling wild areas, as a champion of the national parks and a founder of the Sierra Club, he waged a moral war against the proposed dam with the vigor and rhetoric of an evangelical preacher—which he was, in the gospel of wilderness. However, his passionate message extended well beyond wilderness preservation, calling into question our national obsession with economic growth and development and our dependence on the consumption of natural resources to feed our insatiable appetite for material goods. Echoing the transcendentalist philosophy of Ralph Waldo Emerson and Henry David Thoreau, Muir felt Americans focused too much on material gain and not enough on the more meaningful aspects of life, including contact with nature little touched by human hands. What was progress, he questioned, and what were we willing to sacrifice to achieve it? Perhaps the traditional economic-based calculus could not measure all of its costs.

Muir often looked the part of that evangelical preacher, drawn and disheveled with a scruffy beard. He was the self-made son of a Calvinist zealot, born in rural Scotland along the Firth of Forth but raised on farms in the wilds of central Wisconsin in the mid-1800s as pioneers "civilized" the new state, transforming into private property what they considered in effect to be the vacant, virgin land.

Gifford Pinchot, tall and distinguished, led the proponents. He was a scion of eastern wealth and privilege, possessed of political power played out in the innermost circle of Washington, D.C., and was the father of the U.S. Forest Service and the nation's leading spokesperson for the multiple-use management of our natural resources. He differed profoundly with Muir. "As to my attitude regarding the proposed use of Hetch Hetchy by the city of San Francisco," Pinchot said in 1913, "I am fully persuaded that . . . the injury . . . by substituting a lake for the present swampy floor of the valley . . . is altogether unimportant compared with the benefits to be derived from its use as a reservoir." While sympathetic to the preservation viewpoint, he felt other needs took precedence, and he fought for them with the same evangelical zeal as his philosophical adversary. Pinchot preached the gospel of conservation and consumption, albeit based on wise use and scientific management. Utility, efficiency, and equity were his watchwords. "The delight of the few men and women who would yearly go into the Hetch Hetchy Valley," he said, "should not outweigh the conservation policy, to take every part of the land and its resources and put it to that use in which it will best serve the most people." The question was what use of a special place like Hetch Hetchy would better serve society: development or preservation? Pinchot believed consumptive use took precedent. Muir believed our consumer tendencies should be tempered in such rare landscapes, certainly in national parks, allowing our spiritual needs to be fulfilled.

The proponents prevailed. In 1913 Congress passed and President Woodrow Wilson signed the Raker Act, granting the City of San Francisco the right to dam the Tuolumne River at the narrow mouth of the Hetch Hetchy Valley in the heart of Yosemite National Park to create a water supply reservoir and a source of hydroelectricity. John Muir died shortly thereafter, his death perhaps hastened by the debilitating debate and the devastating defeat. Some politicians apparently had second thoughts about their Hetch Hetchy decision. In 1916 Congress passed and the president signed the Organic Act, creating the National Park Service, in part to stop such consumptive use of natural resources in our national parks from ever happening again. The dam was dedicated with great pontification, pomp, and circumstance on July 7, 1923; the water and hydroelectricity systems came online incrementally over the following decades.

Today O'Shaughnessy Dam stands isolated in the steep-walled, rocky canyon impounding an eight-mile-long reservoir, silent and pristine, that provides crystal-clear water to 2.4 million consumers in the San Francisco Bay Area. A 167-mile-long aqueduct imports the water from its High Sierra holding tank to the mouth of the distant city's distribution network, water so pure that it is usually exempted from federal water filtration requirements, and water so inexpensive that the typical family of four in San Francisco pays less than $14 per month for it. This extraordinary supply fed the Bay Area's phenomenal growth.

However, all is not well with the aging water system. Engineers and administrators have long known about its growing frailties, while for decades city officials siphoned off "surplus" revenues generated by Hetch Hetchy hydropower and transferred them to the city's general fund to finance other municipal needs.

Neither is the aqueduct's vulnerability to earthquake damage a secret. It crosses the Hayward, Calaveras, and San Andreas Faults, yet has never been adequately hardened to withstand eventual seismic events. An earthquake measuring 7.0 on the Richter scale could break a segment, potentially leaving Bay Area consumers without the vital water source for weeks.

Nor is all well with the hydropower part of the system, which today generates about 1,900 million kilowatt-hours annually, enough power for some 325,000 Bay Area households. Bruce Brugmann, the crusading founder, publisher, and editor of the *San Francisco Bay Guardian,* considers the power system the greatest scandal in American urban history. He claims the City of San Francisco has been in continuous violation of those provisions in the Raker Act that govern the hydroelectricity generated by Hetch Hetchy water, and that these violations have probably cost city coffers a billion dollars or more in lost revenues while subjecting customers to decades of higher fees and poorer service.

Brugmann believes San Francisco has never adhered to requirements in the act that prohibit the sale of Hetch Hetchy hydroelectric directly or indirectly to nonpublic consumers, or to the legislative intent that the hydroelectricity forms the core of a public power system for the city. In 1940 the U.S. Supreme Court agreed, ruling forcefully in *United States v. City and County of San Francisco* that the city in fact had been in violation of those requirements and that intent since the power came online in 1925. The problem persists, Brugmann rails, despite the court ruling and the original legislation. He contends that the agreement between the city and Pacific Gas and Electric Company (PG&E) that permits the company to transmit part of the power and profit from that "wheeling" service violates the act's public power mandate. Similarly, he believes the agreement that permitted the Modesto and Turlock Irrigation Districts in the 1940s and 1950s to distribute excess power beyond their needs stretched that spirit.

He might be right. Whether a result of corporate collusion or coercion and municipal malfeasance, or merely benign reasons and historical circumstance, PG&E and the city maintain a working relationship for the handling of Hetch Hetchy power that stretches the spirit, if not the letter, of the law.

When John Muir and others fought the original dam proposal, they believed public pressure would convince Congress to scuttle it, casting aside the vested economic and political interests of Bay Area residents and businesses who supported the plan. They placed their faith in the American people, beyond those directly affected by the project, to decide the issue on philosophical grounds or moral principle. After all, it was *our* national park. Muir was partly right and partly wrong. Despite an outpouring of national outrage, Congress voted decisively in favor of the dam. Those with vested interests held sway in the corridors of capitol power. Perhaps they still do.

A few special places in America—like Gettysburg—tell us much about our character and culture, because these places were once at the center of some extraordinary struggle, physical or philosophical, over our national identity and values. Despite the passage of time, they serve as permanent reminders of that struggle, their presence forever fused with the meaning of the events they hosted. Hetch Hetchy is such a place, a peaceful reservoir isolated in a remote canyon of the Sierra Nevadas, nestled safely in the protective confines of Yosemite National Park. There, a spirited battle raged in the early 1900s over the fate of the pristine valley. There, we argued over whether to dam the Tuolumne River and flood the valley for San Francisco's use far to the west. There, the nation questioned the costs and benefits of resource development for the first time. There, we first challenged the accepted wisdom of growth and expansion and sought to understand our relationship with nature. The debate continues for the fate of the dam, the water it impounds, and the hydroelectric power generated by the system, raise timeless questions.

I've returned to San Francisco to trace the Hetch Hetchy story, a complex story about water, power, politics, and preservation—the greatest environmental debate in American history. Hetch Hetchy was the first national debate on an environmental issue, initially lasting nearly a decade, involving three presidents, Congress, a host of prominent people, and the American public, its significance heightened by the nearly sacred nature of the valley's setting in Yosemite National Park, a place of transcendent beauty and unsurpassed cultural importance. The roots of the debate reach back to fledgling San Francisco in the 1850s, and its results will shape the Bay Area far into the future. Hetch Hetchy exposed the conflict between two tendencies at the core of our environmental stewardship values: our desire to preserve the last vestiges of wilderness and to live as harmoniously with nature as possible, and our need to fully utilize natural resources. It established the basic format for major environmental debates that followed. And it continues to this day, as meaningful as ever, nearly a century later.

The narrative is structured in two parts. The first part traces the history of Yosemite National Park, beginning with the settlement of the Yosemite Valley by the Sierra Miwok people several thousand years ago and concluding with the boundary revision and recession in 1905–06 that established the park's basic configuration we know today. The narrative recounts the arrival of whites in the Yosemite region, their conflict with the indigenous people, and the sequence of steps in the protection of the valley and the surrounding area, beginning in 1864 when the federal government ceded the valley to the State of California as a reserve (state park). In 1890 Congress created Yosemite National Park, which encircled the state reserve. The state ceded the reserve back to the federal government in 1905, and it was added to the national park the following year.

This overview is considered within the context of the Conservation Movement during the late 1800s and the Progressive Era of the early 1900s, periods of mounting anxieties about the rapid pace of social change and environmental degradation as the nation industrialized. Problems posed by modernity, in combination with other forces, fostered new attitudes toward nature and wilderness that prompted civic and political leaders, including Frederick Law Olmsted, John Muir, Gifford Pinchot, and President Theodore Roosevelt, to seek to restrain unbridled resource development and to preserve places of spectacular scenery for pleasure-seeking.

Based on this foundation, Part Two then reconstructs the specific Hetch Hetchy controversy. The story begins with San Francisco's sixty-year struggle, following the 1849 gold rush, to acquire sufficient water to meet the boomtown's surging demand. By the late 1860s the Spring Valley Water Company (initially known as the Spring Valley Water Works) controlled the city's water supply. But people disliked the monopoly, prompting the city's quest to find an alternate water source, whether another private vendor or a public utility. Few people believed the company could meet municipal water needs as the boom in the Bay Area continued, and anger over the monopoly's pricing and business practices was strong.

The decades-long conflict between San Francisco and Spring

Valley came to a head in 1901 when Mayor James Duval Phelan, a staunch Progressive who dreamed of making San Francisco an imperial city emulating the ennobling characteristics of classical Rome, committed the city to the development of a municipal water system that dammed Hetch Hetchy. But the dream had imperialistic implications that Phelan and others overlooked. Its dual connotations—imperial and imperialistic—remain a common dichotomy in contemporary American thinking.

Since Hetch Hetchy was protected in Yosemite National Park, Phelan needed a legal loophole to proceed with his plan. Passage of the Right of Way Act in 1901 offered the answer, granting the U.S. secretary of the interior the authority to approve such a project. In 1902 Phelan promptly submitted a permit application. However, before the secretary made a decision, the corrupt administration of a new mayor, who shared neither Phelan's dream nor his interest in Hetch Hetchy, took office. The secretary did not share Phelan's dream either. He twice rejected the application in 1903.

Bribery would soon buy Mayor Eugene E. Schmitz's support for another water source. The graft probably would have paid off had the great San Francisco earthquake and fire in 1906 not devastated the physical and political landscapes. Reformers aligned with Phelan purged city hall as they rebuilt the city, restoring the imperial dream and renewing the pursuit of water from the upper Tuolumne River. Phelan's plan for Hetch Hetchy was resurrected, though its fate was far from certain as San Francisco again sought its approval by a new secretary of the interior.

The narrative then tracks the political twists and turns from 1906 until 1913 as San Francisco, armed with feasibility studies that portrayed the project as the city's most cost-effective alternative to solve its chronic water supply problem, sought federal permission to proceed with the plan. John Muir, Robert Underwood Johnson, and the Sierra Club led the opponents, advocating the preservation of the spectacular valley and mobilizing widespread public support with a persuasive media campaign. Gifford Pinchot led the proponents, lobbying effectively in Washington for the valley's wise use based on the Progressive concept of conservation. Who would you have sided with?

But the controversy didn't end with the approval of the Raker Act.

Technical complications and legal questions regarding the project have plagued it continuously since 1913. To bring it up to date, I follow the aqueduct from San Francisco to its origin at Hetch Hetchy Reservoir, visiting places along the way that highlight the issues.

First I fly across the country to San Francisco, my final approach into the Bay Area descending low over the suburban sprawl stretching fifty miles down the semiarid peninsula from San Francisco south to Silicon Valley and San Jose, most of the development contingent on the ready availability of freshwater from distant sources like Hetch Hetchy. When constructed, Hetch Hetchy was an engineering and technological marvel, a triumph of Progressive politics. How extraordinary that so large an urban area could develop in so dry a landscape and not want for water.

The drive inland from the San Francisco airport toward Yosemite takes me over Altamont Pass, past a giant wind farm where towering wind-powered turbines silently generate electricity. Like Hetch Hetchy hydropower, and PG&E fossil fuel and nuclear power, the resulting energy is fed into the regional electrical grid for distribution. Each energy source represents a form of municipal imperialism as the city extends its supply tentacles into distant lands, just as it taps remote sources of water and other resources to feed its consuming appetite. Is Altamont Pass wind power more benign than Hetch Hetchy hydropower? Could the former form of energy generation replace the latter?

Beyond Altamont Pass the interstate highway drops abruptly into the San Joaquin Valley, one of the nation's most important agricultural regions and a place dependent on irrigation water drawn from rivers like the Tuolumne that finger into the Sierra Nevada. The valley's settlement story since the gold rush has been tightly entangled with the Hetch Hetchy project. Here farmers pioneered a new type of public cooperation for the development of water resources, forming the nation's first successful irrigation districts. Their dreams challenged Mayor Phelan's dream of an imperial San Francisco. Hetch Hetchy tethered the fates of the two places.

Recently one of the three Hetch Hetchy pipelines that carry in total an average of 220 million gallons of water per day from the reservoir high in the Sierra wilderness to the Bay Area ruptured in the middle of the San Joaquin Valley, shooting a column of water a hundred feet into the air. Over a thousand gallons of pure water gushed per minute onto the irrigated farmland for nine hours, when the flow to the leak was finally stopped. It wasn't the first leak in the system, only the latest.

The geyser highlighted fundamental questions regarding the municipal politics, policies, and practices that govern the Hetch Hetchy system. Born in the aftermath of the 1906 earthquake and fire, the system remains vulnerable to potentially catastrophic earthquake damage that could leave its Bay Area consumers dry, after supplies on the peninsula are exhausted, for the time needed to repair the breaks. Why has this happened, and what is being done about it?

Five days before the break, San Francisco voters finally approved the issuance of $1.6 billion in revenue bonds, among the largest bond authorizations in city history, to repair, upgrade, and expand the eighty-year-old water supply system. Political pressure from the governor and the California legislature motivated the long-overdue action. Several months earlier, the governor had signed into law three bills arising from serious concerns in the legislature about the structural integrity of the system for the 1.7 million Bay Area residents outside San Francisco, who consume about two-thirds of its water and pay a proportional share of the operational costs yet have no representation on the governing board of commissioners. If San Franciscans were loath to properly maintain their essential water supply, that was one thing. But their lack of responsible management also threatened the well-being of people who were outside the city yet equally dependent on the system. The new legislation created a regional water supply and conservation agency to represent their interests, and granted another new agency the authority to issue $2 billion in revenue bonds to fund its share of the capital improvements needed to modernize the system. To make sure the city makes appropriate progress on the capital improvements, the legislation required it to annually report to several state oversight committees. Yet the ruptured stretch of pipeline isn't among the projects scheduled to receive these monies. Funds for the repair of this segment, like funds for routine maintenance, should come from annual operating revenues.

Ironically, beginning in the late 1960s, the city began transferring revenues from Hetch Hetchy Water and Power (HHWP) to the general municipal fund, rather than spending the revenues for utility purposes. Although the city charter permitted the transfers, many public utilities nationwide are precluded from making such transfers, to ensure utility revenues benefit the utility; otherwise, the utility might be used as a politically convenient source of municipal funds in lieu of taxes that must be approved by the voters. In effect, the transfer of HHWP funds in San Francisco violated a canon of municipal finance and governance. Since 1979, the first year records are readily available, those transfers have totaled over $1 billion (in 2003 dollars). In 2000 and 2001 alone the transfers neared $70 million. (This practice may now have come to an end, however: rising public concern has resulted in a charter amendment which requires the approval of three-fourths of the City and County of San Francisco Board of Supervisors to authorize the transfers. The amendment was approved at the same time as the $1.6 billion revenue bond. Another provision enables the board to authorize future bonds on a two-thirds vote without direct voter approval, making it much easier in the future to raise funds for capital improvements.)

Further on, in the foothills of the Sierra, sits Moccasin, a tiny village of low mission-style buildings and bungalows beside one of four Hetch Hetchy power plants. Today Moccasin mostly houses the HHWP division office of the San Francisco Public Utilities Commission. Like Bruce Brugmann, some observers of the commission believe the hydroelectric part of the Hetch Hetchy project has never satisfied a core provision of the Raker Act that all power be owned, distributed, and sold by a public utility. Are they right? How can this suspect behavior persist for decades in apparent violation of federal law and a Supreme Court ruling?

The Big Oak Flat entrance to Yosemite National Park lies about forty miles farther into the mountains. On my way from Moccasin to the park, I'll outline the creation of the National Park Service. The heart of the park—Yosemite Valley—lies about twenty miles beyond the park entrance. A breathtaking view of the valley—breathtaking both because of its wonder and its familiarity—appears suddenly in the distance when you emerge from a short tunnel and round a corner on the narrow, winding entrance road. The entire valley is like that, an American icon, a World Heritage Site.

I'll review the park's use since 1906 as I explore the valley, teeming with tourists from around the world. Have the park's purpose and use changed since its inception? But I'll keep going, past the end of the paved paths where most of those tourists stop, following the Merced River and a tributary higher and higher into the mountains to reach Tuolumne Meadows. Towering peaks encircle the beautiful meadows at the head of the Tuolumne canyon, just below Cathedral Pass, which separates the Tuolumne watershed from the Merced drainage. The fate of the two siblings—Yosemite Valley and Hetch Hetchy Valley—reflects the opposite sides of the preservation-conservation debate: one valley was preserved for recreational use; the other was conserved for multiple resource use. Descending the wild Grand Canyon of the Tuolumne River, I'll explore more of the history and implications of our decision to dam the river and flood the valley.

A movement is now afoot to remove the dam and restore the valley, to undo the past and make a profound statement about the future. Is it economically, ecologically, and technologically feasible? What would we gain by reclaiming the 1,900-acre valley floor now buried beneath 117 billion gallons of water? How would the water and power that Hetch Hetchy supplies to the Bay Area be replaced? Why would we spend so much time, money, and effort to recover this relatively small valley, instead of using these resources to achieve another environmental good of greater urgency and impact? What is "wilderness"? Should the national parks contain it? Can a landscape be restored to wilderness? Would the restored valley be used the same way we now use Yosemite Valley? Perhaps the proposal is simply the latest left-wing fantasy of radical environmentalists and easily dismissed as nonsense; perhaps not.

The story concludes as I stand atop O'Shaughnessy Dam, a still place save for the wind, looking over the glistening water with images of Tueeulala and Wapama waterfalls dancing on the surface in the distance, falls with Indian names of unknown meaning. Their anonymity seems appropriate, reflecting our shallow, at times self-serving, sense of place. Here I'll consider what I've seen and learned. Was the dam a mistake? Should we remedy it? What can we learn about ourselves at this special place in American history and the events it represents, past and present?

PART ONE

The Origins of Yosemite National Park

"General View of the Great Yo-semite Valley"

By Thomas A. Ayres, circa 1860. This was based on the first printed drawing of Yosemite, which Ayres made in 1855, pioneering the now-classic perspective from Inspiration Point. The drawing was published the following year in the inaugural issue of *Hutchings' California Magazine*. Courtesy of the Library of Congress, Prints and Photographs Division

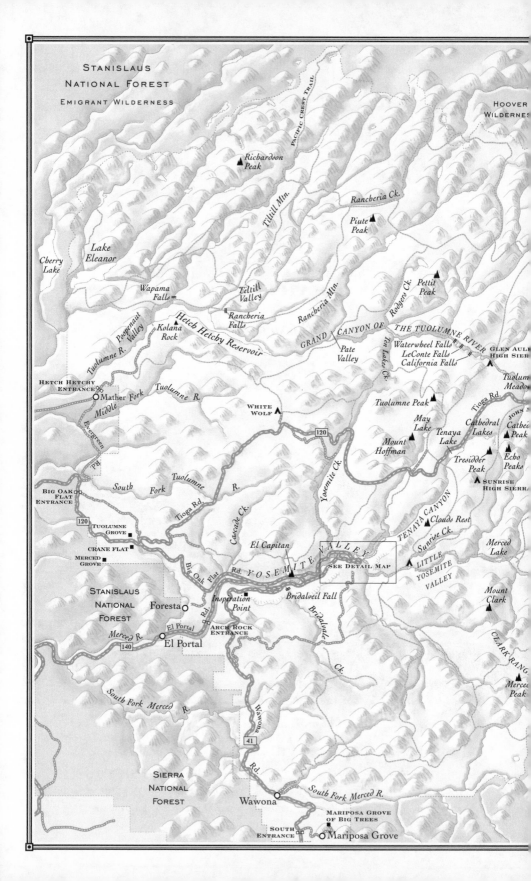

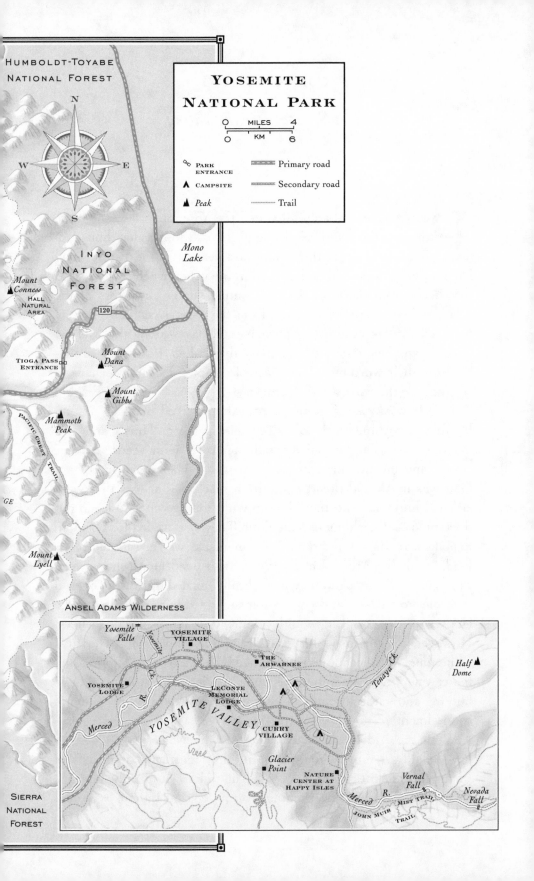

CHAPTER 1

The Struggle for the Valley

People have probably inhabited the Yosemite Valley for more than six thousand years, and perhaps as long as ten thousand. Beginning about three thousand years ago, the Paiutes may have begun to hunt and gather food in the valley when they crossed the Sierra from the east. Several centuries later, ancestors of the Sierra Miwok settled the region from the west. Eventually several hundred Miwok established permanent villages along the Merced River in and below the valley, a place they called *Ah-wah-nee,* probably from their word meaning "place of a gaping mouth," perhaps in reference to the narrow valley entrance.

The *Ahwahneechees* (people of Ahwahnee) lived hand to mouth, hunting grizzly and black bear, deer, small game, and birds, and fishing the river. They supplemented their diet with seeds, berries, clover, and mushrooms gathered seasonally. Their most important food was mush and bread made from black oak acorns that were crushed into meal and then doused with boiling water to leach out the tannic acid, yielding useable flour. They also traded for obsidian to make arrowheads and other implements, as well as salt and other foods, with the Mono Lake Paiutes, who lived along the eastern slopes of the Sierra. And they periodically burned the forest cover in the valley to create a landscape better suited to their needs, a parklike landscape that whites would admire for its pastoral scenery. However, the Indians' purpose was purely functional. The fires maintained open meadows surrounded by black oaks by suppressing the regeneration of competitive plant species. The meadows made hunting and gathering much easier and denied an enemy potential concealment.

While the evidence is sketchy, the Ahwahneechees are thought to have lived tranquilly in Yosemite, until they contracted a mysterious "fatal black sickness" around 1780. The unknown malady, perhaps smallpox, might have been obtained from coastal Indians who had been infected by whites. Immunologically defenseless to European diseases, the Ahwahneechees were virtually exterminated by the epidemic, the few survivors fleeing the valley to live in neighboring villages. Afterward, Yosemite would remain vacant for decades out of a superstitious fear of the mysterious sickness.

Around 1820 the descendents of the Ahwahneechees returned to the valley, led by Tenieya, the son of an Ahwahneechee chief and Mono Lake Paiute mother. An old Ahwahneechee medicine man had convinced Tenieya to ignore the fear of disease and return to their ancestral land. The young leader gathered the remnants of his people, who were scattered on the eastern and western slopes of the Sierra, together with the disaffected from various villages in the region, and they reoccupied the valley. Soon numbering some two hundred people, they became known by whites as the "Yosemite." The origins of the name differ. One account holds that they proudly called themselves the *u-zu'mai-ti,* or *oo-soo'ma-tee,* which means "grizzly bear" in some Miwok dialects; another account believes the name was given them by Indians outside the valley and was based on the Southern Sierra Miwok term *yohhe'meti* or *yosse'meti,* meaning "they are killers." For a generation the Yosemite people flourished in the valley, until contact with whites again shattered their tranquillity.

The search for beaver furs and geographical information first brought whites to the Yosemite area. In the summer of 1833 Joseph Reddeford Walker led an expedition of about fifty hunters and trappers from the Green River rendezvous westward across the Sierra, at the behest of Captain B. L. E. Bonneville, commander of B Company of the Seventh Infantry stationed at Fort Gibson in Oklahoma. Bonneville had been placed on detached service by the government to conduct a private expedition to explore the Rocky Mountains. After meeting Walker at Fort Gibson, Bonneville recruited the famed frontiersman to help conduct and guide the venture. In May 1832, 110 men in a caravan of twenty wagons set off across the Great Plains, up the Platte River Valley, over South Pass in the Rocky Mountains, and into the Great Basin. That winter and spring they trapped and traded in the Green and Snake River Valleys.

Walker's smaller party then left the annual gathering of mountain men in July 1833 with orders to cross the desert west of the Great Salt Lake and make their way to California. By the time the expedition crossed the snow-capped crest of the Sierra Nevada in October, the bedraggled explorers were on the verge of starvation. Below the crest, some scholars believe, they followed the Mono Indian Trail westward along the ridge between the Tuolumne and Merced Rivers, through the heart of what is now Yosemite National Park, quickly descending to a lower elevation in search of food.

"Tuolumne" probably derives from the name given the river by the Central Sierra Miwok people, who lived along the lower Tuolumne and Stanislaus Rivers somewhat west of present day Knigths Ferry. They called it the *taawalimni,* meaning "squirrel place." Fray Pedro Muñoz, the diarist for a Spanish expedition through the San Joaquin Valley led by Don Gabriel Moraga in the early 1800s, called it the *Taulámne,* or *Tahualamne.* The expedition also named the Merced River—*El Río de Nuestra Señora de la Merced*—when they first crossed it on September 29, 1806, five days after the feast for the Our Lady of Mercy celebration.

If the Walker expedition did follow the Mono Trail, apparently few, if any, of the party ventured to the edge of either the nearby Yosemite or Hetch Hetchy Valleys. This means that Walker and the others who kept to the trail saw neither of the wonders just off their path. However, at least one member might have. Zenas Leonard, the clerk of the expedition, described towering waterfalls in his journal that might have been in one of the valleys. The party did see the *Sequoia gigantea* of the Merced or Tuolumne Groves just below the valleys, as Leonard recorded: "In the last two days travelling, we have found some trees of the Redwood species, incredibly large— some of which would measure from 16 to 18 fathom round the trunk at the height of a man's head from the ground." Leonard later returned east to his home in Pennsylvania, where the local paper published his vivid account of the expedition. Several years later the account was reprinted in book form. Word of the treasures waiting in the Yosemite region began to leak out. Yet the treasures hidden in the valley would remain undiscovered by the white world for sixteen years after the Walker expedition passed them by, when the gold rush would bring prospectors to the adjacent foothills in search of other riches.

By 1849 participants in the gold rush swarmed over the Sierra foothills like locusts, devouring the landscape. Yosemite Valley couldn't remain hidden as the forty-niners scoured every creek in the region for gold and eager entrepreneurs scavenged the hills for timber and other profit-making opportunities. On October 18, 1849, William Penn Abrams and U. N. Reamer left from Savage's Trading Post at the South Fork branch of the Merced River, tracking a grizzly bear. Abrams, a carpenter and millwright, had been surveying the area for mill sites to supply lumber for nearby mining camps. His account of their search for the bear is the first definitive written description of the Yosemite Valley:

> Returned to [South Fork] after visit to Savage property on Merced River. Prospects none too good for a mill. Savage is a blaspheming fellow who has five squaws for wives for which he takes his authority from the Scriptures. While at Savage's Reamer and I saw grizzly bear tracks and went out to hunt him down, getting lost in the mountains and not returning until the following evening. Found our way to camp over an Indian trail that led past a valley enclosed by stupendous cliffs rising perhaps 3,000 feet from their base and which gave us cause for wonder. Not far off a waterfall dropped from a cliff below three jagged peaks into the valley, while farther beyond, a rounded mountain stood, the valley side of which looked as though it had been sliced with a knife as one would slice a loaf of bread, and which Reamer and I called the Rock of Ages.

Yosemite had been seen, although Abrams made no mention of Chief Tenieya and his people, who still lived in the valley. Once the valley was seen, its fate and the fate of its inhabitants were cast, despite the area's remoteness—the prevailing attitudes of those caught up in the frenzied race for riches would determine them. Just as San Francisco was beginning its imperialistic quest for water some two hundred miles to the west, the mostly Anglo-American prospectors waged war against the Sierra foothills and Yosemite's inhabitants in their imperialistic quest for resources. Neither the land nor its indigenous people could survive the onslaught intact. Neither the land nor the Indians had rights in the minds of the newcomers; the land was merely property for economic exploitation, and the Indians were merely nuisances to be removed. By the mid-1800s, these ideas were commonly accepted in the dominant white culture as it spread across the continent, conquering what it considered to be wilderness, bringing to it what it considered to be civilization. In so doing they took the gold, the timber, the game, the water, and the land itself. They hunted the inhabitants like animals, burned their villages, desecrated their sacred sites, and even seized their young women for "wives" and servants.

Chief Tenieya and the Yosemites, as well as the other Indian tribal and subtribal groups, differed in their response to the influx of foreigners and the resulting changes, shifting alignments, and the type of resistance or acceptance. At first some Indians stole horses and cattle from the prospectors and pioneers, in place of the food they lost as the game they hunted was eliminated and their territory taken. In late 1850, some Indians raided trading posts and corrals and murdered about a dozen whites before fleeing back into the mountains for sanctuary.

The whites also committed atrocities. By 1851 the brazen behavior of the whites prompted Commissioner of Indian Affairs Oliver M. Wozencraft to publish "An Open Letter to the People Living and Trading Among the Indians in the State of California," stating,

> Since the discovery of gold in this region, the section of the country that was and is peculiarly the home of the Indians has been found rich in the precious metal, and consequently filled with a population foreign to them; and this has been done in most instances without attempting to conciliate or appease them in the grief and anger at the loss of their homes. I am sorry to say that in many instances they have been treated in a manner that, were it recorded, would blot the darkest page of history that has yet been penned. . . . Indians have been shot down without evidence of their having committed an offense, and without even an explanation to them of the nature of our laws. . . . They have been rudely driven from their homes, and expatriated from their sacred grounds where the ashes of their parents, ancestors, and beloved chiefs repose. This is not only inhuman and unlawful, it is bad policy.

His plea came too late to stop the Mariposa Indian War, in which the whites sought to punish the native people in retaliation for their resistance. One of the principal protagonists of the war was James

D. Savage, the colorful entrepreneur who owned the trading post from where Abrams and Reamer had earlier set off in search of the grizzly.

Savage had emigrated from Illinois to California in 1846, following the third expedition of the famous explorer John Charles Frémont. His wife and child died during the difficult journey. About thirty years old with a powerful physique, blue eyes, shoulder-length blond hair, and a beard dangling halfway to his waist, Savage then joined Frémont's battalion and fought under the Bear flag in the war with Mexico. When the war ended and the battalion disbanded in 1847, Savage settled in the Yosemite foothills around Frémont's Las Mariposas estate and started prospecting when the gold rush began. The private estate originated from a Spanish land grant and straddled the southern end of the Mother Lode, making Frémont a fabulous fortune, though he eventually squandered it.

The name "Mariposa" derived from the experience of the Moraga expedition near a creek during its travels through the San Joaquin Valley. "This was called the place of the butterflies *(Llámose este Sitio de las Mariposas)*," wrote Padre Muñoz, "due to its great multitude especially at night and in the morning so unceasingly bothersome that they even reached the point of blocking the sun's rays, pursuing us everywhere so that one of the corporals of the expedition got one in his ear causing him much discomfort and no little trouble extracting it." The name was subsequently given to the creek, two Spanish land grants in the area, and later to a nearby town and the surrounding county, among other things.

But Savage quickly discovered the work was less profitable than trading trinkets and overpriced merchandise to the Indians for gold, or trading essential supplies for gold with white prospectors. So he set up a series of trading posts served by an army of subservient Indians who mined for him. He moved the trading posts around the area periodically to avoid conflict with the influx of white miners.

In late 1849 Savage began business at the South Fork site, fourteen miles southwest of Yosemite Valley. With surging demand and little competition, he made a fortune. Gold had no value to the Indians, so they traded it for what they did value—in some cases necessities and in other cases inexpensive goods, trivialities to the whites, which Savage purchased in San Francisco. He made nearly as much profit trading basic supplies to the white miners who would grudgingly pay exorbitantly for the convenience of obtaining them onsite. Local wisdom held that Savage had barrels of gold dust. He learned the dialects of several tribes, took Indian wives—perhaps over thirty in number—and became the most influential person in the area, revered by some whites and Indians and reviled by others. He was an unofficial intermediary between the various racial, tribal, or cultural communities around Mariposa. Little happened in the area without his involvement.

It was Savage's trading posts and corrals that the Yosemites raided in the hope of dislodging the invaders. He recalled one attack. "While I was located at the mouth of the South Fork of the Merced, I was attacked by the Yosemites, but with the Indian miners I had in my employ, drove them off, and followed some of them up the Merced River into a canyon, which I supposed led to their stronghold, as the Indians then with me said it was not a safe place to go into. From the appearance of this rocky gorge I had no difficulty in believing them. Fearing an ambush, I did not follow them. It was on this account that I changed my location to Mariposa Creek. I would like to get into the den of the thieving murderers. If ever I have a chance I will smoke out the Grizzly Bears [the Yosemites] from their holes, where they are thought to be so secure."

As the violence spread in early 1851 the local sheriff organized a posse to suppress the marauding Indians. Two small skirmishes ensued, ending inconclusively. Fear of a general Indian uprising then prompted local white authorities to appeal to Governor John McDougal for assistance. Like most whites, McDougal had little sympathy for the plight of the indigenous people. (He once told the state legislature that the "extermination of the Indians was inevitable.") He quickly authorized the formation of a volunteer militia known as the Mariposa Battalion to end the insurrection. Two hundred men, mostly local miners, mustered into service on February 12, 1851, with Major James Savage in command.

Before Savage could get his revenge, three U.S. Indian commissioners, supported by army troops, intervened, in the hope of persuading the Indians to accept treaties and move to nearby reservations. Many of the tribes acquiesced; the Yosemites and several others did not.

In March a company led by Savage swept through Yosemite, taking prisoners and destroying property. They were probably the first non-Indians to explore the valley they named after the people they sought to conquer. Tenieya and most of his followers escaped and then eluded recapture by vanishing into the higher reaches of the surrounding mountains. The transcendental scenery of the valley awed some of the troops, as twenty-seven-year-old Private Lafayette Bunnell recalled years later in his popular account of the campaign: "the grandeur of the scene was but softened by the haze that hung over the valley,—light as gossamer—and by the clouds which partially dimmed the higher cliffs and mountains. This obscurity of vision but increased the awe with which I beheld it, and as I looked, a peculiar exalted sensation seemed to fill my whole being, and I found my eyes in tears with emotion." That night as the troops sat around the campfire in view of Bridalveil Fall they discussed what to name the valley. Bunnell recalled that after several suggestions had been rejected he proposed "Yo-sem-i-ty," saying the name was "suggestive, euphonious, and certainly American," and it would perpetuate the memory of the original inhabitants they were in the process of removing. The group agreed, and the name was set.

In May a second expedition set off to "surprise the Indians and whip them well, or induce them to surrender." The force of thirty-five men commanded by Captain John Boling surprised Tenieya and his remaining people at their village near present-day Tenaya Lake. Hungry and exhausted, the Yosemites were rounded up and marched out of the valley with little resistance.

Tenieya and others did not adapt well to their new life at the lower elevation or to mixing with Indians and whites whom they disliked. After several weeks of pleading for his freedom with the agent-in-charge, Tenieya was permitted to leave in late June, provided he pledge to remain peaceful. Other Yosemites quietly slipped away from the reservation and rejoined him in their traditional homeland. No one seemed to care. The last of the Mariposa Battalion mustered out in July.

The peace between whites and Indians didn't last long. A band of Yosemites ambushed a party of eight miners from Coarse Gold Gulch who had entered the valley to prospect in 1852. Two miners were killed; the others made a harrowing escape back to the gulch.

Although the circumstances of the miners' trip and the murders were clouded in intrigue, a new company of nearly forty federal soldiers commanded by First Lieutenant Tredwell Moore, accompanied by Major Savage and a handful of volunteer scouts and friendly Indian guides, was dispatched in June to pacify the resistance. Over the summer, in several forays, the company captured a handful of Yosemites, summarily executing those thought to have participated in the ambush, and they destroyed a village and its acorn stores to starve into submission those that escaped.

The handful of Yosemites who got away, led by Tenieya, fled across the mountains to join his Mono Lake Paiute cousins. Lieutenant Moore made chase with a reinforced company over the Mono Trail, believing almost all the Yosemites had been present at the ambush. The company crossed over Mono Pass and descended onto the plains beyond, becoming the first whites to see Mono Lake. There they found the Paiutes and traces of gold-bearing quartz, obsidian, and other minerals, but no sign of Tenieya and the Yosemites. The company returned empty-handed to their base on the western slope of the Sierra in mid-August. Their reports opened the Mono Basin to exploration and exploitation by white miners and settlers.

Savage returned to his businesses before the end of Moore's campaign and remained active in Indian-white affairs over the summer. That involvement would lead to his death. Earlier in the summer several Indian women and children were murdered under suspect circumstances instigated by a Major Harvey. Angered by the incident, Savage incited Harvey's wrath when the two met in August. A fight ensued, during which Harvey shot Savage to death through the heart. The local court subsequently exonerated Harvey of any crime in Savage's murder.

Tenieya and the remnants of the Yosemites remained with the Monos for a year before returning to their beloved Yosemite Valley homeland the next summer, 1853, after concluding it was safe. Their fate ended tragically just weeks later when several young Yosemites stole horses from their recent Mono Lake hosts for food and brought the animals back to the valley. The Monos had stolen the horses from white settlers to the south, but no matter: the Monos attacked the Yosemites as they feasted on the horses, stoning Tenieya and many of the others to death. Eight men escaped down the Merced River

Canyon, and the surviving women and children were taken back to Mono Lake. Today, several Miwok people living in Mariposa trace their ancestry back to Tenieya or to one of the other Miwok leaders of the day.

While the conflict over the Yosemite Valley and its original inhabitants transpired, Hetch Hetchy received less attention. The Yosemites and at times the Monos hunted and gathered food in Hetch Hetchy, but few lived there. Apparently the Yosemites preferred to live in its larger and drier sibling, probably because snowmelt water each spring flooded the lower portion of the Hetch Hetchy Valley just above the narrow canyon mouth.

The first white to see Hetch Hetchy was likely Nathan Screech, a well-known mountaineer and miner from the Garrotes area. (Garrote was the original name for Groveland, given to the nascent settlement after the lynching of several Mexicans who supposedly stole $200 in gold dust; angry miners selected a sturdy oak tree growing near an adobe trading post there in July 1849 and hanged the thieves. Shortly thereafter, a second lynching occurred in a small town two miles away, prompting that town to be known as Second Garrote.) Screech recalled the events in which he first saw the valley in the distance, and in 1850 when he first explored the valley, probably with his brothers Joe and Bill:

> Once when I was hunting deer and bear in the high Sierras I saw about four or five miles ahead of me a very high mountain and as I had lots of time that particular day I put in the afternoon climbing to the top and after getting on top I had a wonderful view of the surrounding country, especially a passage way of the Tuolumne River from the San Joaquin Plains to far into the Sierra Nevadas and following a deep cut through which the river flowed was surprised to see a wide cut in the mountains that looked like it might be a deep wide valley although I could not see the bottom land or the river from where I was on the peak I had climbed. On getting home I asked the Indian chief the name of the valley and he said Nate there is no valley. It is only a cut in the hills through which the Tuolumne River runs but if you think there might be a valley keep looking and if you find such a place I will give it to you. The old chief claimed all the territory in that neighborhood. [The identity of the Indian chief is not known.]

After hunting a couple of years I finally found the valley and entered it from the lower end and walked up toward the center and faced the Indian chief and his wives. He was surprised a little and said to his women pack up we are leaving. I promised this to Nate when he found it. To me he said I am keeping my promise to you. The valley is yours.

The Screech brothers would shape Hetch Hetchy's early white history in other ways as well. Local legend in the Garrotes area attributes the naming of the valley to Nathan Screech. On entering the valley, Screech asked the Indian chief and his wives who were camped there and cooking a variety of grass covered with edible seeds what they were preparing. They responded it was *hatch hatchy, hatchhatchie,* or *atch atchy,* depending on one's ear for the sound. Another version attributes the name to "Hatchatchie," which was perhaps derived from the Southern Sierra Miwok word *ačcačča,* meaning "magpie." And Joe Screech would blaze a thirty-eight-mile-long trail from Big Oak Flat to Hetch Hetchy, which would become the principal means of access, initially used by stockmen with their sheep and cattle.

By the autumn of 1853 the Yosemite and Hetch Hetchy Valleys stood in wait of new visitors. The calm was short lived. At first only a trickle of white miners and hunters explored Yosemite; however, their accounts enticed others to follow. Two years later the trickle had gradually grown into a steady stream of tourists led by an ambitious gold seeker turned journalist. James Mason Hutchings, a young Englishman, would be among the principal players in the next phase of Yosemite's history, one in which tourist development by private entrepreneurs would predominate.

Hutchings was in the midst of an extended tour of California's wild places in search of material for an illustrated magazine he planned to publish about the new state when word of Yosemite's waterfalls attracted his attention. In July he and an old friend and an artist hired to make sketches for the magazine made the trek to see for themselves. "Descending toward the Yo-Semite Valley," he later recalled as the group reached Inspiration Point, "we came upon a high point clear of trees from whence we had our first view of the singular and romantic valley; and as the scene opened in full view before us, we were almost speechless with wondering admiration at its wild and subtle grandeur." Like so many others who would follow him to Yosemite, the valley entranced Hutchings. He would remain entrapped by it for the rest of his life.

In August the *San Francisco Chronicle* and the *Mariposa Gazette* published Hutchings's description of the valley. Papers around the country picked up the story. The next summer the first issue of *Hutchings' California Magazine* featured an eight-page article on Yosemite, illustrated with four pencil sketches drawn during that initial visit. The word was out, but the valley's remoteness and inaccessibility limited actual visitation. In 1855 just forty people or so reached the valley. Over the next decade eighty people on average made the difficult trip annually.

Reaching the valley from San Francisco required about a week. The trip began with an uncomfortable overnight steamer up the San Joaquin River to Stockton. Early the next morning one set off on a bone-jarring one- or two-day stage ride through the dusty foothills over rutted "roads" to Mariposa. That was followed by several more rigorous days riding on horseback over the steep, narrow, and primitive trails, culminating in the nerve-racking descent down the nearly vertical rocky canyon wall into the valley. Once a visitor arrived, the spectacular scenery certainly must have soothed the pain from the trip, but the rude facilities and the thought of the return trek surely dampened the pleasure. Add to this the considerable time and expense for the trip, including hiring a guide and outfitter, and few were willing or able to make the pilgrimage. However, some of those who did come stayed, placing "claims" on the land and building private cabins and public hotels, resulting in land use and ownership conflicts that still affect the valley today.

In the mid-1800s the policies and practices used by the federal government to manage the public domain were based on several key precepts dating to the nation's birth: that the public domain would be distributed into private ownership as quickly as possible to promote economic growth and development, to secure the borders and foster western expansion, and as a foundation for republicanism; and that the process of transfer would be orderly and managed by the govern-

ment, relying on a systematic survey of land in advance of settlement, and on the auction or sale of parcels with prescribed size,
shape, and location above a set minimum price.

One snag in this approach were people called "squatters," who
sought to claim land from the public domain before it had been surveyed and officially opened for settlement, in effect jumping the gun,
preempting the regular sale of land to settlers. The way the government responded to squatters varied during the 1800s; at times it was
favorable to their claims, and at other times was very hostile to them.
Factions in the government fought vehemently over how to maintain
the orderly distribution of the public domain, trying to balance the
rights of law-abiding settlers with those of squatters and land speculators. Since the nation's founding, land had been its principal
currency; land distribution was among the most important characteristics defining the young nation.

The torrent of people pouring into California, due to the gold rush
and the resulting time lag for establishing federal procedures for land
surveys and distribution, further complicated the settlement process
there, which the state sought to ease with its own land policies. When
white entrepreneurs began entering Yosemite in the mid-1850s, the
controversial Preemption Law of 1841 governed the rights of squatters. The law recognized that pioneers often leaped ahead of the formal settlement process and the sale of land, so it enabled them to
immediately claim up to 160 acres of surveyed land provided they
file an application for the property and they improve and occupy it
for six months, at which time they could purchase it for $1.25 per
acre, the standard minimum price for government land.

The caveat that land must first be surveyed to be eligible for preemption posed another snag, as squatters such as prospectors often
sought claims on nonsurveyed land, usually in remote areas that
would be among the last places surveyed and officially opened for
settlement. Populous and agricultural areas came first, wild lands last.
Yosemite belonged to the latter group. Yet public statements by government officials led local settlers to believe that they could legally file
preemptive claims in the valley even though it would not be surveyed
for years. Between 1856 and 1862 nine officially tried, including
James Hutchings, while others also staked out land, leaving little in
the valley unclaimed. Hotels and other improvements catering to

tourists, and private homes, sprang up at the best sites. By 1860 Yosemite was open for business, if the intrepid tourist could get there.

Three crude trails provided access to the valley until construction of stage roads in the 1870s. From the south, the Mann brothers operated a livery stable and a forty-mile-long toll horse trail from the Mariposa area to the valley. Clark's Station, midway, would become a landmark and its operator, Galen Clark, would become, like James Hutchings, a key person in Yosemite's future. From the north, Lafayette Bunnell, George Coulter (the founder of Coulterville), and several others developed a fifty-mile-long route from Coulterville to Yosemite. A slightly shorter second trail from the north, running through Big Oak Flat and Garrote (Groveland), soon followed. Although the Coulterville and Big Oak Flat trails merged for the last fifteen miles into the valley, the mining towns along their routes would compete for the tourist business for decades.

Horace Greeley made the harrowing trip to Yosemite in August 1859 during his overland journey from New York to San Francisco, to see what all the fuss was about. "The Yosemite Valley (or Gorge) is the most unique and majestic of nature's marvels," the influential founder and editor of the *New York Tribune* concluded, in a popular book documenting his transcontinental trip. "I certainly miss here the glaciers of Chamonix; but I know no single wonder of nature on earth which can claim a superiority over the Yosemite," he wrote. "Just dream yourself for one hour in a chasm nearly ten miles long, with egress save for birds and water, but at three points, up the face of precipices from three thousand to four thousand feet high, the chasm scarcely more than a mile wide at any point, and tapering to a mere gorge, or cañon, at either end, with walls of mainly naked and perpendicular white granite, from three thousand to five thousand feet high, so that looking up to the sky from it, is like looking out of an unfathomable profound—and you will have some conception of the Yosemite."

Greeley foolishly rode the entire Mariposa Trail to the valley in one day, paying the price physically for his late-night arrival at the canyon wall and his descent into the valley.

My friends insisted that I should look over the brink into the profound abyss before clambering down its side; but I, apprehending giddiness, and feeling the need of steady nerves, firmly declined. So we formed a line again, and moved on.

The night was clear and bright, as all summer nights in this region are; the atmosphere cool, but not really cold; the moon had risen before 7 o'clock, and was shedding so much light as to bother us in our forest-path, where the shadow of a standing pine looked exceedingly like the shadow of a fallen one, and many semblances were unreal and misleading. It was often hard to realize that the dark, narrow current-like passage to the left was our trail, and not the winding, broader, moonlighted-opening on the right. The safest course was to give your horse a free rein, and trust to his sagacity, or self-love for keeping the trail. As we descended by zigzags the north face of the all but perpendicular mountain our moonlight soon left us, or was present only by reflection from the opposite cliff. Soon, the trail became at once so steep, so rough, and so tortuous, that we all dismounted. . . . By steady effort, we descended the three miles (four thousand feet perpendicular) in two hours, and stood at night by the rushing, roaring waters of the Merced.

But the reward was almost beyond words as the valley unveiled itself to the exhausted travelers in the early-morning mist and ephemeral light, like the spiritual atmosphere that so often clothes it at dusk.

That first full, deliberate gaze up the opposite height! can I ever forget it? The valley is here scarcely half a mile wide, while its northern wall of mainly naked, perpendicular granite is at least four thousand feet high—probably more. But the modicum of moonlight that fell into this awful gorge gave to that precipice a vagueness of outline, an indefinite vastness, a ghostly and weird spirituality. Had the mountain spoken to me in audible voice, or began to lean over with the purpose of burying me beneath its crushing mass, I should hardly have been surprised. Its whiteness, thrown into bold relief by the patches of trees or shrubs which fringed or flecked it wherever a few handfuls of its moss, slowly decomposed to earth, could contrive to hold on, continually suggested the presence of snow, which suggestion, with difficulty refuted, was at once renewed. And, looking up the valley,

we saw just such mountain precipices, barely separated by interven-
ing water-courses (mainly dry at this season) of inconsiderable depth,
and only receding sufficiently to make room for a very narrow
meadow inclosing the river, to the furthest limit of vision.

Calls for the protection of Yosemite's scenery began in the early
1860s as descriptions, drawings, paintings, and photographs of the
valley amazed people. At the time, many American intellectuals suffered from a nagging sense of cultural inferiority vis-à-vis their
European counterparts. Europeans relished their literary, artistic,
and architectural heritage: Shakespeare, Michelangelo, and Notre
Dame, among so many others. Jealous of that heritage, and spurred
by a growing sense of nationalism and manifest destiny, influential
Americans began to extol an attribute of America that Europe had
little of: wilderness and wild places of spectacular scenery. Greeley,
the famed chauvinistic publisher and politician, was among the most
persuasive advocates for this new view. Romanticism and primi-
tivism now competed with the classicism of the Renaissance and the
Enlightenment in popular preferences.

Since colonization, Americans had waged a moral and physical
war to conquer the wilderness, but by the mid-1800s this alternate
perception and appreciation of our landscape heritage had taken
root. The Transcendentalists were among the first to see the environment as something of meaning and value. Niagara Falls, the
Adirondacks, and Mammoth Cave were early sources of national
pride, although unrestrained commercial development and private
exploitation had already blighted much of Niagara's scenery.

Yet these places were relatively commonplace compared to
Yosemite. Albert Bierstadt's grandiose wall-size paintings of the valley enthralled eastern audiences, capturing and defining the "bold
and true significance" of American scenery, as one critic wrote, as
well as the spirit of "pioneer enterprise and hardy exploration."
Large-scale prints of Yosemite made by Carleton Watkins, a San
Francisco photographer who revolutionized landscape photography
with the use of "mammoth-plate" pictures, became the rage in New
York galleries. Yosemite was indelibly etched into the American con-
sciousness, even though only a handful of people had actually been

there. The valley's importance transcended its scenery to signify our
national heritage and identity, becoming a source of national pride as
had no other place at the time.

The nearby groves of *Sequoia gigantea,* called the "Big Trees," garnered as much attention as the valley. About seventy groves lay scattered along the central Sierra Nevada range, varying in size from a
handful of trees to several hundred in each grove. Their discovery
occurred concurrent with the discovery and initial visits to Yosemite
as prospectors scoured the Sierra foothills. "[The] Big Trees have
been quietly nestled [here] for I dare not say how many thousand
years," Greeley wrote of his visit to the Mariposa Grove following
his Yosemite tour. Two years earlier Galen Clark had named the
grove located several miles from his station. Greeley had spent the
night at Clark's Station after leaving the valley. "That they were of
very substantial size when David danced before the ark, when
Solomon laid the foundations of the Temple, when Theseus ruled in
Athens, when Aeneas fled from the burning wreck of vanquished
Troy, when Sesostris led his victorious Egyptians into the heart of
Asia, I have no manner of doubt. . . . [A] fair measurement of the
largest trees standing in this grove would make them not less than
ninety feet in circumference, and over thirty in diameter, at a height
of six feet from their respective bases, and that several of them have
an altitude of more than three hundred feet."

But Greeley doubted the fate of these "forest mastodons," due to
age, fire, and human volition. "If the village of Mariposas, the county,
or the state of California, does not immediately provide for the safety
of these trees," he proclaimed, "I shall deeply deplore the infatuation,
and believe that these giants might have been more happily located."
For most Americans, the tree stump had always been a sign of "progress," in the national crusade to subdue the land as settlement raced
westward across the continent, ravaging eastern forests in favor of
farms and denuding western forests for lumber and ties. But a new
meaning infused these enormous trees.

Protection of Yosemite and the Mariposa Big Trees followed
quickly and with remarkably little awareness of the novelty, for
never before had the government withdrawn such a large part of the
public domain to protect its scenery from commercial development.
Precedents were few. Congress had set aside the Arkansas Hot

Springs as a national reservation in 1832. That same year a New York newspaper published an article by the famed artist George Catlin proposing that portions of the Great Plains be set aside. "And what a splendid contemplation too, when one (who has travelled these realms, and can duly appreciate them) imagines them as they *might* in future be seen (by some great protecting policy of government) preserved in their pristine beauty and wildness, in a *magnificent park*. . . . What a beautiful and thrilling specimen for America to preserve and hold up to the view of her refined citizens and the world, in future ages! A *nation's park*, containing man and beast, in all the wild and freshness of their nature's beauty!"

Henry David Thoreau asked a similar question in an 1858 *Atlantic Monthly* essay: "why should not we . . . have our national preserves . . . in which the bear and panther, and some even of the hunter race, may still exist, and not be 'civilized off the face of the earth'—our forests . . . not for idle sport or food, but for inspiration and our own true recreation?" America, he concluded, must preserve "a certain sample of wild nature, a certain primitiveness."

And in 1864 George Perkins Marsh's landmark book, *Man and Nature*, linked the protection of critical forest areas, like the Adirondacks, to the maintenance of water quality and soil fertility. The Vermont scholar, lawyer, politician, diplomat, and self-trained naturalist argued that wilderness preservation made "economical" as well as "poetical" sense, such areas serving as "a garden for the recreation of the lover of nature" and as an "asylum" for wildlife, blending practical, utilitarian functions with recreational and spiritual functions. Marsh (1801–82) believed nature, when undisturbed by human interference, always moved toward a balance, a harmony that promoted diversity and stability. Humans, he believed, interfered with that harmony, which then often resulted in waste and destruction. Yet he believed humans existed separate from all other life and were given the earth as home by divine right. Consequently, he believed people had a responsibility not to squander that patrimony: "Man has too long forgotten that the earth was given to him for usufruct alone, not for consumption, still less for profligate waste. Nature has provided against the absolute destruction of any of her elementary matter. . . . But she has left it within the power of man irreparably to derange the combinations of inorganic matter and of

organic life, which through the night of aeons she had been propor-
tioning and balancing, to prepare the earth for his habitation, when,
in the fullness of time, his Creator should call him forth to enter into
its possession."

In *Man and Nature,* Marsh traced the effects of widespread deforestation of European and New England watersheds on soil fertility,
water quality, and even climate, at a time when Americans believed
the landscape was an endless, indestructible resource, one they had
an obligation to civilize. Marsh proposed forest management practices that would lessen the destructive consequences and better maintain the natural harmonies vital to human well-being. His findings
were based on firsthand observations of the profound change occurring in European and New England landscapes, observations made
during years of travel for his political and professional duties. Those
observations he then supported with the latest scientific thinking of
the leading naturalists-scientists of the period.

But the age-old notion of a separation, a disconnection, between
human action and environmental outcome was neither easily nor
rapidly cast aside in America, despite Marsh's monumental work.
Ours was a continent still ripe with resources, a landscape of seemingly unlimited opportunity. Americans then, as now, struggled to
fully comprehend the profound implications of our relationship with
nature. *Man and Nature* was a clarion call for environmental stewardship, a major milestone in environmental planning and conservation
in the United States, for it dispelled the notion that human action
and environmental outcome were separate. In effect it called into
question the prevailing stewardship attitudes and proposed a new set
based on alternate responses to three fundamental components: To
whom is the stewardship obligation or responsibility held? What is
the thing held in trust? And how, or for what purpose, is that trust to
be managed? Whereas the prevailing attitudes identified no real obligation—meaning that little basis for stewardship existed—Marsh
believed God had entrusted humankind with the responsibility to
husband the environment to foster human growth and development.
Consideration of those three components continues today.

Man and Nature was an immediate international best seller. It
made the obvious visible—people affect the environment and it

affects us. The message was most clearly heard in Europe, where the effects of human disturbance on the landscape had had a longer legacy as a result of the centuries of settlement. In particular the book's influence was most immediate on forestry practices there. By the end of the century it had redirected American forestry as well. Gifford Pinchot, the father of the U.S. Forest Service and a leader of the conservation movement, would call *Man and Nature* "epoch-making"; in 1874, the *Nation* said it was "one of the most useful and suggestive works ever published," a work whose message had "come with the force of a revelation."

While the general message of *Man and Nature* remains as timely as ever, some of Marsh's specific forest-management insights were inaccurate or incomplete; in particular, he misunderstood the role of fire as a natural disturbance regime in forests, and other basic differences between forest types. Some scientists realized the errors, but many forest-conservation proponents did not, including John Muir and Charles Sprague Sargent. As Marsh's eastern forest–based ideas were applied unchanged in the west, management problems were inadvertently created that we still struggle to overcome, including efforts to change fire suppression practices.

Hence, the call for the protection of Yosemite arose just as a fundamental change in American environmental values was underway. Nature and wilderness no longer posed the same physical and moral threat that they did to the early colonists and pioneers. People particularly in the more settled eastern landscapes were becoming more appreciative of nature, perhaps based as much on nationalistic pride as on environmental stewardship. Calls by people like Catlin and Thoreau for the protection of wild and scenic places in parks would have been unthinkable a generation earlier to people at war with the land. And the emerging recognition of the environmental effects of human actions by scientists like Marsh enabled people to see for the first time how their economic self-interests were interconnected with their environmental well-being.

Captain Israel Ward Raymond, the public-spirited California representative of the Central American Steamship Transit Company of New York, initiated the idea, having visited Yosemite and been bewitched by its beauty. Fearful of the destructive effects of private exploitation in the valley and on the Big Trees, on February 20, 1864, the recent San Francisco resident wrote John Conness, the junior senator from California,

> I send you by Express some views [mammoth-plate images by Watkins] of the Yosemity Valley to give you some idea of its character. . . . It will be many years before it is worth while for the government to survey these mountains. But I think it important to obtain the proprietorship soon, to prevent occupation and especially to preserve the trees in the valley from destruction and that it may be accepted by the legislation at its present session and laws passed to give the Commissioners power to take control and begin to consider and lay out their plans for the gradual improvement of the properties . . . for public use, resort and recreation and are inalienable forever but leases may be granted for portions not to exceed ten years.

Raymond went on to propose that the properties be managed by a self-appointed commission comprised of five to nine volunteers confirmed by the state senate, that revenues from leases be used to fund the preservation of the properties and any needed improvements, and that the initial commissioners include the governor, an official from San Francisco, Professor Josiah Whitney, "Fred Law Olmsted" (of Mariposa), and George W. Coulter (of Coulterville). The extent to which Raymond consulted any of these people in formulating the proposal is not known.

Olmsted had only arrived at the Las Mariposas estate, located twenty miles southwest of the Yosemite Valley, in October 1863, but would not visit the valley or the Mariposa Grove for the first time until the following summer, after congressional approval of the park. The famed codesigner of New York's Central Park—the nation's first public park—came to California that autumn to manage the sprawling estate on behalf of the New York capitalists who had recently acquired the property and formed a $10 million corporation. He took the position at Las Mariposas as a sabbatical from his landscape-architecture partnership in New York City and his duties as general secretary of the U.S. Sanitary Commission. One of the largest mining operations in the world, the seventy-square-mile property centered on the town of Mariposa and included seven gold mines, four ore-crushing mills, a railroad, a water system, two company stores, lumber-milling and ranching operations, and a mostly male tenant population of three to seven thousand Americans, Mexicans, Chinese, Indians, and Europeans—a management problem worthy of Olmsted's unique skills in land planning and personnel.

Senator Conness forwarded the proposal to the commissioner of the general land office with a request that the appropriate legislation be drafted. Conness also added three additional names to the list of commissioners Raymond had proposed, including that of I. W. Raymond. The resulting bill was quickly drawn and introduced on the floor of the Senate on March 28. The bill was just two paragraphs long and reiterated the provisions Raymond had suggested almost verbatim:

> An Act authorizing a Grant to the State of California of the "Yo-Semite Valley," and of the Land embracing the "Mariposa Big Tree Grove." There shall be, and is hereby, granted to the State of California the "Cleft" or "Gorge" in the granite peak of the Sierra Nevada mountains . . . known as the Yo-Semite valley . . . with the stipulation . . . that the said State shall accept this grant upon the express conditions that the premises shall be held for public use, resort, and recreation; shall be inalienable for all time; but leases not exceeding ten years may be granted for portions of said premises. All incomes derived from leases of privileges to be expended in the preservation and improvement of the property.

The second paragraph repeated the same provisions for the Mariposa Big Tree Grove. The valley part of the reservation consisted of just over 36,100 acres, and the Mariposa Grove added another 2,589 acres about twelve and a half miles to the south; in total the reserve was some sixty square miles. In effect, the bill would create the world's first national park. No one noticed. The Civil War was raging and the bill seemed innocuous and insignificant, mostly a formality; it was certainly not a landmark event.

The Committee on Public Lands reported favorably on the bill on May 17. Conness then requested and was granted its immediate consideration by the full Senate. Discussion was scant. Conness began an explanation of the bill to his colleagues by stating, "This bill proposes to make a grant of certain premises located in the Sierra Nevada mountains, in the State of California, that are for all public purposes worthless, but which constitute, perhaps, some of the greatest wonders of the world." He explained that the purpose of his bill was "to commit them [the Big Trees in the Mariposa Grove, and, by inference, the Yosemite Valley] to the care of the authorities of that State for their constant preservation, that they may be exposed to public view, and that they may be used and preserved for the benefit of mankind." Recognizing the budgetary concerns due to the ongoing war, he continued, "It is a matter involving no appropriation whatever." Nor were any resources of potential value being sacrificed: "The property is of no value to the government," he added. The "application," he explained, "comes to us from various gentlemen in California, gentlemen of fortune, of taste, and of refinement," who requested simply "that this property be committed to the care of the State," and that "there is no parallel, and can be no parallel for this measure, for there is not . . . on earth just such a condition of things. The Mariposa Big Tree Grove is really the wonder of the world, containing these wonderful monarchs of the forest." In closing, he again emphasized the Big Trees: "The purpose of this bill is to preserve one of these [groves] from devastation and injury," as had already happened to another. "The necessity of taking early possession and care of these great wonders can easily be seen and understood."

Few senators had anything to say. Senator Foster of Connecticut commented, "It struck me as being a rather singular grant, unprecedented so far as my recollection goes," although Congress routinely granted land from the public domain to states for various development-related purposes. No mention was made of the nine preemption claims, the two hotels, and the assorted other structures and improvements already in place. Nor were Civil War politics a factor. The Senate approved, as did the House several weeks later. On June 30 President Abraham Lincoln signed the Yosemite Grant Act into law. California governor Frederick F. Low promptly issued an interim proclamation of acceptance on September 28 and appointed the eight other commissioners as specified in the act, until the state legislature formerly accepted the grant and ratified the governor's actions, on April 2, 1866, when it next reconvened.

CHAPTER 2

Olmsted, Muir, and the State Reserve

F orty-two-year-old Frederick Law Olmsted arrived for the first time at the offices of the Las Mariposas estate in Bear Valley at dusk on October 14, 1863. The trip from New York had taken a month. He sailed on the distinctly unglamorous steamship *Champion,* owned by his friend Commodore Vanderbilt, on September 14, arriving at the Isthmus of Panama exhausted in the early morning eleven days later. But the stunning, exotic scenery on the train trip across the isthmus to the Pacific coast that afternoon rejuvenated him. He had never seen anything like it during his extensive travels in the United States or Europe—the thick tropical forest of towering mahogany trees, their dark foliage contrasting with the yellow and green fruit of banana trees growing among cocoa, date, sago, and delicate fan palms, beneath which grew a wondrous garden of brilliant flowers like the crimson hibiscus. By evening Olmsted had boarded the Pacific Mail Steamship Company's *Constitution,* everything in comfort and convenience that the *Champion* lacked, and was soon underway. The change in landscape from tropical to semiarid as the ship sailed northward along the Mexican coast, frequently within sight of land, mesmerized him.

To Olmsted (1822–1903), scenery was all-important, whether natural or designed. "What artist, so noble . . . with far-reaching conception of beauty and designing power, sketches the outline, writes the colors, and directs the shadows of a picture so great that Nature shall be employed upon it for generations, before the work he has arranged for her shall realize his intentions," he wrote. The creation and preservation of scenery, together with the promotion of social welfare, would be the hallmarks of his extraordinary career, which included the pioneering design of New York's Central Park and dozens of other public parks in cities across America; the protection of national wonders like Yosemite and Niagara Falls; the promotion of the suburban lifestyle and landscape by the creation of prototype

housing developments; the articulation of a romantic landscape aesthetic through the site plans for scores of college campuses and institutional landscapes of all types; and the design of landmark projects
like the Columbian Exposition, the U.S. Capitol grounds in
Washington, D.C., and George Vanderbilt's Biltmore estate in
Asheville, North Carolina, where on his recommendation a young,
foreign-trained forester named Gifford Pinchot launched his career.

Olmsted was a renaissance man of immense energy, vision, and
passion, working in the political realm as well. To Olmsted, social
well-being was inextricable from the enjoyment of scenery and the
physical setting. His books and articles were among the most influential attacks on slavery in the years leading up to the Civil War. He
was a key supporter of the Morrill Land Grant Act of 1862, which
began America's grand experiment in public higher education by creating the land grant university system. His work building the U.S.
Sanitary Commission during the Civil War laid the foundation for
the American Red Cross. He enjoyed open access to and close
friendships with several presidents, including Abraham Lincoln,
Ulysses S. Grant, and James A. Garfield, and counted among his
intimates many of America's intellectual and economic leaders.
Perhaps no one has had a more profound and lasting effect on the
character of the American landscape and lifestyle than Frederick
Law Olmsted.

The coastwise voyage north from Panama to San Francisco passed
pleasantly, and the *Constitution* docked on October 11, 1863, among
the scores of ships from around the world that jammed the Golden
Gate. The wharfside commotion reminded Olmsted of New York:
the crush of hackney coaches carrying passengers weaving among
the cargo wagons and stevedores and the tangle of ropes—the familiar sights, sounds, and smells of ports worldwide. And the dry, crude
character of the city, of plank sidewalks, wood-framed buildings, and
dirty streets hastily laid out on a gridiron plan arbitrarily draped
over the rolling hills resembled many western boom towns. It did not
disappoint him, for he expected little of it. Two days later he was off
again, for Stockton by the overnight steamer; and on the 14th he
made the dusty day-long ride by coach to Bear Valley.

The easterner who toured the tiny mining town the next morning
was no inexperienced or unknown man; to the contrary, Frederick

Law Olmsted came with credentials and capabilities matched by few people in the country. His immediate impact on Las Mariposas, on Golden Gate Park, a proposed park in San Francisco on which he would consult, and on Yosemite, was no accident. He arrived with a fully formed set of aesthetic and social values about the importance of scenery and landscape. Las Mariposas proved to be a far greater financial and legal mess than he was initially led to believe, and his management efforts, at times questionable, ultimately had no chance of success. But Yosemite was different.

When Olmsted finally visited the valley in August 1864, camping first at the base of the 2,400-foot-high Yosemite Falls, the highest waterfall in the continent, the pastoral scenery of the valley floor juxtaposed against the raw, majestic canyon walls struck a chord with him. "We are camped near the middle of the chasm on the bank of the Merced," he wrote, "which is here a stream meandering through a meadow . . . like the Avon at Stratford—a trout stream with rushes & ferns, willows & poplars." He continued,

> The walls of the chasm are a quarter of a mile distant, each side— nearly a mile in height—half a mile of perpendicular or overhanging rock in some places. Of course it is awfully grand, but it is not fright- ful or fearful. It is sublimely beautiful, much more beautiful than I had supposed. The valley is as sweet & peaceful as the meadows of the Avon, and the sides are in many parts lovely with foliage and color. There is little water in the cascades at this season, but that is but a tri- fling circumstance. We have what is infinitely more valuable—a full moon & a soft hazy smokey atmosphere with rolling towering & white fleecy clouds.

Yosemite's individual features, although spectacular, did not capti- vate Olmsted as much as its scenery as a whole.

> There are falls of water elsewhere finer, there are more stupendous cliffs, there are deeper and more awful chasms, there may be as beau- tiful streams, as lovely meadows, there are larger trees. It is in no scene or scenes the charm consists, but in the miles of scenery where cliffs of awful height and rocks of vast magnitude and of varied and exquisite coloring are banked and fringed and draped and shadowed

by the tender foliage of noble and lovely trees and bushes, reflected from the most placid pools, and associated with the most tranquil meadows, the most playful streams, and every variety of soft and peaceful pastoral beauty. The union of deepest sublimity with the deepest beauty of nature, not in one feature or another, not in one part or one scene or another, not in any landscape that can be framed by itself, but in all around and wherever the visitor goes, constitutes the Yosemite the greatest glory of nature.

To Olmsted the valley's combination of wildness and seeming domestication most distinguished it. Others sensed it too. Just weeks before Olmsted arrived at Bear Valley, Albert Bierstadt had departed Yosemite after two months sketching the valley. The resulting monumental canvases captured that dichotomy, gaining instant popular success in the East and becoming among the first of his many influential images that extolled the wonders of wild, exhilarating western landscapes as places that were simultaneously safe, nurturing, even inspirational. Yosemite's scenery fit perfectly the emerging American aesthetic that glorified romantic images of untouched nature. This dichotomy, reflected in public preferences for pastoral scenery and pleasure seeking in places perceived as wilderness, would underpin the creation of the national parks and their management, and shape the Hetch Hetchy debate.

Whether or not Olmsted contributed to I. W. Raymond's and Senator Conness's effort to protect Yosemite and the Mariposa Big Tree Grove, the result was certainly consistent with his beliefs. He received official word from Governor Low that he had been appointed to the first board of commissioners in late September, and he immediately assumed a leadership role. But with no budget, no legal powers, and little guidance on duties or purpose, the commission existed mostly on paper. So did the new state reserve. What were the commission's responsibilities? How was the new reserve to be managed in compliance with the vague mandate in the federal legislation? Olmsted quickly set about providing answers.

Typical of his efficient management style and organizational skill, he promptly paid for the preparation of a survey and map of the reserve required by the federal legislation, and began drafting a management plan for the property. The plan took a year to prepare. On

August 8, 1865, Olmsted read his report to the commission. Three days later, with Las Mariposas bankrupt and the enticing opportunities to design Prospect Park in Brooklyn as well as to resume work on Central Park pending, Olmsted left Bear Valley for New York to go back to his landscape architecture practice. He would never return to Yosemite. In October 1866 he would resign from the board of commissioners. (Olmsted would continue to shape American environmental policy and the American landscape until the late 1890s, when his health began a debilitating decline until his death in 1903, after which his son, Frederick Law Olmsted Jr., would carry on.) Even though the commission would struggle for years to implement the unpublished report, Olmsted had nevertheless left his mark indelibly etched on Yosemite's future and eventually on that of the national park system by defining the practical, philosophical, and political bases for those parks.

The Olmsted report began with an overview of the turbulent times in which the reserve was created and an eloquent account of its scenic wonders as context. "It is the will of the nation as embodied in the act of Congress that . . . [Yosemite's] scenery shall never be private property, but that . . . it shall be held solely for public purposes," Olmsted asserted. And when the park would become more accessible, he predicted it would prove an attraction of worldwide attention and a source of significant wealth to California and the United States.

Yet a more important class of consideration than its potential economic worth underpinned Yosemite's value. "These are considerations of a political duty of grave importance to which seldom if ever before has proper respect been paid by any government in the world but the grounds of which rest on the same eternal base of equity and benevolence with all other duties of republican government," Olmsted stated. "It is the main duty of government . . . to provide means of protection for all its citizens in the pursuit of happiness against the obstacles, otherwise insurmountable, which the selfishness of individuals or combinations of individuals is liable to interpose to that pursuit. . . . The establishment by government of great public grounds for the free enjoyment of the people under certain circumstances, is thus justified and enforced as a political duty. . . . It was in accordance with these views . . . that Congress enacted that the Yosemite should be held, guarded and managed for the free use of the whole body of the people forever, and that the care of it, and the hospitality of admitting strangers from all parts of the world to visit it and enjoy it freely, should be a duty of dignity and be committed only to a sovereign state."

Olmsted next argued for the social value of scenery, "It is a scientific fact that the occasional contemplation of natural scenes of an impressive character, particularly if this contemplation occurs in connection with relief from ordinary cares, change of air and change of habits, is favorable to the health and vigor of men and especially favorable to the health and vigor of their intellect beyond any other conditions which can be offered them, that it not only gives pleasure for the time being but increases the subsequent capacity for happiness and the means of securing happiness."

Lastly Olmsted set forth management recommendations for the reserve. "The main duty with which the Commissioners should be charged should be to give every advantage practicable to the mass of the people to benefit by that which is peculiar to this ground and which has caused Congress to treat it differently from other parts of the public domain. This peculiarity consists wholly in its natural scenery." He urged the commission in so doing to keep in mind "the preservation and maintenance as exactly as is possible of the natural scenery; the restriction, that is to say, within the narrowest limits consistent with the necessary accommodations of visitors, of all artificial constructions and the prevention of all constructions markedly inharmonious with the scenery or which would unnecessarily obscure, distort or detract from the dignity of the scenery."

The threats to the park's natural condition and scenery incumbent in accommodating tourists worried Olmsted, so he reminded the commission to consider "the value of the district in its present condition as a museum of natural science and the danger, indeed the certainty, that without care many of the species of plants now flourishing upon it will be lost and many interesting objects be defaced or obscured if not destroyed." He warned them that "in permitting the sacrifice of anything that would be of the slightest value to future visitors to the convenience, bad taste, playfulness, carelessness, or wanton destructiveness of present visitors, we probably yield in each case the interest of uncounted millions to the selfishness of a few individuals."

Yet he knew access to the park was paramount, to enable that "mass of people" to enjoy the healthful benefits of the scenery and to provide revenues to support the park, since it was unlikely that the government would do so. The most expensive part of Olmsted's plan was the construction of an access road.

However, although the park was intended for the mass of people, few of those people could afford to visit a place so remote. While Olmsted and other advocates of setting aside lands of spectacular scenery like Yosemite cited the benefit to the general public, their arguments for preservation had an implied economic class distinction. In principle the social benefit might have been valid, but in practice it would have little merit for decades.

Thus Olmsted had identified the fundamental dilemma confronting the park, and all future national parks: how to promote tourism while maintaining the park's scenery and natural features undiminished in perpetuity. "It is but sixteen years since the Yosemite was first seen by a white man," Olmsted noted, "several visitors have since made a journey of several thousand miles at large cost to see it, and notwithstanding the difficulties which now interpose, hundreds resort to it annually. Before many years if proper facilities are offered, these hundreds will become thousands and in a century the whole number of visitors will be counted in the millions. An injury to the scenery so slight that it might be unheeded by any visitor now, will be one of deplorable magnitude when its effect upon each visitor's enjoyment is multiplied by these millions. . . . It should, then, be made the duty of the Commission to prevent a wanton or careless disregard on the part of anyone entering the Yosemite or the Grove, of the rights of posterity as well as of contemporary visitors, and the Commission should be clothed with proper authority and given the necessary means for this purpose." The report concluded with specific recommendations for the construction of a roadway to the reserve and another in the valley, and for other improvements, together with a request for the $37,000 needed for the projects and initial park management.

Shortly after the state legislature validated acceptance of the grant in 1866 the board of commissioners officially met for the first time. Commissioner Galen Clark was appointed "Guardian of the Yosemite Valley and the Big Tree Grove" with a small annual salary and charged: "to patrol and prevent depredations; build roads, trails, and bridges and maintain them; bestow and regulate leases for hotels and other concessions; use the income from these rentals for improvements; and serve as the commissioners' liaison with local residents." The legislature appropriated $2,000 to fund Clark's salary and the commission's expenses for a two-year period. In effect, from that simple basis the world's first national park was born. Yosemite and the national parks to follow would be maintained under federal jurisdiction for the benefit of the general public while simultaneously protected from spoliation by tourism and development.

Time would prove Olmsted's prescience correct. However, he had asked too much, given the political and financial climate in the state. The 1864 act specified that improvements would be funded by revenues from leases to concessionaires, that the park commissioners would receive no salaries, and that $1,000 per year would be appropriated to pay the guardian's salary and the commissioners' incidental expenses. Olmsted had proposed three times the amount for expenses, $25,000 for road construction, $4,600 for trails, and $2,000 for small hostels. Josiah Whitney and other commissioners were particularly concerned about the road proposal. They doubted Olmsted's amount would be sufficient and noted that the state rarely continued such funding for the number of years it would take to complete the project.

As a result, in its first biennial report, the board revised the Olmsted plan downward to give it a chance to be implemented. Road improvements were left to private companies; $1,200 was needed to buy privately owned bridges and trails to remove charges for their use; and issues related to the settlement of private land claims were left to the courts. Consequently, the commission requested an appropriation of $5,000, "the smallest sum with which the business of the Commission can be carried on for the next two years [1868–69]." There would be no additional appropriations until 1872, due to lawsuits over private land claims in the valley, which cast doubt on the basic validity of the Yosemite Grant. In addition, the state's tax base was a mess, resulting in substantial budget cuts to many state institutions, including schools.

The conflict between promoting tourism and protecting scenery didn't take long to emerge and continues to challenge park managers today. The conflict in Yosemite arose initially from the preemption property claims of squatters like James Hutchings, who were busy building houses, hotels, and other improvements for personal and commercial uses. Were the claims valid? How were the residents of the valley to be accommodated in the new park? What would be the relationship between the park management (the commission and, ultimately, the government) and the concessionaires? How would the improvements made by the concessionaires be regulated to protect the scenery and landscape?

Many of these questions quickly came to a head when Hutchings and two other squatters brought suit against the state and federal governments to have their claims recognized. The legal wrangling lasted several years, eventually reaching Congress in 1868 and 1871, when the Senate rejected bills to grant the claims. The U.S. Supreme Court, in January 1873, ruled in *Hutchings v. Low* (82 U.S. 77) that the claims were invalid and that the government in fact had the right to set aside and regulate such parks for such purposes. By inference the Court ruled that Yosemite and the national parks to follow were constitutional.

But the commissioners and the state were sympathetic to the claimants' concerns, especially to those related to the effort and expense they had gone to in building their hotels and houses, and to the important symbiotic relationship between the resident population, the concessionaires, and the commission in promoting the valley for tourism. The legislature would award generous cash buyouts to several claimants. Hutchings would receive $24,000 in exchange for the rights and title to all his properties and improvements, which he could continue to run as a concessionaire under a ten-year lease. This quid pro quo between the concessionaires and the park continues, as every visitor to the Yosemite Valley today experiences.

And throughout the early years, despite the best efforts of the commission to steward the valley amid the political and legal uncertainties, the financial constraints, competing management plans, and the novelty of their task, the warnings Olmsted made in his report about the damage to the park, as a result of the seemingly small, incremental changes made to accommodate tourists, came true. Little would remain unchanged until the arrival of another person who would become the center of the next stage in Yosemite history.

John Muir arrived on July 15, 1869, giddy with anticipation as he hiked the Mono Trail higher and higher into the Sierra Nevada, mountains he would call the "Range of Light." "After luncheon I made haste to high ground," he wrote of his approach, "and from the top of the ridge on the west side of Indian Canyon gained the noblest view of the summit peaks I have ever yet enjoyed. Nearly all the upper basin of the Merced was displayed, with its sublime domes and canyons, dark upsweeping forests, and glorious array of white peaks deep in the sky, every feature glowing, radiating beauty that pours into our flesh and bones like heat rays from fire. Sunshine over all; no breath of wind to stir the brooding calm. Never before had I seen so glorious a landscape, so boundless an affluence of sublime mountain beauty. The most extravagant description I might give of this view to any one who has not seen similar landscapes with his own eyes would not so much as hint its grandeur and the spiritual glow that covered it. I shouted and gesticulated in a wild burst of ecstasy."

By mid-afternoon he finally gazed down into the valley that would soon become the focus of his life's work. "I came at length to the brow of that massive cliff that stands between Indian Canyon and Yosemite Falls," he recalled, "and here the far-famed valley came suddenly into view throughout almost its whole extent." John Muir had finally found his long-sought home.

> The noble walls—sculptured into endless variety of domes and gables, spires and battlements and plain mural precipices—all atremble with the thunder tones of the falling water. The level bottom seemed to be dressed like a garden—sunny meadows here and there, and groves of pine and oak; the river of Mercy sweeping in majesty through the midst of them and flashing back the sunbeams. The great Tissiack, or Half-Dome, rising at the upper end of the valley to a height of nearly a mile, is nobly proportioned and lifelike, the most impressive of all the rocks, holding the eye in devout admiration, calling it back again and again from falls or meadows, or even the mountains beyond,—marvellous cliffs, marvellous in sheer dizzy depth and sculpture, types of endurance. Thousands of years have they stood in the sky exposed to rain, snow, frost, earthquake and avalanche, yet they still wear the bloom of youth.

The path that brought John Muir to his beloved Yosemite began in early childhood, preparing him for the landmark work that lay ahead. Muir was born in 1838 in Dunbar, Scotland, a small town facing the North Sea near the mouth of the Firth of Forth, thirty miles east of Edinburgh. He was the third of eight children. His father, Daniel, was a hardworking Christian zealot who in 1849 moved his family to the wilds of Wisconsin. They landed in Marquette County as the wave of settlement was civilizing what the pioneers considered to be wilderness. Of his arrival at his New World home Muir later wrote,

> This sudden plash into pure wildness—baptism in Nature's warm heart—how utterly happy it made us! Nature streaming into us, wooingly teaching her wonderful glowing lessons, so unlike the dismal grammar ashes and cinders so long thrashed into us. Here without knowing it we were still at school; every wild lesson a love lesson, not whipped but charmed into us.

He would witness and participate in that transformation, and he would be changed in the process. As a young man, like many people of his day, Muir struggled to resolve his faith with his place in nature as new scientific understanding called into question traditional Christian theology. Muir also strove to find his place in society, leaving life on the farm in search of answers. While wandering the wilds of Ontario north of Georgian Bay, he suddenly, unexpectedly, came upon a rare orchid, a *Calypso borealis,* along the bank of a stream. The flower's two white blossoms illuminated by a stray beam of sunlight glistened like snow against the backdrop of yellow moss. "They were alone," he noted; they stood apart from the other plants, isolated, like him, from the surrounding world. He later wrote, "I never before saw a plant so full of life; so perfectly spiritual, it seemed pure enough for the throne of the Creator. I felt as if I were in the presence of superior beings who loved me and beckoned me to come. I sat down beside them and wept for joy."

There, lost in the most remote corner of the swamp, was that perfect flower, a flower that served no purpose other than its own yet was a thing of wondrous beauty whether or not human eyes even beheld it. "Are not all plants beautiful," he continued, "or in some way useful?

Would not the world suffer by the banishment of a single weed?" That was it—there *was* a grand order, a sublime beauty in all things that result from the hand of the Creator. Science helped reveal it.

From that point on Muir replaced his fundamental religious beliefs with a new set. Nature, he believed, was not just a commodity, nor was it separate from people. The hand of the Creator constructed both humankind and nature. Raw, untouched nature was the most direct reflection of his handiwork. Science did not hide that truth nor shield one from the Creator; instead it served to highlight his wonder, his order, and his purpose. Transcendentalism was only partly right. Nature was good and displayed a universal order, but science, rather than intuition and emotion, offered the key to understanding. Accurate knowledge of nature only heightened one's appreciation of the Creator's majestic master plan.

As his new faith emerged, Muir became infatuated with the famous German scientist and geographer Alexander von Humboldt. "How intensely I desire to be a Humboldt!" he wrote, dreaming of someday traveling to South America to follow in his idol's footsteps, botanizing and living the same scientific life of adventure and exploration in extraordinary places.

Humboldt (1769–1859) had made significant contributions in botany, geology, astronomy, and climatology. He traveled for five years in Central and South America, collecting sixty thousand species new to Europeans, generating vast amounts of climatological data, and producing many important observations and theories, including complete theories of taxonomy, isotherms, and terrestrial magnetism. He climbed many of the Central and South American mountains, mapped many of the rivers, and first described the effect of altitude and physiography on the stratification of plants and animals. On his return trip he stopped in the United States, where he formed a lasting friendship with Thomas Jefferson. A prolific writer and speaker, Humboldt published thirty volumes on his explorations. Of that collected work, volumes 28–30, called *Personal Narrative of Travels*, were particularly influential worldwide. Darwin said it changed his life. In Europe Humboldt's fame was said to be second only to that of Napoleon. Perhaps no other scientist since has achieved the same renown. His books quickly sold out and were reprinted again and again. The scholarly, scientific, and political nobility of the Western world, including Jefferson, sought his company, while common people lined the streets to applaud his passing.

Still unsettled in life and in his beliefs, twenty-nine-year-old John Muir decided to set off on one final grand ramble and walk from the Midwest to Florida with the intent of taking a boat from there to South America to pursue Humboldt's path. That final fling would satiate his wanderlust. It would satisfy his curiosity and leave him ready for domesticity.

Plans, such as they were for Muir, were quickly made. On September 8, 1867, he began his journey outside of Louisville, Kentucky. A few miles south of town he spread out a map, charted his course, and set off on a thousand-mile walk across Kentucky, Tennessee, Georgia, and Florida to the Gulf of Mexico. As he had in Canada, he avoided civilization as much as possible, although practical reasons periodically brought him back. Life in the backcountry refreshed his body; the weeks of quiet contemplation rejuvenated his soul. And there, lost in the landscape, he found his faith:

> The world we are told was made for man. A presumption that is totally unsupported by facts. There is a very numerous class of men who are cast into painful fits of astonishment whenever they find anything, living or dead, in all God's universe, which they cannot eat or render in some way what they call useful to themselves. . . . Not content with taking all of earth, they also claim the celestial country as the only ones who possess the kind of souls for which that imponderable empire was planned. . . . Nature's object in making animals and plants might possibly be first of all the happiness of each one of them, not the creation of all for the happiness of one. Why ought man to value himself as more than an infinitely small composing unit of the one great unit of creation? . . . The universe would be incomplete without man; but it would also be incomplete without the smallest transmicroscopic creature that dwells beyond our conceitful eyes and knowledge.

Although he was spiritually renewed, the ramble left Muir weak from sickness and unable to book passage to South America. After recovering, he headed first to Cuba, next to New York City, and then quickly to California in the hope of pursuing his dream from there. On the morning of March 28, 1868, Muir stepped off the steamer onto the San Francisco wharf, as Olmsted had five years earlier. When he walked up Market Street, the ugliness of gaudy commercialism prompted him to stop a passerby and ask the quickest way out of town. "But where do you want to go?" replied the astonished carpenter. "Anywhere that is wild," Muir responded. But he already knew where he wanted to go. He had heard of a wondrous place in the Sierra Nevada range that he wanted to see. The path he followed went south first, down Santa Clara Valley, then east over the rolling chaparral hills of Pacheco Pass, first crossed by the Moraga expedition in 1805, and into the "knee-deep" flowers covering the San Joaquin Valley. The "floweriest piece of the world I ever walked, one vast, level, even flower-bed, a sheet of flowers," he called it, "a smooth sea, ruffled a little by the tree fringing of the river and of the smaller cross-streams here and there, from the mountains." From the pass he could see the snow-capped High Sierra that embraced Yosemite a hundred miles east.

He spent the summer botanizing and working at odd jobs in the San Joaquin Valley—harvesting crops, breaking horses, shearing sheep. The latter led to the management of 1,800 sheep that fall. Bred for fleece, the sheep were in his eyes examples of humankind's arrogance toward nature, since the breeding process resulted in weak animals inferior in most ways to those of the wild. With the spring thaw of 1869, he led the hated flock, what he called his "hoofed locusts," toward the more succulent grasses higher in the foothills of the Sierra. As John Wesley Powell set off on his famous descent down the Colorado River, and Frederick Law Olmsted worked in New York on Central Park and other projects, John Muir entered the Yosemite Valley.

He knew instantly he had at last found his true home, the one place on earth where God meant him to be. He rid himself of the flock that fall and took a job running a small sawmill for his employer, James Hutchings, at the base of Lower Yosemite Fall. The mill processed mostly fallen timber and was powered by the natural flow of the stream, so it operated only during the wet portions of the year. This left Muir with time to wander the mountains, to botanize, to commune with nature in a virtual temple of wonders. There he disappeared for days, relying on his strength of character and knowledge of the land to survive.

Those were really pilgrimages, journeys to his Mecca, to his holy land. Little in the landscape escaped his keen eye or consuming curiosity during his trips to the altar. He soon knew the mountains intimately. The formative geological forces that shaped the valley particularly intrigued him. To the area's other residents, Muir was harmless, offbeat, and a bit fanatical in his zeal to preach his unique religion in which God was best known through wildness. But he made a great guide for those who could tolerate the endless, enthusiastic proselytizing.

In May 1871, Muir learned from a longtime intimate named Jeanne Carr that Ralph Waldo Emerson, the patriarch of American letters, was going to visit Yosemite with a group of Boston literati. The news was like a blessing from above, and Muir could barely contain his excitement. Emerson was truly a kindred spirit, Muir thought. Surely he was one who shared his religion. Perhaps, then, Emerson might be convinced to stay and commune with him at Yosemite's high altar before he returned to the comfortable parlors of Boston.

Emerson's party stayed at Leidig's Hotel by the base of Sentinel Rock. They found the accommodations too Spartan for their refined tastes, but the magnificent scenery made excellent compensation. Muir hovered about the fringes of the group, too shy to approach the elder Emerson, although Carr had extolled one to the other. However, when Muir learned the group was planning to leave in several days, he left Emerson a note at the hotel making his request: "Do not thus drift away with the mob while the spirits of these rocks and waters hail you after long waiting as their kinsman and persuade you to closer communion. . . . I invite you to join me in a month's worship with Nature in the high temples of the great Sierra Crown beyond our holy Yosemite. It will cost you nothing save the time and very little of that[,] for you will be mostly in eternity. . . . In the name of a hundred cascades that barbarous visitors never see[,] . . . in the name of all the spirit creatures of these rocks and of this whole spiritual atmosphere Do not leave us *now.* With most cordial regards I am yours in Nature, John Muir."

Muir's plea struck a chord with the sixty-eight-year-old transcendentalist. The next morning the venerable man and a companion rode out to the mill to meet their brother-in-nature. By that time

Muir was living in a small room he had constructed that jutted out from the end of the mill, precariously overhanging the stream below. The spectacular views made up for the room's tiny size. South Dome loomed stately above, and to the west the valley floor lay open like a flower. There, in the "hang-nest," the two met repeatedly until the party departed. Muir fussed about the piles of specimens that cluttered in every corner of the room, eagerly, gleefully showing Emerson his treasures and answering the questions they raised with a flood of arcane information. Muir reiterated his invitation. Although tempted, Emerson deferred to his companion and the plans of the entire party and declined. Muir later wrote, "His party, full of indoor philosophy, failed to see the natural beauty and fullness of promise of my wild plan and laughed at it in good-natured ignorance, as if it were necessarily amusing to imagine that Boston people might be led to accept Sierra manifestations of God at the price of rough camping."

Muir did accompany Emerson's group through the Mariposa Big Tree Grove on the last day of its visit, bemusing the easterners with his wide-ranging literary tastes while he also identified every tree species they passed. At the end of the day Emerson bid farewell to Muir with a tip of his hat from a distant ridge; with that polite nod, the leader of the transcendental movement unknowingly passed on the mantle of literary leadership in American environmental philosophy.

Over the next months, still in the afterglow of the encounter, Muir flooded Emerson with letters and packages of specimens and persistently made his plea for the sage to join him in nature's sanctum sanctorum. Emerson responded by inviting Muir to join his group in Concord when the loneliness and solitude of nature became too much, as he had another young protégé named Henry David Thoreau some years earlier. He also sent along two volumes of his collected essays. But surely the wildness of the Sierra had as much or more instruction to offer than the proper parlors of New England, Muir reasoned. Each man remained in his place.

Muir pored over Emerson's work, dissecting it in meticulous detail, and found it filled with technical errors and inaccuracies in its depiction and descriptions of nature. To him Emerson seemed only able to accept nature as a commodity for human use. Nature was only an imperfect reflection of the "Oversoul." Muir's beliefs arose independently; he was never one of the Transcendentalists, although he shared some of their philosophical tenets. He would continue to admire Emerson, not so much for his knowledge of nature but rather for his quiet, granite-like character and the philosophy expressed in the poetry of his powerful writing. Thoreau's work was more to Muir's liking, especially *Walden* because of its more accurate depiction of nature, which he read for the first time in 1872 after Emerson's visit. Still, he felt Thoreau needed a strong dose of Yosemite. Shortly before his death in 1882, Ralph Waldo Emerson added Muir's name as the last on a list he kept called "My Men."

Gaunt and scraggly, John Muir rarely looked the role of a prominent person that influenced presidents and the politically powerful, or the social and artistic elite, or leading scientists. He often looked more like a homeless wanderer, particularly until he settled into domestic life. His role as a national figure started auspiciously when he published his first article in the nation's leading newspaper. On December 5, 1871, shortly after Emerson's visit to Yosemite, Muir's first piece, "Yosemite's Glaciers," appeared in Horace Greeley's *New York Tribune.* The article was not a colorful piece of philosophical prose but a significant scientific explanation of how glaciers carved Yosemite's valleys. Muir based his explanation on physical evidence he gathered while wandering the park, which countered the prevailing wisdom proposed by the famed California state geologist Josiah Dwight Whitney. Whitney believed the valley was formed by "random 'cataclysmic' shiftings and heavings of the Earth's crust." Clarence King, another influential scientist and a former Whitney assistant, thought much the same. Whitney, King, and other scientists had studied glaciers in Yosemite's high country since before Muir arrived in California, but they disagreed with Muir about the extent of glaciation and the role it played in eroding the Sierra.

Muir intuitively made the connection between the glaciers and the valley's formation and then sought physical evidence to support his controversial hypothesis. He found that evidence sprinkled about the valley in glacial scoring, glacial mud (finely ground-up rock), and small residual glaciers in the upper reaches of the Merced River basin. Scientists remained skeptical, so he gathered additional empirical evidence using stakes planted in snow fields to measure the glacial movement of about an inch per day. As he found corroborating evidence and word spread among prominent scientists, friends encouraged Muir to publish his extraordinary findings. Other scientists would expand on his discoveries by explaining how the glaciers were formed, and by linking glacial periods to climate change.

The article would lead to academic and scientific notoriety—not attention Muir particularly sought or approved of, since he viewed much of the formal scientific community with disdain. He thought many academics were too disconnected from the physical world they studied. And it would also lead to a stream of additional publications that described Yosemite's physical makeup, attracting many of the nation's foremost scientists to the hang-nest and the giant living laboratory that lay just outside it.

But Muir's technical-based articles created other writing opportunities that would result in his broader public appeal. Again, friends who noted his unique philosophy and eloquent writing skills encouraged that path. His early articles were modest pieces for the local newspapers and the California-based literary magazine *Overland Monthly,* which paid little but soon opened the door to more significant articles for New York–based national magazines such as *Harper's* and *Scribner's* that (unlike the *Overland*) promptly paid $150 to $200 per article. His interest in writing and preaching his gospel to scores of potential converts nationwide blossomed in the early 1870s, as did his success. Muir discovered he could make a living with his pen. His popular and influential writing would bring him into close contact with leading naturalists, scientists, artists, and authors, as well as politicians.

The *Tribune* article was followed with other pieces about Yosemite's glaciers in the *Overland Monthly,* to which he soon become a frequent contributor; excerpts were reprinted in the *American Journal of Science* and the *Proceedings of the American Association for the Advancement of Science.* The *Overland* articles provided more opportunity for his creative writing talents to emerge and more opportunity to tell his personal philosophy. Additional articles on Yosemite quickly followed in the *Tribune* and the *Boston Evening Transcript.*

While Muir's literary career was quickly gaining momentum, his personal life in Yosemite was disintegrating, largely as a result of his loneliness and personal issues that stemmed from his friendship with

Elvira Hutchings and his stormy relationship with her fiery husband, James Hutchings. What he needed to do as a result became clear by the spring of 1873. Drawn deeper and deeper into a literary career, and with the personal situation in the valley becoming intolerable, Muir decided to move to San Francisco. The troubling thought of leaving his beloved Yosemite for the city probably hung in the back of his mind for months, an unspoken, unpleasant possibility. But by autumn 1873 it was out in the open. He made the move to Oakland in mid-November and spent the next ten months sequestered, penning one piece after another, when he next escaped to the mountains for relief. He returned to civilization in the Bay Area that winter, there to settle into a domestic pattern that would last the rest of his life: relatively long periods in the city, punctuated by trips to the wilderness in Alaska and around the world; he was never again in Yosemite for more than brief visits, although it would forever remain his spiritual home.

Once situated in the city Muir pursued his fledgling literary career to earn a conventional living. His vivid, powerful style appealed to the steadily growing number of Americans, mostly easterners, who read descriptions of nature by authors like Audubon and Thoreau, or those who read wilderness adventure stories like those by James Fenimore Cooper, or those who enjoyed travelogues to America's places of great wilderness scenery, places like the Sierra Nevada, called the "California Alps" by some, including Muir, still competing with their European cousins. Writing in *Harper's*, Muir described a sudden thunderstorm on Mt. Shasta: "Presently a vigorous thunder-bolt crashes through the crisp sunny air, ringing like steel on steel, its startling detonation breaking into a spray of echoes among the rocky canyon below. Then down comes a cataract of rain to the wild gardens and groves. The big crystal drops tingle the pine needles, plash and spatter on granite pavements, and pour down the sides of ridges and domes in a net-work of gray bubbling rills. In a few minutes the firm storm cloud withers to a mesh of dim filaments and disappears, leaving the sky more sunful than before."

Unlike the work of other popular authors, who approached nature as an adversary with suspicion and fear, judged it only according to human use, romanticized and glossed over its infinite detail, Muir's writing embodied a fresh, new perspective. From the early 1870s until his death in 1914 his work advanced American environmental thinking toward a more appreciative, more respectful, and more informed attitude toward nature. Following the path marked by the transcendentalists and George Perkins Marsh, Muir set another milestone in the evolution of American environmental thought, his philosophy the genesis of the preservation movement.

Often uncomfortable in the crowds and civility of urban life, Muir spent the 1870s preaching the virtues of nature and wilderness. The more converts he won, the more environmental souls he saved, the more he also inadvertently created an army of heretics—converts meant visitors to the remote, untouched wilderness he so eloquently extolled. Ironically, the furry "hoofed-locusts" he once shepherded during his first days in Yosemite were replaced with a new hoofed locust of his own persuasion. He was once again a shepherd tending a flock.

At the same time other, less sensitive forms of human intrusion encroached upon his temples, as stockmen and lumbermen also threatened his wilderness sanctuaries. By the 1870s those conflicts created a debate regarding the proper use of the nation's dwindling wild land and with it gave birth to the American conservation movement. As Thoreau, Olmsted, and Muir proposed, and as Theodore Roosevelt would proclaim, wild lands were valuable not just as a potential source of natural resources but as important psychological and cultural resources. By the end of the nineteenth century American values had shifted sufficiently to let people see the dilemma. What was the best use of the scarce wilderness resource? For many people wilderness no longer posed a physical or psychological threat, nor was it so prevalent that it could be used wastefully. The issue became one of finding the greater good between conflicting, competing interests, and defining our stewardship responsibilities.

Muir remained in the Bay Area successfully spreading his gospel and swirling in the currents of the emerging conservation movement until he married in 1880. Children quickly followed, by which time Muir had built a home on his father-in-law's prosperous fruit farm in Martinez, twenty miles as a bird flies northeast of Oakland. Married life and fatherhood apparently gave Muir a long-sought sense of emotional security. He no longer rambled as freely. Perhaps his family obligations, his sporadic writing, and his extensive reading now satisfied his environmental soul.

As the conservation debate gradually intensified during the last quarter of the 1800s, Muir's personal philosophy continued to evolve, shaped by provocative people and ideas, some already circulating in the Bay Area, others gained from books. He began to question the widespread abuses of private land that stemmed from monopolies and the laissez-faire, free-market system that often rewarded greed and short-term return over environmental or social responsibility. Although an affluent landowner, Muir began to support federal ownership of wild, mountain lands that possessed spectacular scenery, in order to safeguard their wonders for public enjoyment.

He read in John Ruskin (1819–1900), the English romantic writer, philosopher, and painter, how environmental degradation resulted from fundamental flaws in the basic economic system. Muir thought little of Ruskin's ideas when he first read them, while living in Yosemite. Ruskin, he felt, needed a good dose of Yosemite to sharpen his romantic ideas—as did Emerson and Thoreau—and to humble him. However, when he reexamined Ruskin's work in the mid-1880s he found valuable ideas, including Ruskin's criticism of cities and technology and his call to reward landowners who maintained their property in "conditions of natural grace."

These influences led Muir to assume a more proactive philosophical stance toward the preservation of the wilderness landscapes he so cherished. He began to advocate more overt governmental intervention to offset private abuse of the public domain, although he remained outside the political fray, not yet acting on his beliefs. Eventually he would be drawn into the battle, and the fight to protect Yosemite would place him at the center of the national debate over the fate of America's dwindling wilderness. Others were beginning to take the same stance as they, too, reacted against the wanton degradation caused by logging, mining, grazing, and farming that encroached farther and farther into the nation's landscape treasures. The American conservation movement was founded out of their concerns, laying the groundwork for the creation of Yosemite National Park and the national battle over Hetch Hetchy.

CHAPTER 3

Pinchot, the Park, and the Conservation Movement

T hrough all the wonderful, eventful centuries since Christ's time," wrote John Muir of his beloved forests, "God has cared for these trees, saved them from drought, disease, avalanches, and a thousand straining, leveling tempests and floods; but he cannot save them from fools—only Uncle Sam can do that." Muir had joined a growing crusade to protect the nation's forests comprised of outdoorsmen who sought to protect the components of wilderness on which their outdoor interests were based; in so doing, they were also sympathetic to the protection of wilderness in general.

Among the first members of the crusade were the mountain and alpine clubs formed in the 1860s and 1870s, such as the Appalachian Mountain Club, founded in 1876 by a group of Boston academics and hikers who wanted to promote and protect their interests in hiking the Appalachian wilderness. Other groups included the Audubon Society, organized by George Bird Grinnell in 1886 to protect birds and their eggs; and the Boone and Crockett Club, a group of big-game hunters from New York City established in 1887 by Grinnell and Theodore Roosevelt to protect wilderness as a means of protecting quarry. Club membership was limited to one hundred men who had killed "in fair chase" at least three species of North American big game.

On the West Coast a group of professors from Berkeley and Stanford and outdoor enthusiasts from the Bay Area met in the office of a San Francisco lawyer on May 28, 1892, to discuss the organization of an alpine club modeled after the Appalachian Mountain Club. The articles of incorporation ratified a week later established the new club's purpose: "To explore, enjoy and render accessible the mountain regions of the Pacific Coast; to publish authentic information concerning them; to enlist the support and co-operation of the people and the government in preserving the forests and other natural features of the Sierra Nevada Mountains." The idea to start a mountaineers club had been suggested by a Berkeley professor six years earlier. John Muir had been quietly at work since 1889 enlisting the participation of worthy members at the urging of his editor and friend Robert Underwood Johnson. Those twenty-seven men formed the Sierra Club that day and elected John Muir its first president, a position he held for twenty-two years, until his death in 1914.

Those who conceived American conservationism were mostly people of great distinction and social position. And most, like the leaders of transcendentalism, were among the liberal, intellectual, and wealthy elite of the East Coast: Charles Sprague Sargent, George Bird Grinnell, and Robert Underwood Johnson among them. A Boston blue blood, Sargent was the director of the Arnold Arboretum at Harvard University and a great friend and supporter of Muir. Following in the footsteps of Emerson and the transcendentalists, he was welcome in the fashionable parlors of Beacon Hill and eastern high society. Sargent was a key matchmaker in the movement, instrumental in connecting Muir with those of like minds in the eastern establishment.

Grinnell was also from a wealthy, well-connected family. Omnipresent in conservation causes, he was editor and publisher of *Forest and Stream,* the leading sportsmen's magazine of the day. His activism likely stemmed from the influence of the man for whom he named his organization of birders. The Grinnells had had a long relationship with the Audubons. George Grinnell grew up in Audubon Park in upper Manhattan, the property once owned by its namesake. He hunted muskrats as a boy with Audubon's grandson along the Harlem River in the 1860s and even attended a school run by the painter's widow.

Robert Underwood Johnson was not a member of the eastern elite by birth; rather, he was a transplanted midwesterner raised in a conservative Scottish Presbyterian and Quaker home in a small rural community in Indiana. Much of Johnson's effect in the conservation movement stemmed from his position as an editor of *Century,* the nation's leading literary magazine and successor to *Scribner's Monthly,* which had published many of Muir's best early works in the 1870s while Johnson was a junior editor. He used the magazine as a forum to promote his proconservation views. By the time Johnson

assumed an associate editorship of *Century* in the 1880s, the magazine was at its pinnacle, paying the highest fees for authors of the cal-
iber of Henry James and Mark Twain. The magazine sought to
promote American literature and culture as separate and distinct
from those of Europe and even to reform national politics. It rarely
shied from social or political crusades. Since the emerging conservation debate was uniquely American, the magazine was naturally
attracted to it and to Muir's distinctive voice.

The first conservation battles fought by those founders usually
concerned the conflict between conserving the beautiful scenery of a
wilderness area for recreational viewing and pleasure seeking, and
the commercial exploitation of its resources. One of the first battles
was fought over Niagara Falls. The conflict there was apparent by
the early 1800s as crass commercialism ringed what many considered the nation's greatest natural spectacle. Alexis de Tocqueville saw
this conflict during his visit to the falls in 1831. He warned its
grandeur was about to be lost and prophesied that a saw mill would
be built at its base within ten years. Few paid heed as calls for
exploitation drowned those for conservation. Frederick Law
Olmsted and Charles Eliot Norton, of Harvard, would finally lead a
campaign to persuade the state of New York to set aside a four-
hundred-acre park around Niagara Falls in 1885. Canada followed
suit on its side about a year later.

The American park soon proved too small to protect the falls from
the effects of nearby hydropower and industrial development. On
visiting the Niagara in 1906 English author H. G. Wells commented,
"Its spectacular effect, its magnificent and humbling size and splendor, were long since destroyed beyond recovery by the hotels, the
factories, the power-houses, the bridges and tramways and hoard-
ings that arose about it." Yet like most commentators of the day he
concluded, "It seems altogether well that all the froth and hurry of
Niagara at last, all of it, dying into hungry canals of intake, should
rise again in light and power." Public preference still valued development over conservation.

The Adirondacks were the focus of another of the nation's early
conservation debates. Like Niagara Falls, the Adirondack region in
upstate New York had long been valued as a place for passive outdoor recreation where people marveled at its spectacular scenery.

Perhaps no other American wilderness was so often written about or was so widely known in the mid-1800s, in part because of the area's proximity to the eastern cities. When settlement and resource exploitation threatened the scenery of the remnant, island-like wilderness that sat surrounded by the advancing sea of eastern civilization, calls were made for its protection. However, the actual proposals that followed were politically justified primarily on utilitarian needs—to protect the timber as a valuable resource and, drawing on the revelations in *Man and Nature,* to protect the forest as a steady source of water for the region's rivers and canals. Big business joined forces with the conservationists in support of protection in the 1870s and early 1880s as water levels in the Erie Canal and Hudson River were purported to be dropping. The supposed crisis made for strange bedfellows as Grinnell's *Forest and Stream* and Greeley's *Tribune* both supported the proposal.

On May 15, 1885, New York State established the Adirondack Forest Reserve, setting aside 715,000 acres as wild forestlands. But the issue was far from over. In 1892 the state revised the reserve and made it a state park of more than 3 million acres in response to growing support for aesthetic values. The new park had multiple purposes: to provide recreation for the public's health and pleasure; to preserve forestland to ensure a future supply of timber; and to preserve the headwaters of the chief rivers of the state.

Fearing that designation as a park might make it susceptible to abuses, Sargent and his supporters in 1894 won a revision in the state constitution to permanently preserve the wilderness. New York declared an area nearly the size of Connecticut as "forever wild." While the heart of the matter remained utilitarian—protection of the watershed for commercial reasons such as supplying municipal water—aesthetic considerations, reasons less utilitarian, also gained recognition.

Throughout the conservation movement's formative years, tourist development in Yosemite Valley grew. The board of commissioners' publicity and promotional efforts succeeded. Yosemite was known worldwide. Concessionaires thrived, with the commission's blessing, although litigation persisted with some to resolve land claims and leases, in particular those of James Hutchings. By the mid-1870s annual tourism topped 2,500 visitors as the valley filled during the summer season with people who stayed at its two settlements: the "Upper Village," centered on Hutchings's hotel, which was soon contentiously taken over by others, and contained a store, a saloon, and a bathhouse; and the larger "Lower Village," which sat less than a mile away and contained several hotels, a toll house, a laundry, a butcher shop, stables, several residences, and other miscellaneous buildings.

As Olmsted had predicted, the vegetation in the valley had begun to change due to the clearing of building sites and the creation of pastures. However, Olmsted also contributed to this change by supporting fire suppression, based on his shallow understanding of disturbance regimes and plant succession, and on his preference for parklike landscape scenery maintained by cutting and pruning. Species such as pines and cedars were invading, forming more forest stands with dense undergrowth as open meadows of native grasses and wildflowers ringed by black oaks were lost. The commission and some observers noted the gradual change, but they were unable to manage it due to political problems, public perceptions, a lack of funding, ecological misunderstanding, and uncertainty over the purpose of a park and the role of scenery within it.

The biggest obstacle to further growth in tourism remained the remoteness of the park and the difficult access. So the commission encouraged the construction of wagon roads to the valley to replace the primitive horse trails. A heated race to complete roadways ensued between three companies formed from businessmen living near the towns from which the three existing trails originated—Big Oak Flat, Coulterville, and Mariposa. The boosters and backers knew the routes would result in more tourists to their towns as well as the park, profiting both. The roadways reached the valley in 1874–75, bringing wheeled vehicles but not the anticipated increase in visitation, due to a national economic depression during the latter half of the 1870s. The number of visitors would not recover until the mid-1880s, accompanied by further development of tourist hotels and facilities in the valley.

Throughout the 1870s and 1880s politics permeated the park's management. The board constantly battled the tight-fisted state legislature for adequate funding and authority, forcing the board to rely on special concessions to private parties to provide park improvements. The board's relationship with the governor's office varied as well. The concessions prompted public charges of favoritism, usually unfounded, which further tightened tensions. The situation came to a head shortly after the state's revised constitution took effect in 1880. The legislature established new regulations governing Yosemite, in particular the terms of board membership, and declared all commission seats vacant. The new board retained two prior members, including I. W. Raymond; the other six members were businessmen from northern California, a majority of whom were likely aligned with the all-powerful Southern Pacific Railroad interests. Ousted members of the old board contested the legislature's action, refusing to acknowledge the new board or to cooperate in the transfer of authority. The U.S. Supreme Court settled the squabbling in the state's favor in 1881, in *Ashburner v. California* (103 U.S. 575).

Among the new board's first actions was the dismissal of Galen Clark as the park guardian and his replacement with the person with whom the old board had had the stormiest relationship—James Hutchings. He had a prickly personality and a difficult management style during those contentious times. Four years later he would be replaced after—according to him—refusing to hire the relative of a commissioner. The next guardian was a disaster, followed after several years by a Southern Pacific Company employee friendly to several commissioners. His short tenure was highlighted by a legislative investigation into the park's management, triggered by Charles Dorman Robinson, an artist who spent summers in Yosemite painting.

The "old crank," as Robinson considered himself, charged the commission with "forcibly breaking and entering private property," when it canceled his lease for studio space, and with "general failure and incompetence." The *San Francisco Examiner* picked up the story, probably motivated by publisher William Randolph Hearst's hatred of the Southern Pacific Railroad and its control of state politics. The paper unleashed its muckraking zeal, capitalizing on the nagging suspicions about the park's management. Hearings were held in the state legislature, which generally vindicated the commission, concluding it could "find nothing more than a difference of opinion between some witnesses and the Yosemite Commissioners as to the best method of management of the affairs of the valley." Several recommendations for management changes were made, but none were ever implemented. The *Examiner* proclaimed the outcome a whitewash. Yet in 1889 the board fired the guardian and rehired seventy-five-year-old Galen Clark to his former position because he was the one candidate on whom everyone could agree. Clark had the widest circle of friends and was the most popular, so his rehiring helped assuage the residual bitterness from the investigation.

By the end of the 1880s, Muir's beloved Yosemite was threatened by tourist development in the valley, despite its protection in 1864 as a state preserve. Dilapidated tourist facilities, saloons, a pigsty, butcher shops, crop land, and vegetable stalls now defiled the temple itself, hardly the sort of scenic protection recommended by Olmsted or envisioned by Congress.

The situation beyond the park boundaries was potentially worse. Like in much of the nation's forest land, logging posed a threat to the mountains surrounding the valley, as did grazing, which reached its peak in California in the mid-1870s. The federal government had yet to control the practice, but stockmen had begun to do so themselves. By the 1890s, grazing on public land in the Sierra had fallen into steep decline, although Muir would continue to excoriate the practice. Threats also arose on private land surrounding Yosemite. The federal government began offering tracts for sale or settlement around 1880, once the land was surveyed. Most buyers wanted the land for lumber, mining, or stream diversion, potentially leaving far greater scars than the transient herds of sheep that had preceded them.

Muir's pen was mute to these threats throughout the 1880s, as family and farm life occupied his attention. That silence was soon shattered by events that thrust him back into the center of the American conservation debate, where he remained for the rest of his life.

In the spring of 1889, Robert Underwood Johnson, while visiting San Francisco to gather material for articles on the gold rush and the state's early settlers, arranged to meet Muir at Johnson's room in the grand Palace Hotel to prod the gentleman farmer out of his self-imposed silence. Muir also had a purpose in agreeing to the meeting. He wanted to enlist *Century*'s support in the defense of Yosemite and other threatened California wildernesses.

That was the first time the two met face-to-face—once Muir finally found Johnson's room, after getting lost wandering the "confounded artificial canyons" of the mammoth hotel. As was Muir's way, he talked. Johnson politely listened. The meeting went well, though, and several days later Johnson visited the Muirs in Martinez. Again the visit was pleasant, but no agreement was reached; however, Johnson, unlike Emerson, accepted Muir's invitation to accompany him to the high altar—to go camping in Yosemite. There, despite the human vandalism they saw about the preserve, Yosemite's inherent wonder worked its magic on both men as they hiked the beautiful meadows of wildflowers and the thundering canyons of the Tuolumne River, and slept on beds of spruce needles beneath a blanket of stars, "the biggest stars I have ever seen," recalled Johnson. He noted, "The first impression is wonder that there should be so much in so small a space . . . the total effect is overwhelming so that you don't take it in at first, but are surprised anew at each new look."

While sitting around the evening campfire along the upper reaches of the Tuolumne River in early June, the two men talked about Yosemite's future. Johnson asked Muir about Yosemite's fate. Muir responded by describing the devastating effects of overgrazing and mismanagement, to which Johnson replied, "Obviously the thing to do is to make Yosemite National Park around the Valley on the plan of Yellowstone." Enclose the state preserve by a much larger national park, he proposed. Muir agreed wholeheartedly, and a deal was struck: Muir would write two articles for *Century* in support of the cause, and Johnson would lobby friends in Washington and write editorials.

In fact, the idea of expanding Yosemite had been proposed by the commission in 1881 when it unanimously adopted a resolution asking the federal government to expand the grant: "The control of the watershed that discharges into Yosemite Valley and its preservation in its natural state, is vital to the future existence of the valley. . . . In our judgment the territory embraced in the watershed of the valley proper, or in other words the entire basin of every stream leading into the valley should be under the control of the Commissioners to the end that the timber, shrubbery, and grasses thereon may be preserved to retain the snow and rain upon which the grandeur and

beauty of all Yosemite streams depend." The request was made to
President James Garfield in June. Three days later he was assassi-
nated. Efforts continued, with Muir merely lending his name in support. Two pieces of legislation were drafted to extend the park's
boundaries and to create a great national park or reservation around
it to protect important woodlands and headwaters. The novel bills
died in the Committee on Public Lands. Perhaps they were too new
in concept, especially for a Congress comprised of men elected with
the support of mining, railroad, and timber barons, who fought any
restriction on the use of natural resources in the public domain. The
board persisted, repeating its request to the state legislature the next
year and again in 1889, when it petitioned Congress.

The creation of Yellowstone National Park in 1872 established
another important precedent for the expansion of Yosemite. The congressional action, however, was not based on a thorough understanding of Yellowstone's natural condition, for only small portions of the
region had been surveyed and little of its physical character or human
history had been studied. Rather, Congress simply sought to protect
the geysers, canyons, and waterfalls from private exploitation. On
February 27, 1872, the U.S. House of Representatives Committee on
Public Lands reported on the proposed Yellowstone bill:

> If this bill fails to become a law this session, the vandals who are now
> waiting to enter this wonderland will, in a single season, despoil,
> beyond recovery, these remarkable curiosities which have required
> all the cunning skill of nature thousands of years to prepare.
>
> We have already shown that no portion of this tract can ever be
> made available for agricultural or mining purposes. Even if the alti-
> tude and the climate would permit the country to be made available,
> not over fifty square miles of the entire area could ever be settled. . . .
>
> The withdrawal of this tract, therefore, from sale or settlement
> takes nothing from the value of the public domain, and is no pecu-
> niary loss to the Government, but will be regarded by the entire civi-
> lized world as a step of progress and an honor to Congress and the
> nation.

And congressional concern was only for the few acres immediately
adjacent those curiosities. The remaining land, the vast majority of

the 2 million acres, was included because other wonders were suspected to exist in the outlying, unexplored acreage, vacant lands also felt to have no other commercial value so they could easily be lumped into the protected zone.

As had the California legislature with the Yosemite Grant, and the Olmsted plan, Congress made no financial provision for the new park's management, due to severe budget problems. Recognizing the potential dilemma, it assumed that the anticipated revenues from visitation and concession fees would be adequate for the secretary of the interior to pay for proper park management. In effect, Congress accepted the park because it thought the park would be financially self-sufficient.

And because the land sat in a territory, Congress could not grant it to a state as it had done with the Yosemite Valley and Big Tree Grant to California in 1864. A territory lacked the appropriate legal basis for receiving such a grant. Consequently the new Yellowstone park had to be a *federal* park, even though the normal government practice for the distribution of the public domain had always been to grant land to a state, a company, or an individual. Not until the creation of Yosemite, Sequoia, and General Grant National Parks in 1890 would government action fully reflect the national park idea.

As had the Yosemite Grant and the Olmsted plan, "An Act to Set Apart a Certain Tract of Land Lying Near the Head-Waters of the Yellowstone River as a Public Park" left unanswered how to balance its two potentially conflicting purposes. The act states:

> [The Yellowstone region] is hereby reserved and withdrawn from settlement, occupancy, or sale . . . and set apart as a public park or pleasuring-ground for the benefit and enjoyment of the people. . . . [R]egulations shall provide for the preservation, from injury or spoliation, of all timber, mineral deposits, natural curiosities, or wonders, within said park, and their retention in their natural condition. The secretary [of the interior] may in his discretion, grant leases for building purposes . . . of small parcels of ground, at such places . . . as shall require the erection of buildings for the accommodation of visitors. . . . He shall provide against the wanton destruction of the fish and game found within . . . , and against their capture or destruction for the purposes of merchandise or profit.

The law left unanswered how a balance was to be achieved between a "public park or pleasuring-ground" and the "preservation from injury or spoliation" of its natural resources in "their natural condition." It also left unresolved how that "natural condition" was to be defined. These issues would challenge the management of Yellowstone far into the future, as they would Yosemite.

Despite the designation as a national park, Yellowstone would continue to suffer from human abuse, as could Yosemite. During the 1870s and 1880s the spread of settlement on the Great Plains decimated wildlife throughout the West. The great herds of buffalo, elk, and other species were driven to virtual extinction within a fifty-year span. Without proper protection and enforcement, Yellowstone was not spared that carnage; nor were the mountains near Yosemite. Poachers hunted in Yellowstone with the same immunity they enjoyed on the Plains, killing elk, bighorn sheep, deer, antelope, and moose by the thousands. By the mid-1880s whites had substantially depleted the park's normal game populations. To stop the poaching and bring order to the frontier chaos, the U.S. Cavalry was dispatched in 1886 to rescue the place. The cavalry would manage the park off and on until 1918, two years after the National Park Service was established. The cavalry's presence in Yellowstone and the other parks it managed left indelible marks on both the parks and the Park Service.

Calls for the expansion of protected land around Yosemite arose out of similar concerns. Those with interests in the protection of forest resources were joined by irrigationists downstream seeking to protect water flows for agriculture and by those seeking to protect the fragile scenery. The ensuing campaign established the prototype for many conservation debates to come. A loose collection of part-time volunteers motivated mostly by philosophical and recreational interests challenged those with vested economic interests directly tied to the issue.

John P. Irish, a powerful political boss and editor of an Oakland newspaper, led the formidable opposition. Appointed to the Yosemite Board of Commissioners in 1889, for which he served as secretary and treasurer, Irish inherited a complicated political situation, given the legacy of the vitriolic Robinson investigation and the rash of accusations flung about by various critics of the board, who castigated it as a failure. Its management efforts were condemned despite the lack of funding, and the only alternative offered by the critics was to remove the grant from the state because of the spoliation of the park. Much of the heat for the board's actions was directed personally at Irish, even though those actions had been taken before he'd become a member. Although widely known by then to favor commercial interests (Irish later served as an agent for the local cattleman's association), he did so perhaps for philosophical reasons regarding the proper purpose and use of the park rather than out of crass profit motives.

To counter the vested commercial interests of the Yosemite concessionaires, real estate promoters and speculators, lumbermen, cattlemen, and sheepherders, and Leland Stanford's Southern Pacific Railroad, which dominated California politics and controlled rail access to the nearby San Joaquin Valley, the conservationists sought to bypass local politics by taking the issue to a more receptive national audience. They quickly enlisted the support of sympathetic people such as Olmsted and California senator George Hearst. Olmsted wrote a letter in support that eastern newspapers reprinted; however, he conditioned his support on the implementation of his preferred form of forest management, including fire suppression, to promote a pastoral character, and he refused to support criticism of the commission. Many papers, such as the *New York Evening Post*, joined the call. By March 1890, California congressman William Vandever introduced legislation (H.R. 8350) proposing a new Yosemite reserve of about 185,000 acres "for the purpose of preserving the forest, and as a recreation ground for the people as a public park." However, key areas Muir wanted included, such as Tenaya Lake, the Ritter Range, Tuolumne Meadows, Tuolumne Canyon, and Hetch Hetchy, were overlooked.

Muir's articles finally appeared in *Century*'s August and September 1890 issues as the bill neared its hearings before the House Committee on Public Lands. His plea to protect a much larger area than Vandever proposed was carried to the magazine's 200,000 readers, many of whom were among the nation's most influential and powerful people. His arguments for protection drew on George Perkins Marsh and described the many utilitarian benefits that would result from protecting the forest, the soil, and the water.

He suggested the area was worthless for mining and agriculture, as had been successfully argued in the Yellowstone debate. And for perhaps the first time in a conservation debate, Muir also argued that Yosemite should be protected solely as a wilderness, to remain untouched for no utilitarian reason other than its own preservation.

"No terrestrial beauty may endure forever," John Muir wrote in the lengthy, richly illustrated *Century* articles, which included maps of the existing reservation and his proposed park boundary. "The glory of wildness has already departed from the great central plain. Its bloom is shed, and so in part is the bloom of the mountains. In Yosemite, even under the protection of the Government, all that is perishable is vanishing apace."

After he gave a lengthy description of the valley and surrounding features, often repeating his earlier published versions, Muir described the wanton destruction of the sequoia groves. "These king trees, all that there are of their kind in the world, are surely worth saving, whether for beauty, science, or bald use. But as yet only the isolated Mariposa Grove has been reserved as a park for public use and pleasure. Were the importance of our forests at all understood by the people in general, even from an economic standpoint their preservation would call forth the most watchful attention of the Government. At present, however, every kind of destruction is moving on with accelerated speed."

Then he made his plea to expand the proposed park to protect the entire drainage. "Steps are now being taken towards the creation of a national park about Yosemite, and great is the need, not only for the sake of the adjacent forests, but for the valley itself. For the branching cañons and valleys of the basins of the streams that pour into Yosemite are as closely related to it as are the fingers to the palm of the hand—as the branches, foliage, and flowers of a tree to the trunk. Therefore, very naturally, all the fountain region above Yosemite, with its peaks, cañons, snow fields, glaciers, forests, and streams, should be included in the park to make it an harmonious unit instead of a fragment."

Muir concluded the articles with arguments reminiscent of Olmsted and Marsh, calling for Congress to enlarge the Vandever proposal to protect a much larger area, including Hetch Hetchy.

I have thus briefly touched upon a number of the chief features of a region which it is proposed to reserve out of the public domain for the use and recreation of the people. A bill has already been introduced in Congress by Mr. Vandever creating a national park about the reservation which the State now holds in trust for the people. It is very desirable that the new reservation should at least extend to the limits indicated by the map, and the bill cannot too quickly become a law. Unless reserved or protected the whole region will soon or late be devastated by lumbermen and sheepmen, and so of course be made unfit for use as a pleasure ground. Already it is with great difficulty that campers, even in the most remote parts of the proposed reservation and in those difficult of access, can find grass enough to keep their animals from starving; the ground is already being gnawed and trampled into a desert condition, and when the region shall be stripped of its forests the ruin will be complete. Even the Yosemite will then suffer in the disturbance effected on the water-shed, the clear streams becoming muddy and much less regular in flow. It is also devoutly to be hoped that the Hetch Hetchy will escape such ravages of man as one sees in Yosemite. Ax and plow, hogs and horses, have long been and are still busy in Yosemite's gardens and groves. All that is accessible and destructible is being rapidly destroyed. . . . And by far the greater part of this destruction of the fineness of wildness is of a kind that can claim no right relationship with that which necessarily follows use.

The conservationists knew the support of President Benjamin Harrison and Secretary of the Interior John Noble, a fan of Muir's writing who was convinced of the necessity to preserve the nation's forested watersheds and scenic beauty, would be essential. Yet even their support, when combined with strong public support across the country, still might not have been sufficient to offset local commercial opposition, who were waging an often nasty campaign in the press to color public opinion. With Irish and the Southern Pacific opposing the plan, congressional approval appeared unlikely.

Realizing Leland Stanford held the key to the entire debate, Johnson called on the Republican godfather of California politics only weeks after leaving Muir in Yosemite. Stanford (1824–93)

began his rapid rise to wealth and power during the gold rush, operating a Sacramento supply store for miners in the 1850s. There he
also became involved in the new Republican Party, befriending three
eager entrepreneurs who shared his political and business ambitions.
In the early 1860s Stanford and partners Collis Huntington, Mark
Hopkins, and Charles Crocker maneuvered Stanford's election as
governor (1861–63), during which he unabashedly used his political
office and influence in the state and national capitals to promote their
business interests in the construction of a transcontinental railroad,
for which the "Big Four" had formed the Central Pacific Railroad
Company. In 1863 Stanford declined to run for reelection, returning
full-time to the railroad as president, a position he held until his
death. Yet during the interim he also served in the U.S. Senate
(1885–93), continuing to mix business and politics.

Stanford was noncommittal to Johnson's overtures, but fate soon
interceded. Over the winter of 1889–90 Stanford and his long-
estranged partner Collis Huntington had a fight to the finish for
control of the Southern Pacific component of their railroad empire.
For years Stanford's brash management style and incessant political meddling had irritated his more business-oriented partners.
Huntington won, replacing Stanford as president and pledging to
clean up the company. Perhaps sensing the potential profit from
increased tourism, the corporate giant quietly shifted its support
behind the Vandever bill, for which another bill (H.R. 12187) had
been substituted that included the additional lands Muir wanted in
the new park, making it five times larger than that proposed in the
initial bill. Meanwhile, Johnson lobbied fiercely and effectively in
Washington.

All the political currents swirling behind the scenes still remain
unclear, but on September 30, 1890, the bill passed both chambers of
Congress with little discussion: "[These lands] are hereby reserved
and withdrawn from settlement, occupancy, or sale . . . and set apart
as reserved forest lands . . . under the exclusive control of the
Secretary of the Interior . . . for the preservation from injury of all
timber, mineral deposits, natural curiosities, or wonders . . . and
their retention in their natural condition. . . . He shall also provide
against the wanton destruction of the fish, and game . . . and against
their capture or destruction, for the purposes of merchandise or

profit." This was done, provided "That nothing in this act shall be construed as in anywise affecting the grant of lands made to the State of California" in the Yosemite Valley and the Mariposa Big Tree Grove. Telltale hints of Olmsted's plan for the valley appeared in the bill, key proponents of which had copies of his plan, perhaps including Muir. Regardless of whether Olmsted's plan directly shaped the drafting of the bill, the authors shared many of his ideas and values. The next day President Harrison made nearly a million acres surrounding the Yosemite Valley the nation's second national park. (Sequoia and General Grant National Parks were, in effect, established simultaneously.)

Muir had little time to celebrate the stunning victory as words once again flowed from his pen in response to another major battle, one at the heart of the conservation debate. The new fight addressed the conflict between the competing interests for control of the nation's remaining forest wilderness.

By the last quarter of the 1800s the vast majority of the most valued public land was forested, and most of that was in the West in places like Yellowstone and Yosemite. Such mountainous landscapes usually possessed the spectacular scenery and natural wonders that were most sought after as public pleasuring grounds. By this time too their commercial value as sources of timber or minerals was apparent. In contrast, the grassland or scrub growth that covered the remainder of the public domain on the Plains, prairies, and deserts were of much less interest. The positive value assigned to wilderness—whether by the consortium of conservation-oriented philosophies espoused by Thoreau and Muir, or Roosevelt, or by those intent on the continued use of wilderness for economic exploitation and development—was only given to *forested* wilderness, not yet to arid or semiarid wilderness. Nor were conservation and stewardship values focused on the commonplace landscapes of typical daily life, whether farmland, suburb, or city in the East or West. Instead, the conservation movement arose mostly from a philosophical battle of wills regarding the use of the nation's remaining forested wilderness, the battleground of which was a proposal to set aside our national forests.

The battle's first skirmish began quietly in 1876 when Dr. Franklin B. Hough was hired by the U.S. Department of Agriculture to collect statistics and distribute information on the nation's remaining forests. The federal action was taken in response to pressure principally from the American Association for the Advancement of Science (AAAS), and from Hough himself, who was the director of the national census and a disciple of George Perkins Marsh. Hough was instructed to develop a report detailing the nation's current and projected forest production and consumption. The first volume of his three-part report, published in 1877 and distributed to twenty-five thousand readers, broadened awareness of the prevailing plunder of the nation's forests, to little result.

Abuse of the nation's forests continued unchecked throughout the 1870s, as did general abuse of the public land laws and land distribution programs. By 1880 Dr. Bernard E. Fernow, a German-trained forester, became the head of Hough's small organization, which was renamed the Division of Forestry. Ironically, though, during his tenure as chief (1880–98), Fernow questioned the federal government's role in large-scale forest management. Under his skeptical management the division received little money (its annual budget was around $28,500) and held little power, so it was of minimal consequence. Fernow was politically unable or philosophically unwilling to implement the scientific forest management practices he had learned in Germany. His division functioned mostly as an information bureau that tacitly tolerated continued clear-cutting of the nation's timberland to satisfy short-term demand as cheaply as possible. The division had little effect on reducing the environmental consequences of logging, or on clarifying the long-term implications of that production. Public and private forestry had not yet incorporated the lessons offered by Marsh's *Man and Nature*. American forestry was neither a profession nor a science.

The origins of federal forest management began with concerned citizens outside the government, especially Charles Sprague Sargent. Inspired by *Man and Nature*, in 1880 Sargent surveyed the forestland remaining in the public domain on behalf of the government. The lack of modern management and the environmental abuses he found shocked him and prompted him to call for federal reform and regulation pending a more complete study by experts. The fledgling American Forestry Association joined his call. Few listened, however, and little progress was made toward either the reform or the study. (*Century* would finally endorse Sargent's proposals nearly nine years later as Muir and Johnson headed into the high country of Yosemite.)

Over a decade passed following Hough's 1877 report and Sargent's 1880 survey before the next rumbles in the gathering storm over the nation's forests occurred. Calls for land reform from the AAAS, the American Forestry Association, the American Forestry Congress, and others found a receptive ear in President Benjamin Harrison in the early 1890s. On March 3, 1891, just before adjournment, Congress passed the Forest Reserve Act (26 Stat. 1095), repealing the widely abused Timber Culture Act and the preemption laws. Attached to the bill was a little-noticed rider proposed by William Hallett Phillips, an obscure Washington lawyer, socialite, and member of the Boone and Crockett Club. The innocuous proposal was supported by other wealthy, influential people, mostly easterners, including Sargent and Johnson, and John Muir. The rider rode through on the bill's coattails without comment. Its enactment, however, precipitated the storm over the nation's forests.

The new amendment contained in the last paragraph of the nine-page bill empowered the president to withdraw forestland from the public domain and set it aside as a "forest reserve" (later called a national forest), "That the President of the United States may, from time to time, set apart and reserve, in any State or Territory having public land bearing forests, in any part of the public lands wholly or in part covered with timber or undergrowth, whether of commercial value or not, as public reservations, and the President shall, by public proclamation, declare the establishment of such reservations and the limits thereof."

President Harrison seized the opportunity and, at the behest of Secretary of the Interior John Noble, over the next two years designated 15 reserves totaling 13 million acres. As it had with the establishment of Yellowstone, Congress left much unsaid in the new Forest Reserve Act. It failed to specify the function of the reserves the chief executive could so easily create with the stroke of a pen. Were they to protect timber and water resources, as in the Adirondacks, or scenic and recreational resources, as in Yosemite and Yellowstone, or wilderness in general?

Muir argued that the intention was clear, since the law followed so closely on the Yosemite debate. The forest reserves were to be like national parks and remain uncut and undeveloped. Secretary Noble generally agreed, as did his successor, Hoke Smith, who dutifully banned sheep grazing in the reserves, despite opposition from stockmen, after Muir and Johnson met with him in 1893 to discuss the matter. The conservationists found a willing audience among key government administrators, often peers who shared their sympathies. Those with vested commercial and political interests received a deaf ear. These conservation decisions were not based on popular public opinion or open debate, but on backroom politics, albeit of a refined sort.

Regardless of interpretation, the new reserves existed only on paper, for, as had happened at Yellowstone, no one was assigned to enforce the rules or regulations. Use of the forest reserves remained a free-for-all. Clear-cutting and exploitation continued unabated despite the efforts of Noble and Smith, Johnson and Muir. By the mid-1890s the chaotic situation became unacceptable to the conservationists.

At the same time timbermen and stockmen were busy organizing opposition to the increasing level of government restrictions on the use of the public domain. In 1892 two bills were introduced at their behest in Congress to cut the size of the new reserves. In one (H.R. 5764), California representative Caminetti proposed to lop off half of the new Yosemite National Park to reopen large areas for private exploitation. Local residents, angry over the loss of tax base, and other settlers, angry over the closing of pastures in the High Sierra, supported his proposal. The other, more radical bill (H.R. 8445) was introduced by Kansas representative Otis, an avowed enemy of forest reserves. It sought to repeal all the recent California reserves. Caminetti's bill drew the new Sierra Club into the world of Washington politics as the club mounted its first campaign to protect the park. More campaigns would soon follow as the club assumed the emerging role as the nation's environmental conscience. Neither bill was ever acted on by Congress.

In the aftermath of New York's constitutional guarantee that the Adirondacks would be "forever wild," Johnson's *Century* organized a symposium in 1894 to examine a Sargent proposal that called for forestry instruction at West Point and for the army to protect forest reserves, as it was doing in Yellowstone and Yosemite National Parks. The symposium attracted many of the nation's leading conservationists, most of whom agreed with the Sargent proposal.

One visionary twenty-nine-year-old consulting forester did not agree, and he voiced a powerful dissenting opinion. Gifford Pinchot fractured the unified conservation movement, splitting it into two factions. The difference in the land management philosophies between the two factions was not one of good versus bad; rather it had become a difference in the definition of the greater good. Both factions loved the land and valued wilderness, only they did so from very different perspectives.

Pinchot and several people from the Division of Forestry proposed that the reserves should be managed not by the army but by "a forest service, a commission of scientifically trained men" (which he would presumably head). While the idea appeared reasonable, the guiding philosophy cut clear through the movement. He proposed that forest reserves be used not just as a onetime supply of a single resource; instead, they should serve as a source of multiple resources managed to extract their maximum sustained yield. Pinchot wanted to generate the greatest possible benefit to the greatest number of people, advocating the utilitarian philosophy of John Stuart Mill and Jeremy Bentham. In his autobiography, *Breaking New Ground*, he wrote:

> Forestry is Tree Farming. Forestry is handling trees so that one crop follows another. . . . Trees may be grown as a crop just as corn may be grown as a crop. The farmer gets crop after crop of corn, oats, wheat, cotton, tobacco, and hay from his farm. The forester gets crop after crop of logs, cordwood, shingles, poles, or railroad ties from his forest, and even some return from regulated grazing. . . . The purpose of Forestry, then, is to make the forest produce the largest possible amount of whatever crop or service will be most useful, and keep on producing it for generation after generation of men and trees. . . . It is true indeed that the forest, rightly handled—given the chance—is, next to the earth itself, the most useful servant of man.

Thus the forests were not to be preserved untouched as Muir proposed; rather, they were to be the source of valuable natural

resources managed scientifically to squeeze out every ounce of benefit. Nor were they only to be pleasuring grounds for hikers and
campers as were the national parks. Instead, the forests were to be
harvested annually like a crop and every resource possible was to be
extracted for the maximum benefit of society. They were to yield an
annual income like the interest on a savings account, and every
penny of interest was to be spent. With enlightened management,
Pinchot preached, natural resource "investments" would even yield
greater rates of return than nature alone would produce. Like
Marsh, Pinchot wanted his treasured forests to be used wisely, not
blindly or wastefully. Pinchot believed a properly managed forest
that supplied many resources and recreational opportunities satisfied more human needs. That was the better use of the prized possession. It achieved the greater good.

The philosophies of John Muir and Gifford Pinchot were, ironically, at opposite ends of the conservation spectrum even though
both arose from the same intention to better husband, to better steward the beloved forests. Pinchot's consumption-based conservation
philosophy of maximum sustained yield quickly assumed the mantle
of the conservation movement and was soon applied to virtually all
of the public domain, whether wilderness or not, whether forest or
not. Applicable to the everyday landscape, it encapsulated the public's prevailing values. Muir's philosophy of recreational use became
the cornerstone of the preservation movement and remained focused
primarily on the dwindling supply of wilderness—initially forested
wilderness but later other wilderness landscapes. Both concepts—
conservation for multiple use and sustained yield; and preservation
for recreation—would be redefined in the latter half of the 1900s by
a new generation of environmental and political leaders.

Pinchot's appearance at the symposium and his proposals were not
out of the blue. Although young and self-employed, like Grinnell and
Sargent, Pinchot was a wealthy, well-connected easterner. And like so
many others in the movement his conservationist inclinations arose
from the opportunities afforded by his economic and social station.

Pinchot's forestry career and his conservation philosophy grew in
large part from his father's quest for personal penance. James
Pinchot, like his own father (Gifford's grandfather), Cyril, was a
successful speculator in the timber industry. For two generations the

Pinchots had profited from New York, Pennsylvania, Michigan, and Wisconsin timberland. As was common in the industry during much of the 1800s they bought land, clear-cut the forest, and then floated the logs tied together in giant rafts down rivers swollen with spring rain to eastern markets. The profits were reinvested in more virgin land, creating a vicious cycle of land exploitation and degradation that left giant swaths of the landscape denuded of forest cover and exposed to the erosive effects of wind and water. This was the short-sighted cycle George Perkins Marsh decried in *Man and Nature.*

In the 1850s, though, James Pinchot left the timber industry and moved to New York City, where he became a successful distributor of domestic and commercial furnishings. His business benefited from the prosperity and economic boom that resulted from rapidly expanding industrialization after the Civil War. His wife, Mary Eno, was also wealthy, adding to the family fortune. Mary was the daughter of Amos Eno, a successful New York City land developer who owned prime properties such as the Fifth Avenue, the city's grand hotel, and other choice real estate along principal avenues like Broadway. Gifford Pinchot was born in 1865 into a family of great wealth and social position; visits to the White House were common; a family trip to Europe could last several years.

By the 1870s James Pinchot retired, even though he was only in his mid-forties, gripped by a growing sense of shame and guilt over the devastation wrought by his, and his father's, timber speculation. James saw young Gifford as the vehicle for his redemption and sought to direct his son along a path that would atone for the landscape sins of the father and grandfather.

That guilt was fostered in part by the European landscapes James Pinchot saw while on holidays in the latter half of the 1800s. Like Olmsted, he fell in love with the picturesque English countryside of quaint villages scattered about a bucolic landscape of green pastures, fields, and forests. In contrast, the abused land around his Milford, Connecticut, home—land devastated by the same shortsightedness he practiced throughout New England and the Midwest—stood in stark testimony to the misuse and arrogance documented by Marsh. So James Pinchot sent his son to restore the American landscape.

Gifford Pinchot's turning point came during his senior year at Yale University as he struggled to choose a career. Amos Eno pressured his grandson to join his business. James Pinchot, impressed by the apparent harmony between people and nature in the English landscape, and bothered by guilt over his landscape malevolence, encouraged the type of modern forestry practiced in Europe as the profession for his son. The father prevailed, and the idealistic son chose forestry as a form of public service instead of continuing the family quest for mammon.

After graduation in 1889 young Pinchot went to Europe in search of forestry training, since no U.S. schools taught the subject. On the advice of eminent foresters there he enrolled at the Ecole Nationale Forestier in Nancy, France. In the classroom and in the French national forests he learned how to manage the forest as a crop that could yield a continuous supply of resources as had been practiced out of necessity for decades on manorial estates and royal forests in Europe.

In contrast, the American attitude toward the forests that covered the eastern third of the continent had been since settlement one of all-out war. Here the goal was the removal of the forest to make room for agriculture and settlement and later to feed the Industrial Revolution's insatiable hunger for fuel and material, especially the ferocious appetite of the railroads. America was understandably slower to adopt concepts of forest management because they considered the supply limitless. When Pinchot returned in 1890 to begin his career he was perhaps the first American formally trained in modern forestry.

While studying European forestry Pinchot also began to believe that natural resources belonged to all the people and should therefore be used for public benefit to achieve social equity—they should serve the greatest good for the greatest number rather than serve only the interests of the social and economic elite. That recognition was accentuated during a tour of a Prussian forest. Pinchot wrote in his autobiography, "I shall never forget the old peasant who rose to his feet from his stone-breaking, as the Oberfoerster came striding along, and stood silent, head bent, cap in hands, while the official stalked by without the slightest sign that he knew the peasant was on earth." The feudal roots of the European landscape remained recognizable. This utilitarian belief would be a hallmark of the Progressive Movement he championed in the early 1900s.

When young Pinchot first returned from Europe he was uncertain about his future. Again benefiting from family contacts he sought the advice of leading conservationists and government officials, including Sargent, Fernow, the secretary of the interior, even Vice President Levi P. Morton. Through those contacts he was employed early in 1891 as a consulting forester by Phelps, Dodge, and Company, a large mining and timber company. Phelps sent the novice to examine its holdings in Pennsylvania. With that work quickly completed he then accompanied Fernow for several weeks as a guest on an inspection tour of the hardwood forests in the southern Mississippi River basin in Arkansas. By March Phelps sent him to Arizona to survey company lands for reforestation. Before returning east he toured California, visiting Yosemite and the Mariposa Grove, and then continued up the Cascades through the old-growth forests of the Pacific Northwest. On return he praised the way John P. Irish and the Yosemite commission managed the park while at the same time he dismissed *Century*'s editorial criticism of the commission. He felt the greater good was achieved by the full exploitation of the park's resources, since the measure he used to calculate benefit relied primarily on tangible economic benefits, not intangible aesthetic and recreational measures.

By late 1891 he returned to New York in search of work. Once again family connections supplied the answer. There his father helped arrange meetings between Pinchot, George Vanderbilt, and Frederick Law Olmsted. As a result Vanderbilt hired Pinchot, on the recommendation of Olmsted, to manage the extensive forests at Vanderbilt's sprawling Biltmore estate, perhaps America's closest cousin to the grand European baronial estates. Olmsted, whose firm had been working on the innovative master plan for the 7,000-acre grounds since 1888, wanted the estate to have a model farm, a great arboretum, and a vast game preserve. He intended the estate to be, as Pinchot recalled, "the first example of practical forest management in the United States." Energetic and idealistic, Pinchot made the most of the opportunity to test his theories on Vanderbilt's forests, which expanded to nearly 200,000 acres; today, that land forms the core of Pisgah National Forest. Pinchot later credited Olmsted with making Biltmore the "nest egg for practical Forestry in America."

Pinchot's landmark work at Biltmore left him time for consulting work; he opened an office in New York in late 1893. His work with privately owned forests steadily grew, as did his influence in the growing forestry and conservation movements. During the debate on the Adirondacks at the New York constitutional convention he opposed the "forever wild" clause because it would prohibit lumbering. Afterward he realized that the greatest opportunity and need for his skills rested in managing the hundreds of millions of acres in the public domain. That understanding led him to abandon his private consulting practice in 1898 when asked to replace Bernhard Fernow as the head of the forestry division in the U.S. Department of Agriculture. There his professional ideals, his political ambitions, and his social agenda blossomed.

When, at the 1894 *Century* symposium, Pinchot countered Sargent's notion that the army should manage the national forests, and proposed instead that the national forests be managed by professionally trained foresters, his viewpoint arose from his family heritage, his European forestry education, and his sense of social responsibility. So did his redefinition of conservation to mean maximum sustained yield for the benefit of society. Still, he joined the rest in supporting Sargent's proposal to form a government commission to propose management guidelines based on a more detailed study of the nation's remaining forests than the one Sargent had conducted in 1880.

The commission was eventually established in 1896 following several years of political maneuvering. After efforts to have Congress establish and fund the body stalled, Sargent, Johnson, Pinchot, and other proponents persuaded Hoke Smith to ask the National Academy of Science to organize it; that would make the $25,000 requisite funding far easier to obtain from Congress. The strategy worked, and a six-person commission set out to survey the nation's forests that summer. Commission members included Sargent, who headed the group, William Brewer of Yale University, Alexander Agassiz of Harvard University, General H. L. Abbott, an engineer, Arnold Hague of the U.S. Geological Survey, and Gifford Pinchot. John Muir joined the group as an ex officio member, much to Pinchot's delight.

Pinchot had met Muir the year before the *Century* symposium and had presented himself somewhat as an acolyte before the revered master. Pinchot sought and Muir offered advice and encouragement. They became friends, sharing a love of the land and a desire to conserve it; unfortunately, their concepts of conservation differed profoundly. Both men had political objectives to see their values implemented and needed to build a constituency to do so, and both were to some extent blinded by their motives. Muir continued to stress the effects of grazing, due to his longstanding hatred of it, even though by the late 1800s it probably posed less of an environmental threat to the Sierra than logging. And he continued to see proper forest management in the Sierra based on some techniques better suited to eastern forests, never accepting the role of fire as a natural disturbance regime. Pinchot continued to discount the recreational value of forests relative to logging and the production of other physical products. Perhaps these positions played well with their supporters. While their differences had surfaced before the commission convened, they were not yet divisive. The tour fostered their friendship. All of that changed when the commission set about preparing its final report.

Sargent and Muir felt the report should identify forest wilderness areas that needed preservation, and they hoped the report would lead the government to set aside additional lands using the existing Forest Reserve Act. Pinchot and Hague felt the report should lay the basis for enlightened forest management open to carefully conducted exploitation under the control of a civilian, professionally trained forest service. The Sargent-Muir faction won as the report limited resource exploitation. The report also recommended the army be given the responsibility to patrol the reserves as it did at Yellowstone and Yosemite. On February 22, 1897, just before leaving office, President Grover Cleveland added thirteen new reserves totaling 21.4 million acres. Like President Harrison before him, President Cleveland made no mention of utilitarian purposes. The apparent preservation victory didn't last.

Acting without the consent of the other commission members, Sargent had persuaded a sympathetic president to make those designations without further consultation or debate. Sargent's action outraged the opposing commissioners, and the president's action outraged Congress and commercial interests all across the country. The issue, far from settled by Sargent and President Cleveland, was carried over to the new McKinley administration. And once again the president and the secretary of the interior were persuaded by personal pleas from Sargent and Johnson not to succumb to mounting political pressure to rescind the new reserves. But the debate by then had spread to Congress, which sought legislation to resolve the issue. Muir, writing in the *Atlantic Monthly* and *Harper's Weekly*, championed the preservation cause: "Much is said on questions of this kind about 'the greatest good for the greatest number,' but the greatest number is too often found to be number one. It is never the greatest number in the common meaning of the term that makes the greatest noise and stir on questions mixed with money. . . . Complaints are made in the name of poor settlers and miners, while the wealthy corporations are kept carefully hidden in the background. . . . Let right, commendable industry be fostered, but as to these Goths and Vandals of the wilderness, who are spreading black death in the fairest woods God ever made, let the government up and at 'em."

On June 4, 1897, Congress finally spoke when it passed the Forest Management Act (30 Stat. 32) and clarified the purpose of the reserves: "No public forest reservation shall be established, except to improve and protect the forest within the reservation, or for the purpose of securing favorable conditions of water flows, and to furnish a continuous supply of timber for the use and necessities of the citizens of the United States." Nor were the reserves to include lands that were more valuable for mining or agriculture than for forest purposes.

Responding to the bulk of popular opinion from western legislators and lumber, grazing, and mining interests, Congress rejected Muir's preservation philosophy in favor of Pinchot's conservation philosophy. National forests were not set aside to preserve wilderness, Congress declared. They were set aside to protect utilitarian needs. The nation's traditional environmental values prevailed. The land was still regarded primarily as a commodity to be used for economic growth and development. Preservation remained a philosophy held by a small minority comprised mostly of elite easterners. Feeling the national forests were a lost cause, Muir thereafter devoted his attention to the care of the national parks, focusing his efforts on the protection of the existing parks from commercial intrusion, other than that necessitated by recreational uses, and on the establishment of new parks where his preservation philosophy might still apply.

Pinchot was rewarded several months later with the appointment as head of the forestry division, where he replaced his lackadaisical colleague Bernard Fernow, who had resigned when asked by Congress to justify the division's existence. Politically astute and aggressive, Pinchot would build the floundering division from a staff of approximately 125 persons with little authority to roughly 1,500 people who managed nearly 150 million acres of federal forest. Working closely with President Roosevelt, Pinchot would become the government's most influential land manager, molding the division over his tenure (1898–1910) to reflect his personal philosophy while spreading his vision over every aspect of federal land policy. In 1905 the division, renamed the U.S. Forest Service, would assume full management responsibility for all the national forests, by which time Pinchot's conservation philosophy of maximum use and sustained yield for the greatest good to the greatest number dominated the government's approach to the entire public domain. Hence, as James Duval Phelan eyed the distant Hetch Hetchy Valley in Yosemite National Park at the turn of the century, it was Pinchot's philosophy, not Muir's, that would guide government action, and the distinction between a national park and a national forest had yet to be resolved.

The philosophical battle lines between Pinchot and Muir, between conservation and preservation, were firmly drawn by 1900 as the two leaders parted ways, personally and philosophically. But the battles over Niagara Falls, the Adirondacks, Yosemite, and the national forests were merely preparatory skirmishes contested by the economically and politically powerful. They were not all-out philosophical warfare, for the American public was yet to join the fray. The two estranged leaders would soon battle for the environmental soul of the country, a fight that would take the war into far more American homes than just those whose inhabitants had vested philosophical, political, or commercial interests. Appropriately, then, their ultimate battle waged over part of Muir's sanctum sanctorum—the Hetch Hetchy Valley.

CHAPTER 4

Theodore Roosevelt; The Park's Revision

Behind him lay the problems of the day as his six-car special train finally departed. Exhausted from the frantic pace of politics since he suddenly assumed the presidency following William McKinley's assassination eighteen months earlier, he could wait no longer for his frequently postponed western tour and respite. Dusk was falling when the Pacific Coast Special swept through the Alleghenies of Pennsylvania on April 1, 1903. The train had reached the physical and cultural divide between the Atlantic seaboard, the nation's cradle, and the vast expanse of America's heartland. A thousand miles of till plains stretched westward, gradually giving way to the vast prairies of the Great Plains and the arid basin and range territory surrounding the Rocky and Sierra Nevada Mountains, until reaching the Pacific coast; these were the landscapes where the nation's future was unfolding. Perhaps the energetic, idealistic president and the adolescent nation he now led had reached thresholds as well.

Forty-four-year-old President Theodore Roosevelt settled into the rich upholstery in the *Elysian,* his sumptuous private car trimmed in velvet plush, mahogany, and brass at the end of the train. He would enjoy its fine food, personal service, and comfort before facing the rigors of the outdoors to come. Never timid, the young president had immediately set to work to redirect the country following his popular and even-tempered predecessor's death. The daunting agenda included improving race relations and immigration policies; continuing tariff, trade, and monetary policy reforms; pursuing antitrust proceedings against the Northern Securities Company, the giant transportation combine that brought together James J. Hill's Great Northern Railroad with E. H. Harriman's Union Pacific Railroad and J. Pierpont Morgan's Northern Pacific Railroad to form the world's second largest conglomerate (only surpassed by U.S. Steel); advancing labor reforms and resolving the devastating United Mine

Workers coal strike; reforming the nation's inconsistent and widely abused policies governing the public domain; preserving law and order at a time of rising public anxiety over incivilities; building a canal across the Isthmus of Panama; upgrading the navy; and asserting American interests in tangled foreign affairs, particularly those in the Pacific Rim and in the Americas, based on the Monroe Doctrine.

Ahead lay an outing into his beloved Yellowstone with John Burroughs and another into Yosemite with John Muir, kindred spirits he had handpicked to join him. The ambitious eight-week trip, reflecting his public and private personas, would cover fourteen thousand miles, cross twenty-five states, and visit nearly 150 towns and cities, during which he would give some two hundred speeches and at least five major addresses. He hoped the wilderness interludes would refresh his spirit and reinvigorate his deteriorating health as excursions into the wilds to hunt and camp had done so often in the past. It was there that he had retreated after his young wife had died tragically while giving birth to the couple's only child in 1884, his mother having died in the same house a few hours earlier. For two years Roosevelt sought solace in writing, hunting, fishing, and working on his ranch in the Dakota Badlands. Now he desperately needed to escape the stifling qualities of civilization again, if only for a few days of solitude in the backcountry, to relieve the burden of the position that weighed so heavily on him.

Perhaps the nation as a whole suffered in a similar way from the growing pressures of modernity and the rapid pace of change at the start of the twentieth century; and perhaps contact with nature could assuage their pain in the same way it would restore the president physically and psychologically. Writing in the *Atlantic Monthly,* John Muir noted in 1898 that "Thousands of tired, nerve-shaken, over-civilized people are beginning to find out that going to the mountains is going home, that wilderness is a necessity, and that mountain parks and reservations are useful not only as fountains of timber and irrigating rivers, but as fountains of life."

George S. Evans, a rising young Bay Area author of short stories about the rugged life and landscape in the unspoiled cattle country of California's northern coast—a place where cougars and deer still found room to roam freely in the mountains and people still exhibited the naturalness of pioneers—captured the same sentiment, writing in *Overland Monthly* just before his death in 1904, "Whenever the light of civilization falls upon you with a blighting power, and work and pleasure become stale and flat, go to the wilderness. The wilderness will take hold on you. It will give you good red blood; it will turn you from a weakling into a man." Go to the wilderness, he urged his readers, so that "dull business routine, the fierce passions of the market place, the perils of envious cities become but a memory." There, he concluded, "you will soon behold all with a peaceful soul." Americans by the thousands headed to the outdoors.

"Naked He Plunges into Maine Woods to Live Alone Two Months," read the headline of the Boston *Post* on August 10, 1913. Joseph Knowles's experiment captivated America. The book retelling his primitive life, *Alone in the Wilderness*, sold 300,000 copies, attracting far more attention than fellow New Englander Henry David Thoreau's account of his own primitive life in a crude hut beside Walden Pond on Ralph Waldo Emerson's land near Concord, Massachusetts, in 1854. The public in the mid-1800s had little interest in Thoreau's two-year-long experience. Wilderness remained primarily a threat in the American mind. However, a generation later attitudes were rapidly changing. By the 1900s less adventuresome nature seekers sought relief in new groups like the Sierra Club, the Boone and Crockett Club, and other outdoor clubs, and even the Boy Scouts. Influential books like Upton Sinclair's *The Jungle* (1906) spoke of the problem; best-selling novels like Jack London's *The Call of the Wild* (1903) and Edgar Rice Burroughs's *Tarzan of the Apes* (1914) suggested the solution, as did more moderate nonfiction books about nature by John Burroughs, John Muir, and Theodore Roosevelt. As the president rode off to the West, other Americans headed to the forests and mountains to hike, hunt, or camp, or simply for pleasure seeking, to enjoy the natural scenery, if only making the trip vicariously.

And following the advice of Frederick Law Olmsted and other tastemakers, more and more people began to flee the failings of urban American as a place to live in favor of the fresh air, romantic scenery, sense of security, and the domestic bliss promised in suburbia. Increasingly, those with the means began to reject the daily assaults on the senses from city life, choosing to live instead in a pastoral "middle" landscape situated geographically and psychologically between the agrarian and urban worlds. Streetcar lines radiating outward from the city center, like spokes on a wheel, enabled the suburbanites to commute downtown to work and shop, while coaches and trains could carry them to vestiges of wilderness in parks like the Adirondacks, Yellowstone, and Yosemite.

But modernity was not all bad. It offered unprecedented prosperity and progress together with the social stress and environmental threats. With balanced management, America's manifest destiny would be realized, Roosevelt believed. Pinchot pointed the way; Muir also offered important guidance. The nation stood at the brink of a brilliant future, indeed the American century, as the train carrying the president raced westward, chasing the setting sun.

Two days later the front-page headline of the *Chicago Tribune* proclaimed, "Speak Softly and Carry a Big Stick, Says Roosevelt," following his speech to the wildly enthusiastic crowd of five thousand who overflowed the Chicago Auditorium. He spoke next on trust policy at a dinner for businessmen at the Plankinton House in Milwaukee; and then on tariff policy in St. Paul. The train continued westward over the tracks of the Northern Securities combine. From the platform at the tail of the *Elysian,* perfect for whistle-stop speeches, he now caught the first glimpse of the Plains and prairies and savored their familiar, distinct scent, making the problems of Washington seem more distant than the miles that lay in between. Several days and several stops later he arrived at Gardiner, Montana, the entrance to Yellowstone. The president quickly mounted a gray stallion and charged off toward the snow-capped peaks with a small escort in tow, just as word arrived behind him in Gardiner that the U.S. Eighth Circuit Court in St. Louis had upheld the government's position in the Northern Securities case.

Yellowstone sat at the core of his being, symbolizing his sense of self and America. Since his first visit seventeen years earlier he had worked for its protection and proper management, initially as a member of the Boone and Crockett Club and then as a politician. "Every man who appreciates the majesty and beauty of the wilderness and of wild life," he stated, "should strike hands with the far-sighted men who wish to preserve our material resources, in the effort to keep our forests and our game-beasts, game-birds, and game-fish—indeed, all the living creatures of prairie and woodland and seashore—from wanton destruction." How could one oppose the protection of our national heritage and the wellspring of American values and identity? "Above all," he continued, "we should recognize that the effort toward this end is essentially a democratic movement. It is entirely within our power as a nation to preserve large tracts of wilderness, which are valueless for agricultural purposes and unfit for settlement, as playgrounds for rich and poor alike. . . . But this can only be achieved by wise laws and by a resolute enforcement of the laws." For him, conservation was essential democracy: government could provide for resource development and economic growth to satisfy current needs while simultaneously conserving resources, including wilderness, for future generations to enjoy their fair share.

Like popular attitudes toward the environment, public environmental policy had reached a turning point as well. Since its inception America had focused on westward expansion and the distribution of the public domain into private ownership. Economic development took precedence. Few questions were asked about the means or the meaning. Now Progressive conservation policy focused on the wise management of the public domain and the reformation of the land laws to reduce abuse, foster efficiency, and promote equity. Roosevelt's foray into the nation's western realms symbolized the crossing of these personal, social, and political thresholds.

Two weeks later the president returned from the wild, beaming with a dark-tanned face and a nose peeling from snow burn. He placed the cornerstone for an immense stone arch through which coaches would now pass on entering the park, climbed aboard the *Elysian,* and was off again. The inscription at the top of Roosevelt Arch reads, "For the benefit and enjoyment of the people."

Small towns and whistle stops in Wyoming, South Dakota, Nebraska, and Iowa passed in a blur. He commiserated with former Rough Riders in Santa Fe and made his first pilgrimage to the Grand Canyon. "I don't exactly know what words to use in describing it," he said. The gaping chasm "is beautiful and terrible and unearthly. Leave it as it is," he urged the crowd of locals gathered in curiosity at the unique presidential character before them. "You cannot improve on it. The ages have been at work on it, and man can only mar it— keep it for your children, your children's children, and for all who come after you."

Southern California came next. Compared to the desolation of Arizona and New Mexico, it struck Roosevelt as fertile and lush. Irrigation had brought the landscape to life. The floral wonder of the Fiesta de Flores in Los Angeles stood in stark contrast to the aridity of the desert Southwest. He headed northward.

"There is nothing more practical in the end than the preservation of beauty," he told the audience in a major address on conservation at Stanford University. California's scenic charms had already enchanted him, with perhaps its best yet to come. Remembering the giant redwoods that dwarfed him near Santa Cruz the day before, he told the students, "I feel most emphatically that we should not turn into shingles a tree which was old when the first Egyptian conqueror penetrated to the valley of the Euphrates." Pinchot's soon-to-be forest service would be central to his vision: "We have a right to expect that the best trained, the best educated men on the Pacific Slope, the Rocky Mountains and great plains states will take the lead in the preservation and right use of the forests."

His themes weren't new. He'd been preaching them since he assumed the presidency in September 1901. Already sympathetic to the conservation cause, Roosevelt had called its leaders to the White House for advice and guidance just weeks after McKinley's death. He then set forth his conservation philosophy and priorities in his first annual message to Congress (now called the State of the Union address) that December:

Public opinion throughout the United States has moved steadily toward a just appreciation of the value of forests, whether planted or of natural growth. The great part played by them in the creation and maintenance of the national wealth is now more fully realized than ever before.

Wise forest protection does not mean the withdrawal of forest resources, whether of wood, water, or grass, from contributing their full share to the welfare of the people, but, on the contrary, gives the assurance of larger and more certain supplies. The fundamental idea of forestry is the perpetuation of forests by use. Forest protection is not an end of itself; it is a means to increase and sustain the resources of our country and the industries which depend upon them. The preservation of our forests is an imperative business necessity. We have come to see clearly that whatever destroys the forest, except to make way for agriculture, threatens our wellbeing.

The practical usefulness of the national forest reserves to the mining, grazing, irrigation, and other interests of the regions in which the reserves lie has led to a widespread demand by the people of the West for their protection and extension. The forest reserves will inevitably be of still greater use in the future than in the past. Additions should be made to them whenever practicable, and their usefulness should be increased by a thoroughly business-like management.

Despite strong opposition from the timber, mining, and grazing interests, by 1903 Roosevelt had already used the executive power granted him by Congress to withdraw millions of acres of western lands as forest reserves, and he showed no signs of stopping. The politics of progress and democracy demanded it. But what was demanded of the national parks? Did he see a difference in purpose between them and the national forests? As Hetch Hetchy would show, the answers would be dictated by his Progressive conservation philosophy.

Yet he also believed in the restorative qualities of wilderness preached by Muir. He continued, "Some at least of the forest reserves should afford perpetual protection to the native fauna and flora, safe havens of refuge to our rapidly diminishing wild animals of the larger kinds, and free camping grounds for the ever-increasing numbers of men and women who have learned to find rest, health, and recreation in the splendid forests and flower-clad meadows of our mountains. The forest reserves should be set apart forever for the use and benefit of our people as a whole and not sacrificed to the shortsighted greed of a few." There was no contradiction, however; like Pinchot the president believed conservation took precedence over preservation if the landscape possessed resources other than scenery that were potentially valuable for commercial exploitation.

And by this time conservation meant more than the multiple-use management of forest and grazing lands. Conservation also called for the construction of dams and reservoirs to irrigate the dry farms and fields of western settlers and homesteaders. The value of irrigation had been proven by districts like Turlock and Modesto in the San Joaquin Valley, the nation's first successful public agencies created to finance and manage the local distribution of irrigation water, an innovative form of public governance unnecessary in the East. Engineering technology had improved, making such projects feasible and affordable; and private business interests could profit from it, creating widespread political support. Whatever the backroom lobbying tactics and motives of its San Francisco proponents were, the loophole allowing water projects in Yosemite created by the Right of Way Act in February 1901 merely reflected the popular attitudes regarding resource use. Roosevelt made the call for irrigation to Congress and to the nation in his first annual message, "In the arid region it is water, not land, which measures production. The western half of the United States would sustain a population greater than that of our whole country to-day if the waters that now run to waste were saved and used for irrigation," he proclaimed.

> The forests alone cannot, however, fully regulate and conserve the waters of the arid region. Great storage works are necessary to equalize the flow of streams and to save the flood waters. Their construction has been conclusively shown to be an undertaking too vast for private effort. Nor can it be best accomplished by the individual States acting alone. Far-reaching interstate problems are involved; and the resources of single States would often be inadequate. It is properly a national function, at least in some of its features. It is as right for the National Government to make the streams and rivers of the arid region useful by engineering works for water storage as to make useful the rivers and harbors of the humid region by engineering works of another kind. The storing of the floods in reservoirs at the headwaters of our rivers is but an enlargement of our present policy of river control, under which levees are built on the lower reaches of the same streams. . . .
>
> Our aim should be not simply to reclaim the largest area of land and provide homes for the largest number of people, but to create for this new industry the best possible social and industrial conditions.

In 1902 he got his wish with passage of the Newlands Reclamation Act, following years of growing concern for irrigation and flood control. John Wesley Powell had originally proposed such an agency in the 1870s, after his pioneering exploration of the Colorado River.

For decades thereafter, as one of the nation's leading scientists work-ing in the U.S. Geological Survey, mapping and inventorying the public domain west of the hundredth meridian, he sought to better align the settlement process with the inherent conditions of the arid landscape, to little avail except for the Newlands Act.

On the surface the act appeared to be a classic Progressive conser-vation program intended to assist farmers and ranchers who worked the arid lands of the West by "reclaiming" marginal lands with irriga-tion. The U.S. Reclamation Service (now the Bureau of Recla-mation) was created to plan, construct, and manage these projects using funds initially provided by the sale of land from the public domain in sixteen western states. Eventually it would dam nearly every major western river. Thus the federal government committed itself to support and control large-scale irrigation and, as a result, placed itself front and center in the transformation of the West's physical landscape, its political and social climates, and its economic well-being.

But beneath the surface, the political waters swirling around the reclamation act, named after Nevada congressman, then senator Francis Griffith Newlands, the bill's principal sponsor, were mud-died with private interests. Development of water resources meant potential windfall profit for insiders. Newlands had lobbied tirelessly to create a government agency to build dams and reservoirs to irri-gate the West; now he would reap his reward. William Hammond Hall, the former California state engineer, would see to it.

Hall had convinced the senator that only the government could afford the huge cost to construct the hydraulic improvements needed to replumb the West. The old laissez-faire business ideology in which private enterprise was thought best able to make such improvements on behalf of the public, when freed from government interference other than the receipt of public subsidies, had become as passé and unpopular as the corresponding environmental attitudes. "Irrigation was then the coming political fad," Hall recalled. "The mining inter-ests and issues with which Mr. Newlands and his predecessors and moneyed connections had heretofore been identified were worn out."

Few people understood western water issues and needs better than Hall. It had been Hall who had taken the lead for Billy Ralston, a flamboyant San Francisco businessman and booster, in the creation of Golden Gate Park in the 1870s and 1880s after Ralston had rejected Olmsted's environmentally sensitive plan. And it had been Hall who had surveyed some of the Sierra Nevada for potential reservoir sites on behalf of Powell's U.S. Geological Survey, contributing to the identification of Hetch Hetchy and the upper Tuolumne River as the answer to San Francisco's water needs. While state engineer, Hall's description of the devastation wrought by hydraulic mining helped stop the practice, and his efforts to reform state water laws challenged the vested interests of leading land barons. But he also confidentially shared or sold his insights to landowners and investors eager to profit from his insider's information—including the PG&E founders, who joined him in a suspect scheme that purchased water rights near Hetch Hetchy that became competitive with those held by the city, forcing the city eventually to buy their rights at great expense. Francis Griffith Newlands was another favorite confidant.

The first project undertaken by the new reclamation service became known as the Newlands Irrigation Project. It dammed the Truckee River in Nevada and diverted its flow to the adjacent Carson River watershed east of Reno, enabling the Carson Valley to bloom with alfalfa and the landowners to reap handsome profits. It also deprived Lake Pyramid of its water source. But this affected only the nearby Paiute Indian reservation and the indigenous wildlife; hardly major concerns in the overall cost-benefit calculations. Few people were concerned that Senator Newlands had earlier hired Hall to investigate the valley's irrigation potential and that Newlands had purchased ranches there in the 1890s, which he sold to settlers or back to the government for substantial profit as the Newlands project came to fruition. Nor did his acquisition of property around Donner Lake, which the reclamation service soon sought as a regulating reservoir, create much notice.

The president continued from Palo Alto up the peninsula to San Francisco, speaking on monetary policy to a conservative audience of business leaders at the opulent Palace Hotel on May 12. William Hammond Hall and James Duval Phelan likely attended. The next morning Roosevelt rallied an audience at the Mechanics Pavilion on American imperialistic interests in the Pacific Rim, proclaiming the nation's manifest destiny to expand its influence ever westward. Two days later, he escaped from it all again, returning to his beloved wilderness, permitting its pristine grandeur and silence to temporarily purge the sights and sounds of civilization from his soul, as Yellowstone had done. "When I first visited California," he wrote in his autobiography, "it was my good fortune to see the 'big trees,' the Sequoias, and then to travel down into the Yosemite, with John Muir. Of course of all people in the world he was the one with whom it was best worth while thus to see the Yosemite."

Roosevelt had sent word to Muir months earlier asking him to be his guide. Muir initially hesitated, having long planned a world tour with Charles Sprague Sargent to begin at the same time of Roosevelt's anticipated arrival. The president prevailed, writing Muir, "I do not want anyone with me but you, and I want to drop politics absolutely for four days, and just be out in the open with you." Muir wrote Sargent of his dilemma: "an influential man from Washington wants to make a trip to the Sierra with me, and I might be able to do some forest good in talking freely around the campfire." Seeing the possible benefits to the preservation cause, Sargent and Muir postponed their trip.

The president continued in his autobiography, "John Muir met me with a couple of packers and two mules to carry our tent, bedding, and food for a three days' trip. The first night was clear, and we lay down in the darkening aisles of the great [Mariposa] Sequoia grove. The majestic trunks, beautiful in color and in symmetry, rose round us like the pillars of a mightier cathedral than ever was conceived even by the fervor of the Middle Ages. Hermit thrushes sang beautifully in the evening, and again, with a burst of wonderful music, at dawn."

The next day Roosevelt and Muir stole away from the group and rode horses to Glacier Point. They made camp without tents in a small clearing ringed by silver fir just back of the canyon rim. "Now this is bully!" Roosevelt proclaimed. As the night deepened, Muir set ablaze a tall, dead pine in the meadow, which lit the blackness like a giant torch, dazzling ashes dancing into the heavens to vanish among the stars. "Hurrah! That's a candle it took five hundred years to make. Hurrah for Yosemite!" roared the president. They talked well into the night as the embers gradually died off. "I stuffed him pretty well regarding the timber thieves, and the destructive work of the lumbermen, and other spoilers of the forests," Muir remembered. He probably harangued the president for federal control of the valley, but made no mention of Hetch Hetchy. Phelan's plan had yet to catch the attention of either camper.

"This is bullier yet!" Roosevelt exclaimed the next morning, discovering that a storm had blanketed them with four inches of snow. "I wouldn't miss this for anything." The next day they descended into the valley wonderland itself. They camped that last night on the southern edge of Bridalveil meadow, El Capitan standing guard over them. "This has been the grandest day of my life! One I shall long remember!" he remarked. "Good-bye, John," Roosevelt said as they shook hands at the end of the outing. "Come see me in Washington. I've had the time of my life." The visit remained a pleasant memory for both leaders. "I shall always be glad that I was in the Yosemite with John Muir and in the Yellowstone with John Burroughs," Roosevelt concluded in his autobiography.

In the aftermath Roosevelt redoubled his efforts to conserve the nation's dwindling forests, although for more utilitarian purposes than Muir advocated. Stopping in Sacramento as he returned to his presidential duties, Roosevelt proclaimed, "No small part of the prosperity of California . . . depends upon the preservation of her water supply; and the water supply cannot be preserved unless the forests are preserved. . . . I ask for the preservation of other forests on grounds of wise and far-sighted economic policy. . . . We are not building this country of ours for a day. It is to last through the ages."

While the implications of Phelan's plan for Hetch Hetchy went unnoticed in the early 1900s by Muir and those intent on preserving Yosemite, or by Roosevelt, Pinchot, and those intent on conserving Yosemite, both groups shared a concern for the management of the state reserve and the national park surrounding it. Two outcomes resulted: the first revised the park's boundary in 1905; the other returned the state reserve to the federal government for inclusion in the national park the following year.

Squabbling over the national park's boundary began as soon as Congress drew it in 1890. Scattered within the park were sixty-five thousand acres and three hundred mining claims in private hands, some of the claims thought to be very valuable. And their owners had

rights for access to and limited use of their property. The in-holdings
disrupted the U.S. Cavalry's efforts to manage the park in a coherent
manner, requiring them to patrol the obscure borders over rugged
terrain and complicating their struggle to control illegal poaching,
grazing, mining, and timber cutting. The presence of property owners working their land enticed wildcat miners, stockmen, and lumbermen to also work within the park. And the remoteness of many
private holdings made it difficult for the cavalry to prevent the
owners from working the land outside their property. In addition,
pressure for revisions of the park boundary came from eager entrepreneurs and businesses who eyed development opportunities for
the park's natural resources or recreation potential.

Bills to adjust the boundary and legal proceedings in response to
private claims appeared every year. Some politicians and park
advocates began to believe that the government needed either to
acquire the parcels or cut as many as possible from the park to sim-
plify management. To purchase them would be very expensive, so
land swaps that required an act of Congress made more sense to
other politicians.

And some leaders felt that most of the problems presented by private claims could be solved by realigning the boundary along natural
borders, like streams and ridge lines, in place of the latitude-
longitude-based borders according to which the existing boundary
was drawn. The rigid rectangular geometry was a product of the
township and range survey system applied to the public domain
nationwide, a practice better suited to the wetter eastern landscape
that John Wesley Powell had sought to replace with the use of watershed boundaries in the arid west. While many people recognized the
many problems inherent in the national survey system, it was the
only practical response to the urgent need and daunting task of surveying the continent into parcels for private ownership as quickly as
possible. When the park boundary was set in 1890, no complete
topographic map of the area was available, so the geometric convenience of the national survey system made sense. By the early 1900s,
detailed maps had been made, permitting the possible revision of the
boundary based on physical features.

In April 1904 Congress acted, directing Secretary of the Interior

Ethan A. Hitchcock to determine "what portions of said park are not necessary for park purposes, but can be returned to the public domain," on the belief that the park contained resource-rich parcels that should not have been included. Congressional thinking toward the nature of suitable park lands had changed little since Yellowstone was created in 1872. Congress had approved the park only because they believed no commercially developable resources would be lost. In the 1890 hearings on Yosemite, the proponents had probably suspected that Congress would hesitate to approve the park if they thought that valuable resources would be foreclosed. So the preservationists played to that utilitarian value, at times suggesting that the proposed park had little economic value beyond its scenery and recreation, although they assumed it did.

In 1904 Congress would hold the preservationists to that same rationale: If the Yosemite did have such lands, then they should be eliminated because they are incongruous with park purposes. The Progressive concept of conservation that promoted the protection of scenery only when no other resources of significant economic value would be foreclosed still prevailed over wilderness preservation for other less quantifiable reasons, whether for scenery and recreation or wildlife protection.

The secretary appointed a three-member boundary commission to study the problem and make a recommendation. Led by Major Hiram M. Chittenden, a respected authority on Yellowstone National Park, the commission toured Yosemite and held meetings with the local stakeholders for several weeks that summer. It then relocated to San Francisco to meet with other interested groups, including local, state, and federal politicians. There Muir and the Sierra Club presented a plan to redraw the boundary, eliminating some areas while adding others.

The commission's final recommendation was as expected. The park boundary would be reset to follow watershed lines as much as possible, cutting 542.88 square miles containing the bulk of the inholdings and claims, mostly toward the western, southern, and eastern boundaries, while adding 113.62 square miles of high country to the north to protect the upper Tuolumne River watershed. "Already a large portion of its waters is appropriated," their report stated, in recognition of San Francisco's permit applications to Secretary Hitchcock for use of Hetch Hetchy, "and the time may soon come when municipal needs will further draw upon them."

Apparently the committee was sympathetic to the city's plan. "There are no patented or mineral lands in this [northern] tract," the report continued. Instead, the watershed was "particularly prized by the people of California for the use that it will yet be to the State," despite it containing "features of great scenic beauty, notably the Hetch Hetchy Valley on the Tuolumne—a second Yosemite—Lake Eleanor, and the Tiltill Valley [part of a tributary of the Tuolumne River that enters the Hetch Hetchy Valley diagonally across the valley from Kolana Rock]." Although torn between protecting the scenery of the upper Tuolumne, as it was the scenery of the entire park, the commission relented to the "overwhelming sentiment" that the watershed be protected from pollution caused by grazing to enable future development of its water resource. Such resource they felt "capable of a use which will enhance the beauty of the park and serve the public as well."

Similarly, the commission concluded that the elimination of the vast acreage on the western, southern, and eastern flanks would not harm the spectacular scenery the park was created to protect. And in removing most private holdings and claims from the park, together with areas that business interests sought for commercial exploitation, the park would also be spared the future temptation to further erode its boundary or to introduce incompatible uses. Ironically, the addition of the new lands in the upper Tuolumne drainage would help make that very temptation too strong to resist.

Congress accepted the commission's recommendation without modification, approving the new boundary with little discussion in February 1905. California representative Gillett, a sponsor of the resulting bill, explained to his colleagues, "when the Yosemite National Park was established arbitrary lines were run and a great deal of territory was taken in not of any value for scenic purposes. Under the rules and regulations governing the park the people can not improve this land, they can not construct sawmills to cut timber; they can not operate and work their mines; they can not develop the water power, and this is to enable them to develop the business enterprises and industries of that county. This bill is intended to take it out of the national park and put it into the forest reserve." And this reserve would be far more open to resource development under Pinchot's supervision. "It is to relieve a large amount of patented land, territory not suitable for a park, and land that is not needed as a part of the national park." Coincidentally, just days before Congress had reconstituted Pinchot's Division of Forestry as the U.S. Forest Service with greater powers.

Concurrent with the gradual building of consensus in the 1890s to revise the park's boundary, consensus also gradually built for the recession of the state reserve to the federal government: return the Yosemite Valley and Big Tree Grove to the American people and incorporate them into Yosemite National Park. Since the reserve's creation in 1864, the stingy California legislature had appropriated on average only about $2,600 per year for the general preservation and improvement of the valley and grove, and another $150,000 over the forty years to settle private claims in the valley, acquire roads and trails, and construct a hotel and water system. With so little funding, commission efforts at consistent management and long-term planning were crippled. The adverse changes in the valley's scenery foreseen by Olmsted were occurring. Constant bickering between the commission and the state legislature over chronic underfunding also promoted an air of suspicion in the press and public over the reserve's management. Politics became incessant in the reserve's governance, especially in the appointment of commissioners. And after 1890 the management differences between the valley and the surrounding national park stood in stark contrast. The commission and the cavalry had little in common. The juxtaposition of the two places, the two management policies and practices for them, and their two governing groups, made no sense.

Muir and the Sierra Club monitored the decline with growing alarm, while trying to work constructively and cooperatively with the commission and the legislature to preserve the valley. But state pride and sovereignty were at stake. Initial efforts to pass a recession bill in the legislature failed, perhaps because the Sierra Club only half-heartedly lobbied for passage due to disagreement among its directors on how best to proceed. Some directors had personal or political ties to the commission, the legislature, and railroad interests, which at the time opposed the recession. However, the club's efforts intensified as its frustration with the endemic problems rose. Resistance from the legislature gradually gave way with the realization that federal control would relieve the state of financial responsibility, and it might actually earn more income for the state and give it greater publicity as tourism to the park would flourish in response to the improved management.

Pressure for recession mounted. By the turn of the century, major papers around the state editorialized in support. The cavalry supported it, as did the preservationists and the conservationists. Muir obtained Roosevelt's agreement when they reveled in the High Sierra and then sadly saw the effects of improper care in the valley. California governor George C. Pardee was among the other dignitaries in the party and probably lent his support to the plan as well. All agreed the action had to be initiated by the state, and only after the legislature had approved it could Congress then accept the recession.

In early 1905 a recession bill drafted by William E. Colby of the Sierra Club, with the assistance of William Mills, head of the Southern Pacific Railroad land department and a former Yosemite commissioner, was introduced in the California legislature. Colby was an enthusiastic young attorney with growing expertise in mining and water law who had joined the club in 1898 immediately after completing school. Attracted to the mountains for respite from academic rigors, he eagerly accepted an offer to be the club's representative in Yosemite Valley that summer. The experience changed his life. In 1901 he would initiate the annual High Trip to the Sierra, which he would lead until 1929, beginning the club's popular outing programs. He would become the club's secretary in 1900 and serve in that position except for two years until 1946; and he would also serve on the board of directors for forty-nine years. Colby was perhaps Muir's strongest ally in the club and next to him its most effective advocate and political player during the early 1900s.

The California Assembly approved the recession bill with little opposition. The boundary commission had heard testimony on recession during its deliberations the year before and helped persuade state officials to support it. The state senate was less sure. Debate raged, led by those aligned with the usual mining, grazing, and lumber interests, especially Senator Curtin of Tuolumne County, who owned several hundred acres at Crane Flat and other sites within the park. Curtin was at odds with the cavalry over his right to drive cattle across park land to reach his property. His tales of the federal government's "czar-like" behavior rallied opposition.

With the vote pending and chances of approval doubtful, Muir asked E. H. Harriman, the president of the Southern Pacific Railroad, to intervene. Harriman was one of the nation's most influential financiers and had added the line to his railroad and shipping empire following Collis Huntington's death in 1900. Although not as dominant in California economic and political matters as it was a decade earlier, Southern Pacific nevertheless retained tremendous clout.

Muir and Harriman had become friends in 1899 when Muir participated in an extensive tour of Alaska sponsored by the magnate. If anything, Harriman knew how to use his wealth and prominence to manage people, whether for business gain or personal interest. Among the large entourage were dozens of leading politicians, scientists, and conservationists, including John Burroughs. Muir's suspicion of his small, nondescript-looking host with an icy manner, an arch-villain in the "gobble gobble school of economics" that Muir so despised, gradually melted away during the two-month-long trip spent mostly in close quarters shipboard. Apparently, opposites attracted; their earthiness, energy, and passion overcame differences in career and lifestyle. The two would remain close, based more on mutual respect than shared intimacy, until Harriman's death in 1909, enabling Muir to call upon Harriman's personal and political assistance from time to time.

Muir's first call to Harriman came as no surprise. Both Muir and the Sierra Club had lost their political naïveté and timidity during the battles on behalf of Yosemite for proper management, for boundary revision, and now for recession. Harriman was happy to help, perhaps realizing the potential profits from increased tourism. Nine senators abruptly changed their votes. The bill passed twenty-one to thirteen on February 23. Congressional acceptance of the recession required Harriman's persuasion as well. Work on the park's boundary revision and legal technicalities also delayed formal approval; but on June 11, 1906, President Roosevelt signed the federal bill just as he promised Muir he would three years earlier in Yosemite.

Muir was overjoyed, writing his close confederate and confidant

Robert Underwood Johnson, "sound the loud timbrel and let every Yosemite tree and stream rejoice! You may be sure I knew when the big bill passed. Getting Congress to accept the Valley brought on, strange to say, a desperate fight both in the House and Senate. Sometime I'll tell you all the story. You don't know how accomplished a lobbyist I've become under your guidance. The fight you planned by the famous Tuolumne camp-fire seventeen years ago is at last fairly, gloriously won, every enemy down derry down." Little did the leaders of the preservation movement know of the change for Yosemite that was in the offing, and little did they see the political forces already aligning to trigger it.

The sequence of steps that ultimately result in congressional action often begin far removed from Washington, propelled by unpredictable and unrelated circumstances, culminating in an outcome unexpected at the outset. Only in hindsight is the sequence visible, and only when seen in its full context is its meaning apparent. So it was with Hetch Hetchy.

PART TWO

The Hetch Hetchy Controversy, Past and Present

"Contemporary View of the Hetch Hetchy Reservoir"

From approximately the same vantage point as the Taber photograph (fron-
tispiece) and the painting by Bierstadt (book jacket). Kolana Rock looms on
the right, with the valley floor several hundred feet below the water surface.
Photograph by the author

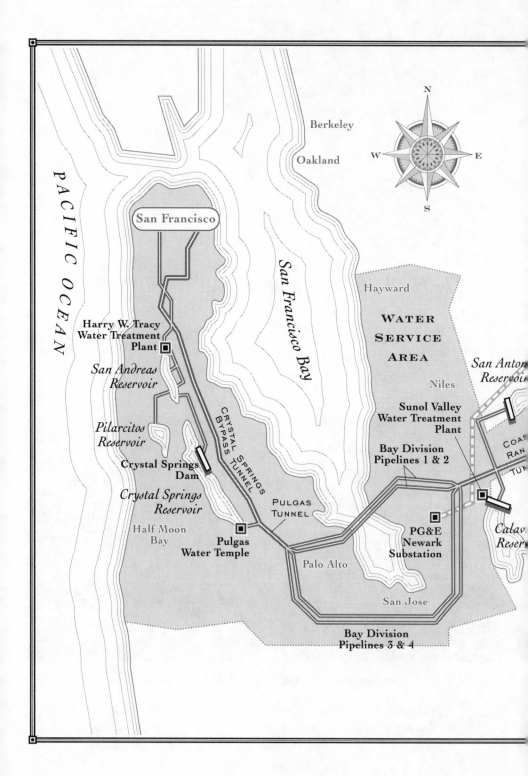

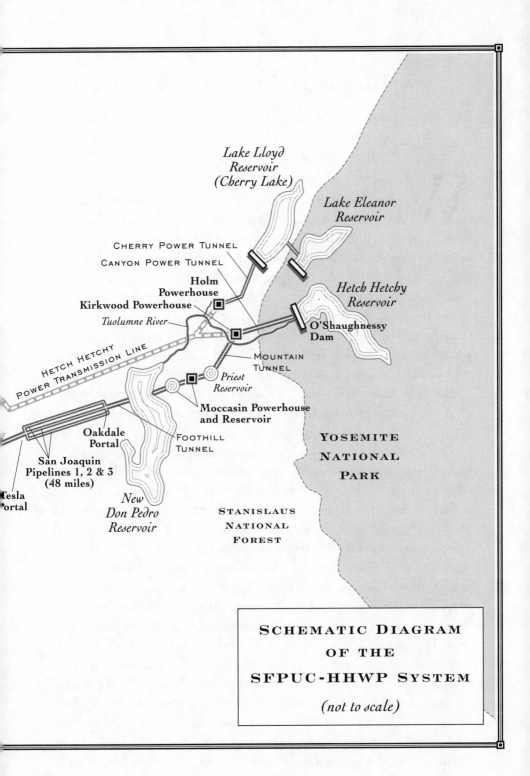

Lake Lloyd Reservoir (Cherry Lake)

Lake Eleanor Reservoir

CHERRY POWER TUNNEL

CANYON POWER TUNNEL

Holm Powerhouse

Kirkwood Powerhouse

Hetch Hetchy Reservoir

Tuolumne River

O'Shaughnessy Dam

HETCH HETCHY POWER TRANSMISSION LINE

MOUNTAIN TUNNEL

Priest Reservoir

Moccasin Powerhouse and Reservoir

Oakdale Portal

FOOTHILL TUNNEL

San Joaquin Pipelines 1, 2 & 3 (48 miles)

Tesla Portal

New Don Pedro Reservoir

STANISLAUS NATIONAL FOREST

YOSEMITE NATIONAL PARK

SCHEMATIC DIAGRAM

OF THE

SFPUC-HHWP SYSTEM

(not to scale)

CHAPTER 5

Spring Valley and the Boomtown Politics of Water

W ater teases and tantalizes San Francisco. Despite the
city's location, surrounded as it is by the sea and bathed
by moist morning fog, it thirsts for freshwater, blocked
from rains and runoff by geography and topography. The search for
reliable sources of freshwater began in the 1850s as the city boomed
during the gold rush. In the spring of 1848, prior to the onslaught,
only eight hundred people or so lived in the ramshackle town called
Yerba Buena at the northeast tip of the peninsula. Local creeks and
streams fed by the twenty inches of annual rainfall supplied sufficient
water for the shabby settlement, though summer droughts were
prevalent. The sandy soils retained scant runoff. Coastal breezes
swept the knobby hills, shaping a desolate, dune-like landscape covered with scrub growth. Little there had changed in years, and few
prospects foreshadowed changes to come.

The boom hit in 1849 with unimaginable force. San Francisco
would rise as a result of an imperialistic quest for gold from the
Mother Lode in the distant Sierra Nevadas. Few American metropolitan areas would experience such explosive and continuous
growth. By year's end the cluster of wood-framed structures housed
a population of nearly 25,000 people, although one could hardly consider it a "city." Urban civilities would come later. Nor were reliable
headcounts really possible. People flooded in so fast, and raced out
so quickly to the placers along the western foothills of the Sierra, that
the population changed daily. But mining-based booms rarely last
long. By the late 1850s, most of the Mother Lode's riches had been
extracted. Hydraulic mining would continue for years, devastating
hillsides and riverbeds in a desperate search for the remaining
ounces of gold. Barring another growth trigger, however, San
Francisco's boom would have petered out with the yields, forcing the
city to find a more stable economic and social basis. An 1860 census
counted 56,802 San Franciscans; another counted more than 83,000.

Development of the Comstock Lode of silver on the eastern slope of the Sierra outside Virginia City, Nevada, reenergized the San Francisco boom, coinciding with the declining yields of the Mother Lode in the 1860s. As the closest major city to the strike, San Francisco supplied most of the capital, labor, and logistical support for the underground mining operations penetrating deep into the two-mile-long vein beneath the shoulder of Mount Davidson, and received most of the wealth in return. The boom continued little abated, with the population reaching nearly 173,000 by 1870, according to local counts. And as the Comstock yield declined, the transcontinental railroad arrived, loaded with more people and more opportunity. Growth around the bay followed suit.

The gold rush boom had hardly begun before water needs surpassed the limited flow of the small creeks and streams at the tip of the peninsula. Entrepreneurs were soon shipping in water by barge from across the bay and selling the liquid gold for premium prices from barrels up and down the sandy streets. Before long, primitive companies formed to tap sources inland on the peninsula. Small diversion dams, flumes, troughs, and pipelines met demand for several years. These were soon insufficient too. The only option: extend the supply tentacles further. The thought of limiting growth to match local sources was inconceivable, of course. The search for water would soon become as imperialistic as the search for gold and silver.

Fires were endemic in the wooden boomtown, burning it to the ground six times between 1850 and 1852 alone. People quickly concluded that a municipal water supply would help combat the frequent fires that plagued the town. They also seethed at the price gouging and poor service of the primitive water companies. Many people thought water should be provided by the city for free, or at least be available at cost. Together the fear of fire and the anger toward the private suppliers would spur a decades-long municipal struggle to control its own water supply and its own destiny.

Private companies jostled for control of the growing market throughout the 1850s, buying the water rights of nearby sources and developing larger storage and delivery systems, though still located near the tip of the peninsula. They also jostled with one another, like commuters, continuously mixing and morphing as companies combined or died in the competitive atmosphere. The Spring Valley

Water Company emerged dominant in the 1860s, acquiring a stranglehold on the city's water supply that would last more than sixty years.

The monopoly was a monster of the city's making, merely reflecting the dominant business atmosphere of the day, an atmosphere that many civic and business leaders profited from handsomely. It was a curious corporate creature, born of legal privileges and loopholes, of vision and ambition, and of greed and personal spite. Control of the water supply meant political power and profit, whether one was in the public or the private sector. As much as any single factor, water would shape the city's future, and those who controlled it could reap great riches through land speculation. Fred Eaton, William Mulholland, and their cronies in Los Angeles would later learn that lesson. The corporate bosses and financial backers of Spring Valley already knew it.

The state legislature granted a water franchise to Spring Valley in 1858, giving it and other privately owned municipal water companies the power of eminent domain so they could acquire land and water rights and lay water mains for the good of the public they served. That public benefit could also make for the greater good of the company owners. The power of condemnation enabled insiders to profit from land speculation along the proposed routes of mains as the extension of water service would increase property values in the new service area. The legislature also exempted the fledgling company from the usual provision for supplying water free for all municipal purposes, except for firefighting, thinking the company's initial daily supply of five thousand gallons insignificant. But Spring Valley didn't stay small for long. The city was booming, and bankers and financiers were flush with capital derived from Sierra mining to pour into water projects to quench the growing thirst.

When local water sources were no longer sufficient, Spring Valley moved aggressively to acquire and develop sources to the south. Rainfall amounts were highest farther down the peninsula on the Santa Cruz Mountains and the shoulders of Montara Mountain, where it averaged nearly fifty inches per year. And there the cleft formed by the San Andreas rift down the spine of the range created a natural reservoir site. In contrast, the annual rainfall on land ringing the bay in the shadow of the mountains dropped to twelve inches.

Few sources of water existed there. If the city needed more fresh-water, it would come first from the mountains on the peninsula; after that, distant sources across the bay would have to be tapped or the city would have to accept the local limits.

Spring Valley dammed Pilarcitos Creek first, on the eastern side of Montara Mountain, diverting to San Francisco its "wasted" flow westward to Half Moon Bay and the Pacific Ocean. The first water arrived in the city on July 4, 1862, concurrent with the news of Brigadier General Fitz John Porter's Union army victory over General Robert E. Lee's Confederate forces at Mechanicsville, Virginia, and President Abraham Lincoln's approval of the Pacific Railway Act, authorizing the transcontinental railroads. Months later, more water was needed. A series of expansions over the next half-dozen years to the Pilarcitos Creek impoundments and pipelines barely kept pace with growing demand.

Next, Spring Valley acquired thousands of acres of land and water rights a few miles north of Pilarcitos Reservoir and dammed the San Andreas Valley, leaving on the peninsula only the long, slender valley formed by the San Andreas rift as a potential impoundment site of any consequence. They dammed it too and expanded it, again and again, from 1867 to 1911, creating the Upper and Lower Crystal Springs Reservoirs. Spring Valley now monopolized all the signifi-cant water sources on the peninsula, forcing potential competitors to pipe in water from distant supplies across the bay. None could do so.

Some people saw the problem and the ultimate solution well in advance. Frederick Law Olmsted did. The answer to San Francisco's water problem appeared obvious to him. He noted in 1865 that the city had no significant water supply closer than the Sierra, "An aque-duct from which," he estimated, "would need to be at least two hun-dred miles in length. It has not as yet been suggested," he continued, "and is not likely to be projected in our time." Events would prove him wrong, and the famous park he helped create and manage would suffer as a consequence.

Barely a month after Olmsted's prediction, the ambitious engineer who designed Spring Valley's Pilarcitos system announced his inten-tion of bringing water from Lake Tahoe—the "jewel of the Sierra"— to the Bay Area, a visionary scheme in direct competition with his employer. The *Daily Alta California* reported the 163-mile-long aqueduct would "throw into shade all similar works of either ancient or modern times, in the old or new world." The engineer boasted it would be "the grandest aqueduct in the world." But he couldn't raise the necessary capital for the costly project. Despite the immense potential profits for San Francisco financiers from water sales, land deals in the Bay Area associated with the proposed project, and the irrigation of vast acreages in the Central Valley, they wouldn't fund the scheme. Many of those same financiers had extensive mining-related holdings in Nevada that might be hurt by the diversion of flow from the Truckee River, the lake's only outflow, never mind the interests of Nevada residents dependent on the river. The Truckee was left untouched, temporarily. The interconnectedness of mining and water imperialism scuttled the engineer's plan. Other entrepreneurs would try to realize it later.

Although Spring Valley had always matched the growing water demand by increasing supply, San Francisco feared the company would be unable to meet future needs, and a steady stream of complaints about poor service poured in from customers. However, Spring Valley's pricing policies and predatory business practices most strained its relationship with the city. Many people felt the company served the public good only insofar as it first served its own interests. San Francisco and Spring Valley were soon at each other's throats, thanks in large part to the legal loophole that exempted the company from providing water free for municipal purposes.

The loophole remained even as the company grew and monopolized San Francisco's water supply, but it had always been overlooked by a gentlemen's agreement of sorts between Spring Valley and city hall. By 1869 Spring Valley felt water usage for public purposes was costing too much, so they put a meter on the municipal spigot. The company president wrote the board of supervisors, "The city has no more right to take the property of said water works without compensation than she has to take the property of the gas company or of any private citizen." No more free water for parks, public buildings, and other municipal purposes, except fighting fires. But the city refused to pay the bills. Eleven years of constant combat and court cases ensued between the city and the company over pricing practices and bills, conflicts that were usually decided in the company's favor. Spring Valley made immense profits for its owners, seemingly at the expense of the public welfare. Profits from mining also flowed freely at the time, providing deep pools of cash for influence peddling as well as for financing further Spring Valley projects on the peninsula.

The new California constitution adopted in 1880 sought to settle the squabbling by making the San Francisco Board of Supervisors responsible for setting rates, to no avail. Rate fixing by the board proved just as problematic. The source of irritation was simply relocated, triggering constant battles between the board, the company, and the public for the next thirty years, when the constitution was amended and responsibility for rates was given to the state railroad commission. Too late: the damage had been done. To the citizens and civic leaders of San Francisco, Spring Valley Water Company was a money-grubbing corporate piranha that had bought privileges for decades.

Making matters worse, Spring Valley repeatedly dodged municipal efforts to purchase it, while city efforts to develop its own supplemental water sources repeatedly failed. When the state legislature granted San Francisco the power to purchase a municipal water supply in 1874, the city immediately initiated a study of options, including sources in the Sierra and Spring Valley's sources on the peninsula. The report recommended the purchase and further development of properties owned by the Alameda Water Company across the bay. Spring Valley was not about to let its profitable monopoly be jeopardized so easily. As negotiations between San Francisco and Alameda began, Spring Valley purchased the critical properties and water rights from beneath the city's feet. Blocked, San Francisco then asked Spring Valley to set its own sale price. The mayor responded curtly to Spring Valley's offensive offer: "We decline the offer, on the ground that the price named is much in excess of the true cost of the works as shown by their own books." Spring Valley rejected the city's counteroffer in 1877, further heightening tensions between the two parties.

Municipal leaders persisted, soon soliciting offers from other private water companies to pipe in water from across the bay, based on several surveys of potential sources. Colonel George H. Mendell, an engineer from the U.S. Army and the engineer for the city water commission, produced the most comprehensive survey in 1877. The

163-page study (excluding extensive appendices) examined existing
sources on the peninsula, including those of Spring Valley, as well as
remote sources in the Sierra, such as Lake Tahoe, and sources drawn
from the American, Mokelumne, and San Joaquin Rivers. Hetch
Hetchy was not specifically considered even though it was yet to be
included in a national park, probably because other options made
more sense. Balanced, practical, and thoughtful, the report surveyed
the general pros and cons for each option based on water quality,
quantity, reliability, cost, and engineering implications. "Quantity
and quality are two well established points for any contemplated
supply from the mountains," Mendell wrote. "On the other
hand . . . the Sierra supply is more expensive than other and nearer
sources."

The first plan to tap the Tuolumne River was apparently drawn up
in 1882 by J. P. Dart, an engineer for the San Francisco and
Tuolumne Water Company in the Sierra foothills. He mapped a
route that diverted water from the Tuolumne fifteen miles northeast
of Groveland and brought it to an East Bay reservoir via an aqueduct across the San Joaquin Valley. Mains would then distribute the
water around the Bay Area. But knowledge of his scheme may have
never spread beyond the Tuolumne County Courthouse in Sonora.

The first person to specifically point out the possibility of the
Hetch Hetchy Valley as a water source and reservoir site was probably George M. Harris. In 1888 he met with San Francisco mayor
Edward B. Pond and other civic and business leaders, offering to sell
the city his rights to the Tuolumne River from the head of the Grand
Canyon to the river's outlet in the bay for $200,000. Nothing hap-
pened. Harris repeated his offer in 1894 in response to a desperate
call for proposals by the board of supervisors published in Bay Area
newspapers. In his letter to the committee on water supply he wrote,
"Here is the greatest storage of the purest water the world ever saw,
in quantity and quality unexcelled. Its bed is the insoluble granite
and gneiss rock. By putting in a dam at the mouth of this canyon it
will safely store at a moderate estimate 1,000,000 gallons of water all
through the year." A half-dozen other offers were also received;
again, none worked out.

Yet underlying assumptions would make every proposal or study
of alternatives problematic, including Colonel Mendell's: How much

and how fast would the city and resulting water demand grow? How would land use change surrounding each source affect its water quality? How would the quantity of each source vary monthly and yearly? What was the cost of developing each source, especially when considering the construction of distant dams and reservoirs and lengthy pipelines and tunnels? How might the various sources be used in combination to meet projected demand as cost-effectively as possible? The colonel made no clear-cut recommendations, although he expected the Spring Valley Water Company would be a part of any eventual municipal system. He did conclude, "It must be clear that the position and circumstances of San Francisco, as compared with other American cities, are unfavorable for a cheap water supply." He continued, "It only remains for the people of the city to use their supply judiciously. While there will always be enough for useful purposes, there is none for waste." Politics and technology would prove him wrong.

Nothing worked out, again and again, in San Francisco's search for an alternate water supply in the 1880s and 1890s. Civic frustration rose. Procedural questions in the city, wrangling over purchase price between the city and potential suppliers, and unruly business practices scuttled potential deals. The search continued for a long-term solution, focusing more and more on a publicly owned and operated supply. Throughout, political and popular support for the cause waxed and waned with alternating years of wet and dry weather, while Spring Valley still continued to meet the city's water needs.

The schemes of those with big money loomed barely behind the scenes during the first decades in the development of San Francisco and its water system. As corporate owners, board members, bankers, and financiers, enriched by mining profits, a handful of power brokers sought to promote their pet real estate projects by guiding the expansion of the city's water supply. Some of the press reported it, and some in politics fought it; however, most people were merely pawns in the game.

Golden Gate Park was one of those schemes and glorious dreams, envisioned by William Chapman Ralston in the mid-1860s. Ralston felt that to be a truly world-class city, San Francisco needed a grand park, like New York's 770-acre Central Park. Coincidentally, his business acquaintance Frederick Law Olmsted happened to be in the Bay Area.

Billy Ralston belonged to that distinctive caste of entrepreneurs who played so prominent a role in the making of urban America in the late nineteenth and early twentieth centuries—energetic and endlessly optimistic, aggressive, and high minded, and little bothered by rules of proper business or political behavior. Billy was a self-made, self-assured dreamer, unable to distinguish his self-interests from the best interests of the city. The founder of the Bank of California and the hub of "Ralston's Ring" of powerful San Francisco bankers and financiers, Billy and his "Bank Crowd" controlled the strings on most of the riches from the Comstock mines. He spread his profits widely, investing in dozens of business ventures, often highly speculative, as well as using them for political and judicial bribes. Community causes also benefited from his largesse. By outward appearances Billy was a prophetic businessman with the Midas touch, a paragon of civic virtue who dreamed of an imperial San Francisco, as would James Duval Phelan twenty years later. Never mind that beneath the façade appeared a different person: not mean-spirited or malicious, but rather someone who ignored propriety in his enthusiastic pursuit of tightly intertwined personal ambitions and civic dreams.

Billy's Bank of California held substantial debt on the Las Mariposas estate, so he knew Olmsted from business dealings about the property. He asked Olmsted to design a huge park for the scrubby, sandy dunes along the western half of the peninsula that would be 150 acres larger than the prototype in Manhattan. Olmsted advised against it. The reason: Billy envisioned a lush, romantic-style pleasure ground, with the pastoral character of Central Park, but Olmsted knew that that style could only be achieved on the windy, desolate dunes by extensive soil enrichment and irrigation. "I do not believe it practicable to meet the natural but senseless demand of unreflecting people bred in the Atlantic states and the North of Europe for what is technically termed a park under the climatic conditions of San Francisco," he argued.

In his report outlining his plan, Olmsted wrote, "The special conditions fixed by natural circumstances, to which the plan must be adapted, are so obvious that I need not recapitulate them here. Determining for the reasons already given, that a pleasure ground is needed which shall compare favorably with any in existence, it must, I believe, be acknowledged, that, neither in beauty of green sward, nor in great umbrageous trees, do these special conditions of topography, soil, and climate of San Francisco allow us to hope that any pleasure ground it can acquire, will ever compare in the most distant degree, with those of New York or London." Olmsted saw an alternate character for the park that would still place it and the city among the ranks of the world's elite. "The question then is whether it be possible for San Francisco to form a pleasure ground peculiar to itself, with a beauty as much superior to that of other such grounds, *in any way,* as theirs must be superior to what it can aspire to in spreading trees and great expanses of turf. I think that it can," he concluded.

Instead, Olmsted proposed an alternate site toward the interior of the city, to be designed in harmony with the topography and climate using indigenous, drought-tolerant species. There the park could offer the same social benefits to the crowded masses of city dwellers as did his Central Park model. Did the idealistic landscape architect try to entice Billy to the plan by appealing to his base instinct— money? After all, Central Park had quickly and dramatically increased the property value of land around its perimeter. Olmsted's report addressed at length the many social and economic benefits of his plan. The implication was clear. Billy and his partners could profit handsomely when the park was built, whether directly by buying up property surrounding the proposed park beforehand, or indirectly by the city's enhanced growth and development. Hence the project could benefit both the public and the prominent, making it a good deal for everyone.

But without having resolved the issue, Olmsted returned to New York in 1865 to resume work on his beloved Central Park and his burgeoning landscape architecture practice. The Las Mariposas estate had gone bankrupt despite his efforts, and opportunities in New York beckoned him more than the variety of possible design projects in the Bay Area. Billy immediately scrapped the Olmsted park plan and pursued his original scheme for an English-style park on the western flank of the peninsula. There the park could better promote his land schemes for the city's expansion, and Spring Valley would provide the water for free, in effect underwriting the plan.

The park came to life in the late 1860s and early 1870s, gradually transforming the dunes into a romantic oasis of sensuously curving paths and coppices over the course of several years. Its insatiable thirst for water cost Spring Valley a fortune, in part forcing the company to extend its tentacles further down the peninsula to find additional sources of supply and to begin charging the city for municipal water. Taxpayers would now underwrite that part of Billy's public dream and private land speculation scheme. The rate Spring Valley charged the city for water use in the park became a sharp thorn of contention, as were the general rates for all forms of municipal water use. At one point the city owed Spring Valley $400,000 for water usage in Golden Gate Park alone.

By the early 1870s Billy had big financial problems of his own. He was a nineteenth-century precursor to a modern-day, highly leveraged speculator who uses junk bonds in a form of circular financing to fund suspect deals. Cash flow, liquidity, and investor confidence were critical to making his convoluted empire work. Driven by his boundless ambition and optimism, however, he overextended and was forced to play a financial shell game. Beneath the outward appearance of stability, the base of his empire sat on very shaky ground. Declining revenues from his portfolio of holdings left him short of cash, and some of his land schemes and imperial dreams for the city—like the Palace Hotel, where Enrico Caruso was sleeping when the earthquake struck—were costing him a fortune.

Billy began building the mammoth eight-hundred-room, seven-story Palace in the mid-1870s in large part to attract buyers for a land deal south of Market Street. He spared no expense on the opulent hotel, intending it to be one of the grandest in the world, befitting both the city's imperial presumptuousness and his own, both based on the newfound riches of Sierra gold and silver. Unfortunately, his revenues from the Comstock Lode were running out, some of his other suspect investments were suffering, and the hotel proved to be a black hole of overruns. He desperately needed cash to stay financially afloat, so he created a scheme to purchase and quickly resell the fabulously profitable Spring Valley Water Company for a 50 percent gain. For example, in 1875, Spring Valley paid a 61 percent dividend on earnings—the years of bribes by the monopoly to city officials and the courts had paid off handsomely. "Water in San Francisco costs more than bread, more than light," wrote famed Bay Area political economist Henry George. "It is a very serious item in the living expenses of every family, and one of the large expenses of every manufacturing establishment. There is no large city in the civilized world where water costs so much. And even then the supply is neither as good nor as plentiful as it should be." The company's profitability likely made it an easy asset to raise capital for, probably enabling Billy to finance its purchase with little of his own money.

Billy's scheme was based on the city's desperate desire to acquire a municipal water supply, as well as his influence in city hall. To start, he bought Spring Valley and concurrently engineered the preemptive purchase of Alameda Water Company assets from beneath the city's feet by a group of private investors, which he headed, thus protecting the Spring Valley monopoly. Spring Valley then purchased the Alameda assets for a handsome markup, making Billy a nice paper profit and expanding the company's supply capacity to satisfy San Francisco's growing demand. For the coup de grace, he would persuade the city to buy Spring Valley from him at an inflated sales price. Since the city would again have no other option for obtaining a municipal water supply, how could it refuse? Plus, Billy would use his influence with city hall to ensure the board of supervisors appreciated the advantages of the offer. He would then pay off the creditors who had financed the scheme, and shore up his floundering balance sheet with the profit.

It didn't work. This time Billy crossed the line, touching too sensitive a municipal and public nerve. City hall couldn't be convinced. Suspicions surfaced about Billy's worsening financial straits. Investor confidence sagged. When the city rejected his offer, Billy's overextended financial empire collapsed. On Wednesday, August 25, 1875, the share value of his Comstock holdings plummeted, and concerns over the solvency of his Bank of California rose. Thursday was worse. Billy's business partner began dumping his Comstock shares, triggering panic in the market. Investors at the San Francisco Stock and Exchange Board ran across California Street to withdraw their cash from Billy's bank. Word of the run spread like wildfire, drawing the general public into the panic. But the bank had too little cash in reserve to cover the frenzy. Billy had allowed the reserves to drop dangerously low, perhaps siphoning off money in the weeks before to settle some of his other debts. With the vaults empty at 2:35 p.m., twenty-five minutes before regular closing time, he ordered the massive bronze doors shut, locking out a throng of screaming depositors in the street. The board ousted him as president Friday morning.

Broke and discredited, Billy went for his usual swim at North Beach that afternoon. Seemingly unaffected by the events of the week, he showered and rubbed down briskly at the Neptune Bath House, walked out to the end of the wooden pier, and dove into the cold water of the bay. A witness saw him swimming vigorously out two hundred yards, past the *Bullion,* a small stern-wheel steamer, and on toward Alcatraz Island. His lifeless body was recovered an hour later.

The throng of mourners in Billy's funeral procession stretched curb to curb for three miles. It seems they had short memories. The *Alta California* eulogized him saying, "His was the vast vision of the Builders and his like shall never pass this way again." The press and those with vested business interests in rebuilding investor confidence in the bank and Billy's other assets they now controlled worked quickly to shape the public's memory of him. It worked. People remembered Billy not so much as a failed financier, but as the embodiment of their hopes and dreams for the city. In many ways he personified the spirit of San Francisco, as would James Duval Phelan.

Spring Valley Water Company continued under new ownership, little affected by his death. His business partner assumed the reins and continued to battle the city over water prices and to buy influence and privileges whenever possible. The Bank of California weathered the storm. The spectacular Palace Hotel opened and for a short time dazzled the world. And Golden Gate Park became a much-loved bit of the pastoral English Midlands set on the semiarid peninsula, an illusion of a lush, semitropical landscape, dependent upon the importation of water from distant places, symbolic of San Francisco as a whole—a hydraulic city fed, like Imperial Rome, by aqueducts.

CHAPTER 6

James Duval Phelan and the Imperial Dream

Mayor James Duval Phelan had had enough of the graft and greed that plagued his city. The unruly boomtown behavior of bankers and businessmen and the backroom deals of political bosses had become endemic, as much a part of the San Francisco culture as the high-mindedness of municipal reformers like him. One behavior necessitated the other. San Franciscans suffered a split personality, torn between the two appealing psyches. They weren't alone. The same schizophrenia affected other imperialistic cities seeking glory at the end of the century. (Perhaps it was true of the entire United States, as well.)

Phelan's dream derived from his father's beliefs and behavior. Business always came first for the father, a practical, calculating, stoic man who had little time for civic causes. But he provided well for his family and instilled a positive set of values in the children. His son attended public schools, not exclusive private schools like his peers. Nor was family life ostentatious. The Phelans certainly lived comfortably and enjoyed cultural refinement, but they retained an earthiness unusual for people of their prominence. Did James Phelan completely avoid the shady business and banking practices of his rivals, like Billy Ralston? Perhaps part of the son's passion for municipal reform was a reaction to the sins of the past from which the prior generation profited, and perhaps part of his obsession stemmed from the continuing sins of the present, whether those of the Bay Area nouveau riches or those of the second generation of boomtown wealth.

It was Phelan who had brought Daniel Burnham, the famous architect and urban planner, to San Francisco two years earlier to prepare a master plan that would etch that dream on the city land-scape. Elegant stone-and-steel buildings in the ornate beaux arts style would line grand boulevards radiating out from nodes containing classical civic monuments to link with public parks. San Francisco would be a showcase of the latest "City Beautiful" concepts of urban design, an enlightened city in physical form, social structure, and cultural refinement—a twentieth-century Rome, a modern imperial city standing on the hills overlooking the bay, Mediterranean in climate and character, based on Progressive political thinking. That was Phelan's dream. "There is much to be done to make San Francisco an ideal city," he wrote. "There are citizens utilitarian in their lives, as well as in their aspirations, and this class must be educated to an appreciation of the beautiful, before they will give their vote and support to any movement whose end is beauty." He continued,

The rough work of the building of a city has been successfully accomplished in San Francisco. The forest, as it were, has been cleared, the land has been tilled, [and] the promise is abundant. . . . San Francisco must act on the theory; that the future is on her side; there is no good reason to doubt it, and no progress can be made without it. . . . San Francisco is in the position of a young merchant, whose future depends on the clearness of his vision, the boldness of his enterprise, the steadiness of his hand. He borrows with confidence, knowing his ability to repay; he surveys the field in which he is to make his operations, and satisfies himself that it will yield abundant returns. . . .

With money San Francisco can reduce its death-rate by improved sanitation; it could possess its own public utilities, as water and artificial light, and save us the moral humiliation of perennial corruption, which dims our civic pride and embitters our political life.

It can make the streets afford pleasure to all who use them. It could, imitating Paris, Berlin and Vienna, wed our superb [Golden Gate] Park to the city, by connecting it with the business and residence portion by beautiful boulevards, green with foliage; and, by thus holding and attracting a large population, it would bring business and profit to every industry. . . .

Then would follow museums, galleries of art and theaters, until San Francisco, by reason of its remarkable meteorological advantages, would assume the position of the most beautiful city in America, and its population the most artistic and pleasure-loving, drawing to its realm myriads of strangers from year to year.

As a three-term mayor, from 1896 to 1902, Phelan championed the city's new charter in 1900, which cut the bothersome political umbilical cord tethering the youthful city to its state parent. Now home rule gave San Francisco greater control over its destiny. Now a mayor with clearly defined executive powers could work with various boards and commissions to chart its course, reflecting the Progressive agenda. Now honest, reformed government, led by devoted civil servants responsive to the wants and wishes of their constituents, could depose the self-serving, backroom politics of personal greed and corporate meddling. Municipal utilities could replace private monopolies. Great public projects could remake the city, assuring its future growth and prosperity, embracing the welfare of all its citizens. A sense of civic responsibility could foster constructive cooperation between the public and private sectors. San Francisco would then stand as a monument to American achievement, an American Renaissance rivaling New York, Washington, D.C., and the great cities of the world.

San Francisco was James Duval Phelan's mistress, the city his only true and lasting love. Phelan would never marry, perhaps because no woman could compete for his attention and affection like San Francisco and his business and civic interests, on which he would lavish the gifts of his time and money.

But his dream of an imperial city had imperialistic implications. How was the city to obtain the resources needed to enable that development when the local landscape was so short of them, especially water? New York City had gone far to find it, tapping watersheds well to the north, reaching upstate into the Catskill Mountains. Los Angeles had begun the process in the distant Owens Valley. So San Francisco's quest for water from remote sources would not be unique.

Phelan's answer was consistent with typical American thinking: get the needed resource from wherever it can be obtained most easily. Technology would make it possible, and the political clout of the powerful and the profit motive of the private sector would support it. Yet like most politicians, corporate leaders, civic boosters, and the general public, Phelan assumed the wants and wishes of the city justified the appropriation of whatever resource it required, with little thought given to the consequences for the affected landscape. What else was the environment for, if not to supply resources? Why should one let local limits dampen dreams?

Urban imperialism assumes many forms, in this case the colonization and exploitation of a distant landscape in order to obtain water. Rarely does a city of significant size satisfy its needs for food, energy, capital, labor, and other necessities within its boundaries. Few metropolitan areas limit themselves to immediate sources found in the local landscape. Most live beyond their means, requiring that resources be obtained from far away. However, American cities and American society have had particular difficulty accepting such limits. Our settlement history and our western expansion were predicated on the opposite behavior of growth and development dependent on the unbridled consumption of resources. This behavior becomes imperialistic when the quest for distant resources runs roughshod over the places and people who are appropriated to fulfill faraway needs.

The line separating imperialistic behavior from cooperative, mutually beneficial behavior is a fine one, often a matter of degree. Motives might be as important in drawing it as outcomes. Like many leaders of his day, a sense of manifest destiny drove Phelan. "On the map of the world," he preached, "the great bay and harbor opening onto 76,000,000 miles of ocean was stamped by the hand of Fate and destined for Empire." He attended the glorious Columbian Exposition held on the Chicago lakefront in 1893, where he was in charge of California's exhibit as the vice president of the California Commission. Neoclassical in architectural design and layout, the exposition celebrated the nation's self-perceived ascendancy to the pinnacle of the Western world. San Francisco's ascendancy to world prominence would surely follow; fate and destiny, and James Duval Phelan, would see to it.

Daniel Burnham was one of the exposition's principal planners. "Make no little plans," he wrote, "they have no magic to stir men's blood and probably themselves will not be realized." Burnham led the City Beautiful movement (circa 1890–1920), drafting grand redevelopment plans for cities across the country, including Chicago. "Make big plans," he continued, "aim high in hope and work, remembering that a noble, logical diagram once recorded will never die, but long after we are gone will be a living thing, asserting itself with ever-growing insistency. Remember that our sons and grand-sons are going to do things that would stagger us. Let your watch-word be order and your beacon beauty." Phelan returned from Chicago energized, his dream for San Francisco defined. The next year he chaired the city's Mid-Winter Fair, modeled after what he loved about Chicago's "Great White City" built on the sandy flats of Jackson Park.

Politics called the rising young civic leader in 1896, when the thirty-five-year-old neophyte was elected mayor. No surprise; Phelan was a very appealing candidate to both the prominent and the general public. For the prominent, he belonged to all the correct clubs, among them the Pacific Union Club and the Bohemian Club, for which he served as president. In their finely appointed dining and drawing rooms, cigar in hand, he made lasting friendships with the city's economic and civic leaders. His business record and rank among the city's wealthiest people garnered additional influence. Success managing civic affairs, like the state's participation in the Columbian Exposition and the city's Mid-Winter Fair, won him fur-ther respect and support among the city's elite. Like many of his Progressive Democratic peers, he was also increasingly offended by the chronic corruption that plagued city hall, and became a vocal advocate for municipal reform. And he was a man with a vision and a voice who could mesmerize an audience as perhaps the city's fore-most orator.

He appealed just as much to the general public, who perceived him as a brother despite his elite status. Phelan was of Irish-Catholic lineage, a member of the city's largest and most politicized voting bloc. People of Irish ancestry made up the city's second largest ethnic group, only several thousand fewer than the mostly Protestant peo-ple of German extraction, and over 80 percent of the public was Catholic. Phelan cherished his Irish heritage, though he wasn't devout in his faith. His father, also James, was a self-made man, an original forty-niner who immigrated to San Francisco from Cincinnati to capitalize on the gold rush, not by panning for gold, but by selling vital supplies and services to those who did. The elder James helped build the city during its infancy. His son would lead it through its adolescence, having inherited his father's business acu-men as well as his financial empire. (James Duval and sister Mollie, and married sister Alice, had split their parents' $12 million fortune, the money saved by James and Alice [Kelly] Phelan, both first-generation Irish Americans.)

In what better role than mayor could the rich banker, business-man, and real estate magnate realize his dream for his beloved city? He would clean up and streamline municipal government, and he would solve the nagging water supply problem that threatened San Francisco's future. By 1900 the cause for municipal reform and the quest for a public water supply had become a personal crusade for the young mayor. His new city charter, full of the popular Pro-gressive ideas of the time, established commissions and boards to direct civic affairs, and in response to the prevalent frustration with Spring Valley, it mandated the municipal ownership of utilities. The legal requirement for a public water supply now replaced the previ-ous civic desire for one. Phelan promptly set to work on the issue, ably assisted by two loyal engineers who shared his dream, Carl E. Grunsky and Marsden Manson. From 1900 until 1912 the three-some directed the city's pursuit of the dream. It then came to fruition under the guidance of city engineer Michael M. O'Shaughnessy (1912–32) and Mayor James "Sunny Jim" Rolph (1912–31).

Knowledge of Hetch Hetchy's potential along with that of other water sources had grown in bits and pieces over the past quarter cen-tury, although Colonel George Mendell's report remained the most comprehensive study of alternatives. In early 1900, Colonel Mendell, A. B. Maguire, and Marsden Manson were made San Francisco's first board of works and were immediately charged by the board of supervisors to make a report and recommendation on a municipal water supply. They were given one year and a small budget. Grunsky served as city engineer. The time and budgetary constraints imposed by the board of supervisors forced the board of works to restrict their initial inquiry to the solicitation of offers for the sale to the city of either an entire company or a major water sup-ply. A half-dozen offers were quickly received, drawing water from the North Yuba River, the American River, the North and Middle Yuba Rivers, the Eel and Russian Rivers, Coyote Creek and the Middle Fork of the Stanislaus River, and several artesian sources. None worked out.

The board of supervisors then directed city engineer Grunsky to make plans and cost estimates for the construction of a municipal water system based on four alternative water sources, all from northern Sierra watersheds: Lake Tahoe; the American River and its forks; the Yuba River and its forks; and the Feather River. At the urging of the board of works, the list was expanded to examine sources from other rivers, including the Mokelumne and the Tuolumne, as well as the existing Spring Valley system, which was then supplying the city with about 30 million gallons of water per day and potentially expandable to over 60 million gallons.

Grunsky already knew the solution, however. He had no need for another study. He had known of Hetch Hetchy since completing a survey for the Modesto Irrigation District years earlier that recommended the Stanislaus and Tuolumne Rivers as sources of irrigation water for the district. He knew the quantity and quality of the available flows. If there was insufficient supply for irrigation and the city, then surely the city's needs would take precedence.

Grunsky's study of Hetch Hetchy and alternative sources didn't take long. He delivered a progress report to the board of supervisors on August 12, 1901, with the expected result. Three sites on the upper Tuolumne River were the clear preference: the Hetch Hetchy Valley and sites on two tributaries that joined the river slightly downstream—a modest-size natural lake on Eleanor Creek five miles to the northwest of Hetch Hetchy, and a site nearby on Cherry Creek. Never mind that the Hetch Hetchy Valley and Lake Eleanor lay in Yosemite National Park (Cherry Creek lay just outside). The thirteen other alternatives received little serious consideration in the cursory study. The Tuolumne simply seemed ideal for practical and political reasons: water purity; water quantity; best potential reservoir sites; few complicating water rights; and hydroelectricity potential. These were all indeed sound reasons; however, little mention was made of the site's national park status or the potential effect on the scenery. San Francisco's desire for Hetch Hetchy water was the only real consideration. The principal drawbacks to the proposed scheme, Marsden Manson reported, were the remote distance and the resulting cost and difficulty required to deliver the water, understating the huge challenges these posed. In response to the nature of Bay Area politics, he noted there was "one almost insurmountable obstacle. There are no private interests to be served by the acquisition and development of this source." On the surface, he was right, although private interests continued to loom just beneath.

While Grunsky worked on the study for the board of supervisors, discussions regarding potential water sources continued between the city engineer, the mayor, and the board of works. When they read in the year-old 1899–1900 annual report of the U.S. Geological Survey that a Hetch Hetchy reservoir could "furnish the city of San Francisco with an unfailing supply of pure water," they concluded the valley posed the solution to San Francisco's nagging water problem. They apparently needed little nudging.

The survey's conclusion arose from a canvas of rivers west of the 100th meridian for potential dam and reservoir sites. Stream flow data were collected for hundreds of drainages in the West, including the rivers of the Sierra Nevada, the Tuolumne River among them. The 1890–91 annual report alone identified 147 sites in California, Colorado, Montana, New Mexico, and Nevada, of which California site #29 was Cherry Valley and site #33 was Hetch Hetchy. (Lake Eleanor, the Tuolumne Meadows, and scores of other sites throughout the West had been identified the year before.) But these surveys were little more than preliminary feasibility studies. Sites were not compared or ranked, and specific recommendations were not made, although the 1899–1900 report examined the probable use of a reservoir at Hetch Hetchy for irrigation, with a brief discussion of hydropower potential, and it presented a schematic dam design and a basic cost estimate. No mention was made of the reservoir's use for water supply beyond the single statement quoted above, nor did the report include any mention of the aqueduct needed to convey water to the Bay Area.

Grunsky, Phelan, and the board of works apparently paid little attention to the author's description of the spectacular valley. John Wesley Powell, head of the U.S. Geological Survey when the stream flow data were collected, did, advising at the time that "such a wonder spot of nature" should only be dammed as a last resort. "Hetch Hetchy Valley is a mountain meadow at an elevation of 3,700 feet above the sea," reported the author. "It is a veritable Yosemite Valley on a small scale. The Hetch Hetchy Falls, near the lower end of the valley, are fully equal in beauty and grandeur to many of the falls in Yosemite Valley," he noted at a time when the Yosemite Valley was world famous for its scenery and had been protected as a state reserve for thirty-five years. At that time too, the Hetch Hetchy Valley had been protected for nearly a decade in a national park surrounding the Yosemite state reserve. He continued,

> The valley proper is about three and one-half miles long, and its width varies from one-quarter to three-quarters of a mile. The rugged granite walls, crowned with domes, towers, spires, and battlements, seem to rise almost perpendicularly upon all sides to a height of 2,500 feet above this beautiful emerald meadow, which, seen from the trail approaching it from the east, is a sight never to be forgotten. It was visited in May, when the snows on the glacier meadows at the higher altitudes were rapidly melting, and the river was bank full and overflowing the lower part of the valley. The water is here dammed up, owing to the narrow outlet between high mountains of granite. At one place in this gorge, below the valley, the granite walls on either side approach so as to confine the river at low water to a width of about 20 feet, and this has been selected as a dam site.

The board of supervisors now directed the city engineer to prepare a plan for a Hetch Hetchy system and estimate the project costs: $39.5 million, Grunsky quickly calculated, for a system that would supply 60 million gallons a day, separate from the existing Spring Valley system. It's a curious plan and estimate, delivered in a forty-six-page report on July 28, 1902. Although the merits of expanding Lake Eleanor and damming Cherry Creek were discussed in detail, including their capability of satisfying the full water requirement, they were excluded from the estimate, apparently because of the board's preference for a reservoir at Hetch Hetchy. "It has seemed important to call attention to these features," Grunsky noted, "in order to show that the accepted project of utilizing at this time Hetch-Hetchy Valley alone for storage purposes is not the only feasible means of securing an ample supply of stored water in those portions of the high Sierras tributary to Tuolumne River. Lake Eleanor is equally favorably located and the water liberated from it would reach Tuolumne River and would be diverted from the river and brought to this City along the same route that would be followed by the water from Hetch-Hetchy Valley."

Grunsky also explored—at least superficially—the cost implications of absorbing portions of the Spring Valley system into the
Hetch Hetchy scheme. Several months later he would comment in
his final report that the Spring Valley system "can not be ignored
when an earnest move is made toward the acquisition by the city of
municipal water works. In their entirety they are comparable with
the other projects that are or have been under consideration." Then
he would state, "no proposal has been submitted for a sale of properties of the Spring Valley Water Works or any portion thereof to the
city, and no definite project for the acquisition of these works has yet
been formulated."

Why focus initially on Hetch Hetchy and not Lake Eleanor and
Cherry Creek? Why these Tuolumne sources and not other Sierra
sources further north and outside the park, sources explored in
greater detail by Colonel Mendell's report and sources that the city
had been repeatedly offered by water companies? And why not build
a long-term plan around the acquisition of Spring Valley first, with
other remote water sources added in the future as increased water
demand warranted? Grunsky's progress report and subsequent cost
estimate provide only partial responses at best, leaving many of the
basic questions regarding San Francisco's long-term water needs
unanswered. The city's focus on the construction of a new municipal
system based on the upper Tuolumne River in the High Sierra rested
on a shallow foundation.

In fact, Grunsky had made his choice even months before the
progress report, writing to the board of works on January 23, 1901,

> The water supply investigation has been advanced sufficiently to jus-
> tify the conclusion that San Francisco will ultimately be in need of a
> source of water supply from the Sierra Nevada [M]ountains, either
> with or without the utilization of the established and nearer sources.
> Preliminary examinations demonstrate the practicability of bringing
> in such a supply.
>
> Under these circumstances, the acquiring of necessary water rights
> and storage facilities should not be overlooked. They should be
> secured as opportunity offers to the end that when the time comes
> works may be established adequate to meet the future needs of this
> city.

To prevent certain privileges and rights that may be of vital importance from falling into the hands of speculators, private individuals or private corporations adverse to the interests of this city, and as the regulations of the Department of the Interior permit filing of applications and the setting apart to individuals or corporations of reservoir sites in the public domain, application should at once be made to the Secretary of the Interior to set apart for the use of this city the Hetch Hetchy valley and Lake Eleanor reservoir sites.

If this can not be done at once, it may be possible to have these lands which lie entirely within the Yosemite National Park, withdrawn from entry for reservoir purposes for a reasonable time in order that this city may have an opportunity to perfect a formal application therefor.

It will undoubtedly be at once recognized that the use to which the waters to be stored are to be put is the highest possible beneficial use to which water can be put.

Grunsky, Phelan, and Manson had committed San Francisco to the Tuolumne even though the watershed's legal status as a national park apparently protected it from such use and even though other sources might well have been cost-effective alternatives. With no public debate, they were free to move ahead.

The timing of Grunsky's letter wasn't accidental. Its recommendations reflected pending legislation in Congress that would provide a legal loophole opening the door for water projects in Yosemite, legislation for which the city had lobbied. Several weeks later, on February 15, Congress passed the Right of Way Act of 1901. The act stated,

[T]he Secretary of the Interior . . . is, authorized and empowered . . . to permit the use of rights of way through the public lands, forest and other reservations of the United States, and the Yosemite, Sequoia, and General Grant national parks, California, for electrical plants, poles, and lines for the generation and distribution of electrical power, and for telephone and telegraph purposes, and for canals, ditches, pipes and pipe lines, flumes, tunnels, or other water conduits, and for water plants, dams, and reservoirs used to promote irrigation or mining or quarrying, or the manufacturing or cutting of timber or lumber, or the supplying of water for domestic, public, or any other beneficial uses . . . provided that such permits shall be allowed within or through any of said parks . . . only upon the approval of the chief officer of the Department under whose supervision such park or reservation falls, and upon a finding by him that the same is not incompatible with the public interest.

Did Congress really mean to subordinate the sanctity of Yosemite National Park? In establishing the park just eleven years earlier, in 1890, it instructed the secretary of the interior "to make and publish such rules and regulations as he may deem necessary or proper for the care and management of the same. Such regulations shall provide for the preservation from injury of all timber, mineral deposits, natural curiosities, or wonders within said reservation, and their retention in their natural condition." Certainly a project the scope of the proposed Hetch Hetchy dam and reservoir would violate that mandate.

Yet Congress had rarely, if ever, approved the preservation of public land if that protection would limit economic growth or resource development, not in the national forests, which were in fact set aside to provide for sound resource exploitation; nor at national parks like Yellowstone and Yosemite, which were thought to have no significant value beyond sightseeing. Congress said nothing about the apparent conflict in its consideration of the Right of Way Act, passing the bill without debate. After all, it was just one of many pieces of legislation at the time that promoted resource and infrastructure development, like railroads, on public land, and it was consistent with the emerging Progressive concept of conservation. Phelan must have assumed the Right of Way Act superseded the provisions of the law that preserved Yosemite. Only the act's last provision raised any doubt: "any permission given by the Secretary of the Interior under the provisions of this Act may be revoked by him or his successor in his discretion." Perhaps Congress intended the magnitude of the right-of-way projects to be relatively minor, even temporary, rather than monumental and permanent.

With the loophole in hand, Grunsky, Phelan, and Manson in July and October 1901 secretly filed for the water and reservoir rights around Lake Eleanor and in the Hetch Hetchy Valley in the name of James D. Phelan, as a private citizen. They paid the considerable cost for the preparatory surveys and filings out of their own pockets, in the belief that the clandestine tactics were needed to avoid competitive land speculation and price gouging if their motives became public. The Spring Valley–Alameda Water Company fiasco remained fresh in their minds. Phelan then petitioned Secretary of the Interior Ethan A. Hitchcock in April 1902 for a permit to proceed with the project, as required by provisions of the act.

On November 24, 1902, Grunsky finally delivered his completed report on options for a municipal water supply to the board of supervisors. The twenty-two-page report was purely perfunctory by then, and its estimates of the cost for a 60-million-gallon water system based on four options were merely self-serving: for the acquisition and complete development of Spring Valley, $37 million; for a Yuba River supply, $48.2 million; for a Lake Tahoe supply, $47.4 million; and for Hetch Hetchy, $39.5 million. However, Grunsky noted, "construction of a water works system entirely independent of the water works which are now supplying the city with water from nearby sources, would not be productive of the best results. The best available sites for water storage in large quantity near home— Crystal Springs Reservoir and Lake Merced . . . —are already in use. They should be a part of the municipal system." Purchase of Spring Valley should be a part of any municipal plan, he felt, but it would not constitute the core.

To what extent was it a case of three visionary leaders acting for the public good versus shortsighted politicians and power brokers acting expediently? This was a time of great municipal water projects in Los Angeles and other major cities, just as these men envisioned for their own city. Many of the grand projects blended true civic vision with backroom politics. Civic pride and democratic feelings abounded in the aftermath of the new city charter, and Mayor Phelan proudly led the parade. Trust busting was also popular as part of the emerging Progressive agenda. Whatever their motives, while they awaited the secretary's decision, Eugene E. Schmitz succeeded Phelan as mayor, and the new administration would come to different conclusions about the best solution to the city's chronic water worries. Schmitz, a violinist and president of the musicians union, had been hand-picked to be mayor by Abraham Ruef, the city's most powerful political boss.

Secretary Hitchcock announced his decision on January 20, 1903, rejecting Phelan's petition on the grounds "that a considerable portion of the right of way desired was over patented lands, over which the Department had no authority to grant privileges; and, furthermore, that it appeared that the survey of the sites in question had been made surreptitiously, and without securing the consent of the Department to entering the reservation for that purpose." Hitchcock apparently balked at the city's tactics and felt uncertain that the Right of Way Act gave him the authority to supersede the will of Congress when it preserved Yosemite as a national park. Other secretaries of the interior who would hold the fate of Hetch Hetchy in their hands would share the same uncertainty.

A holdover from the McKinley administration, the elderly and conservative secretary wasn't a true believer in the new Progressive gospel of conservation. Hitchcock belonged more to the traditional business-oriented thinking of the past, the religion of laissez-faire, free-market capitalism based on unregulated resource exploitation. Those compulsions had laid waste to the continent's riches on an unprecedented scale, thought the true believers. Private profiteering was plundering the nation's vast forests, fertile grazing lands, and rich mineral deposits, leaving a rapidly dwindling supply for future generations. Those with foresight saw shortages looming ahead, where to previous generations the nation's resource wealth had seemed limitless. Meanwhile, opportunities to dam rivers for flood control, navigation, irrigation, and hydropower went untapped.

Science and government held the keys to progress for believers in the new conservation gospel. Government could manage the exploitation of natural resources based on the latest scientific methods better than the private sector, whether the resources lay in private or public land. Government could rise above America's historical compulsion for resource use based on expediency and short-term profit and so better steward resources to ensure their maximum benefit to society. And government regulation could avoid and in some cases remedy the sinful practices of the past: waste, inefficiency, inequity. Enlightened management based on cooperative public-private exploitation led by the government could satisfy national needs while maintaining the resource base in perpetuity. Although President Theodore Roosevelt (1901–09) championed the Progressive gospel of conservation, he had yet to purge all the heretics left over from the previous administration. Until then, Hitchcock was not about to approve the city's petition.

Phelan persisted even though he was no longer mayor, transferring the water rights to the city in 1903 and lobbying behind the scenes. The new Schmitz administration was initially supportive. Franklin K. Lane, the city attorney, petitioned Secretary Hitchcock for a rehearing. The chief engineer of Spring Valley Water Company reached the secretary first, receiving an audience before the city could meet with him. The irrigation districts also voiced strong opposition. Nonetheless, the rehearing was granted, around the time that John Muir and President Theodore Roosevelt toured Yosemite, blithely discussing the fate of the wondrous place, neither apparently aware of the application. Instead, their attention focused on the chronic management problems with the state reserve and the surrounding national park. Several months later, such concerns would trigger a federal commission to investigate the boundary problem and propose a revision.

Nothing of substance had changed for the secretary, who denied the permit on December 22, 1903, on the grounds both that the project would exceed an acceptable level of intrusion in the park and that he lacked the authority to grant the permit, with a referral to Congress for further appeal. Secretary Hitchcock explained,

The Act [which created Yosemite National Park], makes it obligatory upon the Secretary of the Interior to preserve and retain the "natural curiosities and wonders" in the park in their "natural condition." . . . If natural scenic attractions of the grade and character of . . . Hetch Hetchy Valley are not of the class which the law commands the Secretary to preserve and retain in their natural condition, it would seem difficult to find any in the park that are, unless it be the Yosemite Valley itself. In the absence of the clearest expression to the contrary, it is inconceivable that it was intended by the [Right of

Way] Act of February 15, 1901, to confer any authority to be exer-
cised for the subversion of those natural conditions which are essential to the very purposes for which the park was established.

San Francisco promptly appealed to Congress, but the effort died
in the Committee on Public Lands for lack of standing. A final appeal
to Secretary Hitchcock was rejected on February 5, 1905, on the
grounds that the permit "could not be granted without further legislation by Congress."

A flurry of important actions occurred within days of the secretary's final decision: Congress expanded the national park boundary
northward to encompass the entire upper Tuolumne drainage for
Hetch Hetchy, probably at the urging of Phelan and other Bay Area
proponents of his plan; the State of California approved the recession of the Yosemite grant back to the federal government for incorporation into the national park; and Gifford Pinchot became head of
the new U.S. Forest Service, asserting greater influence over the
Roosevelt administration's land-use policies. Frustrated with
Hitchcock's denials and congressional lack of interest, Phelan's
group immediately sought Pinchot's help to bring the matter before
President Roosevelt for the first time.

Pinchot had known of Phelan's plan since the original permit
application was denied in 1903 and apparently decided then that its
benefits overshadowed any damage to the park's scenery. No place
was sacred in his mind. No place was safe from development—not
his national forests, and, if he had his way, not the national parks.
"The object of our forest policy," he told the Society of American
Foresters that year, "is not to preserve the forests because they are
beautiful or wild or the habitat of wild animals; it is to ensure a
steady supply of timber for human prosperity. Every other consideration comes as secondary." And it made no difference to him whether
the timber stood in a forest reserve or a national park. A year later he
traded philosophical jabs with Robert Underwood Johnson, writing
in Johnson's *Century* magazine that no lands would be permanently
held in reserve for pleasure seeking if they could be used to serve
people better.

Thus by 1905 the battle between the conservationists and the preservationists for the president's support had been joined, as Pinchot noted in a letter to William Colby:

> I have just received your confidential letter of February 10, and I want to reply in the same way because Congressman Needham [in whose district the park lay] has asked me not to make public my recommendations to the President. This letter is therefore strictly confidential. I reported to the President more than a week ago, recommending: first, the use of Lake Eleanor whenever the city shall make the necessary application and acquire the necessary rights. Second, the reservation of the Hetch Hetchy and Big Tuolumne Meadows reservoir sites for the eventual use of San Francisco and the other adjacent cities, provided a time comes when they need them. This recommendation seems to me to fit almost exactly with that expressed in your letter. I feel very strongly that San Francisco must have an adequate water supply, and it has seemed to me that the action of the Secretary of the Interior was based purely on a technicality and entirely failed to meet the needs of the situation. On the other hand, I agree with you fully as to the extreme desirability of preserving the Hetch Hetchy in its original beauty, just as long as that can be done without serious interference with a matter of such large importance as the water supply of a great group of communities. From what I can gather, it will be not less than 50 years before any supply further than that which can be derived from Lake Eleanor is required, and perhaps twice as long.

Previously unaware of the issue, Roosevelt was caught in a political bind. He agreed with Pinchot's recommendation but thought the matter was not his to decide; the secretary of the interior had already made the decision. So Roosevelt sought an opinion from the secretary of commerce and labor on the matter. Hetch Hetchy would no longer be a local matter between the city and the secretary of the interior. It would become a national issue to be decided on national politics and policy. Unfortunately, this would too often pit the preservation philosophy against the conservation philosophy in simplistic terms: beauty and recreation for personal refreshment against progress and prosperity; good versus bad; right versus wrong.

However, the questions posed by the Hetch Hetchy proposal were far more complex.

Like many participants, including the Sierra Club membership and board, Marsden Manson was torn between the two sides. He had joined the club in 1895 and had contributed several pieces to its *Bulletin*, yet throughout the controversy he tried unsuccessfully to convince John Muir that the loss of Hetch Hetchy would not defile the park's scenery but rather would provide significant benefits to the city (and even remove a bothersome breeding ground for mosquitoes).

The secretary of commerce and labor opinion affirmed the right of the secretary of the interior to deny the city's application, although casting doubt on the reasons for the denial. In response the San Francisco city attorney again gained access to the president, sending Marsden Manson to meet with him in June 1905. At the meeting Roosevelt granted the city permission to file a brief in response to the Hitchcock rulings and the secretary of commerce and labor opinion, suggesting that the brief be in a format for referral to the U.S. attorney general. Manson delivered the brief to the White House in July.

In October Attorney General M. D. Purdy advised the president, "I have carefully considered the language of the [Right of Way] act . . . and am clearly of the opinion that Congress thereby intended to vest in the Secretary [of the Interior] a discretionary authority to grant or refuse applications of this kind. I would, therefore, respectfully suggest that, if you desire further consideration or different action, the matter may be taken up with the Secretary of the Interior." Even though the president and Pinchot supported the application, they were unable to overrule Hitchcock and were either unable or unwilling to pressure him to reverse his position.

Purdy's opinion was not communicated to the city; but events soon made it moot. Three months later, in January 1906, San Francisco formally abandoned its pursuit of Hetch Hetchy when the board of supervisors passed Resolution 6949 and the Schmitz-Ruef administration began pursuit of a scheme proposed by the Bay Cities Water Company, although the city had not necessarily forfeited its claims to the upper Tuolumne River originally filed by Phelan and subsequently transferred to the city.

Mayor Schmitz and the new administration wouldn't pursue

Hetch Hetchy any further—it wasn't their dream. The board of works had been reconstituted with entirely new members (Mendell had died in 1902, and Manson wasn't reappointed in 1903), and Grunsky had been replaced as city engineer. The new administration was now free of the three men who dreamed of Hetch Hetchy. Landowners in the San Joaquin Valley also attacked the plan, submitting a petition against it signed by more than 1,200 residents of the Modesto and Turlock Irrigation Districts. With that final straw, on January 29, 1906, the board of supervisors, now completely controlled by the Schmitz administration, adopted Resolution 6949: "Resolved, that the city refrain from expending further money, energy or time in the futile attempt to acquire the so-called Tuolumne system." Those in power felt development of Hetch Hetchy would take too long and was too tenuous, while the pressing need for a public supply to combat the Spring Valley monopoly compelled the search for other sources. End of story, it appeared.

CHAPTER 7

The Private Debate over Hetch Hetchy

Enrico Caruso was in fine form that Tuesday night at the Tivoli Opera House in San Francisco, performing his popular role of Don José, a naïve but passionate corporal bewitched by a sexy, sultry femme fatale in Georges Bizet's *Carmen.* April 17, 1906. It was the second night for the visiting Metropolitan Opera Company's performance. Caruso's silky tenor voice surely thrilled the packed house. James Duval Phelan and his younger sister Mollie sat captivated in their season seats—good seats, for the forty-five-year-old patrician was one of the city's leading patrons of the arts, as well as one of its wealthiest and most prominent citizens.

After the gala, perhaps they joined patrons from other theatrical productions around the sparkling city that night for a late dinner at Luna's or Coppa's in the fashionable North Beach District. Cast members from the shows arrived to the applause of diners from the Columbia Theater who had just enjoyed Victor Herbert's *Babes in Toyland* and others whom the dashing John Barrymore had enchanted with his performance in Richard Harding Davis's *The Dictator.* Did table conversations proclaim the grandeur of the day, despite troubling news of yet another political scandal from city hall involving Mayor Eugene E. Schmitz and Abraham "Boss" Ruef? Perhaps a bottle of Chianti directed the conversation to the latest news about the ongoing eruption of Mt. Vesuvius, its lava flows once again destroying much of Naples and the Neapolitan countryside on the infamous volcano's flanks. But that environmental and human disaster was half a world away, hardly a worry here. With no volcanoes in the Bay Area, San Francisco was surely safe from such catastrophes.

Or perhaps Phelan and his sister simply enjoyed the fine evening by strolling from the theater back to the family mansion at Valencia and Seventeenth Streets, on the flats of a family-oriented neighborhood in the Mission Dolores District. Along the way they might have envisioned Phelan's dream of an imperial city. When he left office in 1902 he thought his goal was well in hand. Three terms as mayor were enough. Besides, the political tides were turning and he was losing support in the all-powerful labor unions. Time to refocus on his businesses and on his patronage of the arts, he thought.

But as he left the grand opera house on Mission Street this night, he knew his dream had been perverted. Graft again plagued municipal government and turned the new administration away from his water supply solution. His work had been corrupted, though circumstances were not yet ripe for him to intervene. Nor did circumstances that April evening bode well for the new Burnham plan. The fractured configuration of private property holdings in the city undermined Burnham's and Phelan's vision of broad boulevards cutting diagonally across the urban fabric to stitch together civic nodes and parks with residential and business districts. Did Phelan think of those difficulties as he returned home?

The two-story Phelan mansion, modest by the standards of their snobbish peers on Nob Hill, sat amid lush gardens in a three-and-a-half-acre compound. The bachelor and his mentally fragile spinster sister Mollie now occupied the home in which they grew up, their parents having died several years earlier. Despite the setbacks in municipal affairs, the spring found Phelan in good spirits. His businesses were flourishing; his home life was comfortable; his personal life was settled as recent tensions with a longtime lover had passed; and his civic life as the city's leading citizen was without criticism in the press. He reveled in the fruits of his success, enjoying opera and fine art, fine food, fine wine, fine clothes, and a cultured, refined lifestyle, and sought to share that success and those values with the community. On the surface all was well, mirroring general life in the city. James Duval Phelan slept well that night, after retiring late.

Enrico Caruso also slept well that night, in his fifth-floor room at the Palace Hotel. "I went to bed feeling very contented," he recalled, for the show met with fine éclat. "But what an awakening!" he wrote. "You must know that I am not a very heavy sleeper," he noted. "I always wake early, and when I feel restless I get up and go for a walk." Early Wednesday morning, he continued,

I wake up about 5 o'clock, feeling my bed rocking as though I am in a ship on the ocean, and for a moment I think I am dreaming that I am crossing the water on my way to my beautiful country. And so I take no notice for the moment, and then, as the rocking continues, I get up and go to the window, raise the shade and look out. And what I see makes me tremble with fear. I see the buildings toppling over, big pieces of masonry falling, and from the street below I hear the cries and screams of men and women and children.

I remain speechless, thinking I am in some dreadful nightmare, and for something like forty seconds I stand there, while the buildings fall and my room still rocks like a boat on the sea. And during that forty seconds I think of forty thousand different things. All that I have ever done in my life passes before me, and I remember trivial things and important things. I think of my first appearance in grand opera, and I feel nervous as to my reception, and again I think I am going through last night's *Carmen*.

Later that day Caruso and his valet made their way to the Oakland ferry to flee the devastation. "We pass terrible scenes on the way," he said, "buildings in ruins, and everywhere there seems to be smoke and dust." In Oakland he booked train passage to New York. While en route east he wrote, "the trip to New York seems very long and tedious, and I sleep very little, for I can still feel the terrible rocking which made me sick. Even now I can only sleep an hour at a time, for the experience was a terrible one." Caruso never returned to San Francisco.

The hands of the clock on the Ferry Building at the foot of Market Street froze at 5:16 a.m., Wednesday, April 18, 1906. A great spasm in the earth's surface that would have measured about 8.3 on the Richter scale (Professor Charles F. Richter of the California Institute of Technology did not develop the scale until 1935) radiated out from Tomales Bay, about thirty miles north of San Francisco, as the Pacific oceanic plate suddenly lurched twenty-one feet against the North American continental plate, releasing immense tectonic pressures pent up by the inexorable movement of one plate against the other. The resulting wave of subterranean energy spread from the suture, liquefying land in San Francisco made by filling marshes and inlets to create building sites. Structures on the made land in the Financial and Mission Districts stood little chance. Farther to the south, down the peninsula, the San Andreas rift jumped eight feet. The dam spanning the rift to impound Crystal Springs Reservoir, one of the city's primary water sources, held, but the violent movement sheared most of the rigid iron pipes carrying water from the reservoir to the city.

James Duval Phelan awoke with a start. As it did with the ordinary and extraordinary lives of thousands of other San Franciscans, the earthquake and three days of subsequent fires destroyed the placid surface of his life. Circumstances in the city shifted as suddenly as the boundary between the two tectonic plates. The time for his intervention in municipal affairs had come. However, his personal and business interests demanded his immediate attention.

He quickly dressed, checked the household for damage, and organized the staff to shut off the gas and electric lines and make other precautions. Thinking the earthquake damage was localized to his neighborhood, he then went out to look around. "Going to the Valencia Street gate," he wrote, "I met three men and two women who were weeping." He continued,

> I asked what was the matter; and they pointed south to a five-story wooden hotel building on the west side of Valencia Street, south of 19th, which had fallen across the street and crumpled. All they said was, "Everyone is killed!"
>
> I immediately went there, and could see men and women imprisoned by the fallen timbers; and, returning to my stable, I got my men, with axes and saws, and took out the family carriage, a vis-à-vis with two horses, and Barry, the coachman, (My automobile being garaged in some other part of town) and went to the scene of the hotel disaster.

The morning dawned mild beneath a calm, clear sky; there was no hint of things to come. Although the initial damage of the quake ran 270 miles along the San Andreas Fault, Phelan had no immediate sense of its extent. A city employee broke the bad news to him. "The city is wrecked, and fires have broken out," he told Phelan. The patrician had his carriage readied, and the two men promptly set off downtown to see. Perhaps Phelan could somehow help; his businesses and properties probably required his attention too. Damage and devastation lined the streets as they left the Mission District and passed through the South of Market District. The collapsed ceiling of the Tivoli Opera House covered the stage on which Caruso had sung hours before, as well as the seats from which Phelan and Mollie had listened. Fire would later consume the rest of the building. "But, not until we reached the City Hall," Phelan recalled, "did we realize the magnitude of the calamity. The City Hall was completely wrecked, large parts of the dome having fallen, leaving the cap in the air and the brick structure, on every side, ruined, with here and there a column standing, resembling the ruins of the Temple of the Dioscuri in the Forum in Rome."

To Phelan the crumbled city hall symbolized the broader impact of the quake on San Francisco. He detested the building and what it reflected of the city's political and cultural past. Started in 1871, when Phelan was ten years old, construction of the building took twenty-seven years to complete, a monument to bad planning, bad management, bad government, and bad taste. Bribes, kickbacks, and shoddy construction plagued the project as it passed from one administration to the next. Phelan was the first mayor to occupy the gaudy, overpriced, structurally suspect monstrosity. When it fully opened in 1900, it was the most imposing public building in the city. Good riddance to it. Now its destruction would give him the chance to remedy the lingering effects of the past while rebuilding the city to better reflect his dream.

From the ruins of the city hall he moved on to check the damage to the Phelan Building, the centerpiece property in his real estate port-folio at the intersection of Market, Grant, and O'Farrell Streets. Thankfully he found the prominent building still standing when he arrived early that morning. But aftershocks continued to shake the city and fires were spreading, threatening further destruction. He worked quickly in his fifth-floor office to secure the safety of impor-tant family papers, business records, and personal possessions, in-cluding private letters, bonds, a jewelry collection, and various pieces of art, among them a portrait of his father, paintings by William Keith and Benjamin Constant, and a marble sculpture by Auguste Rodin purchased the year before from the artist's Paris studio. Good thing; fire consumed the building the next day. He would construct a new Phelan Building on the site, larger, more modern, and more prominent than its predecessor, just as he hoped a bigger, better city would arise from the rubble. The new ten-story tower would be among the first major buildings reopened after the disaster, anchoring the Commercial District and protecting Phelan's property values while demonstrating to the city and the nation that San Francisco was on the mend.

In mid-morning he walked to the Financial District to check the bank he owned, Mutual Savings, and others in which he held major interests. The news was not good. Most of his fortune lay or would soon lie either in ruins or in ashes, including the family mansion. "We have lost all our income property here and about half in San Jose," he wrote his cousin in New York. (His San Diego assets were unaffected.)

Like thousands of other people, Phelan and his sister became temporarily homeless, wandering refugees who joined the "endless procession of wagons and trundle carts, men and women of all descriptions carrying various objects and seeking places of safety," he recalled. They camped in Golden Gate Park, near the Japanese Tea Garden, well to the west of the raging fires and billowing smoke, though hardly roughing it like most of the other refugees, and staying only briefly, until suitable accommodations could be found. The Phelans preferred refined comforts, which their servants tried to provide as best they could from the caravan of cars and wagons that carried the family's possessions, including the grand marquee tent formerly used to shelter large outdoor receptions and lawn parties at the estate. The evening sky glowed, "so brilliantly illuminated by the fire," Phelan wrote, "that one could read the newspaper out of doors." Mercifully the glorious spring days bathed in sunshine and mild temperatures benefited the displaced, though the dryness fueled the fire. Did he notice the perfect weather? How could he, given the horrendous circumstances? Nor was he an outdoorsman who enjoyed the strenuous life, like his friend President Theodore Roosevelt or other friends in the Sierra Club.

Throughout the crisis, as throughout his life, Phelan wasn't blind to the needs of those around him, nor to his privileges. He often exhibited a noblesse oblige–like concern for his personal and professional staffs and for common people in need. "The calamity is overwhelming but everybody is game and making a good fight," he told his cousin. "All our friends are well and have a superabundance of health, good appetites and low diet, and attenuated purses," he wrote a friend in London. "There is a splendid spirit among the people to rebuild on better lines," he continued. "[It] is something to have lived through the tragedy and the fall of a great city in a few hours and to take part in its reconstruction."

That effort began immediately at the behest of the person whom Phelan would want to replace first. As fires swept the city, engulfing it in a conflagration that surpassed the damage done by the quake, Mayor Schmitz sent an aide to solicit Phelan's assistance, asking him to join the Citizens Committee of Fifty, a group of community leaders being hastily organized to take charge of the rising crisis. The request was probably perfunctory, as Schmitz and Phelan were at opposite ends of the political and philosophical spectrum. Schmitz embodied all that Phelan despised about sleazy city government. The current administration and its underlying style of political behavior would have to be destroyed and a new administration and behavior built, just as the city hall they occupied and the city they ruled had been destroyed and now needed reconstruction. Again, fate and destiny, and James Duval Phelan, would see to it.

The work of the Citizens Committee of Fifty ignited with nearly continuous meetings in the days immediately following the fire. Phelan was quickly elected chairperson of the finance subcommittee and was personally designated by the full committee and President Roosevelt as the sole trustee for the $10 million in relief funds that would be received by the city from various sources. The city's main relief effort was soon placed under the auspices of a specially incorporated joint venture between the American Red Cross and the committee's relief fund. Phelan controlled the disbursement of its monies and directed the overall relief and reconstruction effort. Three parts of his dream for San Francisco conjoined in the cause: the restoration of responsible municipal government, the realization of Burnham's grand City Beautiful plan, and the securing of an adequate public water supply from Hetch Hetchy to protect the city's growth potential. The fourth part—patronage of the arts—would follow. In the next few years, as a private citizen always working behind the scenes of elected public office, if just barely, Phelan would wield considerable influence to win political reform, set in place large pieces of the city's physical and cultural fabric, and quench the city's nagging thirst for public water by tapping the wilderness in the distant Sierra Nevada Mountains of Yosemite National Park.

The earthquake and fire on April 18 brought Phelan's Hetch Hetchy dream back to life, seemingly arising from the city's ashes in response to public anger at the failure of the water supply during the crisis. Of course, no supply would have withstood the earthquake. The Spring Valley Water Company wasn't to blame for broken pipes. It didn't matter. The fire fueled long-standing antagonism toward the monopoly and rekindled public interest in Hetch Hetchy. The Schmitz administration took political heat, too. Amid scandalous accusations, the courts and the public swept the administration from office, replacing it with reformers aligned with Phelan's preference for Hetch Hetchy.

Tensions between San Francisco and Spring Valley over water prices flared in the aftermath of the disaster as both worked to rebuild damaged infrastructure. The Federated Water Committee, a citizens committee, urged the board of supervisors to purchase the monopoly. Instead, the board once again solicited proposals from private companies across the bay to sell the city their Sierra water systems. It noted, "the necessity for the acquisition of a municipal water supply is more urgent at the present period than ever before in the city's history. It has become almost axiomatic that if the city had proceeded with diligence . . . [it] would not now be in ruins." The procrastination and delays, they stated, could be attributed to many causes, including the "active opposition of the existing water monopoly of San Francisco," and the "obstinacy of certain municipal officials in favor of a single pet idea."

Eleven offers were received by the June 21 deadline. The board narrowed the list to five finalists: three offers that drew water from the American River; one that drew water from the American and the Consumnes Rivers; and one that drew water from the Mokelumne River. In July Mayor Schmitz appointed a three-member board of engineers to make the final recommendation. When the engineers, chafing under the mayor's meddling, reported that it needed a year to conduct the study, the board of supervisors simply accepted the

Bay Cities Water Company's proposal to sell its American and Consumnes River water system to the city for $10.5 million. The board of engineers resigned in protest.

The press picked up the story, and pent-up fury over the general behavior of the Schmitz administration exploded. Several of San Francisco's biggest power brokers, including business and banking friends of former mayor Phelan, and Phelan himself, clamored for an investigation into charges of widespread municipal corruption. Phelan spearheaded the inquiry with the support of the Roosevelt administration, while directing the city's reconstruction on behalf of the San Francisco Red Cross and Relief Corporation.

Boss Ruef stood in the eye of the storm. Ambitious and brilliant, Ruef graduated as the class valedictorian from the University of California in Berkeley at age eighteen. The stylish attorney rose through the ranks of the local Republican Party in the late 1880s and 1890s by building a vast patronage network based on doling out favors. By 1901 he tried unsuccessfully to take control of it. But Ruef wasn't a peer of the party's big-money and big-business bosses, who were dominated by backers of the Southern Pacific Railroad. Despite his network, the class difference might have prevented him from gaining further importance. Nor would the Progressive reformers of Mayor Phelan's Democratic Party accept his political behavior. However, the balance of power in the Bay Area was changing. Popular support had been split between the Democrats and the Republicans when the reformers alienated the labor unions, which were gaining political strength in the aftermath of a teamsters strike on the waterfront.

Ruef saw opportunity for greater power in the infant Union Labor Party, so he shifted allegiance and quickly took control. He wrote the party's platform for the upcoming mayoral election and persuaded a law client—Eugene Schmitz—to run for the office. After Schmitz won the close election, Ruef retained tight control over the mayor and the administration, using his law practice as the vehicle to solicit bribes and peddle his favors and influence in city hall to the highest bidder. "Clients" would "hire" Ruef for legal services, though none would be performed; instead, Ruef would use the money to bribe city officials, including the mayor and the board of supervisors, for rulings favorable to his clients' interests. The graft ran rampant after

Schmitz's surprising reelection in 1905, despite being repeatedly excoriated by Fremont Older, the crusading editor of the *Bulletin*. The Union Labor Party took full control of the board of supervisors, effectively eliminating the last remnants of Phelan's reformers.

City hall now nestled snugly in Boss Ruef's back pocket. Big business lined up to buy influence, delivering bags of cash to Ruef every month. PG&E, the Home Telephone Company, and United Railroads (which had interests in the operation of trolleys powered by overhead electric lines) were among his favorite patrons. One client pursued a speculative land scheme similar to the one Billy Ralston began around Golden Gate Park. A group of investors led by William H. Crocker—son of Charles Crocker, the founder of Crocker Bank—formed the Parkside Realty Company to develop a four-hundred-acre parcel a mile south of the park. For the project to succeed, it needed a streetcar line to link the twenty-block-by-five-block development to the center of the city. The company "retained" Ruef to see that the board granted them the necessary streetcar line franchise.

The administration's preference for the purchase of the Bay Cities Water Company was also bought by bags of bribery money months before the great fire and the search for a new water source it supposedly spurred. In fact, when the board of supervisors passed Resolution 6949 in January, they may have done so with the expectation of a payoff to favor the Bay Cities scheme, which was being hatched at the time. Yet the board also had legitimate technical, economic, and political reasons to abandon Phelan's pursuit of a Hetch Hetchy solution. When the supervisors subsequently solicited new water purchase proposals after the fire, narrowed the set to five finalists, then selected Bay Cities without waiting for the board of engineers to make a final recommendation, those actions were bought by Bay Cities and Abe Ruef—those decisions were fixed all along.

The scheme was simple, like Billy Ralston's earlier scheme involving Spring Valley and Alameda. Bay Cities president William S. Tevis paid Ruef $1 million to persuade the city to buy his company for the inflated price of $10.5 million. The company existed mostly on paper, planning to build a water system originating near Lake Tahoe for $7.5 million; the $3 million profit would line the pockets of Tevis, Ruef, and other participants in the scheme. Ruef paid $75,000 to each lead supervisor on the board who supported the purchase, and $25,000 to every other supervisor who voted favorably for the proposal. Boss Ruef split the remaining $500,000 with his puppet mayor, Eugene Schmitz. The plan probably would have worked, had tensions with Spring Valley not rekindled in the aftermath of the fire and had public scrutiny of municipal behavior not been ignited. Ironically, despite the bribery the proposed Bay Cities water system might have been a sound alternative to Hetch Hetchy.

As Phelan toured eastern cities about a year after the fire, speaking to business and banking leaders to rebuild confidence in San Francisco's future and to acquire capital for reconstruction, Mayor Schmitz was indicted and removed from office, and sixteen members of the board of supervisors resigned after confessing to various improprieties. (They were granted immunity by the grand jury in return for their testimony.) The deal with Bay Cities evaporated. Mayor Schmitz was convicted, although the conviction was reversed on appeal. Boss Ruef would serve five years in San Quentin. While visiting Boston in 1907 Phelan told the *Sunday Herald,* "the conviction of Mayor Schmitz and the rout of Ruef, the political 'boss,' who made a confession which has criminally involved his followers and 'patrons,' have at last brought the government of graft, which existed for several years in San Francisco, to an end." He continued, "the grafting officials are not, however, the only culprits. The officers of the telephone, street railway, gas and electric companies must answer to charges of bribery. These corporations were not 'held up'; they sought privileges, and they are suffering now from the consequences of ordinary corporate greed."

Although bribery determined the board and the mayor's decision to pursue Bay Cities, the board had a valid criticism of Phelan's obstinate pursuit of Hetch Hetchy. The potential of the upper Tuolumne River as a water source had been identified as early as the 1880s, yet no feasibility study found the valley to be the preferred source until after Phelan, Grunsky, and Manson committed the city to develop it. The schemes to develop the river and the reports pointing out the valley's potential in the 1880s and 1890s were either a simple statement of potential or an opportunistic proposal, rather than a serious plan based on a careful comparison of alternatives. Only Colonel Mendell's study examined the feasibility of alternatives, including the development of the water sources from northern Sierra rivers such as the American and Mokelumne, but he made no mention of the Tuolumne. And some of the proposals made to the city in response to its repeated solicitations over the previous three decades were certainly viable. Some alternatives were probably less expensive, less technically challenging, and less politically complicated. Hindsight proves as much, but the indications also existed at the time. Unfortunately, the threesome could not consider the alternatives objectively. Too many circumstances clouded their perspective.

Like a phoenix, Phelan's dream for an imperial city was reborn in the devastated political and physical landscapes following the great earthquake and fire. With city hall in rubble, reformers reasserted control and resumed pursuit of a Hetch Hetchy permit. The dream had never died, despite the Schmitz-Ruef regime and the Hitchcock denials. Phelan, Manson, and proponents of the Hetch Hetchy plan had effectively lobbied President Theodore Roosevelt, persuading him to support the proposal, assisted by Gifford Pinchot, as the Yosemite Valley was finally added to the park that bears its name. At the same time James Garfield, the commissioner of corporations in the U.S. Department of Commerce and Labor, discovered the Purdy opinion. In May the city learned of it, and the Roosevelt administration let them know that it would look favorably on a new application. Pinchot wrote Manson, "I hope sincerely that in regeneration of San Francisco its people may be able to make provision for a water supply from the Yosemite National Park. . . . I will stand ready to render any assistance which lies in my power."

Action on the matter had to wait until the physical and political landscapes in San Francisco stabilized. In March 1907 seventy-two-year-old Ethan Hitchcock resigned as the secretary of the interior, enabling Roosevelt to appoint someone who shared his conservation philosophy. The president found his man: forty-two-year-old James Garfield, an ally of Pinchot with close ties to San Francisco business and civic leaders. Unlike his predecessor, Garfield was a true believer and, along with Gifford Pinchot, a member of the president's conservation coterie who enjoyed direct access to the Oval Office. Others in the youthful and passionate inner circle included William A. Richards, commissioner of the general land office;

Frederick H. Newell, chief engineer of the reclamation service; and WJ McGee (he always dropped the periods), secretary of the inland waterways commission.

Pinchot wrote Manson again, suggesting the new secretary would approve the city's application: "My advice to you is to assume that his attitude will be favorable, and to make the necessary preparations to set the case before him." Proponents of the Phelan plan finally found a receptive ear in Washington. The supervisors quickly repealed the Ruef-controlled board resolution abandoning pursuit of the Hetch Hetchy plan and authorized the new mayor to re-petition for permission to proceed with the plan.

The rehearing was held quietly on the evening of July 27 in the San Francisco Board of Supervisors' old chambers on Eddy Street. At the mayor's request, Manson made the city's case to the handsome secretary. Phelan was among the dozen people in attendance. The Turlock and Modesto Irrigation Districts sent representatives, who voiced concern for the plan, as did several representatives of companies who had alternate sources of water to offer. Participants were allowed to submit follow-up briefs. But no one from the Sierra Club knew of the meeting—many were camping in the mountains during a High Trip led by William Colby—and so the preservationist arguments were not heard. About a month later, Muir went camping in the Sierra, spending a week in the high-walled wonder of Hetch Hetchy Valley, no doubt thinking about the fight ahead to preserve it.

In the aftermath of the missed meeting, Muir wrote his Yosemite camping companion from 1903 urging that the region "be saved from all sorts of commercialism and marks of man's works." While San Francisco's water needs had to be met, he suggested other viable sources of water were available outside "our wild mountain parks." Supporters of the plan, he said, "show forth the proud sort of confidence that comes from a good sound irrefragable ignorance." Muir warned the president that when the public learned the facts, they would overwhelmingly oppose the plan. "As soon as light is cast upon it," he concluded, "nine tenths or more of even the citizens of San Francisco would be opposed to it. And what the public opinion of the world would be may be guessed by the case of the Niagara Falls." Roosevelt had already sought independent confirmation of the plan's necessity, requesting advice from government engineers earlier that summer; they had reported that Hetch Hetchy was the city's only practical source.

Still, the president passed Muir's letter to Garfield and Pinchot with a note asking them to reconsider. "Please look over the enclosed letter from John Muir," he requested. "It does seem to me unnecessary to decide about the Hetch Hetchy Valley at all at present. Why not allow Lake Eleanor, and stop there?" They stood steadfast. Roosevelt responded to Muir that he thought the great majority of people would favor the material needs of growth and development over the preservation of wilderness. "So far everyone that has appeared has been for it," he would write, "and I have been in the disagreeable position of seeming to interfere with the development of the State for the sake of keeping a valley, which apparently hardly anyone wanted to have kept, under national control. (P.S.: How I do wish I were again with you camping out under those great sequoias or in the snow under the silver firs!)"

Pinchot had no problem with the plan, writing his boss and tennis partner, "I fully sympathize with the desire of Mr. Johnson and Mr. Muir to protect the Yosemite National Park, but I believe that the highest possible use which could be made of it would be to supply pure water to a great center of population." In May 1908 Secretary Garfield granted the permit with Pinchot's and Roosevelt's blessing, although the president remained uncomfortable with the decision. Hetch Hetchy was "one of those cases where I was extremely doubtful," he confessed several months later to Robert Underwood Johnson, "but finally I came to the conclusion that I ought to stand by Garfield and Pinchot's judgment in the matter." The battle had begun.

Two days later the Governor's Conference on the Conservation of Natural Resources convened at the White House. Organized by WJ McGee and Gifford Pinchot, who funded much of it personally, the conference extolled the virtues of the administration's conservation philosophy to the governors and various national leaders. It also sought to calm the concerns of mining, timber, and grazing interests who contested Roosevelt's withdrawal of land open to commercial exploitation from the public domain to place it in national forests. Even though the forests would be open to government-sanctioned exploitation, the private sector chafed at the interference. Andrew

Carnegie and James J. Hill were among the industrialists who spoke, in addition to politicians and resource experts. Most speeches emphasized the nation's need to exploit natural resources and the specific circumstances in various states. The conference was a seminal event before the birth of the American environmental movement, focusing public and political attention on conservation issues as never before. Two important outgrowths resulted the following year. In 1909, Roosevelt and Pinchot established the National Conservation Commission, comprised of representatives from the states and federal agencies; and Pinchot led the First National Conservation Congress, an assembly of private conservation interests.

Surprisingly John Muir, Charles Sprague Sargent, and most preservationists were purposely not invited to the governor's conference. Even Robert Underwood Johnson, who had originally proposed the conference to Pinchot, was only invited as a member of the press. Still, a few attendees voiced concern that utilitarian goals should not drive policy everywhere. In some special places the preservation of scenery or wildlife should take precedence, they argued. As the conference concluded, two things were clear: Progressive conservation was the national policy; and the management of natural resources was becoming a mainstream national issue for the first time. Hetch Hetchy would keep it on the national agenda for years to come.

Secretary Garfield approved the petition, contingent on certain restrictions and congressional approval. "Congress [by way of the Right of Way Act] has given power to the Secretary of the Interior to grant the rights applied for by the City of San Francisco," he said, "if he finds that the permit 'is not incompatible with the public interest.' " Garfield continued,

> "[T]he public interest" should not be confined merely to the public interest in the Yosemite National Park for use as a park only, but rather the broader public interest which requires reservoir sites to be utilized for the greatest good to the greatest number of people. . . . I appreciate keenly the interest of the public in preserving the natural wonders of the Park[;] . . . domestic use, however, especially for a municipal supply, is the highest use to which water and available stor-

age basins therefor can be put. . . . Hetch Hetchy Valley is great and beautiful in its natural and scenic effects. If it were also unique, sentiment for its preservation in an absolutely natural state would be far greater. In the mere vicinity, however, much more accessible to the public and more wonderful and beautiful, is the Yosemite Valley itself. Furthermore, the reservoir will not destroy Hetch Hetchy. It will scarcely affect the canyon walls. It will not reach the foot of the various falls which descend from the sides of the canyon. The prime change will be that, instead of a beautiful but somewhat unusable "meadow" floor, the valley will be a lake of rare beauty.

Garfield's conditions included four that proved critical for the eventual outcome. First, he sought a no-cost means of reducing the amount of nongovernment-owned land in the park, and thus proposed a trade between the city and the federal government. "The City of San Francisco practically owns all the patented land in the floor of the Hetch Hetchy reservoir site and sufficient adjacent areas in the Yosemite National Park and the Sierra National Forest to equal the remainder of that reservoir area," he noted. "The city will surrender to the United States equivalent areas outside of the reservoir sites and within the National Park and adjacent reserves in exchange for the remaining land in the reservoir sites, for which authority from Congress will be obtained if necessary." The idea seemed straightforward, yet it would ultimately prove the most contentious, as it opened the door for congressional and public intervention in the debate. The seemingly innocuous clause would affect the course of American environmentalism. City officials were dumbfounded by the eventual outcry.

Second, as a compromise to concerns for the loss of Hetch Hetchy, Garfield specified "the City and County of San Francisco will develop the Lake Eleanor site to its full capacity before beginning the development of the Hetch Hetchy site." City engineer Grunsky's report broached the possibility. Even Pinchot agreed, forecasting that Lake Eleanor alone could satisfy the city's needs for fifty years or more and urging that the damming of Hetch Hetchy be postponed as long as possible to preserve the valley's original beauty, as John Wesley Powell had also recommended. The secretary concurred, and few opponents to Hetch Hetchy contested the change to Lake

Eleanor even though it lay in the national park; similarly, no one opposed the potential damming of Cherry Creek, just outside the park. Hetch Hetchy would be the last resort. Garfield further stipulated that construction of Lake Eleanor Dam must begin within three years following public approval of the plan and progress in five years "with all reasonable diligence" to completion.

Third, the irrigation districts in the San Joaquin Valley vehemently opposed the entire proposal out of fear that the city's use of Tuolumne River water would deplete the flow for their use during critical dry months of the growing season. The districts comprised about 258,000 acres, of which about 235,000 acres were irrigable. In response to these concerns Garfield ruled that the petitioners "will not interfere in the slightest particular with the right of the Modesto Irrigation District and the Turlock Irrigation District to use the natural flow of the Tuolumne River and its branches to the full extent of their claims, as follows: Turlock Irrigation District, 1500 second feet; Modesto Irrigation District, 850 second feet; these districts having respectively appropriated the foregoing amounts of water under the laws of the State of California."

And fourth, in light of the trust-busting Progressive thinking of the day, the secretary stipulated that San Francisco would sell to the irrigation districts "any excess of electric power which may be generated such as may not be used for the water supply herein provided and for the actual municipal purposes of the City and County of San Francisco, (which purposes shall not include sale to private persons nor to corporations) at such price as will actually reimburse the said City and County for developing and transmitting the surplus electrical energy thus sold." By implication, Garfield required the creation of a public utility in parallel with the much broader public water supply, albeit with the limited capacity to generate, transmit, and sell electric power directly to the city for the needs of the water system and other municipal uses, and to the irrigation districts for pumping groundwater. However, he made no mention of the utility servicing the power needs of the general retail consumer as would a true public power system.

Yet Garfield hedged on the overall necessity of the project, stating, "I do not need to pass upon the claim that this is the only practicable and reasonable source of water supply for the City. It is sufficient that after careful and competent study the officials of the City insist that such is the case." He effectively dodged a core question, shifting responsibility for its resolution to the people of San Francisco by requiring them to approve the proposal by a two-thirds majority within two years. Was the use of Yosemite National Park by the City of San Francisco necessary? If San Franciscans deemed the use desirable, the secretary would grant them that use. The concerns of the American people would not be heard in the local debate. National interests were subordinated to local self-interests. Were the environmental costs that would be borne by the American people warranted by the benefits that would be enjoyed by Bay Area residents? Garfield alone judged them to be. The role of public input in determining resource policy was much different then. The outcome of Hetch Hetchy would help change that.

However, only Hetch Hetchy mesmerized the dreamers, not Lake Eleanor or Cherry Creek, regardless of the reversal of roles in the Garfield permit. To Phelan and Manson, only Hetch Hetchy could ultimately solve San Francisco's water needs. The other Tuolumne reservoirs and Spring Valley were merely supplemental sideshows. To dam Lake Eleanor and Cherry Creek and pipe their water to San Francisco while leaving the Hetch Hetchy Valley untouched simply made no sense. The extraordinary steep-walled valley set within a wilderness watershed, pinched to such a narrow throat at its outflow, through which flowed millions of gallons of pure water was perfect for a dam and reservoir. Ironically, what distinguished the valley to Phelan and Manson was what entranced the preservationists. Both groups stood in awe of the area's natural wonder, although they saw it from totally different perspectives.

CHAPTER 8

A National Cause Célèbre

T he Garfield permit would mobilize John Muir, the Sierra Club, and other wilderness and outdoor advocates across the country. Even though Lake Eleanor would be dammed first, Hetch Hetchy remained vulnerable at a later date. The issue quickly transcended local politics to become a national controversy as Muir and the opponents took the debate to the American public during congressional hearings triggered by the right of Congress to approve the exchange of public land for private land.

To a great extent the American environmental movement began during the December 1908 and January 1909 hearings. No public policy affecting the environment had ever triggered such public concern. For the first time a broad consortium of nonprofit groups coalesced around an environmental issue of mutual concern to raise public awareness and influence national policy. Using the media of the day—magazine articles, newspaper editorials, printed pamphlets, letters, and telegrams—they tapped into the national sentiment for the outdoors and anxieties over modernity, arousing an unprecedented outpouring of public support for an environmental issue, flooding Congress with their concerns. Across the country groups joined in the cause: the Sierra Club, the Appalachian Mountain Club, the American Civic Association, the newly formed Society for the Preservation of National Parks, the General Federation of Women's Clubs, the Saturday Walking Club, the Chicago Geographical Society, the American Scenic and Historic Preservation Society. Tens of thousands of Americans mobilized to have their voices heard in Washington. And the organizers testified at the congressional hearings, bringing the message directly to the policymakers, countering the testimony of those from San Francisco and California with vested interests in the proposal and the politicians who supported their position. Certainly some of the opponents had vested personal or financial interests too, such as the Sierra Club and

Spring Valley Water Company. But the basis of their concern and the nature of their voice differed fundamentally from the proponents', as they would in many environmental debates to come.

The proponents were comprised more of public agencies with local economic interests, and private corporations in later cases, who sought government approval to disturb the environment for resource development, albeit perhaps for valid public purposes. On the other hand, the opponents were mostly poorly funded, nonprofit, member-based groups who sought to prevent the disturbance and protect the environment as much on philosophical grounds as personal interest in the actual use and enjoyment of the jeopardized landscape.

Both sides presented closely reasoned arguments, yet few people found cause to set aside their preconceptions. The debate played out in the media and documented in hundreds of pages in the *Congressional Record* at times degenerated into one of us versus them, progress versus preservation, development versus environment, practical versus philosophical, necessity versus luxury, material versus spiritual, right versus wrong. Passions ran hot on both sides. Sound arguments had little effect on opinion.

Writing in *Outlook* during the debate Muir proclaimed, "everybody needs beauty as well as bread, places to play in and pray in where Nature may heal and cheer and give strength to body and soul alike." Yet he ascribed the plan to "mischief-makers and robbers of every degree from Satan to Senators . . . trying to make everything dollarable."

Lyman Abbott, editor of *Outlook* and a staunch opponent of the Hetch Hetchy plan, wrote, "if this country were in danger of habitually ignoring utilitarian practice for the sake of running after sentimental dreams and aesthetic visions we should advise it . . . to dam the Tuolumne River in order to instruct its citizens in the use of the bathtub. But the danger is all the other way. The national habit is to waste the beauty of Nature and save the dollars of business."

J. Horace McFarland, the influential president of the American Civic Association, noted that if Hetch Hetchy were vulnerable, then no place in a national park would be secured from commercial development. Yet such scenic places would become increasingly valuable for recreation to the nation as it became more and more urban and industrialized. Whenever wilderness preservation conflicted with material interests, he asserted, those with financial stakes cried foul: "that is sentimentalism; that is aestheticism; that is pleasure-loving; that is unnecessary; that is not practical," they would claim. And they would win, with wilderness sacrificed for development as a result. But "it is not sentimentalism," he told Secretary Garfield, "it is living." Writing later in the Sierra Club *Bulletin,* he elaborated, "the primary function of the national forests is to supply lumber. The primary function of the national parks is to maintain in healthful efficiency the lives of the people who must use that lumber. . . . The true ideal of their maintenance does not run parallel to the making of the most timber, or the most pasturage, or the most water power."

Phelan countered at the congressional hearing, belittling Muir: "I am sure he would sacrifice his own family for the preservation of beauty. He considers human life very cheap, and he considers the works of God superior." California congressman William Kent would later tell a colleague not to take Muir and his concerns about Hetch Hetchy seriously, "for he is a man entirely without social sense. With him, it is me and God and the rock where God put it, and that is the end of the story."

Could the debate have been otherwise? Were the two sides mutually exclusive? Must it always be so? And if the split is inevitable, what is the basis of compromise and resolution? Where does the public interest and the public good lie? Both sides claimed to represent them. Neither side could persuade the other with reason. Congress was split on the issue, despite the nation as a whole clearly favoring preservation. Roosevelt wavered in his support, stating in his eighth annual message to Congress just a week before the start of the hearings that "Yosemite, is a great wonderland, and should be kept as a national playground. In both [Yellowstone and Yosemite], all wild things should be protected and the scenery kept wholly unmarred."

Although the House Committee on Public Lands approved the plan by a single vote, a strong dissenting minority report noted, "there has been an exceedingly widespread, earnest, and vigorous protest voiced by scientists, naturalists, mountain climbers, travelers, and others in person, by letters, and telegrams, and in newspaper and magazine articles." Confronted with such opposition, the House tabled the application. Congress made no final decision on the right-of-way land exchange. Hetch Hetchy received a temporary stay of execution.

Supporters in San Francisco were incensed. How could "hoggish and mushy esthetes," wondered the *San Francisco Chronicle,* deny the city this righteous cause? Marsden Manson, now the city engineer, called the opponents "short-haired women and long-haired men." The war of words raged, though the truth was at times overshadowed by emotionalism.

The city proceeded, undaunted. After the Garfield permit had been granted, Manson had immediately moved forward to satisfy the most pressing provisions of the permit: the status of the city's rights filed some seven years earlier by Phelan, Grunsky, and Manson but not acted upon since, and possibly abandoned by the Schmitz administration resolution, had to be affirmed and supplemented where necessary; additional lands and water rights in the Hetch Hetchy Valley, Lake Eleanor, and Cherry Creek sites had to be secured; a plan and cost estimate for the system had to be developed and the plan approved by the voters; and a construction bond issue had to be passed.

Manson quickly refiled for the original Phelan rights, and in November 1908 he won passage of a modest bond issue to purchase privately held properties in Hetch Hetchy; 86 percent of the voters also approved the general Hetch Hetchy plan, far exceeding the two-thirds majority required by the Garfield permit: "To acquire by purchase the lands and water rights in and about Hetch Hetchy and Lake Eleanor: Yes, 34,950. No, 5,708. To incur a bonded debt of $600,000 for the purpose: Yes, 34,572. No, 5,647."

Acquisition of the additional rights for the Lake Eleanor and Cherry Creek sites would prove acrimonious, costly, and time-consuming. After Phelan, Grunsky, and Manson had originally filed for water rights around Hetch Hetchy and Lake Eleanor, William Hammond Hall had quickly acquired competitive rights around Lake Eleanor and Cherry Creek, intending to develop his own water and power company. In 1902, three founders of PG&E bought into his scheme, forming the Sierra Ditch and Water Company in 1905 to accomplish it. But the company actually served as a front to hide the identities of its owners and the PG&E connection, since the monopoly had a vested corporate interest in competition with the city's plan for a municipal water system that might also produce electricity. The three PG&E silent partners also needed to keep a low profile after they were indicted in the 1906 Boss Ruef graft and corruption hearings for having bought off the board of supervisors to keep gas rates low.

When the Garfield permit required Lake Eleanor to be developed first (instead of creating a dam at Hetch Hetchy, as had been Phelan's dream when he made the filings), the change played perfectly into the holding company's position. Now they would make the city pay. The company offered the city its rights for $300,000; the city refused, thinking the amount outrageous. Too bad; after several years of heated negotiations, San Francisco in 1910–11 finally paid the speculators $1 million in total to acquire their rights.

Manson had also drawn up plans for the new dam and water system in response to the provisions of the Garfield permit and made a cost estimate on which to base the construction bond. In 1910 voters approved the $45 million bond for a Lake Eleanor system, separate from any Spring Valley supplies, by an overwhelming twenty-to-one margin.

The city had also negotiated a $35 million purchase price for the Spring Valley Water Company, assuming that if the acquisition occurred, portions of the Lake Eleanor system would not be needed, such as the construction of a duplicate water delivery network in the city; hence, only $23 million of the $45 million in bonds would be issued. However, after a contentious campaign leading up to the same election as the construction bond, only 65 percent of voters would favor the Spring Valley bond issue, tantalizingly close to the required two-thirds majority. Suspicion that the price for the water company had again been inflated undermined public support. Some civic leaders also worried that the level of resulting city indebtedness would be too high. And some voters simply didn't want to pay the added tax. Spring Valley also might have had a hand in the result by lobbying political leaders to remain silent on or to be vocal opponents of the purchase. Unexpectedly, Mayor P. H. McCarthy (1910–12) campaigned against the bond issue, as did several labor groups. Although the Lake Eleanor plan enjoyed phenomenal public support, Spring Valley remained the city's nemesis.

As Manson prepared his plan and cost estimate the spring following the congressional setback, the fate of Phelan's project and the Garfield permit appeared further in doubt when President William Howard Taft (1909–13) assumed office. Many Republicans assumed the new president would continue the Progressive conservation policies of his popular predecessor. He didn't. The new president wasn't a true believer in the cause like his rambunctious predecessor.

To the Progressives, conservation meant the protection of valuable public lands from private ownership and potential abuse, and the wise development of timber, minerals, grazing, water, and recreation on those lands through cooperation directed by government scientists and enlightened bureaucrats. Both presidents appreciated Hetch Hetchy's spectacular scenery, and both struggled with how best to manage it. Roosevelt's Progressive conservation values led him to favor the utilitarian, multiple-use approach. Taft's preference for resource development by the private sector along with legal concerns led him to hesitate in permitting such uses in national parks or forests, or in creating new ones. Roosevelt fumed, overreacting to Taft's resource policies in the belief that they necessarily favored the interests of big business over public and environmental welfare, backsliding to the short-sighted policies of the 1800s.

As Taft took hold, Pinchot and the other true believers became increasingly angry about the policy changes and their lessened influence. They tried unsuccessfully to convert the new president to their gospel or to bypass his policies. Some in the former Roosevelt coterie resigned in protest. The powerful chief forester chose to stay and fight. Hetch Hetchy reflected the widening rift. Pinchot had lobbied hard to win approval of the Garfield permit; now, to the dismay of many Progressive Republicans, Taft appointed Richard A. Ballinger, a like-minded land attorney, as secretary of the interior.

Pinchot had never approved of the new secretary, and had contested his appointment. Ballinger was a respected attorney and former mayor of Seattle, who had worked to reform the notoriously corrupt General Land Office during a short tenure as commissioner several years earlier. But integrity aside, Pinchot fundamentally disagreed with Ballinger's (and Taft's) land management philosophy. Likewise, Ballinger thought some of Pinchot's freewheeling agreements were illegal.

Tensions between Taft and Ballinger and the holdovers from the Roosevelt administration tightened, quickly straining their working relationship to the breaking point. It all snapped during the so-called Ballinger-Pinchot affair, which unfortunately evolved into a public debate argued in the national press and focused more on personality and politics than the men's important underlying policy differences.

In autumn 1909, Ballinger's critics accused him of indirectly asserting pressure for the approval of a potentially fraudulent Alaskan coal claim without sufficient investigation; the land claim had been submitted by some of his former law clients. The complicated issues dated to Ballinger's term as commissioner of the general land office and involved nuances in several land laws. Whether or not the accusations were founded, personal vindictiveness and politics clearly motivated some participants. Accusations of wrongdoing were hurled back and forth between Ballinger and his accusers, especially Pinchot. President Taft had little patience for the mudslinging, accepting his attorney general's belief after a cursory investigation that Ballinger had not breached any ethics.

The controversy exploded in early 1910 when Iowa senator Jonathan Dolliver read to the body a letter written to him by Pinchot that defended Ballinger's accusers while extolling the policies of the forest service under Pinchot's leadership. President Taft promptly fired Pinchot for insubordination. Pinchot struck back, leading a public attack to discredit Secretary Ballinger and the Taft conservation policies. Meanwhile, Congress conducted its own investigation, hearing forty-five days of conflicting testimony, contentious cross-examination, and partisan wrangling. The result: Secretary Ballinger was exonerated of any wrongdoing by a narrow vote along philosophical lines. But it didn't matter in the court of public opinion. Ballinger had been effectively smeared, and the Republican Party began to fracture between those who supported Roosevelt and those who favored Taft. (Discredited, Ballinger resigned from office in 1911 due to poor health. He never recovered politically or physically from the damage done to his integrity. Another investigation conducted in 1940 by Secretary of the Interior Harold Ickes again exonerated Ballinger and criticized Pinchot for his overzealousness.)

Concurrent with Manson's preparatory work on the plan and the escalating tensions in the Taft administration over conservation policy, the preservationists quickly petitioned Secretary Ballinger to void his predecessor's permit. They also mounted a national media campaign to strengthen public opposition to it, in part because Ballinger was initially inclined to uphold Garfield's decision. William Colby invited several congressmen and members of the administration to join the Sierra Club on its ninth annual High Trip that summer. The stout president declined, but he and Ballinger toured the Yosemite Valley with Muir in October.

As the group descended into Yosemite, President Taft teased Muir that the flat valley floor would make a fine farm. "Why!" Muir replied, "this is Nature's cathedral, a place to worship in." To which the president responded, "But don't you think that since these valleys are so far from the centers of population, they might just as well be used commercially?" Pointing to the extraordinary mouth of the valley, he continued, "Now that would be a fine place for a dam!" Muir went apoplectic. "A dam!" he exclaimed, "Yes, . . . but the man who would dam that would be damning himself." Taft chuckled, his guide having fallen into the trap. "I suppose you know, Mr. Muir, that several people in San Francisco are very much worried because I asked you to come here with me today." Muir showed the president a map detailing his plan for a trail system linking Yosemite Valley, Tuolumne Meadows, Tuolumne Falls, and the Hetch Hetchy Valley, forming perhaps the grandest compact sightseeing loop in the world. Taft was impressed and made clear his opposition to the proposed Hetch Hetchy dam.

The next day Muir toured Ballinger, George Otis Smith, director of the U.S. Geological Survey, and several government engineers around the Hetch Hetchy Valley. The engineers gushed about the suitability of the site for a dam and reservoir, partly in jest. The press accompanying the group missed the levity and reported the comments and Muir's predictable response out of context. Shortly after his return to Washington, President Taft appointed a three-member board, comprised of Smith as head and two engineers from the reclamation service, to study the Hetch Hetchy scheme.

"Everything in the Hetch Hetchy Yosemite Park battle looks fine for our side, & black for the robbers," Muir rejoiced. With the Ballinger-Pinchot affair heating up in the press, casting doubt on the

chief forester's influence and the course of national conservation policy, and giving the secretary of the interior further cause to reverse
the permit, Phelan's dream looked dead. But the battle was not won.

While the Smith board conducted its study, the City of San
Francisco was moving successfully forward with preliminary work
on the project, preparing a cost estimate for it, bond issues and a ref-
erendum on it for voter approval in January 1910, and negotiating
for the purchase of Spring Valley, which San Franciscans narrowly
rejected in the election. Within days of the vote, President Taft fired
Pinchot for insubordination, and the Sierra Club membership voted
four to one in opposition of the Hetch Hetchy plan after a long and
divisive internal debate.

The Smith report was issued a month later, concluding the plan
was technically very weak, with the valley better used for recreation
than as a reservoir, and that other sources of water were available,
noting that Lake Eleanor was "amply sufficient to meet the present
and prospective needs of the city." The report even speculated that
the entire scheme was merely a ploy to drive down Spring Valley's
water rates.

After reviewing the Smith report, Ballinger ordered the city to
show why the Hetch Hetchy part of the Garfield permit should not
be revoked. And he asked the president to appoint a three-member
board of army engineers to act as advisors during the review. Taft
and Ballinger apparently agreed with the preservationists' concerns
and felt the eventual damming of the valley was simply unnecessary
or contrary to the purpose of a national park, as had Secretary
Hitchcock. When the rehearing on the Hetch Hetchy part of the permit was held in May 1910, Secretary Ballinger stood ready to officially revoke it.

Yet the secretary took no action at the hearing. Why didn't he act
on his threat? A form of subtle political blackmail likely contributed
to his hesitancy. When Manson and the city proponents of the Hetch
Hetchy plan examined the Smith report, they found a number of
improprieties in the work and false statements made by the reclamation service engineers that cast doubt on the report's objectivity,
making it an embarrassment to the secretary. However, Manson kept
quiet on the findings until the Ballinger hearing began.

San Francisco mayor Patrick H. McCarthy and city attorney

Percy Long spoke on behalf of the city. Manson presented technical data, which John R. Freeman had helped prepare, before the army advisory board. The opponents relied prominently on the Smith report for technical support of their case. In the face of the report's damning evidence, the proponents stalled for additional time to produce a more detailed study of Hetch Hetchy, Lake Eleanor, and Cherry Creek, and a favorable shift in their Washington fortunes. Long asked the secretary to grant the city a year to investigate whether a dam could be built at Lake Eleanor, as suggested by the Smith report, before taking any action on the permit. The opponents cried foul, claiming the proponents had had years to study the options. Throughout, Manson had sat patiently as the suspect findings from the Smith report were presented, allowing the potentially incriminating testimony to be made public, and then he privately whispered to the secretary that he had evidence of the irregularities; but, "without waiving any rights to bring it out later," he would permit the secretary "to act as his best judgment indicated."

The outcome: Ballinger announced he would appoint a new commission of army engineers to restudy the scheme, to which the city had to supply data on Hetch Hetchy as well as alternative water sources and examine the "extent of damage to the scenic features of the National Park that will result from the proposed works." The new study was due June 1, 1911. The army advisors concurred with his decision, reporting to Ballinger as the hearing concluded that, "from the information received, the Board is of the opinion that sufficient accurate data on Lake Eleanor and adjacent watersheds is not available; that as the City of San Francisco will not be permitted to do any development work in the Hetch Hetchy Valley during the interval, nor to acquire any additional rights, there is no valid reason why the year's delay asked for by the city should not be granted." Ballinger's order would result in the city's hiring Mr. Freeman to produce its study, and in the preparation of an associated report by the new Special Advisory Board of Army Engineers, comprised of the same threesome that participated in the hearing.

The city was none too eager to push its study forward, delaying the hiring of John Freeman for months while officials considered their political options in Washington. Throughout the autumn and winter leading into 1911, both the proponents and opponents continued the war of words in the media for political and public support. In March President Taft named Walter Fisher as the secretary of the interior following Secretary Ballinger's resignation. The appointment sent mixed messages to the Hetch Hetchy players.

On the one hand, Fisher was a friend of Pinchot and Garfield, given the position by Taft in an attempt to curry political favor with western Progressives. But the new secretary soon accepted an invitation by the preservationists to visit Hetch Hetchy in September to see for himself the source of all the fuss. J. Horace McFarland replaced John Muir as the spokesperson for the preservation side during the tour. Marsden Manson presented the conservation viewpoint. The group argued the issues around campfires late into the night, while during the days they toured Hetch Hetchy, Lake Eleanor, and the other sites figuring prominently in the debate. Afterward, Secretary Fisher remained tight-lipped on the proposal, not revealing his position to either side as they all awaited Freeman's report. And as had happened at each step in the sequence of events culminating in congressional approval of Hetch Hetchy, both sides carefully plotted new strategy in response to changes in the political tides, often arguing internally over the most effective course of action.

Preparation of the Freeman and army studies moved deliberately, with the completion of the Freeman report postponed first to December 1, 1911, then to March 1, 1912, to June 12, and finally to November 1912. The Advisory Board of Army Engineers awaited his report before making its recommendation.

Fifty-five-year-old John Riley Freeman was finally giving Phelan's dream full engineering form. The prior Grunsky and Manson plans were schematic and shaped by imposed political limitations. Freeman's visionary plan, set forth in his four-hundred-page report, including appendices, had no such constraints. Stern faced, fastidious, sporting a goatee and a handlebar moustache, and devoted to his work, Freeman provided the city with exactly what it sought—an unassailable expert who enthusiastically supported its position. They probably knew he would, since the city had hired the easterner from Providence, Rhode Island, to help prepare its case and give testimony on its behalf at the Fisher hearing. It was no surprise that they then hired him on the recommendation of President Taft to prepare

the definitive justification for the project. A noted authority on
hydraulic and seismic engineering, and also on fire prevention,
Freeman would turn down two professorships at Harvard and the
presidency of MIT, his alma mater. Prestigious universities around
the world, including Yale, Penn, Brown, and prominent German
programs, would confer on him honorary degrees for his lifetime of
engineering achievements. That work would help shape the municipal water systems of Boston and New York. More importantly, he
shared Phelan's dream and the imperial and imperialistic values it
represented.

The lengthy title to the July 15, 1912, Freeman report was telling:
"On the Proposed Use of a Portion of the Hetch Hetchy, Eleanor
and Cherry Valleys within and near to the Boundaries of the
Stanislaus U.S. National Forest Reserve and the Yosemite National
Park as Reservoirs for Impounding Tuolumne River Flood Waters
and Appurtenant Works for the Water Supply of San Francisco,
California, and Neighboring Cities, a report to James Rolph, Jr.,
Mayor of San Francisco, and Percy V. Long, City Attorney." Clearly
the report was intended to justify the city's dream for a Hetch
Hetchy water supply, not to evaluate alternatives, so it bore little pre-
tense of objectivity.

"There can be no question that some day the [Bay Area] cities
must have water from the [Sierra] mountains," the report stated, "the
only questions are, how soon? and which source first?" It presumed
Hetch Hetchy to be the answer. Alternative sources received page-
length discussions at the end of the report, but they were summarily
dismissed as viable options for the same reasons and with the same
shallow depth of consideration given in the earlier Grunsky and
Manson plans.

The Freeman report also abandoned the bothersome constraints
imposed by the Garfield permit, stating, "the scope of the Hetch
Hetchy water supply problem and the scope of methods for solving it
have become greatly changed [since the Grunsky and Manson plans
were produced] and the scope of the Garfield Permit is insufficient
for present needs and for future conservation." Why limit the system
initially to 60 million gallons a day, as had the Grunsky and Manson
plans and the Garfield permit? Instead, Freeman recommended that
the city construct the entire system at once, noting, "it costs relatively

little more to drive a tunnel for 400 million gallons daily than for 60 million gallons daily. . . . So long a project must be a large project with broad scope in order to work out well; in other words, in order to make an aqueduct 172 miles long into this difficult region commercially successful it must be of large capacity and planned on a generous scale."

The most troublesome constraint in the Garfield permit was the requirement that Lake Eleanor be dammed first, followed by Hetch Hetchy only when future water needs warranted. To postpone development of Hetch Hetchy, Freeman felt, "would be, under light of the present day, an economic blunder of the worst kind, wasteful of the city's funds and in gross violation of the principles of conservation of water supply. Seldom, if ever, has an economic fact been more plain than that it is logical, economical and in all ways proper to build the Hetch Hetchy dam first and to defer building any high masonry dam upon the unfavorable, expensive Lake Eleanor site for fully half a century."

Scenic and recreational concerns remained the only arguments against the plan, so Freeman attacked them head on. The first illustration in the report, a full-page retouched photograph on page six, showed a shimmering reservoir reflecting the magnificent surrounding canyon walls and cascading waterfalls, with a scenic drive snaking around the perimeter. The caption read, "The depth of water would not lessen the apparent height of cliffs. On the contrary, the reflection would increase it." Similar images conveying the same message followed for Hetch Hetchy and reservoirs around the world, as the report extolled the project's scenic and recreational benefits, including the construction of a summer tourist hotel near the dam site.

"The Hetch Hetchy Valley has no conceivable important value except for two purposes: 1)Scenery; 2)Water supply. By care in the designs, the use for water supply can be made to add greatly to the scenic value, and . . . can bring the scenic beauties of the Hetch Hetchy Valley within reach of a hundred-fold more people than would otherwise find it possible to enjoy them during the next quarter or half century." Visitation counts attested to the swampy, mosquito-infested conditions that plagued the remote valley during the summer season, Freeman said: 269 persons in 1909, 16 in 1910, and

185 in 1911. "If a beautiful region can be brought within the vision of a hundred appreciative nature lovers instead of closed by time, hardship and expense of the trip to all but one or two, the enjoyment of this beauty has been fifty or a hundred-fold increased, and it is so simple as to require no argument that the two beautiful cliffs in the Hetch Hetchy Valley would become more beautiful when mirrored in a deep, placid lake more than half a mile in width and several miles long. . . . What one finds there today is beautiful, but it is relatively tame and uninteresting in comparison with the far more grand and varied Yosemite."

These were sound arguments in some cases, but none were supported with any factual evidence; instead, they derived only from personal opinion and a Progressive-utilitarian perspective. By that line of reasoning, would any place be safe from resource exploitation, including the national parks?

CHAPTER 9

The Political Outcome

U ltimately, politics would settle the fate of the Hetch Hetchy Valley, rather than economic, engineering, environmental, or philosophical concerns. As preparation of the Freeman report neared completion, and the 1912 presidential election neared, the rift in the Republican Party widened further. The Taft faction was failing the party and the country, Roosevelt proclaimed. Unable to win the party's presidential nomination at its raucous convention in Chicago, Roosevelt's supporters stormed out of the hall and formed the Progressive "Bull Moose" Party to run him for president on a platform that shared many of the same planks as Wilson and the Progressive Democrats. The split doomed the Republicans to defeat.

Wilson's platform differed significantly from his Republican predecessor's. Not since President Grover Cleveland's second term (1893–97), sixteen years earlier, had the Democrats occupied the White House, and rarely during this drought had they controlled Congress. Hetch Hetchy had been tightly entangled in the political turmoil that gradually built during the sequence of presidential administrations that eventually brought the dramatic change in power. Wilson would easily win the acrimonious election, for which former San Francisco mayor James Duval Phelan organized his campaign in California and served during it as the Democratic Party state treasurer. In hindsight the fate of Hetch Hetchy appears to have been cast.

By autumn 1912 the Freeman report was complete, setting the army board to work on its report and the preservationists to write extensive rebuttals. The frequently postponed rehearing on the city's application was finally held before Secretary Fisher in Washington from November 25 through 30. Representatives for San Francisco included the new mayor, James Rolph, and the new city engineer, Michael M. O'Shaughnessy, the city attorney, Percy Long, and John

Freeman. Spring Valley sent a contingent, as did the irrigation districts. J. Horace McFarland, Stephen Mather (later to be the first director of the National Park Service), and Robert Underwood Johnson, among others, represented the "nature lovers." The army engineers sat and listened as the sides had at it day after day.

William F. Badè, the Sierra Club representative, noted that "Freeman got several awful 'jawings' from the Secretary for his lack of candor and his desire to dismiss all other sources [of water than Hetch Hetchy] with a wave of the hand. . . . The Army Engineers said they had for weeks tried to get Freeman to equalize his [cost] estimates on the same unit basis—but without avail. The Secretary practically served notice on the city that their failures along these lines was presumptive evidence against them." As a result, the secretary ordered Freeman and the city to prove more adequately that the Tuolumne was in fact the only reasonable source, as well as to submit new cost estimates that fixed discrepancies in labor rates that favored the Hetch Hetchy plan over other alternatives. The city was given about two months to revise the estimates and furnish additional data. Beyond that, the secretary still had not tipped his hand.

The city delivered its revisions to the Freeman report to Washington in mid-January 1913, and a month later the army board delivered its 146-page report, with attachments, to Secretary Fisher on February 19. While a bit more balanced than the Freeman vision, the board's report concurred with each of Freeman's recommendations, including the project scope and timing; this was no surprise, since they based their evaluation on Freeman's data, and, as engineers, they were naturally inclined to support Freeman's and the city's utilitarian position. "The board is of the opinion," they concluded, "that there are several sources of water supply that could be obtained and used by the city of San Francisco and adjacent communities to supplement the near-by supplies as the necessity develops. From any one of these sources the water is sufficient in quantity and is, or can be made, suitable in quality, while the engineering difficulties are not insurmountable. The determining factor is principally one of cost. . . . The project proposed by the city of San Francisco, known as the Hetch Hetchy project, is about $20,000,000 cheaper than any other feasible project for furnishing an adequate supply. . . .

The Hetch Hetchy project has the additional advantage of permitting the development of a greater amount of water power than any other."

The advisory board also responded to the opponents' arguments against the plan on scenic and recreational reasons with the same utilitarian counterarguments used by Freeman. "The relative beauty of the Hetch Hetchy Valley in its two conditions—as it is at present or dammed up into a reservoir—seems to be a matter of individual opinion. It is admitted that the Yosemite Valley is as a whole more wonderful than the Hetch Hetchy Valley, but the floor of the latter is more diversified in its trees and flowers, and of at least equal beauty. Flooding the valley will destroy this floor and the falls of the Tuolumne at the head of the valley. The surrounding cliffs and falls would not be affected." On balance, the engineers concluded the effects on the scenery and the loss of camping sites on the valley floor would be more than offset by the creation of new recreation opportunities resulting from the construction of the scenic highway, new campsites, and other facilities. In addition, these improvements would bring more people to enjoy the little-visited valley.

Letters and lobbying efforts on behalf of each side inundated Washington as Secretary Fisher pondered the issue. But his term was about to end. On March 1, 1913, just three days before he left office, he announced his decision to not decide, writing to Mayor Rolph and the San Francisco board of supervisors,

> If it were clear that I should issue to the City of San Francisco a permit of the general character it requests, it would have been and would now be absolutely impossible within the time available to embody the details of such a permit in a properly considered document. This is a matter of the greatest regret to me as I had hoped to be able at least to draft a permit embodying the provisions which, in my judgment, should be contained in any permit for the use of the Hetch Hetchy Valley as a reservoir site by the city of San Francisco and the communities around San Francisco Bay. The importance of doing this, however, is much reduced by the fact that I have reached the conclusion that a permit for this purpose should not be issued by the Secretary of the Interior under the existing law.

Noting in his official explanation that the army engineers' report in effect placed a $20 million value on the scenery of Hetch Hetchy, he felt "that in order to save the expenditure of a certain sum of money by the people of San Francisco the people of the whole country should consent to change the present condition of the Hetch Hetchy Valley. It may well be that such consent would be justified," he continued; however, it "should not be taken by the Secretary without a clear authorization by Congress that I am to believe was consciously intended when the act of 1901 was passed."

Despite the Right of Way Act and the attorney general's opinion, Fisher still questioned whether he held the administrative authority to grant a revocable permit that would result in such significant damage to an important part of a national park. Did Congress really mean to give the secretary that individual discretion when it had also passed legislation protecting the same land? Like Hitchcock and Ballinger before him, Fisher would not exercise that authority. "In view of the language of the Yosemite reservation act of 1890," Fisher concluded, "as a matter of broad public policy . . . the natural condition of so important a natural curiosity or wonder as the Hetch Hetchy Valley should not be radically changed without the express authority of Congress."

The city was all too happy to make its case to Congress with the installation of the Wilson administration and Franklin Lane as secretary of the interior. It's not clear whether Fisher anticipated this, realizing his non-decision was in effect one that granted the city its entire request. However he was fully versed on both sides of the controversy and likely torn between the compelling arguments each offered.

Circumstances for the city had changed significantly since the Garfield permit was originally issued. With the pending Wilson administration so supportive, the proponents were now in the political driver's seat. And they balked at some of the limits imposed by the permit. "The outlook and the state of the art have moved so fast that the Garfield Permit has become practically worthless for the needs of the city," Freeman had concluded. "A new permit should be drawn in accordance with the scope of the works [desired by the city]," he argued. The city was also fed up with the fickle politics that influenced secretaries of the interior. Tired of being subject to their whims, and unnecessarily constrained by the permit, the proponents now sought direct congressional approval for the entire Hetch Hetchy project, confident that it could muster the votes. Legislative action, although not required, would finally end the controversy in the city's favor, permanently. When the new president quickly appointed Franklin K. Lane, the former San Francisco city attorney who had worked on the initial Hetch Hetchy proposal, as his secretary of the interior, the valley's fate was no longer in doubt, even if Lane would also forward the proposal to Congress for resolution as had Hitchcock, Ballinger, and Fisher.

So the city made its case to the new Wilson administration and a Congress already predisposed to agree, pointing to the Freeman and army board reports. Clearly San Francisco needed water delivered by a public utility to break up the Spring Valley monopoly, they argued. Not only was Hetch Hetchy perfect to meet their water quantity and quality needs, it was also the only viable option, and it was the least expensive one as well, saving money required for other options to acquire water rights on private land, or build longer aqueducts, or provide more water treatment. Besides, they boasted that the proposed reservoir would improve the scenery of the valley and open up that spectacle to a hundred-fold additional visitors a year. And since the valley had a famous nearby sister, there was no need to retain this little-seen sibling intact. Never mind the valley's location in a national park; the Right of Way Act gave the secretary of the interior the power to grant park easements for water and power projects. The sanctity of a national park was yet to be established. The needs of progress took precedence, argued the proponents. How could the opponents counter? The proponents blocked them at every turn.

The city immediately dispatched a contingent including city engineer O'Shaughnessy and city attorney Long to help draft a bill. California congressman John Raker introduced the first version in the House on April 7 (he had unsuccessfully introduced a bill on the city's behalf two years earlier), beginning the "dance of legislation" as Congress, the city, and the irrigation districts sought an acceptable version and the opponents fought to stop it. The proceedings of the five different versions of the bill fill hundreds of pages in the

Congressional Record. Everyone seemingly had an opinion, in Washington and across the nation. Yet for all the verbiage and ink, few minds were changed. The outcome was predetermined. Despite another outpouring of public outrage during the floor debate in the Senate, Congress and the Democratic president were convinced.

As the Freeman report recommended, the project rushing head-long toward congressional and presidential approvals differed significantly from that approved by the Garfield permit. A reservoir at Hetch Hetchy Valley was no longer the last resort, only to be built at some distant time if San Francisco water demand warranted. Instead it would be built immediately as the backbone of the plan. Reservoirs would also be built when demand warranted at Lake Eleanor and Cherry Creek, yielding a potential daily water supply of 400 million gallons, far beyond the 60 million gallons previously considered. Spring Valley could be purchased to yield additional supply, storage, and other benefits, but its acquisition was not essential to his plan. Now the city would unite other Bay Area municipalities into a single water service area under its control and so influence the region's growth. And the new plan enabled the eventual generation of significant amounts of hydroelectricity, in contrast to the minimal amounts needed mostly to pump water over mountains envisioned by the Grunsky and Manson plans. San Francisco wanted it all, in one grand scheme free of bothersome constraints; Phelan's dream from the beginning.

As the political debate over the plan and its alternatives had progressed in the months leading up to the Raker Act, the city had made more and more of a case for Hetch Hetchy due to its potential for generating hydroelectricity, effectively using the findings of the Freeman and army reports. No other alternate site had such potential, the proponents argued. And during the decade since the original plan had been envisioned, electrical usage had grown. But the supporters' use of the hydroelectric potential in their argument might have been as much a political ploy to justify their prior commitment to Hetch Hetchy as it was a serious intention. The PG&E electric monopoly was much less problematic than the Spring Valley water monopoly, and future events would cast doubt on the city's sincerity about the PG&E breakup. Regardless, none of the alternative water sources offered the opportunity to generate the desired amounts of hydroelectricity because they lay at lower elevations. Proponents would emphasize this fact to a Congress eager to break up electric power monopolies in favor of public power.

The initial congressional hearings began on June 25 before the House Committee on Public Lands and ran intermittently until July 7 in the sweltering heat of the committee room. Participants were permitted to remove their coats and work in their shirtsleeves. The proponents brought all their big guns: Secretary Lane, Gifford Pinchot, Percy Long, Michael O'Shaughnessy, and James Duval Phelan. The opponents were caught off guard and had few leaders present due to chronic budget problems to pay for travel, poor organization, and lackadaisical preparation. Muir, Johnson, Colby, and McFarland were noticeably absent. Politicking raged concurrently in the Capitol corridors, in the Bay Area, and in the media across the country.

On July 12 the *New York Times* reported on the hearings in an editorial titled "A National Park Threatened": "Why the City of San Francisco, with plenty of collateral sources of water supply, should present an emergency measure to the special session of Congress whereby it may invade the Yosemite National Park is one of those Dundrearian things that no fellow can find out. The Hetch Hetchy Valley is described by John Muir as a 'wonderfully exact counterpart of the great Yosemite.' Why should its inspiring cliffs and waterfalls, its groves and flowery, park-like floor, be spoiled by the grabbers of water and power? The public officials of San Francisco are not even the best sort of politicians; as appraisers and appreciators of natural beauties their taste may be called in question.

"It is the aggregation of its natural scenic features, the Secretary of the Interior declared to the would-be invaders of the park when a decade ago they presented their first petition, that 'makes the Yosemite Park a wonderland, which the Congress of the United States sought by law to preserve for all coming time.' Their application was rejected. Now they have obtained from the Board of Army Engineers a report approving their project as an emergency measure which is based on incomplete, erroneous, and false evidence. The engineers say in their report that they have merely passed on such data as were presented by the officials of San Francisco, since they had neither time nor money to investigate independently the various projects presented. But San Francisco's officials have withheld from these data the report upon the Mokelumne River and watershed submitted April 24, 1912, in which Engineers Bartel and Manson declare that this system is capable of supplying to the City of San Francisco between 280,000,000 and 430,000,000 gallons daily, the larger amount if certain extinguishable rights are disposed of. Even on their insufficient data, the army engineers report that San Francisco's present water supply can be more than doubled by adding to present nearby sources, and more economically than by going to the Sierras.

"The suppressed report, showing that the Mokelumne River is a better and cheaper source than the Hetch Hetchy, says that between 600,000,000 and 700,000,000 gallons of water outside the park may be delivered daily into San Francisco and the adjacent bay region, supplying their growing needs for perhaps a century to come. Representative Scott Ferris, Chairman of the Park Lands Committee, has been apprised of the existence of this report. A receipt of the copy is worth waiting for. If the water-power grabbers are put off this session, or two, or three, or many more sessions, before gaining an entrance to the Hetch Hetchy Valley, the dwellers of San Francisco will not go thirsty."

The claims in the editorial of a suppressed report documenting the advantages of a water system using the Mokelumne River were mostly true. On April 24, 1912, Max J. Bartel, a brilliant young assistant engineer, delivered his study of the Mokelumne to his boss, city engineer Manson. But Manson never had any interest in an alternative to Hetch Hetchy and was certainly not inclined to give attention at that time to such a report, prepared by an assistant on his own initiative. (In the late 1920s several East Bay cities would tap the Mokelumne for their water source with far greater technical ease and at much less cost than Hetch Hetchy, just as Bartel, and others, had proposed.)

Unfortunately, the opponent's case was undermined at the hearing by another claim of the Mokelumne's suitability made by Eugene J. Sullivan, the president of the Sierra Blue Lakes Water and Power Company. Acting on knowledge of the Bartel study, Sullivan also claimed to have sound engineering data that proved the Mokelumne could supply the city with all the water it needed and that the city had deliberately lied about the river's possibilities. The committee devoted a full day to his inflammatory claims. By the end of the session Sullivan was found to be a fraud, even though the study was real and its findings sound. As had the Smith report during the Ballinger hearing, for the second time self-serving testimony had shattered the opponent's case and credibility. The House committee unanimously reported the Raker bill forward on August 5.

The floor debate on the bill began on August 29, concluding September 2. On September 3 the House overwhelming approved it. The next day the *New York Times* editorialized: "The only time to set aside national parks is before the bustling needs of civilization have crept upon them. Legal walls must be built about them for defense, for every park will be attacked. Men and municipalities who wish something for nothing will encroach upon them if permitted. The Hetch Hetchy Valley in the Yosemite National Park is an illustration of this universal struggle.

"The House of Representatives yesterday passed a bill of the politicians of San Francisco who are nurturing a power project under the guise of providing a water supply for San Francisco. The attempt has been made to suppress a report that the Mokelumne River would furnish a better and cheaper source than the Hetch Hetchy. The army engineers who passed favorably on the data presented to them by the officials of San Francisco—they made no investigation themselves—declared that the present water supply of the Far Western city can be more than doubled by adding present nearby sources and more economically than by going 142 miles to the Sierras.

"But the nearer sources do not provide the water power found in the magnificent valley which John Muir describes as a 'wonderful counterpart of the great Yosemite.' The politicians of San Francisco care nothing for matters of natural beauty and taste. They have an eye only for utility, a utility that flows their way. The chief newspapers and organs of public opinion throughout the country have spoken in opposition to the 'grab.' We trust that the Senate will heed their expression of public sentiment, and, failing that, that President Wilson will veto the measure."

The Senate Committee on Public Lands held one day of hearings on September 24, and then voted unanimously to send the bill to the floor, by which time the war of words waging in the national media had reached a new level of ferocity. That autumn hundreds of newspapers nationwide published editorials on the controversy. Magazines including *Century, Outlook, Nation, Independent,* and *Collier's* joined the crusade to stop the dam. Congress received tens of thousands of protest letters. But the war was taking a heavy toll on its primary combatants. "I'll be relieved when it's settled," John Muir would write one of his daughters, "for it's killing me."

A *Times* editorial on October 2 titled "The Hetch Hetchy Steam Roller" tracked the debate: "The Senate of the United States, designed by 'the Fathers' to afford a wise check upon presumably impulsive action by the lower house and called 'the most august deliberative body in the world,' now has a chance to put a spoke in the wheel of the steam roller by which San Francisco's official lobby has heretofore crushed opposition to the Hetch Hetchy bill. An inkling of the tactics of the city's officials is given in *The San Francisco Chronicle* of Sept. 12, which says editorially:

> While we all desire and expect to get the Tuolumne water, it is not desirable that the bill shall be rushed through without a full and free discussion of the rights of the States. The water which we shall need for the next few years will have to be got by the development of the Spring Valley property, [the present chief supply,] and we should make a very poor trade to surrender the rights of the State within its own boundaries in order to get glory for our municipal officials just as an election is coming on.

"A prominent advocate of the project has confessed privately that 'there are bad things in the bill, but they were put there to get votes.' The House debate gives reason for thinking that the measure is a clumsy and probably unworkable attempt to partition the flow of the Hetch Hetchy watershed between the city and such of the San Joaquin Valley farmers as could thus be bribed to forgo their opposition.

"The local strength behind the city's rushline is not difficult to understand when one realizes that the bill involves contracts amounting to $120,000,000, with opportunities of 'honest graft.' For months the project has been presented to Congress with persistence

and specious misrepresentation. Urged first as a measure of human-
ity, it has been shown to be a sordid scheme to obtain electric power.
Urged as providing the only available source, it is confronted by the
conclusive statement of the Board of Army Engineers that 'there are
several sources of water supply' and that 'the determining factor is
one of cost.' Urged on the ground that it cannot injure Hetch Hetchy
because that valley is inaccessible and altogether negligible, it is
shown by Mr. Long, the city's attorney and advocate, that nine miles
of roadway would make it accessible, and by Mr. Pinchot's confession that it is 'one of the great wonders of the world.' Its altogether
reputable official sponsors are Secretary Lane, who ten years ago as
attorney of San Francisco became an advocate of the project, and
Secretaries Houston and Garrison, who half-heartedly join in
approval, besides three bureau heads who have the temerity to agree
with their chiefs. In Congress the bill finds strong support in the two
Public Lands Committees, composed as they are preponderatingly
of trans-Mississippians, who have a natural and proper bias in favor
of the local use of the forest reserves, and who apply this theory illog-
ically to the national parks.

"The act creating Yosemite National Park sets forth the importance and duty of reserving these wonders 'in their original state,'
and the world has a moral right to demand that this purpose shall be
adhered to. The 'beautiful lake' theory deceives nobody. An artificial
lake and dam are not a substitute for the unique beauty of the valley.
Senators cannot transfer to a committee the grave responsibility that
rests upon them."

Intervention in early October by California senator John Works
postponed the proceedings due to concerns raised by the irrigation
districts, as the *Times* noted on October 9 in an editorial titled "The
Steam Roller Halted": "The Hetch Hetchy steam roller did not work
smoothly on Saturday and therefore on Tuesday it was withdrawn
for repairs. In other words, the Senate voted to postpone to the regular session in December the bill to give over a large part of the
Yosemite National Park to the tender mercies of the San Francisco
Philistines who know how to 'improve' the handiwork of the
Creator. The $45,000,000 electric power franchise must wait, despite
the appeals of the two Senators from Nevada. Senators Borah,
Gronna and Poindexter, all Westerners by the way, were not satis-

fied, but exhibited a Missourian desire 'to be shown' and an unwillingness to be swept off their feet. They asked embarrassing questions, and showed a creditable sense of Senatorial responsibility for a
piece of legislation of which Mr. Mondell in the House debate said
that its conflicting provisions made his head fairly whirl.

"The determining factor in the postponement was this telegram
from Senator Works of California, who apparently went home to get
in touch with his constituents:

Coronado, Cal. Oct. 2, 1913

Hon. Reed Smoot: I have sent the following telegram to
Senator Myers. I have satisfied myself that the Hetch Hetchy
bill should not pass without further investigation. Ninety-nine
per cent of water users in the irrigation districts are strongly
opposed to it, and claim that they were betrayed by those who
consented to the compromise measure. They claim that thousands of acres of land in their districts and outside of them will
be deprived of water to which they are entitled, and that they
can show that this sacrifice of the best and most fertile lands in
the State is not necessary to the interest of San Francisco.
Because of this compromise, that they indignantly repudiate,
this phase of the question has not been investigated. The bill
should not be rushed through this session under such circumstances. It is too serious not only to the parties directly interested but to the whole State.

John D. Works

"The plain fact is that mid-Western, Southern and Eastern
Senators have been culpably inclined to leave to the determination of
some of their Far Western colleagues a measure involving millions
upon millions of dollars, grave constitutional questions, revolution-
ary policies concerning franchises and conservation, and the higher
interests of a people proud of our noble scenery. They cannot too
promptly set themselves at work to study the question in its broadest
and highest aspects: the immense value of great natural wonders, the
folly of giving away valuable national resources."

The Senate resumed floor debate on December 1. On it went. All the arguments stated, restated, and restated again. The *Times* noted on December 4: "Does President Wilson know that the enterprising lobbyists for the seizing of the Hetch Hetchy valley in the interest of the power companies of San Francisco call their bill an 'Administration measure'? The leading newspapers from Maine to California have expressed the strong public sentiment that exists against the spoliation of this national park. Will President Wilson let his name be used as favoring a local and very selfish interest against the best opinion of the country?

"The lobby has had its effect with the Interior Department. Bureaucratic influences are at work in Washington to make it appear that the Administration stands back of the selfish measure. President Wilson can put a stop to this business by a word seasonably spoken."

The decision was made to finally hold the vote on Friday, December 6. As the chamber filled in the morning for the last day of proceedings, senators found a "Special Washington Edition" of the San Francisco *Examiner* on their desks. "The Real Facts about Hetch Hetchy," the headline read, beneath an artist's striking depiction of the dam and reservoir, complete with cars driving on a scenic road ringing the steep-walled canyon. Hotels arose from the sheer cliffs like temples at Llasa. "Does This Beautiful Lake Ruin This Beautiful Valley?" asked the caption.

Just before midnight, at 11:57 p.m., the Senate also approved the bill: forty-three in favor, twenty-five opposed, twenty-nine abstaining. Only nine Republicans favored the bill. There was strong support among southern Democrats for the administration's position, and the California contingent carried the day.

By inference, the value of Hetch Hetchy's extraordinary scenery had been determined to be some amount less than $20 million combined with the opportunity to generate hydroelectricity. When Congress finally agreed to sacrifice this natural wonder, it did so on the condition that the citizens of San Francisco would enjoy the benefits of water and power owned, distributed, and sold by a public utility, not by a private company. Were the public benefits and cost savings to San Francisco worth the national sacrifice? O'Shaughnessy, Rolph, and Phelan watched from the gallery. Afterward they adjourned with a senator to the bar at the Willard Hotel to celebrate. Being after midnight, now on a Saturday morning, meant all they could get was water. Nonetheless they toasted their long-fought success with the liquid at the center of the commotion. Hetch Hetchy would be dammed; only President Wilson could stop it now.

The *Times* responded on December 9, 1913, in "One National Park Lost": "Any city that would surrender a city park for commercial purposes would be set down as going backward. So far as we are aware, such a case is unknown. Any State Legislature that would surrender a State park would set a dangerous and deplorable example. When the Congress of the United States approves the municipal sandbagging of a national park in order to give some clamorous city a few dollars, against the protests of the press and the people, it is time for real conservationists to ask, What next?

"The Senate passed the Hetch Hetchy bill by a vote of 42 to 25. The bill converts a beautiful national park into a water tank for the City of San Francisco. The San Francisco advocates of the spoliation handsomely maintained at Washington, month after month, quite openly, a very competent and plausible lobbyist, and save for a few hearings and protests he occupied the Washington field most comfortably alone and unopposed. For this first invasion of the cherished national parks the people of the country at large are themselves to blame. The battle was lost by supine indifference, weakness, and lack of funds. All conservation causes in this country are wretchedly supported financially, and this one seems not to have been supported at all.

"Ever since the business of nation-making began, it has been the unwritten law of conquest that people who are too lazy, too indolent, or too parsimonious to defend their heritages will lose them to the hosts that know how to fight and to finance campaigns. The American people have been whipped in the Hetch Hetchy fight. They had the press and enlightened public opinion and all men of public spirit on their side. The lobbyist was too much for them, although at the end the bill was rapidly losing support. If the people had set up a lobby they might have won."

Last-ditch appeals to President Wilson fell on deaf ears. On approving the Raker Act the president reported to Congress, "I have signed this bill because it seemed to serve the pressing public needs of the region concerned better than they could be served in any other way, and yet did not impair the usefulness or materially detract from the beauty of the public domain." He continued,

> The bill was opposed by so many public-spirited men, thoughtful of the interests of the people and of fine conscience in every matter of public concern, that I have naturally sought to scrutinize it very closely. I take the liberty of thinking that their fears and objections were not well founded. I believe the bill to be, on the whole, in the public interest, and I am the less uncertain in that judgment because I find it concurred in by men whose best energies have been devoted to conservation and the safeguarding of the people's interests, and many of whom have, besides, had a long experience in the public service which has made them circumspect in forming an opinion upon such matters.

Days after the devastating decision Muir wrote a friend, "As to the loss of the Sierra Park Valley it's hard to bear. The destruction of the charming groves and gardens, the finest in all California, goes to my heart. But in spite of Satan & Co. some sort of compensation must surely come out of this dark damn- dam-damnation." On Christmas Eve one year later, John Muir died.

Ironically, in the 1920s Pinchot began to question some of the tenets he instilled in the forest service. He challenged the agency's allegiance to the timber industry and emphasis on production at the expense of other, less quantifiable benefits like recreation, aesthetics, and spiritual refreshment. Forests, Pinchot came to believe, were not simply abstract commodities or a crop. Instead, they were "a living society of living beings, with many of the qualities of societies of men." Yet he held on to the belief that forests are resources that should yield multiple benefits for all people, resources that could advance human well-being and social equity. His views of resource development remained essentially the same ones that Muir had con-tested in the Hetch Hetchy debate. Pinchot concluded *Breaking New Ground* stating, "The earth, I repeat, belongs of right to all its people, and not to a minority, insignificant in numbers but tremendous in wealth and power. The public good must come first. The rightful use and purpose of our natural resources is to make all the people strong and well, able and wise, well-taught, well-fed, well-clothed, well-housed, full of knowledge and initiative, with equal opportunity for all and special privilege for none."

Hetch Hetchy water finally flowed into the Pulgas Water Temple at 10:12 a.m. on October 24, 1934, nearly twenty-one years after passage of the Raker Act. The project had been shaped from the outset as much by those with big money and political power as those with noble civic intentions. The Roman Renaissance revival pavilion was built at the terminus of the 167-mile-long aqueduct to commemorate the water's arrival at the southeast side of Crystal Springs Reservoir, where the Hetch Hetchy pipeline linked into the former Spring Valley water system on the peninsula, 30 miles from San Francisco. Filoli, the palatial estate of William Bourn II, stood about a mile away, set in the midst of his 654-acre property abutting Spring Valley land around its principal reservoir. Bourn had acquired a controlling interest in the water monopoly in 1908. At one time Spring Valley owned some 100,000 acres on the peninsula and across the bay. But Bourn's company had been absorbed in 1930 by the City of San Francisco's new municipal water system. Filoli was all he retained. (The estate is now open to the public, the regal mansion and extraordinary gardens operated by the National Trust for Historic Preservation and the Filoli Center.)

Like Billy Ralston's fortune, Bourn's fortune came from the imperialism of mining in the Sierra Nevada Mountains. Bourn owned the hard-rock Empire Mine, a gold mine in Grass Valley, California. He bought the mine with riches inherited from his father, who was president of Fireman's Fund Insurance Company. The father's fortune derived from the Imperial Silver Mining Company of Gold Hill, Nevada. He poured those Comstock Lode profits into other banking, real estate, and diverse business interests. And like Billy Ralston, William Bourn II appreciated the profitability and power inherent in the ownership of San Francisco's utilities. In the early 1900s he became president of San Francisco Gas and Electric Company and merged it with several major rivals, then sold out, in a complicated set of transactions, to the owners of California Gas and Electric in late 1905, resulting in the formation of the Pacific Gas and Electric Company. Three years later he expanded his holdings in the Spring Valley water monopoly to acquire a majority interest.

What were Bourn's feelings as he watched the city celebrate the arrival of Hetch Hetchy water—municipal-controlled water—outside the gate of his Eden-like estate? He would die two years later.

James Duval Phelan didn't live to see his dream of a municipal water supply fully realized. He died in 1930. Throughout the controversy he triggered, Phelan remained active in political and civic affairs, serving one term (1915–21) in the U.S. Senate as a Progressive Democrat from California. While serving in the Senate, Phelan settled into his magnificent new home, called Villa Montalvo, in the foothills west of San Jose. "I will build a villa and bask in the eternal sunshine," he wrote his sister; he said he wanted to enjoy the Mediterranean climate and lifestyle he so admired. Broad verandas surrounded the sprawling home set on 175 acres overlooking the fields of fruit trees of the Santa Clara Valley. The house and the elaborate gardens and grounds blended Spanish and Italian Renaissance motifs, creating a casual, sophisticated setting he filled with art. From there until his death he continued to promote his dream for the imperial city by the bay, lavishly entertaining the elite of politics, business, and culture, and championing the causes dearest to his heart. Today Villa Montalvo remains a cultural center, donated to the people of California and endowed by James Duval Phelan in his will, just as the dam at Hetch Hetchy stands as a testament to his municipal dream.

Nor did Michael M. O'Shaughnessy live to see his work completed. The enormously powerful city engineer who championed the complex project from 1912 until 1932, and after whom the O'Shaughnessy Dam across the mouth of the Hetch Hetchy Valley was named, had died just twelve days before the official celebration on October 28. The festivities had been postponed for several weeks due to scheduling problems with another dignitary. Also absent was John Ripley Freeman, the engineer whose 1912 design for the system so closely reflected Phelan's dream and so shaped the final constructed version. He had died two years earlier, in 1932.

The cost of the system dwarfed Grunsky's $39.5 million estimate in 1902 and the $45 million Manson budget prepared in 1910 in response to the Garfield permit. This comes as no surprise, since those estimates were based on a system of 60 million gallons a day with far fewer tunnels. But the Freeman plan was never as cheap or as easy as the proponents made it out to be. The $45 million bond voters approved in response to the Garfield permit and the Manson plan was woefully inadequate for the system Freeman envisioned: beyond the $400,000 spent in 1910 on land and water rights in the Lake Eleanor basin, the $600,000 spent on land and water rights in the Cherry Creek basin, and the $45 million for the first construction bond, an additional $10 million construction bond was approved in 1924 for the Foothill and Coast Range Tunnels; a $24 million construction bond for the Coast Range Tunnel and the San Joaquin pipelines was approved in 1928; $40 million was spent to buy the Spring Valley Water Company in 1930; a $6.5 million construction bond to finish the aqueduct was approved in 1932; a $3.5 million construction bond issue was approved in 1933 to enlarge O'Shaughnessy Dam; and another $12.1 million bond was approved to construct the second pipeline crossing the bay and make other improvements. Time after time the city returned to the voters for additional funding. They did so by choice, thinking incremental funding would be less politically offensive and more responsive to actual needs, as well as by circumstance as design changes and local politics affected progress. The public chastised O'Shaughnessy, calling him "More Money" O'Shaughnessy. The total cost of the system as of the celebration: $142.1 million (roughly $2 billion in 2003 dollars), including the cost to purchase Spring Valley.

And that was just the beginning. A $25 million bond issue was approved in 1947 for further pipeline construction; a $4 million bond issue was approved in 1949 for Cherry Creek Dam (plus $9 million in federal aid); a $54 million bond issue was approved in 1955 for power system construction; a $115 million bond issue was approved in 1961 for general water system needs; and $104 million in revenue bonds was approved in 1984 for water treatment facilities. The list of expenditures continues to the latest $3.6 billion in bonds approved in 2002—and this isn't even a full accounting of the system's costs.

Certainly many of these costs fell outside the requirements of the plans envisioned by Phelan, Grunsky, and Manson. The completed system supplied much more water and power than had been originally proposed. Yet much of the additional cost should have been anticipated, because it stemmed from the problems posed by the terrain between the water source and the consumer. Those costs were

likely one reason no engineer studying alternate water sources for
the city had selected Hetch Hetchy until after the threesome focused
on it. Neither does this accounting compare these costs to the hundreds of millions of dollars in revenues that the Hetch Hetchy water
and power systems have contributed to municipal coffers over the
years. Nor does it calculate the project's costs and revenues relative
to alternative systems that might have been built instead. Some of
these figures may be impossible to measure accurately.

Yet Hetch Hetchy can be compared to two water systems developed concurrently in California. Los Angeles completed its Owens
Valley water system below the original estimate of $24.5 million and
did so within five years, even though its aqueduct was nearly one
hundred miles longer than the Hetch Hetchy aqueduct. However,
the route of the Los Angeles aqueduct avoided the complications
posed by the mountain ranges that the Hetch Hetchy system had to
cross. A twenty-five-mile-long segment of Hetch Hetchy's Coast
Range Tunnel was the longest in the world when completed. The
Hetch Hetchy Valley may have made an ideal dam and reservoir site
from an engineering and water supply viewpoint, but the valley's
remoteness and the topography between it and the Bay Area also
made construction of the aqueduct an immense engineering challenge.

The other comparable system lies just across the bay from San
Francisco. Fearful of being administratively swallowed by San
Francisco if they were to join in the Hetch Hetchy project, and frustrated with the snail's pace of the proposal's progress, several East
Bay communities banded together to pursue their own water supply.
Engineers had always known that an aqueduct from the Mokelumne
River could bypass the mountains. The East Bay consortium looked
to the north, and in 1929 they completed their own water supply
aqueduct. The project took just six years from site selection to delivery of water, tapping Sierra water from the Mokelumne River as had
been proposed repeatedly to San Francisco. And it was good that the
East Bay system came online so quickly—in 1931, San Francisco ran
short of water, and was forced to obtain it from the East Bay system
three years before Hetch Hetchy water finally arrived at the Pulgas
Temple.

Standing in Hetch Hetchy's circular temple in October 1934,

Mayor Angelo Rossi toasted Secretary of the Interior Harold Ickes with a glass of crystal-clear Sierra snowmelt water. The *San Francisco Chronicle* reported the new temple was "a little bit of Rome out there in the California meadow, a sort of reminder that aqueducts made Roman civilization." Aqueducts made San Francisco, too, an imperial city predicated on the imperialistic extraction of mineral wealth and water from the Sierra.

CHAPTER 10

Competing Claims for Water

T he Nevada desert, then the Sierra Nevada Mountains, and then the San Joaquin Valley, pass by on my approach to the Bay Area. Reservoirs and the effects of life-giving irrigation dot the otherwise dry landscape. As I fly across the country, it's hard to comprehend the strange landscapes below. I know buttes, box canyons, mesas, and dry riverbeds only secondhand or from occasional glimpses. They don't seem real.

For most people in the East, water remains a nonissue, or at least that was true until recently. In the East, we have few constraints imposed by the environment. Life revolves around other factors. In the West, life ultimately revolves around access to and control of water. There, people have always dealt with limits imposed by environmental conditions. Technology only hides that truth.

My plane descends in a gentle right-hand turn to the north, passing by San Jose and the southern end of the bay. It's been several years since I last visited San Francisco. Suburbia sprawls down the bay side of the peninsula, now forming an unbroken mess of development from San Francisco fifty miles south past Millbrae, San Mateo, Menlo Park, and Mountain View to San Jose—paradise lost, I think. The megalopolis surrounds the bay like a bathtub ring, although the peninsula remains rural west of Interstate 280, which runs down its spine. Our final approach passes over Silicon Valley, a cause and effect of it all. Water was key to the valley's development—water obtained in part from Hetch Hetchy.

"Generally speaking," Margaret Bruce, who directs environmental programs for the Silicon Valley Manufacturing Group, the valley's principal trade organization, told me, "high-tech manufacturing (which can now be said to include bio-tech and pharmaceuticals) relies upon water, sometimes large quantities of water. Very high quality is good, but predictable and consistent is better. Whatever the process is, systems are set up to pretreat or 'condition' incoming water to meet production standards for conductivity, for purity, for temperature, etc. The systems that perform this conditioning are set to handle the incoming water, whatever that is. When that changes, the whole system must be changed. For some facilities, this means retooling a capital/facility investment to the tune of several hundred thousand to several million dollars. The reason high-quality incoming water is such a plus is that requirements to condition water are minimal. The harder the water, or the more impurities in it, the more elaborate the pretreatment system needs to be. Of course, the costs of basic resources are a factor in business decisions. The cost of operations is always part of the bottom line."

She said the availability of high-quality, inexpensive, reliable water was an important serendipitous bonus to other factors that facilitated the valley's phenomenal growth, including close proximity to Stanford University, NASA/Moffett Field, Lawrence Livermore/ Lawrence Berkeley laboratories, Stanford Research Institute, and the synergy resulting from being near other "hot" technology companies emerging here. Add to that an attractive housing market at that time, an idyllic climate, close proximity to cultural and recreational resources, and abundant finance capital in the Bay Area, and the boom was born, the second in the Bay Area's young municipal life.

The jet sweeps lower, flying barely above rooftops. Some of the homes below have backyard pools. The water gleams against the irrigated emerald green landscaping. Housing developments with cul-de-sacs and loop roads cover the bay side of Santa Clara County like a floral-patterned carpet. Silicon Valley brought jobs here, which brought people and suburban sprawl, each of which was contingent on the ready availability of water in a semiarid world.

When Stanford college pals Bill Hewlett and Dave Packard partnered to form a fledgling engineering company before World War II in the wood-framed garage behind the modest house at 367 Addison Avenue in Palo Alto, vineyards, fruit orchards, and cropland covered the countryside surrounding the small town. The region remained agricultural, and food processing dominated the economy. San Jose, the largest city and county seat, had fewer than 100,000 residents. By the time baby boomers Steve Jobs and Steve Wozniak formed another garage partnership a generation later, in a new, nearby suburban tract development, San Jose's population had surged to

450,000 and South Bay cities were growing significantly in area by annexation. But uncontrolled growth in the "valley of heart's delight," as it was known during the early economic boom, was rapidly despoiling the quality of life in paradise: traffic congestion, overwhelmed municipal services, inadequate schools, and insufficient parks all abounded.

"In response," Stan Ketchum told me, "the city and county enacted an urban growth boundary in the 1970s within which municipal services would be provided; beyond the line, no services." Ketchum is a principal planner with the city and oversees the master plan process. "The boundary effectively contained growth, enabling the city to grow up, not out, causing construction of more multifamily housing and less single-family housing. Our density has been rising ever since, especially along designated transit corridors. 'Smart growth,' we call it." Today the city population nears 900,000, with 1.5 million in the county. "Water supply has never been an issue during this spectacular growth, even though this is a semiarid place," Ketchum said. "Water hasn't been a constraint in past master planning and doesn't look to be a factor in the foreseeable future."

While development within municipal boundaries exploded around Silicon Valley and the South Bay, outside municipal boundaries the explosion was tightly controlled, according to Ann Draper, the planning director for the county. "In Santa Clara County," she explained, "we have protected the agricultural areas outside the growth boundaries by restricting new development to rural types of uses and very large acreage minimums, such as a 160-acre minimum lot size. Today, all of the cities combined only occupy about 24 percent of the county land area. Development in the nonincorporated areas of the county remains very rural in character, and it relies on well water, not piped water, as no urban infrastructure is allowed. The only exception to this is in pockets of county land that are surrounded by a city; piped water is allowed there." Like many public officials, Draper believes California will experience a huge influx of people in the future. And, like Ketchum, she thinks that building up, not out, is a good thing; with proper planning, the amount of water used per capita in her county has significantly decreased over the past years.

The Santa Clara Valley Water District provides the water in the

South Bay to water purveyors, who in turn sell it to individuals. "In a normal year less than half of Santa Clara County's water is drawn from local groundwater aquifers or rainwater captured in the district's reservoirs," the water district states. "More than half originates hundreds of miles away, first as snow in the Sierra Nevada range of northern and eastern California, then as river water that empties into the Sacramento–San Joaquin River Delta. This imported water is brought into the county through the State Water Project, the federal Central Valley Project, and to a small degree, San Francisco's Hetch Hetchy system."

"Don't assume from your eastern perspective that everyone out here hates Hetch Hetchy," Draper told me. "Not so. In California we ship water all over the place, mostly from the north to the south, namely to the Los Angeles area. The debate about shipping water around the state usually occurs at the regional or statewide level, not at a city level. The only major concern around the Bay Area with Hetch Hetchy water is the lack of system maintenance by San Francisco water works and their management relationship with the suburbs. Whenever a city or the county has turned to the water purveyor and asked if water was available to service a new development, the answer has always been yes, so we move on to other considerations."

With the degree to which California has been replumbed, it's impossible to anticipate all the implications. One unexpected result in San Jose has been a problem for South Bay ecology. So much water was imported to satisfy growth, and then discharged after use and treatment into the bay, that the salinity in the bay was lowered sufficiently to affect the saltwater ecosystem. To reduce the discharge of freshwater into the bay, a multimillion-dollar recycling system now pumps treated wastewater throughout the city for irrigation on suitable municipal lands such as parks, golf courses, and landscaped areas.

Water management is now carefully planned, regionwide. Draper described how the Santa Clara Valley Water District recently updated its Integrated Water Resources Plan, which included plans for providing water to the county until 2030, the use of recycled water, and the introduction of conservation methods to reduce the need for nonrecycled water. "Our land use patterns also help to provide a systemwide means to reduce per capita demand for water," she noted. "The San Jose water treatment plant provides a source for recycled water. The cities, the county, and the water district all use adaptive management to monitor our local water resources and to be sensitive stewards of our watershed. We are all part of a Water Resources Collaborative and a Water Management Initiative. We are doing this," Draper concluded, "because it is the right thing to do."

The runway at the San Francisco International Airport extends into the bay, giving me an uncomfortable, sinking feeling as we descend ominously closer and closer to the water. At the last moment before splashdown, land finally appears beneath our wheels—land that was created by filling in the bay.

By force of habit, I always get a drink from a water fountain when I get off a plane. The habit has given me pause in some cities where the source of the municipal water supply might be suspect. Old industrial cities in an eastern megalopolis strike the most fear. Here I pause for the opposite reason. This is mostly pristine Hetch Hetchy water delivered unfiltered to the fountain directly from the distant source, mixed with a bit of water obtained from other sources downstream from the mountain reservoir, and subject to chlorine or chloromine treatment for bacteria. Snack bars along the concourse sell expensive bottled water, in part catering to such fears. Labels proudly proclaim the liquid to be crystal clear, purified, or from a mountain spring: safe, healthful, and chic. What I slurp from the fountain was snowmelt or rainfall in a High Sierra wilderness not long ago. Where did the bottled water originate? People queue up behind me at the fountain, taking for granted the free resource, most of them unaware of the water's source or quality. Since the construction of Hetch Hetchy, water has always been available for development, or for drinking, making it easy for the Bay Area to ignore the resource even in a dry world dependent on imported water.

Mayor Willie L. Brown Jr. noted the irony while dining at an exclusive San Francisco restaurant several years ago. Watching people pay several dollars for imported bottled water, he thought they might do the same for city water, which comes from the pristine glacial streams of the Tuolumne River. "Even when it comes from the tap," the mayor said, "[Hetch Hetchy water] is better than all those other waters." Why not bottle and sell it at city outlets like the airport, the zoo, the port, and the city hall? "Hetch Hetchy has a cachet," he said, "everyone will pay for this water. It is worth drinking." His dream came true recently when he paid $1.25 for the first half-liter plastic bottle of Hetch Hetchy Mountain Water.

The pilot program hopes to sell 31,000 bottles of Sierra water. It is drawn directly from Hetch Hetchy Reservoir, then micron filtered and treated with ozone to meet state and federal regulations. The small revenue will help finance the maintenance of the municipal water system. The bottle's pretty label depicts the shimmering blue lake lapping against the 2,500-foot-high granite walls that form the Hetch Hetchy Canyon, with a spectacular waterfall cascading into the reservoir, as if directly filling your bottle with the crystal-clear liquid. The goal of the program is to promote the city and "the idea that San Francisco has the best and purest water in the country, if not the world," according to one member of the city's public utilities commission (SFPUC). However, another commissioner believes the water "tastes very different up at Hetch Hetchy—it's much sweeter" than the slightly mixed municipal water. That might be true, but I can't tell the difference in taste between the water from the fountain and the bottled versions, whether from Hetch Hetchy or other sources. I'll keep the $1.25 for other uses.

Reaction to the project has been mixed. "It is pretty odd to think about the Tuolumne River water being bottled and sold, because it is Yosemite's water," commented Deb Schweizer, a ranger at Yosemite National Park. "It brings back the history of the fight over whether Hetch Hetchy should have been dammed at all." Ron Good, executive director of Restore Hetch Hetchy, believes the revenues should be used to finance a study of alternative ways to remove the dam and restore the valley. "This is another example of San Francisco exploiting the natural resources of Yosemite National Park," he thinks. The *Sacramento Bee* agrees, editorializing, "Why not use the proceeds from it to pay for this study? That would make this water venture something that everybody in California could swallow." The *Los Angeles Times* wrote, "Shame [on] San Francisco, that self-proclaimed wellspring of environmental passion . . . Hetch Hetchy may be as fresh and tasty as bottled water goes, but any good environmentalist with a sense of history would rather drink irrigation runoff. . . . Someday, perhaps San Francisco will recognize that its pride in Hetch Hetchy is misplaced and that dismantling the dam is something that is really worth San Francisco's image of itself." Even the *New York Times* ran a feature article on the project.

Tear down the dam and restore the valley: a radical, impractical pipe dream? Perhaps not. Ron Good leads a grassroots, nonprofit campaign to remove the dam by 2013—the one hundredth anniversary of the Raker Act—and begin the long-term process of restoring the valley. As a first step, he lobbied (unsuccessfully) in the 2002 election for $600,000 from the city's $1.6 billion bond issue to repair and upgrade the Hetch Hetchy system be set aside to fund a feasibility study of the "win-win" options for removing the dam and restoring the Hetch Hetchy Valley. The mayor and board of supervisors couldn't be convinced to adopt the plan.

Yet we currently pay to remedy other environmental mistakes. We routinely spend billions of dollars to reclaim abandoned mine lands and clean up Superfund sites. We conduct extensive programs to protect or replenish endangered populations of plants and animals, including the removal of small dams to restore fish habitat. We've even begun to "deplumb" watersheds in Florida, including the removal of canals and water projects that adversely affect places like the Everglades. In urban areas we now reclaim abandoned "brown field" sites for redevelopment and spend billions to bury an aging elevated freeway in downtown Boston. Why shouldn't we reclaim a wondrous place in a national park for the scenic enjoyment of millions of people worldwide?

On a Tuesday in early August 1987, Mike McCloskey, the chairman of the Sierra Club, got a call from a former law school classmate, Secretary of the Interior Donald Hodel. The call surprised McCloskey, one of the leaders of the environmental movement, as Reagan administration policies hadn't endeared the secretary to the movement. The latest contention arose from the president's plan to exploit resources in places dear to the environmentalists, such as coastal waters and the Arctic National Wildlife Refuge. "Hello, Mike, this is Don Hodel," a dumbfounded McCloskey heard. "Hello, Don," he responded. Pleasantries completed, the secretary then dropped a bombshell: he wanted to tear down the O'Shaughnessy Dam at Hetch Hetchy and restore the valley. He told his stunned adversary that he intended to initiate a study of the possibilities.

Speculation regarding the secretary's motives swirled about the Sierra Club and environmental circles. Public reaction was equally suspect. San Francisco mayor Dianne Feinstein felt the "beautiful" dam and the water it provided San Francisco were the city's "birthright." She called the secretary's idea of its removal "crazy," "the height of folly," "dumb, dumb, dumb," and "the worst idea since the sale of weapons to the Ayatollah." The *San Francisco Chronicle* editorialized, "The Secretary's vision is terribly flawed," and went on to state in a booster-like tone that Hetch Hetchy "is a whirring core that produces water, energy, and capital for millions."

In response, the Sierra Club's board of directors, meeting nearly ninety years after the Hetch Hetchy battle erupted, reaffirmed the club's commitment to continue its battle for Hetch Hetchy, recalling the words club secretary William Colby wrote to Gifford Pinchot in 1909: "Let me assure you that we have only begun the fight . . . [and] are going to keep up the good fight without fear or favor, 'if it shall take until doomsday.' " The club created a task force to pursue the cause.

Hodel persisted despite the public reaction, resulting in a preliminary concept study conducted by the Bureau of Reclamation for the National Park Service. The findings reported in 1988 considered alternatives to remove the dam, replace its water and power supplies, and restore the valley, and concluded several were promising. The report stated, "The restoration of Hetch Hetchy Valley to its natural environment would be a stunning acknowledgment of technological man's ability not only to recognize the usefulness of restoration, but also to accomplish such a feat. . . . Such restoration would renew the national commitment to maintaining the integrity of the national park system and keep in perpetual conservation an irreplaceable and unique natural area." But federal funding for further study was defeated in congressional committee, the Reagan administration left office in January 1989, and the issue fell from public attention. Despite the energetic rhetoric, Sierra Club interest also waned. Club efforts focused on other, more pressing environmental issues.

Ron Good and a few other club members resurrected the dream several years later, reinvigorating the task force in 1997. However, many members of the task force, together with colleagues in other environmental groups, soon decided their cause could be advanced more rapidly by an independent nonprofit group. In 1999 they founded Restore Hetch Hetchy, with the same goals as the original task force: in the short term, to obtain outside funding for an objective feasibility study of dam removal and valley restoration in the belief that a win-win outcome exists; in the long term, to remove the dam and restore the valley. Independence gave Restore Hetch Hetchy greater freedom of action than the task force had, since the task force was restricted by the club's organizational structure, operating procedures, and priorities.

Like Secretary Hodel's concept study, Restore Hetch Hetchy's in-house studies suggest that the dam can be removed, the water storage relocated to other existing reservoirs downstream, the hydropower replaced with alternate renewable energy sources, and the valley eventually reclaimed to its prior wild condition. And the studies estimate that the cost of this might not be significantly more than pending maintenance and expansion costs for the aging infrastructure. Obviously, the technical, legal, political, and economic implications of the feat would be immense; but so too might be the results.

Their cause is gaining ground. The *New York Times* recently editorialized, "In 1913, in defiance of established law and the wishes of millions of Americans, Congress foolishly approved the construction of a dam and an eight-mile-long reservoir in a lush valley known by its Indian name, Hetch Hetchy, in the northwest corner of Yosemite National Park. The dream of righting this wrong has never really died. . . . [T]he least we can do is endorse a feasibility study. It may well lead to something remarkable." The *Los Angeles Times* added, "Replacing the lost water and power would be complicated and costly, but it could be done. Would it be worth it? Consider the value of Yosemite Valley to the nation. Think of the possibility of having a second such valley, free of cars and development, that would be the temple of nature John Muir saw before the dam was built. That too would be priceless."

The battle has been joined, though not by the established environmental movement. "One would think the dam-busting environmental movement would be all over this idea," the *Sacramento Bee* stated in an editorial, to "leverage San Francisco to get a feasibility study of demolishing its dam that submerges Yosemite's second valley, Hetch Hetchy. Curiously, the groups hottest to arm-twist San Francisco are ones with zip codes outside the city." While some national groups supported the call by Restore Hetch Hetchy and other local groups for a city-funded feasibility study as a part of the recent bond issue, none has taken the lead and put the dam removal–valley restoration proposal atop its pecking order of projects. Organizations like the Sierra Club and the Wilderness Society prefer to fight other environmental battles they consider to be of greater potential success and benefit. Tear down the dam and restore the 1,900 acres now submerged, at what political and economic expense, for what ecological and psychological benefits? Aren't issues like air and water quality, suburban sprawl, deforestation, population control, global climate change, and species diversity of more pressing concern? Shouldn't we focus on protecting existing wilderness areas, national parks, forests, and wildlife refuges, and the addition of new areas? It's hard to fault the groups' practicality. Yet if they won't make a philosophical stand and fight, who will?

With one last free drink of Hetch Hetchy water from the municipal water fountain, I'm off to see the source of all this contention. I pick up a rental car—I get a free upgrade to a red Mustang convertible—and begin the drive to Yosemite. You hardly need a map to find your way once you're on Interstate 580 heading east from Hayward. The route is well marked, and on a Friday you can follow the pilgrimage heading to the park. Look for outdoor-themed bumper stickers, roof racks of camping equipment, and carriers filled with off-road bikes. Yosemite is tantamount to a private park, and is a personal playground for many people in the Bay Area. They dash off there by the thousands for weekend getaways and annual summer holidays. Couples have been married or honeymooned in the valley, and their children have grown up enjoying family adventures there. Person after person will share with you a favorite story about the place. Half of the park's 3.5 million annual visitors come from within California, and many of those come from the Bay Area. Few venture beyond the Yosemite Valley floor, never exploring the wilderness that makes up 93 percent of the park's 761,266 acres. From the beginning, "Yosemite" has been synonymous with the Yosemite Valley, leaving its sister, Hetch Hetchy, overlooked and easily abandoned.

A cool Pacific breeze follows me inland on Interstate 580, eastward from Hayward and up into the Coast Range. The landscape changes abruptly here: the dense, urban Bay Area abuts the vast expanse of the irrigated fields, orchards, and pastures of the San Joaquin Valley. Behind, parts of San Francisco lie shrouded in fog this morning, its rolling hills remaining cool all day, the climate tempered by the ocean. Ahead lies one of the world's most productive agricultural regions, stark, hot, and dry. The juxtaposition of the two distinctive worlds jars the senses.

Altamont Pass divides the two, its sensuously rounded landforms seemingly sculpted by the constant twenty-five-mile-per-hour summer wind. It's a haunting place, timeless in some way: windswept, desolate, with a coastal-like stillness despite the freeway traffic and breeze. One of the world's largest wind farms rises out of the treeless grassland. The giant slender blades of its 4,788 turbines turn in slow motion, silhouetted against the sky, generating 957 million kilowatt-hours a year. The ghostly apparitions feed the PG&E system with enough power for about 170,000 homes at a cost—five cents per kilowatt-hour—competitive with natural gas sources. Construction began on the complex in the 1970s, when federal energy policy encouraged the development of alternate and sustainable sources of power. California has led the nation ever since, with 60 percent of the nation's current wind-generation capacity. Just three sites, including Altamont Pass, generate 95 percent of the state capacity and 11 percent of the world output. Much more could be generated with new technology. And California ranks only seventeenth among the states in wind energy potential. The winds that sweep the Great Plains provide those states with sufficient potential to theoretically meet the electricity demands of the entire country.

Where and how do we generate power? It's an economic and political question with profound environmental implications, and in the Bay Area, it's inextricably linked with the corresponding question for water. Perhaps that's part of the problem. We ask the wrong set of questions. Were the debate framed differently, as the opponents of the Hetch Hetchy proposal tried to focus on the human and ecological implications in addition to the political and economic outcomes, our decisions might be much different. The San Joaquin Valley spreads before me as I descend Altamont Pass, another place shaped by the nature of these decisions. The valley constitutes the heart of California's four-hundred-mile-long Central Valley, which extends roughly from Bakersfield northward to Redding, one of the nation's most productive agricultural regions, thanks in large part to irrigation.

"Paradise Valley," the early settlers called the landscape here, bordered by the Stanislaus, Tuolumne, and San Joaquin Rivers. "Our road was now one of continued enjoyment," observed John Charles Frémont on March 24, 1844, as the thirty-one-year-old lieutenant in the U.S. Army Topographical Engineers, Kit Carson, "Broken Hand" Thomas Fitzpatrick, and the others in their group crossed the valley. "It was pleasant riding among this assemblage of green pastures with varied flowers and scattered groves," he continued, "and out of the warm green spring, to look at the rocky snowy peaks where lately we had suffered so much." Frémont was leader of an expedition exploring routes across the Sierra Nevada Mountains into California. Just weeks earlier, nearly starved, the expedition finally broke free from a month spent snowbound in the high country. Now the lushness of Paradise Valley, lying along the western flank of the range, enchanted their senses. "The lupine [is] a beautiful shrub in thickets, some of them being 12 feet in height," Frémont wrote. "Occasionally three or four were clustered forming grand bouquet about 90 feet in circumference and ten feet high. The whole summit was covered with spikes of flowers, the perfume of which is very sweet and grateful. A lover of natural beauty can imagine with what pleasures we rode among these flowering groves, which filled the air with a light and delicate fragrance." Frémont fell in love with the region and would return to the nearby Sierra foothills in 1847 as owner of the vast Las Mariposas estate.

Without irrigation, little grows in this parched place, despite some of the most fertile soil in the world. Twelve inches of annual precipitation suffices for the few row crops in the San Joaquin Valley. Summers are bone dry, often with no rain for several months. Droughts are common. A vast, open prairie of perennial bunchgrasses, wild rye, and other associated grasses covered the flat valley before pioneers colonized the region. A riparian forest lined the rivers; otherwise only scattered oaks and groves broke the plain.

While the young lieutenant from Savannah surveyed Paradise Valley, Daniel Webster prepared to reenter the U.S. Senate after serving as secretary of state for Presidents William Henry Harrison and John Tyler. Imposing in stature and demeanor, the black-haired, stern-faced Whig statesman from New England typified a prevailing American sentiment toward the "Great American Desert," as many people perceived the West during the first half of the 1800s, when he asked his colleagues, "What do we want of this vast worthless area, this region of savages and wild beasts, of deserts of shifting sands and whirlwinds of dust, cactus and prairie dogs?" How should the young nation respond to the recently acquired West? How should the distant land be stitched into the national fabric socially, politically, and economically? Should it be slave or free? How should western expansion and settlement interests be balanced with the development interests of the East? "To what use could we ever hope to put these deserts or these endless mountain ranges, impenetrable and covered to their bases with eternal snow?" Webster wondered. Like the brilliant and brooding orator, the nation struggled to find answers.

Horace Greeley found a use for the western wasteland: fill it with the huddled masses living in crowded eastern cities and the torrent of immigrants pouring daily into the urban portals. "Go West, young man, and grow up with the country," the influential founder and editor of the *New York Tribune* told them in his oft-quoted sentiment. Greeley urged the hopefuls to settle on the plains and prairies of the nation's hinterland, but to little avail. Few of the would-be yeoman farmers knew how to prosper in the alien world. Many would try; most would fail and return east. But his plan would become national policy, reflected in programs like the Homestead Act of 1862, and part of our western mythos, in which humble pioneers and intrepid homesteaders crossed the prairie sea in canvas-topped schooners to civilize the western wilderness.

"What use have we for such a country?" Webster asked. None, he answered himself. With so little water, the land initially had few uses beyond a bit of fur trapping and cattle ranching and as a repository for the urban poor, outcasts, and Indians. The California gold rush would change that, of course.

Yet the West did have water, just not in the right amounts at the right time in the right place. Spring floods routinely inundated ten-mile-wide swaths of the San Joaquin Valley as local rivers swelled with runoff and snowmelt water from the nearby Sierra Nevadas.

The floodwaters nourished the fleeting spring lushness that prompted Frémont's admiration—or, at least, they did before hydrotechnology, in the form of dams and irrigation, ameliorated the droughts and floods and asserted a semblance of human control over the vagaries of nature. Water, its presence or absence, its movement across the land, and its several forms, defines the West far more than it does the East.

Like the West, the Bay Area and the San Joaquin Valley have always been lands of contradiction, lands of fact and fiction, lands where illusion, wants, and wishes have tainted perception as often as it has been shaped by a firm grasp of reality. Where Frémont saw lushness, Webster saw wasteland, and Greeley saw political and social possibilities. No one was entirely wrong, and no one was entirely right. Few Americans really understood the western landscape free from the tints of their eastern bias. We still struggle with this.

Approximately 25,000 Yokut Indians once flourished in fifty tribes scattered throughout the San Joaquin Valley from Bakersfield to Stockton—a land of plenty, they must have thought. Trappers like Jedediah Smith marveled at the plentitude of beaver and salmon in the rivers. The Spanish colonizers, however, had little use for the native population or the dry land, beyond cattle ranching. By the early 1800s the Indians had been mostly evicted and a handful of ranchers ran huge spreads on vast land grants given by the Spanish overlords. An epidemic in the 1830s decimated the remnant Indian population. Awareness of the fabulous soil fertility slowly grew among the new occupants, although few of the aliens could see beyond the weather extremes to recognize the real potential of the place.

The chaos of the gold rush changed many things in California, but it did not change the common illusions of the land; nor did statehood. Certainly these brought a wave of people and a flourish of activity to the San Joaquin Valley. By the mid-1800s hordes scoured the land and riverbeds for quick riches—mostly prospectors infected with "yellow fever." A few found their dreams, but most failed, though they triggered change in land use. Some of the disillusioned joined perceptive ranchers and pioneer farmers who discovered the real gold: wheat to feed the surging Bay Area and valley populations.

Cycles of drought and floods had doomed cattle ranching, together with the advent of fencing laws and the arrival of the railroad, enabling pastures to be quickly converted. In 1860, 22,500 bushels of wheat were produced in Stanislaus County alone, the central portion of the valley; in 1870 the yield topped 4 million bushels. A local newspaper reported in 1868 that "That part of the county between the Stanislaus and Tuolumne Rivers, an area of 125 square miles known as 'Paradise,' is one unbroken field of grain." By 1878 the harvest in Stanislaus County topped 7 million bushels, most grown on sprawling farms in the central plain, some the legacies of the original Spanish land grants and others accumulated by purchase from the federal government through various land distribution programs. Small farms struggled to compete. Yet the underlying landscape contradictions and illusions remained, perhaps even intensified. Water remained the problem, becoming permanently entangled with politics.

Recurrent droughts and floods caused by the fickle weather frustrated farmers, especially those with small fields, who were less able to benefit from the substantial economies of scale and mechanization enjoyed by the giant wheat operations. And the reliance on a single crop made the valley economy more vulnerable to market swings and manipulation than it would be if a diversified crop were grown. It also depleted soil fertility more rapidly than would a varied crop rotation. In short, the wheat era was no more sustainable over the long term than the cattle ranching it replaced. Agricultural practices in the San Joaquin Valley were as imperialistic as the boom-bust cycle of mining along its rivers and in its adjacent foothills.

The genesis of irrigation districts in the valley arose in the 1870s from these pressures. The need for irrigation and the potential benefits gradually became apparent, but the method to achieve it remained unclear, especially since the practical and political circumstances varied throughout the valley. Initial attempts to form corporate and cooperative irrigation companies failed in many places. By the mid-1880s a proposal to enable the formation of public irrigation districts gained support as nagging disputes between cattle barons, miners, and farmers over the legal basis of water rights in the state were resolved. Enabling legislation drafted by newly elected assemblyman C. C. Wright, a young attorney from Modesto, paved the way with its passage in March 1887. On May 28 voters established the Turlock Irrigation District, followed days later with the approval of the Modesto Irrigation District. Today the districts irrigate about 210,000 acres on which almonds, grapes, walnuts, tomatoes, peaches, poultry, and beef and dairy cattle are grown or raised, making the prosperous region one of the global centers of agriculture, a triumph of technology and cooperation.

Hetch Hetchy threatened that cornucopia. When San Francisco's intention to dam the upper Tuolumne River and divert its water became known to farmers in the San Joaquin Valley, a new army of vocal opponents joined the fight to stop the project. Fears ran rampant among valley farmers dependent on irrigation water drawn downstream from the city's proposed impoundment that the diversion of normal flow would leave them dry at critical times during the growing season. Farmers felt their water claims took precedence, legally and morally. The *Stanislaus County News* captured the sentiment of many when it stated that a "beneficent and Divine plan" ordained that water from the High Sierra irrigate the dry plains through which it flowed. "God gave to San Francisco the Pacific Ocean; the rest of the world to the Standard Oil Company; but the waters of the Tuolumne River belong to Stanislaus County," someone said. After thirty years of fighting to establish the irrigation district, and the adoption of taxes to finance its development and operation, they weren't about to put all that at risk.

Local papers fueled the rising outrage. The front page of the *Stanislaus County News* called upon the people of Paradise Valley to "seize their swords and bucklers in preparation for a more desperate defense" of their rights. The *Modesto Evening News* ran the headline "Chronicle Thinks We Are Farmers," and reported that the San Francisco paper depicted the directors of the irrigation district as "honest and substantial farmers without much knowledge of the water needed by their district." Bay Area papers fired back. The *Chronicle* urged the city to take the Tuolumne River water with or without valley consent. Loggerheads. No room for discussion, compromise, or cooperation. Neither side would budge. The valley thought it had prevailed in early 1906 when the San Francisco Board of Supervisors voted to abandon the Hetch Hetchy plan after receiving the petition signed by 1,200 valley residents.

The victory was short lived; the earthquake and fire in April and further lobbying in Washington saw to that. The city had effectively pursued its cause in Washington since then secretary Hitchcock rejected its initial permit applications, swaying President Roosevelt to its position with the support of Gifford Pinchot, laying the groundwork for Secretary of the Interior Garfield's approval of the city's petition in 1908, with the approval of the irrigation districts. The districts had actively participated in the negotiations leading to the permit and were satisfied it protected their primary concerns for the rights and use of Tuolumne River water. But those concerns would resurface each time the city sought approval of Hetch Hetchy. After 1908 the districts watched events surrounding the city's pursuit of Hetch Hetchy with interest, not alarm. In August 1912, however, the Freeman report reawakened old fears and animosities.

When Freeman rejected the guarantees granted the districts by the Garfield permit, substantially increasing the amount of water the city planned to withdraw from the river and seeking future reservoir sites that had been reserved for the districts, opposition to the plan erupted in the districts. Crews of engineers were immediately sent into the field to gather data to counter claims made in the report. The showdown between the districts and the city occurred at Secretary Fisher's hearing in November, ending inconclusively, since revisions were required in the Freeman study and the army engineers' report was not yet complete. Over the winter both sides pressed the case in Washington.

Political pressure mounted for the city and irrigation districts to reach a mutually agreeable compromise when the army report was completed in February 1913, concluding "that there will be sufficient water if adequately stored and economically used to supply both the reasonable demand of the bay communities and the reasonable needs of the Turlock [and] Modesto Irrigation District[s] for the remainder of this century." Bolstered by the army report, the city made a last-ditch effort to gain approval from outgoing secretary Fisher and president Taft; they declined. A major cause of Fisher's hesitancy stemmed from his concern that the plan did not adequately protect the rights of the districts. The new secretary, Franklin Lane, although predisposed to approve the plan, shared his predecessor's belief that only Congress should authorize it. The Raker Act resulted. The Wilson administration pushed the project forward, and congressional hearings loomed ahead.

The irrigation districts joined the preservationists in the effort to fight the bill, but finding the politics in Washington strongly behind it, they quickly opened negotiations with its backers. When guarantees similar to those contained in the Garfield permit were restored, together with other compromises, district directors telegraphed Congress their endorsement of the bill in August 1913. The House of Representatives Committee on Public Lands soon reported the draft to the floor in the belief that the bill had the support of the Departments of the Interior and Agriculture, the army engineers, both of California's senators and eleven of its congressional representatives, the governor and the state legislature, the landowners in the irrigation districts, the Commonwealth Club of California, and even members of the Sierra Club board. The only dissenting voices, the report asserted, were a "small group of nature lovers."

But that "small group of nature lovers" wasn't so small after all, nor was the rank-and-file membership of the irrigation districts happy with the compromise. All hell broke loose. California senator John D. Works requested a delay in further debate on the bill, stating, "Ninety-nine per cent of water users in the irrigation districts are strongly opposed to [the bill], and claim that they were betrayed by those who consented to the compromise measure." Action on the bill was postponed until December, when hearings were held. In the meantime, the Bay Area and valley papers had at it again. The *Chronicle* and the *Modesto Morning Herald* traded initial swipes. Papers throughout the San Joaquin Valley chimed in. The Modesto Irrigation District repudiated its earlier endorsement of the Raker bill and funded a campaign to lobby against its passage. Other local groups joined the fight, including the county board of trade, the board of supervisors, and even the local chapters of the Federated Women's Club. The Turlock Irrigation District held firm, however; its board and its chief engineer were unwilling to change their minds, out of principle.

The resulting public uproar became deafening. As the local turmoil and the Senate hearing heated up, Senator Works repeated his claim that the people in the districts had repudiated the bill. San Francisco mayor Rolph wired an insider in the districts to check the allegation and was told in response that "public sentiment has greatly changed in the irrigation districts. . . . The people of these two districts are unquestionably against the bill or any bill permitting water to be taken out of the Valley." The Turlock board wrote Rolph that "the people are greatly agitated" and vehemently against the city's taking of any water from the San Joaquin Valley. Turlock finally released Congressman Church, who had been representing them in the debate and was a leading proponent of the bill, to act as he saw fit.

The next day he apparently recanted his support, asserting it had always been reluctant and only because he believed the districts had been in favor. Too late, the proponents pointed persuasively to the districts' earlier endorsement, diverting attention from the last-minute reversals. Most senators ignored the reversal as they cast their vote. Suspicions created by the squabble between the city and the irrigation districts over the issue would take years to overcome, although today the groups cooperate for their mutual benefit. The board of army engineers was apparently right: the Tuolumne River had sufficient flow for both the Bay Area and the irrigation districts, although the necessity of damming Hetch Hetchy to tap that flow remains unclear.

Unfortunately, the farmers and preservationists never effectively joined forces even though they both opposed the Hetch Hetchy plan, in part because the irrigation districts eyed the upper Tuolumne River for reservoir sites of their own. Had the groups combined, the outcome might have been different. Today that difficult lesson has been learned. The "environmental movement" isn't a centralized, unified set of organizations that work jointly on a single agenda. Rather, it consists mostly of disparate groups who from time to time share a common goal despite differing agendas; the "movement" is therefore a constantly changing consortium of groups with local, regional, national, or global concerns who sometimes coalesce around a specific issue of mutual interest.

Resolution of the Hetch Hetchy proposal meant different things to the different stakeholders. From the perspective of San Francisco and the federal government, Hetch Hetchy was an appropriate project, wholly consistent with the Progressive concept of conservation. Perhaps Hetch Hetchy wasn't the city's "birthright," as Mayor

Feinstein would later claim, but few San Franciscans thought they had been granted a special exemption or privilege for the project. The city had been granted a reasonable request, so the outcome was not so much a victory as it was the work of good government.

From the perspective of the irrigation districts the Raker Act meant they would be forced to share Tuolumne River water with the city, inextricably tethering their fates to the wants and wishes of San Francisco and the federal government.

And from the preservationist perspective, the outcome of the battle for Hetch Hetchy was a great defeat. The economic benefits derived from resource development were given preference over the scenic and recreational benefits of untouched wilderness. Yet at least, for the first time, the argument had been debated by the public, and they supported the preservation of this special place. Wilderness preservation had lost the political battle in Washington, but the stage was set for future victories.

CHAPTER 11

Mismanaging the Dream

The geyser erupted with frightening force, like Old Faithful, suddenly in the early hours one Sunday morning in 2002, shattering the stillness of the irrigated fields in Paradise Valley, about twenty miles west of Modesto. Usually all you hear standing in the treeless farmland is the wind, not the roar of water escaping under tremendous pressure. The jet shot 1,050 gallons per minute one hundred feet into the air, until Pipeline #3 was drained to enable the leak to be patched nine hours later. Hetch Hetchy Water and Power engineers chafe at depictions of the event as anything more serious than a leak. After all, the hole in the thirty-five-year-old, seventy-eight-inch-diameter high-pressure pipe was only two inches across and was easily repaired. And relatively little water was lost. At the time, over 150 million gallons per day was rushing through the pipeline. The small leak only reduced that flow by 1.5 million gallons a day, not even enough for the sensors to detect. Still, the spectacular column of water that gushed skyward as if by magic assaulted the senses, so discordant with the peaceful surroundings, mysteriously arising, tall, deafening, and wet from beneath a cow pasture in an otherwise flat, quiet, dry landscape.

Leaks like this in a primary pipeline occur once a year or less, but are more common in the aging distribution system in the city. A month earlier a major water main burst in San Francisco, flooding streets beneath a shallow lake. The stretch of the San Joaquin aqueduct that sprung the latest leak had been problematic for years. Farmers sometimes plow too deep and hit one of the three pipelines that comprise the aqueduct, not necessarily breaking the pipe but often weakening it; and fertilizers applied to the fields covering the pipes corrode their metal more rapidly than normal. In 2001 maintenance crews surveying the much older Pipeline #1, built in 1932, with a new corrosion-detecting device found a suspected leak or two, "weeping" around many rivets, and up to 100 weakened spots where leaks were possible. At the time of the latest leak, only Pipeline #3 was in service; #1 was in stand-by, and #2 was out of service.

The leak wasn't the only problem. To repair it, the water flow to the remote rupture first had to be adjusted by closing a diversion gate at the bottom of an intake shaft at the Red Mountain Bar West gate-house about thirty miles to the east, just downstream from the system's Moccasin Powerhouse. And Pipeline #1 had to be brought online in place of #3. The twelve-by-twelve-foot metal diversion gate regulates the flows to all the pipelines downstream. When the gate is raised in the "open" position, water from the afterbay reservoir below the powerhouse flows unimpeded through the shaft, on its way to the three San Joaquin pipelines, which carry on average 220 million gallons a day from Hetch Hetchy to the Bay Area. (Total daily water demand in the SFPUC service area averages 260 million gallons; the remaining 40 comes from sources around the bay.) When the gate is lowered in the "closed" position, it blocks the flow, diverting the water up the forty-foot-deep shaft until it gushes over a spill-way and races into the New Don Pedro Reservoir. A small engine housed in the control booth hovering over the shaft raises the flat metal gate up and down in tracks.

Even though the gate is repositioned up to fifteen times a year, it wouldn't budge when crews tried to raise it to restore the flow into #3 after the leak had been patched. Stuck half closed by a broken pin, the supply of Hetch Hetchy water to the system's 2.4 million Bay Area consumers was reduced to #1's capacity of 70 million gallons a day—a manageable short-term problem, because water demand was low during the late autumn three-day weekend, and the reduction in Hetch Hetchy water could be offset by an increase in the use of supplemental water from the peninsula and other sources around the bay, in combination with minor cutbacks in consumption. But the problem would quickly escalate in severity the longer it persisted.

Yet some of those supplemental sources of water were also offline. Two treatment plants needed to filter water from these sources happened to be partly shut down at the time for repairs, so the amount of available supplemental water was about half the normal amount.

When the initial efforts to open the gate proved futile, contract divers from San Francisco were sent down into the surging, swirling water flooding the shaft to survey the problem. They discovered the broken pin. A special underwater arc welder needed to be brought in from outside the region to fix it. Nearly four days after the geyser's eruption, a diver strapped to a chair and lowered by crane down into the dark water made the final repair. Beyond tasting a slightly different water flavor during the crisis, few consumers noticed the change in service.

The leak symbolized an underlying systemwide problem: for decades, system maintenance and funding had been lax. The problems were no secret. Elected city officials, San Francisco Public Utilities Commission administrators and engineers, and wholesale water customers around the Bay Area all knew of them, although the latter group was largely powerless to effect change—the SFPUC was governed by a board of commissioners comprised of San Francisco residents appointed by the mayor. Coincidentally, just weeks before the leak, the *San Francisco Chronicle* had published a series of critical articles on the management and maintenance of the Hetch Hetchy system, concluding, "Over the past twenty years, San Francisco officials raided the city's vaunted Hetch Hetchy Water and Power system of hundreds of millions of dollars, leaving the Bay Area's largest water supply vulnerable to earthquake, drought and decay. Despite increasingly serious warnings about the need for expansion and seismic upgrades, city officials postponed the costly work and used profits from Hetch Hetchy's hydropower electricity sales to bankroll city programs and salaries for everything from the Municipal Railway to health care for the needy."

A SFPUC managing engineer concurred with the paper's assessment, stating matter-of-factly that "the system has not been adequately maintained over the decades and is in need of repair, upgrading, and hardening for earthquakes. Like owning an old car," he explained, "things eventually start breaking. The car still functions, but you eventually have to replace the brakes and suspension, and rebuild the engine. Proper seismic precautions, including flexible joints, were never designed into the system, although they built a wonderful system for the time.

"Have we spent an appropriate percentage of the cost of the infrastructure, say 5 percent of $5 billion, or $250 million, on maintenance and upgrades?" he asked rhetorically. "No," he answered.

"The city has been spending less than that. Is it enough? Probably not," he thought. "There just weren't enough people in city government who were willing to come out and address the problem. When the city builds something, it builds it very well. But it doesn't budget for repairs. They don't budget based on lifecycle expenses.

"Why would a city official go before the public and either raise taxes or water rates to pay for maintenance," he questioned, "when every time someone turns on the tap, the water flows? It's not politically sexy to spend money on utility infrastructure. In comparison to the total replacement costs for the HHWP system [from O'Shaughnessy Dam to Tesla Portal, where the water lines link into the water department lines], less than 1 percent of that cost has been spent annually on maintenance when perhaps 5 percent or more should be spent based on the rate of depreciation for the infrastructure." According to a study of the SFPUC conducted by the state auditor in 2000, the SFPUC had completed fifty-four capital projects in the previous ten years, totaling $270 million, leading the audit to conclude, "Given the size, complexity, age, and declining condition of the commission's water delivery system, this project completion rate appears low."

A recently retired operations manager noted that repairing or replacing a segment of pipe like the one that sprung the leak in the San Joaquin Valley is not a major capital improvement. Funds for routine maintenance should come from the annual repair budget. Too often, they don't. A former SFPUC general manager knew that that part of the pipeline had been a problem for years, yet when he asked staff members why it wasn't being properly maintained, "I didn't get an answer," he said. "The money wasn't there." Revenues from water rates supplied insufficient funds for routine maintenance, and surplus revenues generated from the sale of hydropower had been transferred to the city's general fund for other municipal purposes. The former operations manager said that such maintenance projects were relatively low priorities as long as the water kept flowing. Monies weren't available to replace the pipe. "In general, sufficient staffing has not been put in place in the Hetch Hetchy system to support a comprehensive preventive maintenance program, partly because no one wanted to spend the money," he explained. Presumably, "spend the money" meant either raise water rates, or use the hydropower surplus to fund maintenance, or both. When a SFPUC general manager during the time of the transfers pushed for funds to be used for repairs before the funds were declared surplus and transferred, he felt "there was a tremendous amount of pressure put on the [SFPUC] by city hall, which wanted as much revenue out of Hetch Hetchy as possible."

It hasn't always been the case. A longtime SFPUC general manager noted that before Hetch Hetchy revenues began to be transferred to the city's general fund, "we never had anything like this. Every single stretch of that pipe was patrolled at least once a week or more often." Funds from internal sources—water or hydropower revenues—supplied sufficient monies for proper maintenance.

Why would this deterioration be permitted by those in public power? First, for money: big projects cost big bucks. And second, for politics: elected officials have a variety of problems to deal with, some of them immediate. Rarely are the reasons so sinister that they include financial and political gain in neglecting the problems.

San Francisco mayor Willie Brown's longtime press secretary explained the lack of political will to address these problems this way, "In the 1970s and 1980s, the city had strong leadership in the mayor's office with Mayors Joseph Alioto [1968–76], George Moscone [1976–78], and Dianne Feinstein [1978–88], who were able to pursue political agendas, despite the usual volatility between the mayor's office and the board of supervisors that has existed since incorporation of the city. During their terms, San Francisco grappled with some high-profile, fundamentally life-affecting issues and social traumas, including the political and social causes of the 1960s as the city changed from a conservative to a liberal slant. The women's liberation and gay liberation movements had a profound impact in the 1970s, as did the Moscone and Milk murders. The Jonestown tragedy a month later [which involved a number of Bay Area residents] also rocked the city. Mayor Feinstein had to come in and stabilize a city shaken and torn by those events and deal with major new issues. By the late 1980s land use emerged as a dominant political issue, and continues today as the defining political issue, rather than party affiliation [more than 70 percent of San Francisco voters are registered Democrats]. The body politic, the press, and the public at large have been distracted by those hot-button issues over the years. Mayors Art Agnos [1988–92] and Frank Jordan [1992–96] were less formidable and struggled to move their programs forward while they encountered worsening financial problems.

"When Mayor Brown took office following Mayor Jordan, many city service and infrastructure issues had been long neglected, including Hetch Hetchy. San Franciscans weren't clamoring about it because the sweet-tasting water always flowed when you turned on the tap. Rather, they screamed about public transit, parks, streets, and sidewalks, because those were the problems they were experiencing. The political will to push politicians to do something about Hetch Hetchy didn't exist until recently, even with knowledge of earthquakes.

"Yet San Franciscans live with the threat of an earthquake all the time, so the threat forms a cultural backdrop of sorts rather than being right at the forefront of our minds. So, it takes an event like the 1989 Loma Prieta quake to wake people up to the vulnerability. The Hetch Hetchy debate picked up in the aftermath, but an even stronger question was what to do about the Bay Bridge, and it was the more high-profile, more visible issue and thus received the higher priority.

"It takes a mayor and a board of supervisors on the same page to push through big-ticket infrastructure and capital improvement projects. It also requires a reasonably good economy so they're not just responding to immediate budgetary crises. And because these kinds of projects require voter approval, it takes politicians who are willing to risk their political capital in support of these issues. In San Francisco, most elected officials prefer to spend that capital on immediately popular issues, like social programs. They get more bang for the buck with them, especially in the short term."

A SFPUC commissioner during the Feinstein administration concurred with this assessment: "There is nothing wrong in my view with using the [Hetch] Hetchy power resource to generate money for the general fund, which pays for cops, parks and recreation, and everything that people hold dear." Former mayor Jordan explained, "I walked into office with a $300 million deficit and was having to consolidate services. The public was clamoring for health care for AIDS, social services for the homeless, Muni [mass transit], affordable housing, [and] the libraries." He toured the Hetch Hetchy system and saw the needs, "but it wasn't something I could take on as an immediate priority given what I was dealing with." These are indeed tough choices, yet the public entrusts city government with the responsibility for protecting health, safety, and welfare—all at the same time. Should short-term political expediency jeopardize the public's long-term security?

This political hesitancy to address infrastructure needs, common in many municipalities, led in the Bay Area to three interrelated problems: the lack of proper maintenance on the system due to a shortage of funds resulting from a general unwillingness to raise water rates to pay for repairs and improvements and from the transfer of "surplus revenues" from the utility to the city's municipal fund; the lack of proper long-term planning and a capital improvement program for major projects, especially related to earthquake vulnerability; and an antiquated organizational structure for governance of the utility.

While voters demand sound infrastructure, they often reject the requisite funding, and few politicians will go before the public to promote a tax increase or higher utility service fees. As a result, many politicians are forced to use circuitous means of "revenue enhancement" in lieu of taxes or simply neglect prudent spending on basic infrastructure. For years increases in San Francisco retail water rates lagged behind the rise in costs. Perhaps the public and the politicians had grown complacent with their extraordinary water system because it had been built and initially paid for several generations earlier. While new, the system needed little care. Now the needs for maintenance and upgrades to the aging system were escalating, like the mounting repair needs of an aging car. However, accustomed to the system's smooth operation, the owners' attention focused on pressing social issues.

The transfer of surplus money—excess revenues generated by HHWP hydropower—from the SFPUC to the city's general municipal fund apparently began in the late 1960s as a convenient source of nontax dollars to subsidize shortages in the city budget. Since 1979, the first year for which SFPUC records are readily available, transfers totaled $678 million (over $1 billion in 2003 dollars). Transfers in 2000 alone were nearly $40 million and nearly $30 million the next year—all apparently legal, although based on political and semantic sleight of hand, and in violation of municipal finance norms.

The sleight of hand stems from a set of provisions added to the city charter in 1935 as the Hetch Hetchy water and hydropower systems were initially coming online. Recognizing that additional work on both systems was likely in the future, the charter established the San Francisco Water Department and the "Hetch Hetchy project" as separate entities until the board of supervisors declared the Hetch Hetchy project completed. At that time, the project would be merged into the water department, which provided water collection, storage, treatment, and delivery in and immediately around the city, as a carryover of the Spring Valley Water Company. The Hetch Hetchy project managed the new construction and functions resulting from the Raker Act.

A second provision required that receipts from each utility be kept separate and used first to fund operating expenses, then, in order of priority, repairs and maintenance, depreciation, interest on bonds, improvements, and, finally, as surplus.

The next provision required each utility to maintain a depreciation account to provide funds for "reconstruction and replacement due to physical and functional depreciation . . . on the basis of an appraisal of the estimated life and the then current depreciated value" of its assets, and to monthly pay into that account one-twelfth of the annual amount of the depreciation.

And, lastly, the charter enabled the board of supervisors to transfer excess revenues from a utility to the general municipal fund provided the excess "exceed 25 per cent of the total expenditures of such utility for operation, repairs and maintenance for the preceding fiscal year."

No problems here. All the provisions appear reasonable and clear-cut. Revisions in the charter in 1994 and 1996 made only minor adjustments.

Today the SFPUC retains the two departments as separate utilities. The water enterprise captures, stores, and treats a modest amount of freshwater on the peninsula, and sells that water in combination with the primary water supply received from Hetch Hetchy to 700,000 retail consumers in the city and 29 wholesale customers in the Bay Area, who then distribute and sell the water to their 1.7 million retail consumers. Retail water rates are set by the board of supervisors; wholesale rates are calculated based on a twenty-five-year master contract contained in a settlement agreement reached in 1984 between San Francisco and the wholesale customers, as a result of the 1977 federal appeals court ruling in *City of Palo Alto v. City and County of San Francisco,* which held the benefits of the Raker Act should apply to wholesale customers as much as to retail consumers.

The Hetch Hetchy project—now known as the Hetch Hetchy Water and Power Enterprise—collects freshwater in and around Yosemite National Park, generates hydropower from it, and conducts the water and power toward San Francisco, where the water lines link into the water enterprise and the electric lines feed into the PG&E distribution grid (other electric lines run directly to the Modesto and Turlock Irrigation Districts). About 85 percent of HHWP's revenues from operations come from the sale of hydropower; the remaining 15 percent, roughly $20 million, comes mostly from a set fee, calculated every few years, charged to the water enterprise to recover HHWP's costs for the water it delivers to them.

The city has never declared the Hetch Hetchy project complete, so the utility has never been merged with the water department. Had the two units been merged, the revenues from one part of the combined department would first have to be used for any other part in need of additional funds before the funds could be declared surplus. Today the division between the two water units convolutes the accounting and management structure by somewhat arbitrarily segmenting the costs of and revenues from the supply, long-distance transmission, treatment, and local distribution of water. It complicates integrated systemwide management and clouds transparent accounting. The city also has subdivided HHWP into a water component and a hydropower component, reflecting the fundamental difference in products—water and power—and the timing of their construction.

Yet the historical basis for these separate units has lost relevance—so why not merge them? Primarily, the reasons are, once again, money and politics; maintaining the units as separate entities enabled the transfer of revenues generated by the hydropower component to the general municipal fund at the same time that the water component and the water department lacked sufficient monies for routine maintenance and repairs because annual revenues from operations were inadequate to fund those needs. The transfers also occurred while incremental funding for the eventual replacement of infrastructure due to normal depreciation was inadequate.

From some perspectives, these actions appear to be administrative and accounting contortions, mere political ploys to rationalize questionable institutional beliefs and behaviors. From other perspectives, they appear appropriate. Just as in Mayor Phelan's day, reasonable observers, politicians, and public administrators often share common goals regarding municipal governance but have differing views on the best ways to achieve them. The difference between enlightened governance and unethical governance can be very vague.

Nationwide, many municipalities prohibit the transfer of excess utility revenues to the general fund for a number of sound reasons related to equity and efficiency. As a charter city, San Francisco sets its own water rates; hence, without safeguards that prohibit excess water revenues from being transferred to the municipal coffers, city officials could purposely overcharge for water and use the excess revenues as a nontax-generated source of funds to finance whatever municipal purpose they saw fit. Or the city could simply permit the infrastructure to deteriorate while it siphoned off revenues needed by the utility.

The rate payers might enjoy benefits as a result of these actions—or they might not. Either way, they do not have as direct a say in the setting of the rates the board of supervisors charges as they do when they vote on a tax, nor do they have a choice for an alternate source of water if they are dissatisfied with the rates. In effect, city officials could use their water monopoly to hold the public hostage, raising water rates above the need and/or siphoning off revenues for municipal uses without the direct approval of the rate payer: Spring Valley incarnate; James Duval Phelan's dream perverted. Public utilities were never intended to be cash cows for city budgets.

Proponents of the transfers argued that they reflected a fair return on the equity held by the city in the system because the city paid for the system; therefore they believed it was appropriate that the city enjoyed the profits generated by the system. They also argued that the surplus revenues simply returned to the city monies that originally came from the city, since the city was the primary customer and rate payer for the hydroelectricity. Of the some $110 million in annual hydropower revenues, about 70 percent comes from the sale of electricity to the city. Most of the remainder comes from the sale of power to the Modesto and Turlock Irrigation Districts. Power is sold to nonenterprise municipal divisions at or below cost, while enterprise divisions, in particular the airport, pay rates comparable to those they would be charged by PG&E—that is, well above the cost of service.

Some proponents also believed that the use of surplus hydropower revenues on the repair and replacement of water system infrastructure was less equitable than distributing the money back to city coffers to fund current programs. They argued that some components of the water system have long useable life spans; therefore, repair and replacement costs come sporadically, not incrementally. These timing characteristics make an annual work program based on some prescribed percentage amount of depreciation in the asset value impractical. They suggested it was better to fund such work when the need for the work arises, using long-term debt to distribute the costs to future users since they will most benefit from the expenditures. However, care must be taken to avoid the political temptation to undercharge for water to curry political favor with voters, while relying totally on periodic revenue bonds to fund repairs and improvements.

Despite these arguments, the transfers violated an important canon of municipal finance, which holds that long-term capital funds should not be used to finance short-term operating expenses. When the city transferred excess utility revenues to the general fund, it used that money to finance short-term operating expenses normally funded by tax dollars. Had the excess revenues been retained by the utility, the monies could have been used to finance annual maintenance needs or system improvements, which the utility was later forced to fund with revenue bonds, for which it pays interest to the bond holder. Long-term debt is intended to finance capital improvements—big-ticket projects with long depreciation periods—but it is too costly to use for annual operating expenses. A household equivalent might be the use of a thirty-year loan or credit card debt to pay daily expenses for necessities like food or luxuries like entertainment: need or enjoy now, pay (more) later. The financial pitfall of this practice can easily bury one beneath a mountain of debt that reaches far into the future, while promoting a comfortable lifestyle beyond one's means. Perhaps manageable during periods of prosperity and economic growth, unfortunately the practice often leads to financial collapse during economic downturns. (Just ask Billy Ralston.)

Long-term planning for general repairs, replacement, and improvements, and to meet demand during droughts and from future growth, was lax as well, at least until recently. The 2000 state audit concluded the SFPUC "has been slow to assess and upgrade its water delivery system so it can survive catastrophes such as earthquakes, floods, and fires. It also has been slow to estimate the amount of water it will need to meet future demand and to seek additional sources of water. As a result, the nearly 2.4 million customers in four Bay Area counties who rely on the commission for their drinking water are at greater risk of disruptions and water shortages if an emergency or a drought occurs." The audit also claimed the commission was "slow to develop its water supply master plan" and criticized its "slow pace in completing capital projects aimed at upgrading its aging water delivery infrastructure." The report cited several causes, but beneath each was a lack of political will to effectively address the out-of-sight, out-of-mind needs of the infrastructure.

Politically it is easier to envision a great infrastructure project like Hetch Hetchy than it is to properly maintain it once created. The dream can be clothed in civic pride, patriotism, and personal profit, while the reality is seemingly more mundane: turn the tap or flip the switch for water or power on demand, delivered inexpensively through a little-seen labyrinth of pipes and wires, a triumph of technology, long since forgotten, that supplies a basic necessity for daily life in a semiarid world. For many San Franciscans this wonder has bred a sense of complacency and an arrogance of sorts. Ample water has become their birthright, a matter of fact made possible by technology and the colonization of the remote Hetch Hetchy landscape. "It's this idea San Franciscans have," noted Kevin Starr, the California state librarian, "that this isn't a real city dependent on maintenance but . . . a Monte Carlo, an Oz, the Club Med of American cities"—the imperial city envisioned by Phelan.

Technology overcomes many environmental obstacles, such as the scarcity of water in a dry landscape, shielding us from the daily implications and hiding them from regular view. But it cannot change the underlying truth in California: San Francisco depends on the importation of water from the distant mountains. While no city of significant size escapes the dependence on technology to overcome local shortages of vital necessities, San Francisco appears to have lost sight of that dependence, taking for granted the supply of water that underpins the city's existence, as if the supply was always present and the scarcity merely a faint memory, perhaps even an illusion.

This mindset appears in their governance of the Hetch Hetchy system. After all, they envisioned it, they designed it, they fought for it, and then they funded it and built it. Hetch Hetchy belongs to San Franciscans. They consider it their birthright alone—even though the Freeman report expanded the original Phelan-Grunsky-Manson plans for a city-only system, to yield sufficient water to supply other Bay Area communities. Approval of the system by the Raker Act assumed that sharing. Today San Francisco consumes about 84 million gallons per day, well within the amount that would have been produced by the original plan for which Secretary of the Interior Garfield granted a permit (60 million from Lake Eleanor and 60 million from the acquisition of Spring Valley), while the 29 wholesale customers consume 175 million gallons, roughly two-thirds of the supply made possible by the Freeman plan and the Raker Act. Of these wholesale customers, eighteen are wholly dependent on Hetch Hetchy water and three others are at least 75 percent dependent. Most of them have no choice for an alternate water supply. Yet the SFPUC and HHWP remain governed by a board of five commissioners appointed by the mayor of San Francisco from city residents. The wholesale consumers have no representation on the board or in the governance of the system even though they consume most of the water and pay a proportional share of the costs.

A 2001 study on water governance in the San Francisco Bay Area by the California Policy Research Center at the University of California stated, "Other studies recently identified substantial deferred maintenance of physical infrastructure, some explicitly postponed, some requiring seismic upgrades, and some inadvertent.

While recent estimates for these deferred costs run to the billions of dollars, most customers have few means to hold SFPUC accountable for the risks these backlogs represent." The report continued,

> One explanation for the SFPUC's limited accountability to its wholesale customers is that it has many characteristics of an unregulated monopoly. Many wholesale customers are dependent on the SFPUC for a majority of their water, yet have little if any political authority or regulatory protections. Because the SFPUC is a charter-city department, the California Public Utilities Commission does not regulate it. Its commissioners are appointed by the mayor of San Francisco. The absence of regulatory oversight and alternative water sources for suburban water customers presents substantial accountability and responsiveness challenges.
>
> The SFPUC and its wholesale customers have a water rate pact for the next few years, the result of an out-of-court settlement that appears agreeable to all parties. However, the SFPUC appears to lack the same electoral or regulatory incentive to plan and maintain infrastructure and service levels outside its municipal boundaries that it has within them.

As a result of the maintenance, planning, and governance issues, core components of the system remain unnecessarily vulnerable to earthquake damage, and other portions are prone to failure due to age and deterioration. System engineers worry most about the tunnels. At the Irvington Tunnel, for example, only one conduit carries Hetch Hetchy water to the city. "If that tunnel fails," the managing engineer warned, "then nearly 90 percent of your water is cut off. How do you rebuild a tunnel? That's a big problem." He continued, "Calaveras Dam has major problems too. The reservoir has to be maintained at an extremely low level due to the risk of dam failure during a seismic event. The three San Joaquin pipelines are another big problem. When all three are in service, during summer months, and a problem occurs, the broken pipeline has to be shut down for repairs, cutting off water, creating almost a crisis mode. A fourth pipeline is needed to provide some backup." The recent San Joaquin Valley leak illustrated his point. The water department's assets on the peninsula, at the other end of the system—which the managing engineer doesn't deal with—have additional problems with water mains and century-old water storage and delivery components.

Could a seismic event of 7.0 on the Richter scale prove disastrous? "Oh, yeah," the engineer replied. "There would be outages all over the place. If the system would be drained down, we'd go in an emergency mode. Hopefully there will be contractors available to put everything back together, like putting Humpty Dumpty back together. But regardless of what you spend, if you get a big enough seismic event, no system will withstand it." A technical study of such potentials prepared by the Bay Area Economic Forum in 2002 concluded, "The system's limited capacity, its age and its vulnerability to serious damage and service disruption in an earthquake, flood, fire or other catastrophic event, present major implications for the region's economy if not addressed." It continued,

> Based on recent experience in droughts, SFPUC can only assure its customers a total supply of 239 mgd [millions of gallons per day], and currently operates 21 mgd above that assured supply capacity. The current shortfall will grow to 64 mgd by 2030 and 71 mgd by 2050.
>
> Hetch Hetchy's major dam, reservoir, pipeline, tunnel and pump station components are all at least nearly 50 years old, and many are 60–80 years old. Key structural assessments, maintenance and upgrades have been deferred for decades. Major components have no bypass capability in the event of failure.
>
> Hetch Hetchy crosses at least five active earthquake faults. Facilities located near these points of intersection are at risk of failure in the event of a major earthquake, an event considered likely in the next 30 years.

Beyond the human hardship resulting from such a catastrophe, the report concluded, "Potential economic losses to the region from a water supply interruption total at least $28.7 billion for a major earthquake on the San Andreas Fault and $17.2 billion for a similar event on the Hayward Fault. In addition to quantifiable near-term damage," the report continued, "the Bay Area economy would suffer irreversible long-term damage due to the failure of many businesses to reopen because of losses incurred during a disruption, the permanent relocation of other businesses outside the region due to water security concerns, and the reluctance of new businesses to locate here for similar reasons. These permanent economic losses are difficult to estimate without more study, but would almost certainly be on a large scale."

As awareness of the maintenance and management problems grew in the 1990s, pressure for change mounted, more from the wholesale water customers than from within the SFPUC board or San Francisco city hall. And frustration with the nonresponsiveness of city officials eventually prompted wholesale customers to direct that pressure toward the state legislature.

One of the first calls for change was voiced in 1994 by a management audit report of the water department prepared by the budget analyst for the board of supervisors. The report noted that the city's water system suffered from an aging infrastructure that required increasing facilities maintenance and was badly in need of large-scale, general capital improvements. The report criticized the SFPUC for not having developed a capital improvements plan and urged that one be prepared as quickly as possible. It also noted the increasing need to fund facilities maintenance from annual water rate revenues, and the eventual need to issue revenue bonds to fund capital improvements, both of which would create upward pressure on water rates.

City hall and the SFPUC commission responded tepidly. In the mid-1990s, the bond-rating agencies on which municipalities like San Francisco depend to finance long-term debts announced that they would no longer rate SFPUC water bonds because the agency had no capital improvements plan nor had it shown the will or ability to adequately maintain the system. SFPUC dutifully developed a basic plan, yet when the plan was presented to the utility's governing commission for approval and adoption, the commission ignored the recommendation, preferring instead to simply send the draft to the bond agencies. The agencies weren't impressed. Although they resumed rating SFPUC water bonds, they did so at a lower grade than would have been given had the SFPUC formally adopted and committed to the improvement plan. Why did the commission balk at adopting the plan? Because of the plan's economic and, hence, political implications: water rates would have to be raised signifi-

cantly to pay for the improvements, and no one had the political will
to push for those increases.

By 1996 the city had voluntarily "frozen"—not raised—retail
water rates, perhaps to be consistent with Proposition 13, the
statewide initiative in 1978 that limited tax increases a city or county
could impose on its residents to finance non-income-generating
branches of city government. Yet "enterprise" units, like the water
department and HHWP, are self-financing through service fees, so
they are exempt from the limits. While politically popular, the water
rate freeze placed a financial straitjacket on the utility: maintenance
and labor costs were rising, but revenues were fixed. Something had
to give. Maintenance could be postponed; the city and public were
accustomed to overlooking those needs. But rising labor costs could
not be avoided, as they were tied to set escalators in contracts. And
city hall clamored for the "surplus" hydropower revenues to cover
other operating expenses.

Passage of Proposition H in 1998 confounded the funding problem. San Franciscans formally froze water rates, with some minor
exemptions. The politics behind the vote were complicated. Many
voters were angry with the general cost of government. Others were
outraged at the transfers of hydropower revenues to the municipal
fund and thought the freeze would force the city to leave those revenues in the SFPUC to cover rising internal costs. The bond agencies interpreted the vote negatively, promptly lowering their ratings
for water bonds due to heightened concerns for the city's commitment to proper system maintenance and improvement, potentially
costing the city tens of millions of dollars in increased interest
charged over the life of future capital improvement bonds. Efforts to
save consumers money in the short term by freezing water rates and
postponing improvements would now cost them dearly in the long
term. City hall and the SFPUC board heard the cumulative cries for
change, grudgingly. Work began on a comprehensive capital
improvements plan, although the funding shortage for routine maintenance remained and the transfer of surplus hydropower revenues
continued.

By the late 1990s pressure from the Bay Area wholesale consumers for change in SFPUC operations intensified, motivated by
deepening concerns about the security of the water system on which

their well-being depended. The state audit, the water governance study by the California Policy Research Center, and the Bay Area Economic Forum report corroborated these concerns. The SFPUC staff responded as best they could while the commitment from the board and city hall gradually grew. A detailed, long-term capital improvements plan was developed in conjunction with the wholesale customers in the early 2000s.

Yet when the completed plan went before the board in August 2001 for formal approval and adoption, election-year politics postponed the vote for months. Frustrated by the delay and deeply concerned about the danger of disruption in the water supply to the entire region, the state legislature intervened, drafting bills the following winter and spring to compel the city to move promptly ahead with the needed repairs and improvements. In May 2002 the SFPUC board finally adopted the capital improvements plan, but it was too little, too late. In August the state legislature passed A.B. 1823 with only one dissent, A.B. 2058 with only two dissents, and S.B. 1870 unanimously, despite lobbying against the bills by San Francisco mayor Willie Brown, who had served fifteen years as speaker of the assembly. Governor Davis signed the bills into law several weeks later.

The bills established three interrelated actions intended to achieve the needed improvements as quickly as possible. Together the bills created a regional water agency to better represent the concerns of the wholesale customers to San Francisco, created another agency empowered to issue revenue bonds to finance the wholesale customers' share of the capital improvements needed to once again set the water system on sound footing, and required San Francisco to annually report its work on the capital improvements to various state agencies to ensure that proper progress is being made. The legislature cast off concerns about its intervention in local affairs and the modest burden of implementing its proposed oversight role out of overwhelming concern for public health, safety, and welfare. The time had come to fix the problem, setting aside partisan politics and blame. San Francisco city hall had shirked its public responsibilities for too long, for whatever reasons. Its indifference could not be permitted to further jeopardize the region's and the state's future.

With that prompting, two months later San Franciscans approved several charter reforms affecting the management of the SFPUC, and also a revenue bond to finance the city's share of the capital improvement plan. City hall and past players in the events leading up to the vote backed the proposals, including former mayor Dianne Feinstein. "The voters in San Francisco have spoken," proclaimed the general manager of the SFPUC in response. "[They] have determined having a safe and reliable water system is of the ultimate importance."

Among several revisions, one charter reform enables the SFPUC to issue revenue bonds without voter approval, like most public utilities, streamlining the prior cumbersome process that required approvals by the SFPUC board, city hall, the board of supervisors, and the public. Another revision reaffirmed the existing mandate to "use surplus funds from its utilities to operate and maintain the utilities before transferring any surplus to the General Fund." A third revision tightened restrictions on the transfer of surplus revenues, requiring approval for a transfer by three-quarters of the board of supervisors. And a fourth provision established a rate fairness board to review proposed water rate increases, helping to reduce the role of politics in rate setting. To pay for the $1.6 billion revenue bond, monthly water rates in San Francisco for the typical family of four will almost triple, to about $43 over the course of the capital improvements, while the corresponding monthly fee for most suburban customers will rise, from about $31 per month to about $71, to pay for the bonds to cover the wholesale providers' $2 billion share of the costs.

As the spectacular leak that gushed water skyward underscored the endemic problems with the Hetch Hetchy water system just five days after the November vote, the general manager of the Bay Area Water Supply and Conservation Agency noted, "Clearly, it's a sign of weakness in the system." His new agency represents the twenty-nine wholesale customers of Hetch Hetchy water and was formed from a prior association that spearheaded the campaign for legislative intervention. "This is not a good situation," he said. "We know it, and San Francisco knows it. It emphasizes why the work [upgrading the Hetch Hetchy system] needs to be done." A district manager for a wholesale customer of Hetch Hetchy water agreed, saying, "This is what people who argued for the [Hetch Hetchy renovation] bond initiative have been warning about." The general manager of SFPUC agreed, too. Noting the vulnerability of the water supply system, she emphasized, "that's one of the major issues we tried to communicate to the public about the need for our capital program. Frankly, I feel like the Dutch person sticking my finger in the dike."

Have the revisions finally remedied the long-standing, fundamental political issues and public attitudes that created the problems in the management of the water system? Skepticism abounds. Engrained institutional behaviors change slowly. Will the capital improvements be fully implemented before the next major earthquake again shakes the Bay Area from its environmental complacency, reminding residents of their dependence on remote water sources, as did the great quake of 1906? No one knows. Like all imperialistic landscapes, San Francisco lives precariously balanced on a thin technological edge between security and disaster.

CHAPTER 12

Constructing the Engineering Marvel

The original Moccasin Powerhouse stands empty and silent like a cathedral. It is a monument to the technological marvel of the Hetch Hetchy system, reflected in the mirror surface of the power plant's afterbay reservoir along its flank. The small reservoir fills most of the narrow valley floor formed by Moccasin Creek, whose flow is diverted upstream to bypass the impoundment of pure Hetch Hetchy water headed for the Bay Area. The air feels cool in the shade beside the water, in stark contrast to the bright aridness of the surrounding foothills.

Moccasin Powerhouse is a handsome structure, seventy yards long and nearly seven stories tall, constructed of creamy-colored concrete, designed in the California mission style with a terra-cotta tile roof and arched arcades. A dramatic arched window at the end, standing nearly the height of the structure, fills the nave with light. Grand lettering over the window proclaims the building's name; a plaque beneath tells its parentage. Opened in 1925, the powerhouse's four 20-megawatt generators whirred away until replaced in 1969 by two 50,000-kilovolt generators housed in a bland building just to the rear. Priest's Grade rises on the opposite side of the powerhouse from the still reservoir. Giant penstocks plummet the 1,200 feet from the forebay reservoir atop the hill to the powerhouse at its foot, carrying the hydraulic force of Hetch Hetchy water into the turbines, which convert the potential energy of gravity into a form usable for human purposes. High-voltage electric lines carry off the resulting power over the opposite hills toward San Francisco.

The town of Moccasin nestles quietly in the remainder of the tiny valley. There's not much to it: a few small shops, a handful of bungalow-style homes, and the offices of Hetch Hetchy Water and Power. You can tell it's a company town, like Norris, Tennessee, and others built during the 1920s and 1930s in conjunction with a great Progressive Era water project. The town's origin is told by the common architectural style of the bungalows, the gently curving lanes, and the simple parklike landscaping interspersed with mission-style institutional buildings that look like lodges at a California summer camp. The main HHWP office stands in the center of the town, overlooking Moccasin Reservoir, a block from the old powerhouse. The historic building has a grand lobby beneath a ceiling supported by elegant wood beams, with a large, rarely used stone fireplace at one end. Workers are busy restoring the tile roof with loving care. Nearby a cluster of flimsy single-story wood buildings, resembling a series of attached modular trailers, houses the overflow of engineering staff. The difference in style between the original buildings and the faceless newer versions seems to reflect the change in public and political perception of the system. The grand visions and civic pride that gave rise to the Hetch Hetchy project in Mayor James Duval Phelan's day have been replaced by political and economic expediency.

Remnants like these convey the wonder of the system and its birth, so easily forgotten over the years of reliable operation and the proliferation of new anonymous-looking engineering projects. Hetch Hetchy was magical when it was constructed. The monumental effort to realize the Freeman plan began immediately after approval of the Raker Act. By then a dynamic new mayor, James "Sunny Jim" Rolph Jr., ruled San Francisco, until he resigned in 1931 to become governor. Charismatic, popular, and very powerful, Sunny Jim shared many of Phelan's dreams for their beloved city, including Hetch Hetchy. And like Phelan, Rolph never lacked energy, enthusiasm, optimism, or a benevolent but dictatorial political will. Sunny Jim was a larger-than-life character in a city and time that seemed to breed them.

Beginning in the late 1800s as an office boy in a Bay Area commission house, Rolph rose by the early 1900s to become a successful banker and entrepreneur with various shipping and shipbuilding interests. Like Phelan, he moved in the right business and civic circles, forming alliances and allegiances with like-minded elite. And like other leaders of the day, he periodically ignored bothersome political norms when they stood in the way: when he suffered financial downturns, he relied on "loans" from wealthy friends to bail him out, debts he reputedly paid off with political favors; he openly flaunted Prohibition, once sending a case of whiskey to a condemned man; and most infamously, while governor he refused to call out the National Guard to protect two men who had kidnapped and bludgeoned the son of a prominent and very popular San Jose family, then pronounced that justice had been served and a lesson learned after an angry mob stormed the jail, extracted the confessed murderers, and lynched them in St. James Park.

Shortly after assuming office in January 1912, Rolph hired forty-eight-year-old Michael M. O'Shaughnessy, a fiery Irish American, to direct the burgeoning Hetch Hetchy project, with the charge that the new city engineer answer only to the new mayor. O'Shaughnessy was an ideal choice. He had immigrated to San Francisco from Ireland in 1885 with a bachelor's degree in engineering from the Royal University of Dublin. Once in the Bay Area he refined his technical skills as he learned the basics of project management while working on various infrastructure projects around the region.

O'Shaughnessy was chief engineer for the Southern California Mountain Water Company in San Diego when Rolph recruited him. Called "the Chief" out of fear and respect by the army of staff and workers he soon commanded, O'Shaughnessy directed the massive water project like a general waging war—which it was at the time, a righteous war against a hostile environment for a noble public cause. He could be dapper and eloquent at one moment, enthralling the audience at congressional hearings with his technical competence, his command of the facts and issues, and his unassailable confidence in the project, his sweet Irish brogue lilting like a song. At other times the person and the brogue could be as coarse and crude as the construction troops chiseling the tunnels through solid granite, or those pouring concrete for the dam, or those laying track for the supply train. Together Rolph and O'Shaughnessy formed the perfect pair to win the political and technical war over Hetch Hetchy, with Rolph as commander-in-chief, fighting the political battles in San Francisco, and O'Shaughnessy serving as his field commander leading the troops.

Immediately following approval of the Raker Act, O'Shaughnessy set about refining the Freeman plan sufficiently to guide mobilization for the massive project and begin actual construction. Teams of engineers were sent into the High Sierra to reconnoiter the terrain and finalize surveys of dam sites, routes for pipelines and tunnels, and the location of support facilities. The resulting work plan specified the general sequence and timing of tasks within an overall project strategy intended to minimize logistical complications, construction problems, and cost.

The Hetch Hetchy Dam (later renamed O'Shaughnessy Dam) initially would be built only to three-quarters of its ultimate height, creating a reservoir of 60 percent final capacity. Water would be released from the reservoir at about 3,500 feet in elevation and flow twelve miles down the Tuolumne River, where it would be diverted into a tunnel at Early Intake, a small powerhouse built along the riverbank at 2,300 feet in elevation to supply electricity during construction of the project. However, the Hetch Hetchy Reservoir would not be completed for several years after completion of Early Intake. In the meantime the normal river flow would not have the force or the constant volume needed to operate the power plant's three turbine generators. Consequently, a diversion structure would be quickly built across a nearby tributary called Cherry Creek. Its outflow, combined with supplemental water diverted from a small lake on adjacent Eleanor Creek, which would be dammed to deepen the natural impoundment, would be piped to the edge of the river canyon above Early Intake, then plummet through penstocks to the plant, thus providing the hydraulic head and reliable volume needed for the turbines. Discharge from the power plant would be released back into the Tuolumne River.

The tunnel at Early Intake would carry Hetch Hetchy water about nineteen miles westward toward Moccasin, where it would empty into a small holding reservoir at the top of Priest's Grade before descending to a main powerhouse at 929 feet two miles beyond the end of the tunnel. The Moccasin facilities would be brought online as fast as possible to earn income for the overall project. From Moccasin the aqueduct would carry the water to the Bay Area, totally enclosed in pipes and tunnels to protect its purity.

Hetch Hetchy Dam would be raised to full height after the initial system was completed. At some later date, a tunnel could be driven from the dam to Early Intake, where a larger, permanent powerhouse could be built. That Canyon Tunnel would provide the hydraulic head needed for power generation by a plant set in the canyon bottom along the riverbank, and it would protect water purity. Outflow from the plant would continue to Moccasin through the Mountain Tunnel.

Eventually a third permanent power plant could be built to tap the flows of Cherry Creek, which could be dammed as well, and Lake Eleanor. In the late 1940s the city decided that discharge from this plant would be returned to the Tuolumne River rather than added to the Hetch Hetchy flow diverted to the Bay Area. Hence, Cherry Creek and Lake Eleanor would never supply freshwater for San Francisco as originally specified by the Garfield permit. (The reservoir on Cherry Creek, called Lake Lloyd, would become a part of a cooperative plan between the city and the Modesto and Turlock Irrigation Districts that culminated in the New Don Pedro Reservoir.)

Thousands of workers employed by the city and numerous contractors waged the war at dozens of sites. The army included engineers drawing detailed plans and construction documents; lawyers negotiating contracts, drafting and marketing bond issues, and acquiring rights-of-way; purchasing officers buying equipment, supplies of all types, and trainloads of materials; accountants keeping track of the budget chaos; laborers digging tunnels deep underground, laying pipe across flat fields and the bay bottom, and pouring a concrete dam; and countless other logistical support personnel needed to maintain the massive campaign.

As construction of the complex Hetch Hetchy system began, the O'Shaughnessy plan called for the city to finally acquire Spring Valley Water Company and fully develop and bring into service its East Bay properties by constructing an aqueduct across the southern end of San Francisco Bay. These new sources would satisfy increases in water demand during the years needed to tap Hetch Hetchy, and they would earn income as quickly as possible to help defray full project costs. The aqueduct would eventually carry Hetch Hetchy water too, on completion of the reservoir in the park and pipelines linking it to East Bay, which was expected to occur simultaneously with water demand in the city finally exceeding Spring Valley capacity, but not before, to save costs. Therefore, the war would be fought simultaneously at multiple fronts scattered along the full length of the 167-mile-long aqueduct, coordinated to link precisely at the designated time and place. That was the plan. But few projects so complex and so political go according to plan.

When San Francisco voters approved the Hetch Hetchy project in 1910, and approved the issuance of $45 million in bonds to pay for it, they did not approve, by the narrowest of margins, the $37 million bond issue intended to purchase Spring Valley. So negotiations to acquire the bothersome monopoly resumed shortly after Mayor Rolph assumed office in 1912, spurred by a renewed sense that the Spring Valley system suffered from neglect and was nearing its capacity. The board of supervisors passed a resolution calling for the acquisition of the company, and the new mayor created an advisory water committee to represent the city in negotiations. In August the committee and company reached agreement on a price of $38.5 million, but the board of supervisors hedged, asking for a $37 million price, and then rejected it without justification when Spring Valley agreed. In frustration, city efforts then switched to acquire the company via condemnation in the courts. These proceedings were abandoned after preliminary steps were completed out of fear that the remaining steps would take too long.

By this time, in the spring of 1913, the Freeman report was circulating in Washington, where the political winds were changing with the coming of the Wilson administration, and negotiations had begun to resolve the concerns of those opposed to the Raker Act, including Spring Valley's concerns about protecting the value of its assets should the city build its own system. As a result, a special provision was added to the act that required all local sources of water around the Bay Area to be developed to their full capacity before any Tuolumne water could be diverted to the city; this would also limit the city's impact on irrigation development in the San Joaquin Valley. Spring Valley's owners dropped their opposition, safe in the knowledge that their investments would be fully recovered when the city bought them out.

Negotiations between the city and the company resumed once again in the aftermath of the Raker Act and the city's formal acceptance of its provisions. However, the tone differed from the prior decades of hostility and distrust, for two reasons. First, the ultimate outcome of the negotiations was no longer in doubt: Spring Valley would be absorbed into the new municipal water system, but after the company had fully developed its assets. The only remaining questions regarded cost and timing.

The second change in circumstance came about when the California constitution was revised in 1910, granting the state railroad commission the power to set water rates. (The commission didn't actually begin to do so for San Francisco until 1916, due to various legal and court complications.) This change ended the decades-long legal battle between the city and the company over rates. Now a single independent public body would set rates and the profit margin from water services in combination, reducing the opportunity for corporate price gouging and further motivating Spring Valley's owners to reach an accord with the city. They did, in 1915 agreeing once again on a price of about $35 million. Once again, San Franciscans rejected the deal, the public vote of 54 percent in favor falling short of the required two-thirds majority. Opposition from the *San Francisco Chronicle* and several civic leaders affected the outcome. Old suspicions remained in the minds of some.

Six years later another purchase proposal was made, this time for $37 million. The state railroad commission certified the price as fair, and the proposal had the support of four mayors, including James Duval Phelan and James Rolph. Yet nothing of substance had changed in the minds of the naysayers: the issue failed, receiving only 58 percent of the vote. After this, Spring Valley remained cooperative, giving the city a ten-year purchase option for $37 million which would expire on December 31, 1931, later extended by two years. Support for the acquisition gradually grew as additional components of the water system were completed. San Francisco tried again in June 1927, placing another bond issue on the ballot to finance the buyout, but it garnered only 59 percent of the vote. Throughout all this, cooperation grew between the city, the company, and the railroad commission, in part out of mutual self-interest as the company sought to fully develop its assets and as components of the Hetch Hetchy system came online, enabling the two systems to share infrastructure and costs, and in part out of goodwill and recognition of the inevitable.

And the inevitable finally happened, on March 3, 1930, when Spring Valley president S. P. Eastman gave a beaming San Francisco mayor Sunny Jim Rolph the deeds to his company while standing beneath the glittering rotunda of the "new" city hall—the first part of Phelan's dream for a municipal water system realized in the place that most symbolized that dream. The struggle begun some sixty years earlier, in the 1870s, was over. In return, Mayor Rolph handed Mr. Eastman a check for $39,962,606.51, then told the audience that he considered this the crowning achievement of his eighteen years in office. The reluctant voters had formally approved the purchase in May 1928 with a 70 percent majority, but the bonds could not be sold in the downmarket until the Bank of Italy bought the entire $41 million issue eighteen months later. The long-lived opposition to the purchase had finally died off. It had to; the Hetch Hetchy Dam was complete and pipelines were about to link it with the Spring Valley network. The grand engineering dream was about to be realized. Victory was at hand, technology triumphant. Progress could no longer be denied.

What were the consequences of the lengthy delay in acquisition? Did the city ultimately pay a fair price for the monopoly? Probably: although some observers still suspected the sale price was too high, it had not inflated significantly between 1910 and 1928, while some Spring Valley assets had been more fully developed and others liquidated, and the terms had been scrutinized for years by the public, the state railroad commission, and independent groups. The opportunity for a sweetheart deal that would unfairly enrich inside participants likely had diminished years earlier.

Once Mayor Phelan focused on Hetch Hetchy in the early 1900s, would it have made a difference in development of the city's water system if Spring Valley had been acquired in 1910, 1915, 1921, or 1927? Doubtful: San Francisco had already irrevocably committed to a regionwide water system predicated on the damming of Hetch Hetchy and the acquisition of Spring Valley. The delay in acquisition had no effect on that overall scheme.

Yet had the acquisition occurred before the 1901 point of no return, would San Francisco's entire quest for a municipal water system have differed? Had the city purchased Spring Valley in the 1870s, 1880s, or 1890s, would Hetch Hetchy have ever been dammed, even as demand for water around the bay exceeded Spring Valley supplies? Probably not: Yosemite National Park visitors today could gaze in wonder at the spectacle around them as they walk about the Hetch Hetchy Valley in the footsteps of John Muir. San Francisco's water supply would likely be based primarily on Spring Valley's sources on the peninsula and sources around the bay that were later tapped by the monopoly, supplemented with some Sierra water. But the city's wholesale customers in the surrounding counties today most likely would have formed their own water district in the early 1900s and sought their own sources in the Sierra, other than Hetch Hetchy, as did the East Bay consortium.

Now, reservoirs in the foothills impound Sierra water on most major drainages. Hetch Hetchy was not the only site and probably not the cheapest. Phelan and his followers alone were fixated on the valley, overlooking its scenic wonder and national park protection. Concern for water quality and quantity, the engineering suitability of the valley for a dam and reservoir site, and the ease of acquiring water rights predominated Phelan's original thinking. Only later in the Freeman plan did Hetch Hetchy's value as a source of hydropower and the opportunity to construct a gravity-based system gain importance as distinguishing characteristics from alternate sites and sources. Of Phelan's initial justifications, water quality most distinguished Hetch Hetchy from other options. His decision in effect weighed the loss of the valley against the possible future cost of constructing a water treatment plant. No one else seemed willing to make that trade-off. Colonel Mendell's report never mentioned Hetch Hetchy. Mayor Phelan was the first person willing to take on the inherent engineering challenges of damming the remote valley and piping the water to the Bay Area, and to confront the political complications posed by its protection after the creation of Yosemite National Park in 1890.

From the outset, the primary problems facing San Francisco's quest to find sufficient water were money and politics. The engineering challenges, despite their complexities, were ultimately more manageable than the financial and political ones. Nothing has changed today.

Armed with the $45 million war chest approved in the 1910 vote, O'Shaughnessy commenced the campaign. Before actual construction could begin, an army of workers had to be hired, hundreds of construction contracts bid and signed, and an extensive logistical support structure created. Access roads and a sixty-eight-mile-long standard-gauge railroad had to be built eastward from the foothills into the rugged High Sierra to move a huge amount of material and thousands of people in and out. Hundreds of project workers and facilities of all sorts poured into the tiny lifeless town of Groveland, an important staging area, reviving for a decade the prosperity and vitality it had enjoyed half a century earlier during the gold rush. Homes, hospitals, schools, shops, and bars flourished. The remote region around the western flank of Yosemite once again pulsed to life. Quarries had to be opened and a saw mill constructed to supply the millions of board feet of timber needed for ties, forms, and supports. The Hetch Hetchy Railroad was completed in 1917, operating as any other regulated commercial railroad from 1918 to 1925 with set time tables and tariffs; however, Mayor Rolph served as its president and the Chief as its vice president and general manager. Like the gold rush, the Hetch Hetchy project brought another brief boom to the Sierra foothills before it, too, petered out.

Provision of electricity to power the construction effort, especially drills for boring through the granite bedrock, posed another immediate need. Nothing was easy. Electricity would have to be provided onsite, not transmitted from the Bay Area, so a power plant had to be built. The small plant at Early Intake would be located at the lower end of the steep-walled Tuolumne River canyon downstream from Hetch Hetchy Valley, with electric lines then strung to the various construction sites and logistical centers like Groveland. To create the reliable, continuous flow of water for the plant, a dam 1,260 feet long by 70 feet high was needed to deepen Lake Eleanor, a glacial lake several miles away. Water from the lake and from nearby Cherry Creek would then flow through a three-mile-long series of flumes, pipes, tunnels, and concrete-lined canals to the hillside 350 feet above the power plant sitting in the Tuolumne canyon. Construction of the plant required that all the heavy machinery and materials be lowered into the deep canyon via a funicular tramway. Early Intake Powerhouse came online in 1918.

As this preliminary work began, financial problems slowed progress. The bond market had dropped as the Western world waged war on itself. After the war was over, the national economy slumped.

San Francisco had difficulty selling Hetch Hetchy bonds to fund construction, a financial and political obstacle that would plague the project for decades.

Preparatory work for the Hetch Hetchy Dam began concurrent with the other preliminary projects. Once access roads reached the site, a twenty-three-by-twenty-five-foot diversion tunnel was bored a thousand feet through the valley's solid granite wall to carry the Tuolumne River around the dam site. When the tunnel was done, a small coffer dam was poured across the river, diverting the flow through the tunnel and leaving the former river channel at the dam site dry and exposed. Work on the actual dam began in autumn 1919. Again, nothing was easy.

The remoteness, the terrain, the weather, and the inherent nature of the work itself posed immense challenges. To reach solid bedrock for the dam's foundation, a hundred-foot-deep layer of glacial debris—rock fragments ranging in size from sand to giant boulders—had to be removed from the river channel, then the granite floor and side walls prepared for contact with concrete. The pour for the arched gravity dam continued day and night, year-round, for nearly four years, its cyclopean concrete containing a mix of granite blocks up to six cubic yards in size imbedded in the plain concrete. Summer temperatures of over one hundred degrees baked the valley, the blazing sun searing the bare canyon walls. In winter workers fought fierce High Sierra blizzards. At its dedication in 1923, the 226½-foot-high dam was acclaimed the largest structure on the West Coast; fifteen years later it was raised 85½ feet, thickened to 308 feet at the base, and lengthened to 900 feet at its crest. While other great dams of the Progressive Era would soon surpass Hetch Hetchy in size, few water projects would eclipse Hetch Hetchy in complexity or encounter a comparable range of challenges during their construction.

Work on the aqueduct connecting the reservoir to the Spring Valley network on the peninsula was perhaps more difficult than work on the dam. The battle raged at several sites: the nineteen-mile-long Mountain Tunnel, connecting Early Intake to the top of Priest's Grade; the Foothill Tunnel, running about sixteen miles from Moccasin Reservoir to the mouth of the San Joaquin pipelines at Oakdale Portal; the forty-seven-mile-long pipeline spanning the valley from Oakdale to Tesla Portal; the twenty-nine-mile-long Coast Range Tunnel, connecting Tesla to the edge of the bay; and the twenty-five-mile-long underbay pipeline linking the aqueduct to the peninsula storage and distribution system at Crystal Springs Reservoir.

Mountain Tunnel would run at an average depth of 1,000 feet below the surface and range in diameter from 10 feet to a bit over 13 feet, much of it drilled through solid granite. The nightmares in its construction began shortly after work commenced in 1917. Two vertical access shafts first had to be dug down to reach the elevation of the tunnel, one shaft descending 786 feet, the other 646 feet. Excavation of the actual tunnel then began horizontally in opposite directions from each shaft, proceeding simultaneously on multiple faces. But water drained into the deeper shaft from every seam and fissure in the rock. Men in oilskins worked in the airless, damp depth night and day for four years to complete the shaft while giant pumps, lifting up to two thousand gallons of water per minute, strained to keep up with the seepage. Backup generators stood by to ensure the pumps remained in constant operation to protect the lives of workers at the bottom of the shaft. Mountain Tunnel was completed in 1925.

The Coast Range Tunnel posed other complications. The tunnel was composed of two sections connected by a short segment of pipeline: one tunnel section was twenty-five miles long, the longest in the world when completed; the other was three and a half miles long. Construction began in 1927, two years after the scheduled start specified in the O'Shaughnessy master plan, due to funding problems and concerns about the plan's safety and feasibility. Critics feared that gases, groundwater, quicksand, and ground swells would be encountered. Instead they proposed that the aqueduct pump the water over the mountains, as the original Grunsky plan specified, rather than tunneling through them. O'Shaughnessy stood steadfast, concluding as had Freeman that a gravity-flow tunnel for 200 million gallons a day could be safely dug for about the same cost that an aboveground pipeline could be laid to carry 60 million gallons a day; in addition, the tunnel would save the perpetual cost of electricity for pumps required by the pipeline over the mountains. Concern about earthquakes affected both schemes, forcing features in the tunnels to minimize potential damage from tremors. O'Shaughnessy's plan followed the basic route proposed by Freeman in his 1912 report, although O'Shaughnessy moved the tunnel a bit south from the Freeman route to avoid marshy areas thought to contain hydrogen sulfide and methane gas.

Unfortunately, the critics' worst fears came to fruition. As the tunnel cut through Crane Ridge at a depth of 2,500 feet, ground swell constricted the eighteen-foot-in-diameter shaft to an opening three feet in diameter in one day. The massive eighteen-inch-square timbers used to brace the tunnel walls snapped like matchsticks. Several days later the tunnel was so constricted that a worker could barely squeeze through it. To solve the problem, the tunnel was rebored at a larger diameter and three-foot-thick gunite ringlike bands were set inside every few feet. The bands were about a foot in diameter smaller than the new shaft, allowing their concrete to harden as the ground swell constricted the tunnel around them. The tunnel was then lined with concrete several feet thick. The gunite supports have held ever since.

On July 17, 1931, the Coast Range crew tunneling from the Mitchell shaft encountered methane gas. The resulting explosion killed twelve workers. Investigations found no fault. Every safety precaution had been taken since methane gas had been detected first in the Mocho shaft. Electrical sparks had not triggered the blast, nor had the locomotive used to carry debris out of the tunnel, the inquiries concluded. But both Wolf Safety Lamps used to detect dangerous gases in the shaft were broken, and two of the victims were found to have matches and smoking materials in their pockets, in violation of safety rules.

Finance problems persisted, too. Work on the Coast Range Tunnel was suspended on several occasions to conserve funds as the bond market crashed together with the stock market. At times the city simply could not find buyers for the bonds needed to finance the project.

The politics of the project took their toll as well. O'Shaughnessy's irascible personality had rubbed many people raw. He had little tolerance for doling out jobs to family of friends and city officials. And he never curried favor with the board of supervisors, which he often challenged, or the press, whom he could treat curtly. When Mayor Rolph resigned to become governor, his longtime field commander was left politically unprotected. Critics seized the opportunity, pointing to the engineering and funding problems. They forced the Chief from power in 1932 as the city charter was revised—the new charter eliminated the city engineer position and the board of public works, replacing them with the public utilities commission to manage the soon-to-be-completed municipal water system.

The Coast Range Tunnel was finally finished in 1934. In January the last of the tunnel faces were joined when the Mocho shaft linked with the Mitchell shaft. Dignitaries at the "holing through" included the new mayor, SFPUC commissioners, and the new general manager of the SFPUC. But the ceremonial drilling of the final foot was delayed for the arrival of the seventy-year-old Chief, who reached through the holed tunnel first to shake the hand of tunnel foreman Peter Peterson. O'Shaughnessy would die in late October, just days before the first drops of Hetch Hetchy water would reach the peninsula. And Sunny Jim Rolph would die, after several heart attacks, on June 2, 1934, four months before his chief lieutenant.

Gradually, incrementally, the segments came together, connecting the pieces of the project like a giant jigsaw puzzle. As planned, the pipelines linking Spring Valley's East Bay assets to the peninsula came online first, in 1924–25. At the other end of the system, the Moccasin Powerhouse came online in 1925, enabling water to flow from the Hetch Hetchy Reservoir, down the Tuolumne River to the mouth of the Mountain Tunnel at Early Intake, then through the tunnel to the forebay reservoir on Priest's Grade, before jetting down the penstocks to the plant. Discharge was released back into the Tuolumne River until completion of the remaining segments: the Foothill Tunnel was completed, after three years of digging, in 1929; and San Joaquin Pipeline #1 was buried about nine feet beneath the fields and orchards spanning the valley in 1931–32. The welded and riveted pipeline, 56 inches to 78 inches in diameter, could carry 70 million gallons a day. (Pipeline #2 would add another 80 million gallons of capacity in 1953, and #3 would increase capacity another 150 million gallons in 1968.) The agonizing completion of the Coast Range Tunnel in 1934 completed the system, finally enabling Hetch Hetchy water to reach consumers in San Francisco and the Bay Area. Phelan's dream for a public water system had been realized, but the corresponding dream added by others for a public power system had not.

CHAPTER 13

The Raker Act's Ignored Mandate

T urn on a tap in San Francisco, and Hetch Hetchy water flows from it, public water owned and managed by the municipality, from the dam and reservoir that impound it, to the aqueduct that transports it to the Bay Area, to the local distribution system that pipes it to the faucet, just as James Duval Phelan envisioned and as the Raker Act specified. Can the same be said if a San Franciscan flips on an electrical wall switch? No. Should it be the same? Was the Hetch Hetchy project intended to create a public power system in parallel with the municipal water system? Not in Phelan's mind—water was his obsession, and electrical use was only in its infancy when he originated the scheme.

To the extent that the resulting Grunsky plan identified hydropower potential, the electricity was only intended to power the pumps needed to lift Hetch Hetchy water over mountains between the source and the consumer. Grunsky stated, "The power development included in this project has been restricted to that required for lifting the water over Livermore Pass. To develop additional power and bring the same into San Francisco for use, would become practically an independent project." Perhaps some excess power could be generated for limited municipal use, he thought. "There can be more water delivered through the canal system above the power station than required in San Francisco for many years, and by installation of pressure pipes, water power and electrical machinery, the energy represented in the descent of this surplus water can be converted into electricity and sent to San Francisco." But the costs would be too great for such minor municipal use. "There would be required for such delivery an independent pole line and transmission wires. The cost of installation would, owing to the length of the line, 150 miles, and consequent loss of power in transit, be relatively large; and when interest on investment, an allowance for deterioration and operating expenses are all taken into account, this scheme of saving a few dollars on the fuel account for power required in operating the city pumps and for other municipal purposes, does not appear attractive, and has appeared to be an unnecessary addition to the water works system." Clearly the Phelan-Grunsky plan focused on water, with electricity merely as a by-product commodity. The original plans for Hetch Hetchy never envisioned a public power system comparable with the water system.

The Garfield permit and resulting Manson plan shared the same focus, although the potential to generate sufficient electricity to power other municipal needs beyond those of the water system was more clearly defined as electrical usage was growing. In justifying his decision, Secretary Garfield identified several beneficial uses of the hydroelectricity to be generated by the project: "the irrigable land in the Tuolumne and San Joaquin Valleys would be helped out by the use of the excess stored water and by using the electrical power not needed by the City for municipal purposes, to pump subterranean water for irrigation of additional areas"; and, "the City would have a cheap and bountiful supply of electric energy for pumping its water supply and lighting the City and its municipal buildings." Beyond those limited municipal uses, a public power system to provide electricity for the retail consumer was never mentioned.

The Freeman plan enlarged the potential role of hydropower, yet it foresaw that expanded role only in the future and presumably as a means of saving money on the cost of electricity consumed by city services, rather than as a source of public power for residents and businesses. "The city does not propose in the immediate future to build any plant for the development of hydro-electric power," he noted in his report, "but it plans to carefully conserve all reasonable opportunities for power development against the time when it may become expedient for the city to undertake such matters." Consequently, Freeman designed his system around the future addition of three hydroelectric plants, which in total would yield "157,000 mechanical horsepower available 24 hours per day and 365 days in the year," he calculated, while at peak the output could reach 200,000 horsepower; that's equal to a constant current of 117,000 kilowatts, or 1,025 million kilowatt-hours annually. (In fact, the

Hetch Hetchy system today has four hydropower plants that produce an average of 1,900 million kilowatt-hours.) Was the potential
power production Freeman foresaw significant?

In 1913 the San Francisco population topped 425,000 people.
Electrical usage remained relatively minor. Beyond lighting, houses
had few appliances. The municipality needed electrical power primarily for streetcars, with a small amount needed for streetlights and
office lights. The electrical demands of business and industry were
small as well. PG&E dominated the turbulent San Francisco market,
with Great Western Power Company as its nearest rival. Similar to
the struggle for control fought by Spring Valley against other fledgling Bay Area water companies, PG&E wrested control of the
Central Valley and northern California power markets throughout
the late 1800s and early 1900s as it acquired or merged with one
competitor after another. Its monopoly became complete when it
absorbed the San Joaquin Light and Power Company and the Great
Western Power Company in the early 1930s.

In 1918, as the first Hetch Hetchy power became available from
Early Intake, the total amount of electrical power delivered to San
Francisco was about 360 million kilowatt-hours, or roughly one-
third of the potential Hetch Hetchy output Freeman calculated. The
municipal street railway system was by far the biggest consumer
(63.6 percent), followed by general commercial use (21.2 percent),
commercial lighting (9.4 percent), streetlighting (2.2 percent), and
3.5 percent for all other uses. But the amount of excess power from
Early Intake was negligible compared to the total demand in the city.
Not until Moccasin Powerhouse came online in 1925 would Hetch
Hetchy supply a significant amount of electricity. Moccasin alone
could generate a maximum of 460 million kilowatt-hours, enough to
meet city demand at all but peak hours. Thereafter, Hetch Hetchy
could satisfy San Francisco's nascent electricity needs well into the
future if the other proposed power plants were completed in step
with the city's growth.

However, in 1912–13, what should Freeman, city officials,
Congress, and other participants in the Hetch Hetchy debate have
concluded about the amount of potential hydropower? They must
have speculated about the future for electricity and the value of
hydroelectricity versus other sources of power like coal and gas. It's

doubtful they would have anticipated the extraordinary levels of electrical use today—levels that are due to the advent of unforeseen technologies a generation later which led to the proliferation of electrical appliances, air conditioning, and computers. Still, they should have concluded that Hetch Hetchy could be a significant source of electricity, certainly one capable of supplying more than limited municipal needs, and probably one capable of forming the core for a public power system in parallel with the public water system.

In 2003 the San Francisco population neared 760,000 people. Total power demand was 4,924 million kilowatt-hours. Hetch Hetchy hydropower could provide about 35 percent of that demand were it part of a public power system comparable to the public water system.

Yet what was Freeman's priority for the plan? Water. "Power development should be subordinate to domestic water supply at every point," he wrote, "and I have designed the works with this as a fundamental idea." Like Grunsky, Freeman worried about the cost-benefit analysis of hydropower. "At all three sites the cost of [a] power house and that of the hydro-electrical machinery will be exceptionally small and the flow of water uncommonly constant and dependable. On the other hand, the transmission line, although laid mostly over the aqueduct rights of way, would be 150 miles long to San Francisco and 135 miles to Oakland, and cost a large amount of money. Today, with cheap oil fuel and with three large hydro-electric enterprises bringing electrical current to the city and competing actively for business under the oversight of a public service commission, no occasion appears for the municipality to go into the power business." Nor did he believe the city charter would permit it.

Still, the advantage of Hetch Hetchy for hydropower development over other alternative reservoir sites was critical to Freeman. "It is plain," he concluded, "that this valuable asset of about 200,000 mechanical horsepower and presenting with the first installation of the aqueduct and pipes 70,000 horsepower of constant 24-hour mechanical power, an amount greater than is developed today at any one hydraulic power house outside of Niagara, ready for quick and cheap development, should be reckoned into the balance sheet when comparing the Tuolumne source with others that present no such potentiality."

City engineer Michael O'Shaughnessy summarized San Francisco's thinking about Hetch Hetchy hydropower during hearings before Secretary of the Interior Fisher in November 1912, stating in a January 1913 *San Francisco Examiner* article, "One of the questions brought forth by the Secretary's investigation in Washington was to what use the City was going to make of power. A proviso in the proposed permit makes it possible, after the City's requirements of 20,000 or 25,000 horsepower are provided for, that all surplus power above this quantity may be disposed of by the City so as to procure an equitable return on the investment in dams, reservoirs and aqueducts above a point at which the power would be created. This would relieve the City from the expense of going into wholesale power investment, while it would be compensated at the same time for its enterprise in creating the storage dams and making the conduits, while engaged in the development of a domestic water supply." The city saw Hetch Hetchy hydropower primarily as a means of earning income to help defray the cost of the water system, rather than as a source of public power in the same sense it considered the public water system.

Congressional intent differed dramatically. To a Congress caught up in the conservation, public works, and trust-busting milieu of the Progressive Era, the sacrifice of a scenic wonder in a national park could only be justified if the loss of Hetch Hetchy realized multiple public benefits: municipal water to replace the corporate monopoly; municipal power in competition with the corporate suppliers; and recreational opportunities for the public. The resulting Raker Act granted San Francisco the necessary rights for "conveying water for domestic purposes and uses to the city and county of San Francisco and such other municipalities and water districts as, with the consent of the city and county of San Francisco . . . may hereafter participate in the beneficial use . . . ; [and] for the purpose of constructing, operating, and maintaining power and electric plants, poles, and lines for generation and sale and distribution of electric energy."

Yet those rights were contingent on the benefits accrued from them falling only to the public: "That the grantee is prohibited from ever selling or letting to any corporation or individual, except a municipality or a municipal water district or irrigation district, the right to sell or sublet the water or the electric energy sold or given to it or him by the said grantee: *Provided,* That the rights hereby granted shall not be sold, assigned, or transferred to any private person, corporation, or association, and in case of any attempt to so sell, assign, transfer, or convey, this grant shall revert to the Government of the United States."

The will of Congress was crystal clear: *public* water and *public* power. No private person or corporation could ever profit from either resource. Given the history of the Hetch Hetchy proposal, the meaning of "public water" was equally clear. Hetch Hetchy would yield sufficient water to quench the needs of *all* San Franciscans and other Bay Area customers far into the future with water captured, stored, transmitted, distributed, and sold directly to consumers by the municipality at the lowest possible cost. To do so the city would purchase the existing water monopoly to acquire its supply capacity around the peninsula and its local distribution system.

Did Congress interpret "public power" to mean the same? That is, the generation, long-distance transmission, local distribution, and sale of sufficient power directly to consumers to satisfy the demands of *all* municipal and retail customers in the city and perhaps some surrounding communities? If so, how would the city meet a shortfall in supply if one occurred in the future? Did Congress assume that the city would supplement Hetch Hetchy hydropower if needed with electricity purchased from wholesale suppliers or that the city would build additional power plants? Or did Congress envision that the city would eventually supply only a portion of the overall amount of electricity needed, while private companies supplied the rest? And did Congress assume the city would purchase PG&E's existing electric power distribution grid in San Francisco, or build its own grid in competition with the burgeoning monopoly? Given the limited role of hydropower prescribed in the Grunsky plan, the Garfield permit, and the Freeman report, the legislative intent for the public power proviso could have differed from that for public water. But it didn't.

The Raker Act recognized that Hetch Hetchy's hydropower potential would be developed incrementally, requiring the city to bring at least 10,000 horsepower online in three years for either "municipal or commercial use"; at least 20,000 horsepower in ten years; at least 30,000 horsepower in fifteen years; and no less than 60,000 horsepower in twenty years; hydropower, the act stated, "for the use of its [the grantee's] people."

Testimony during congressional hearings on the bill and during the floor debates in the House and Senate shed light on its authors' intent. When California representative John E. Raker, the bill's principal sponsor, was questioned by other representatives during a floor debate on the draft bill, Raker clarified his intent:

> Mr. Sumners: "Does San Francisco own its own lighting plant now?"
>
> Mr. Kahn: "No; it does not."
>
> Mr. Raker: "I understand it does not."
>
> Mr. Kahn: "It does not own its own water supply. Its present water supply is furnished by a private company."
>
> Mr. Raker: "The Spring Valley Water System."
>
> Mr. Sumners: "Is it the purpose of this bill to have San Francisco supply electric power and water to its own people?"
>
> Mr. Raker: "Yes."
>
> Mr. Sumners: "Or to supply these corporations, which will in turn supply the people?"
>
> Mr. Raker: "Under this bill it is to supply its own inhabitants first. It is to supply the public utilities, the courthouse and schoolhouses, the street lights, and such things as that for its own citizens. Next, it is to supply those around the Bay, some ten cities, that may . . . become beneficiaries of this system and pay their proportion."

The same intentions were heard in the Senate debates. "San Francisco needs electric power," stated Senator Thomas, a member of the committee reporting the bill to the full membership, "and California needs development in electric power just as much as she needs ownership in water. . . . She is anxious to extend her spheres of municipal usefulness, but she is in the grip of a power monopoly as well as that of Spring Valley Co." He continued, "This scheme appeals to me, so far as the power is concerned, because the city of San Francisco as a municipality will be the owner of it, the manufacturer, the distributor of it." Representative Bailey concurred, stating colorfully that the intent of the act was to free San Franciscans from the "galling bondage to a merciless taskmaster" and the "thrall-dom . . . [of] a remorseless private monopoly."

Nebraska senator George W. Norris, new to the body but a member of the reporting committee and a leading sponsor of the bill, highlighted the bill's intent to the full chamber on the day of the bill's passage. "I said that I was in favor of this bill to a great extent for the reason that it developed this power," he stated. "This power will come into competition with the various water-power companies of California. . . . [It will] harness that power and put it to public use. . . . Here is an instance where we are going to give it directly to the people. . . . It is going to come into direct competition with power companies and corporations that have, or will have, if this bill is defeated, almost a monopoly not only in San Francisco but throughout the greater portion of California. . . . This bill, if passed, will bring into competition with them one of the greatest units for development of power that has ever been developed in the history of the world. It means competition."

During his thirty-year tenure in the Senate, Norris would become the champion of public power and a leading voice to bring economic progress to America's rural regions. He believed the nation's rivers should be harnessed for flood control, navigation, and hydroelectricity. During the Great Depression in the 1930s, Norris would father two of the most important New Deal programs: the creation of the Tennessee Valley Authority (TVA) in 1933, and the Rural Electrification Act in 1936. Critics like Henry Ford and other industrialists assailed such programs as socialistic and un-American, to which Norris responded, "Every stream in the United States that flows from the mountains through the meadows to the sea has the possibility of producing electricity for cheap power and cheap lighting. This natural resource was given by the all-wise Creator to His people and not to organizations of greed." In honor of Senator Norris, TVA's Norris Dam bears his name, as does the small town of Norris, Tennessee, which was built to house workers during the construction of the dam. His staunch support for the Hetch Hetchy project was an early example of his lifelong fight for Progressive conservation programs.

"Conservation does not mean dealing out these resources to private capital for gain," Senator Norris continued. "It is not necessary to accuse those corporations of doing any wrong; but here will be an instance where the cheapest power on earth will be developed and where it will be sold at cost." Looking to the future, the great liberal summarized, "The people who ride on street cars, the people who use electric lights, the people who are now using gas, those who eventually will use coal for purposes of heat, and those who use water for washing purposes will all receive the benefit there is in this legislation without any rake-off by any corporation or monopoly."

To Congress, Hetch Hetchy was as much about public power as public water. They envisioned the two systems as coequal in extent and importance. Some members even placed greater emphasis on the public power benefits. Senator Smoot proclaimed during the floor debate that "the principal object of this bill is to provide for the creation of power." Perhaps his personal opinion was more focused on public power than most, but it offered insight into the city's political strategy for gaining congressional approval for the project by emphasizing the hydropower potential of Hetch Hetchy over alternate dam-reservoir sites. "It is my opinion," he proclaimed, "that the reason San Francisco wants this particular dam site is for the power she thinks can be developed cheaper than from any other source, and at the same time get a large supply of water." William Kent, an influential California congressman during the debate and a leading proponent of the plan, later recalled, "From the very beginning I urged, as did others who took part in that fight before Congress, that the water-development side of the plan was minor in importance to the hydro-electric aspect."

And Congress presumed San Francisco would either purchase the PG&E electric distribution grid to deliver the public power or develop its own grid, just as it presumed the city would acquire Spring Valley to obtain the monopoly's local water delivery system. In 1925, as the city balked at acquiring an electricity grid when Moccasin Powerhouse was about to come online, Representative Raker recalled that San Francisco had known for years "that as soon as provision was made for the development of power it would be required to provide for [its] distribution." Angered at the city's hesitancy, he retorted, "Distribution systems exist. There is a method of condemnation. I would say, give the men [of PG&E and Great Western Power] who own these systems a fair price, but do not let them hold you up. If they will not sell at a reasonable figure, dig down in your pockets, raise your tax rate if you must, and build your own system."

In 1940, when ruling that the city's agreement with PG&E to distribute and sell Hetch Hetchy power violated the Raker Act, an agreement that had been in place for fifteen years, the U.S. Supreme Court concluded, "Opponents of the bill themselves recognized that its regulatory conditions were designed to insure distribution of power from Hetch Hetchy through a municipal system in San Francisco. Before final passage in the Senate, opposition had practically narrowed down to the power provisions of the measure, and these provisions contemplated a publicly owned and operated power system." In fact, the court noted, immediately before the final vote, an amendment that would have deleted all the provisions related to the generation, sale, and distribution of Hetch Hetchy power offered by opponents of the public power provisions was voted down.

But the city has never acquired its own distribution grid, and it sells virtually no power directly to the public today. Perhaps as Phelan, Grunsky, Garfield, and Freeman intended, Hetch Hetchy hydroelectricity primarily powers San Francisco streetcars, streetlights, municipal buildings, and other municipal functions, in particular San Francisco International Airport. Excess power is sold to the Modesto and Turlock Irrigation Districts and other government agencies. Why has the congressional intent for a true public power system never been achieved? Money, politics, and PG&E.

The Raker Act had little effect on San Francisco's view that the hydropower potential simply serve as a source of electricity for limited municipal uses like streetcars and streetlights, and as a source of income derived from the sale of excess power to defray the cost of the water system. The act's public power proviso apparently meant little to the city officials who represented the city during the negotiations leading to the act. Robert M. Searls, the city's special counsel for the Hetch Hetchy project and a key representative of the city during the legislative process, later stated snidely that "The Raker Act emerged from Congress loaded with a hodgepodge of conditions which had been inserted by every department clerk and every member of the House of Representatives who had some theory of natural resource conservation, protection of irrigation interests, or public ownership, to exploit. . . . [Section 6, which contains the public water and power provisions] was originally drafted to prevent San Francisco from turning the project over to the Spring Valley Water Company. Some Congressmen from Arkansas were afraid that it might be turned over to a power company, and inserted the words—'or electric energy.' That didn't suit some of the others, so they added a forfeiture clause."

Gifford Pinchot saw the mandate differently, believing the Raker Act required that Hetch Hetchy hydropower potential be developed and distributed as part of a public power system. "All parties to the [Hetch Hetchy] grant are under the obligation to see to it that the consuming public receives the full benefit of all the water and power available, at cost, solvently calculated," he wrote. "Congress definitely protected San Francisco against weak-kneed surrender to [private] interests by the clear and definite forfeiture clause of Section Six."

Consequently, as work commenced on the water system after the act's passage and as negotiations resumed for the acquisition of Spring Valley, no corresponding work began on the acquisition or development of a power distribution grid in the city. City engineer O'Shaughnessy might have thought differently, extolling the value of fully developing Hetch Hetchy's hydropower potential and urging the issuance of additional bonds to fund it. He expressed those intentions in a series of articles on which he cooperated published by the *San Francisco Examiner* in 1918, "City Engineer O'Shaughnessy tells of enormous work being done, but the City needs millions to bring it to completion. Power to run all street cars, operate factories, light streets and homes, drive riveters in ship plants to be harnessed. Power sufficient to drive all the wheels of industry in San Francisco—this is the amount of 'juice' that is running to waste through the Hetch Hetchy Valley. That explains why municipal officials and particularly City Engineer O'Shaughnessy are so desirous of selling sufficient Hetch Hetchy bonds to complete that part of the construction that will make this force available."

The articles proclaimed the cost-effectiveness of the public power system in Seattle and the value of Los Angeles's hydropower production. The message was clear: San Francisco should construct a power system that would supply all municipal, industrial, commercial, institutional, and residential needs, and to do so additional funding beyond the $45 million in Hetch Hetchy bonds was needed to develop it. If the economics favored acquisition of PG&E's distribution grid or construction of a separate, competitive municipal grid, so be it; if the economics didn't favor it, the city could contract with PG&E to distribute the power. O'Shaughnessy focused first on the profit potential for the municipality, then on the cost savings to industry, and only last on the direct benefits to the public. A pragmatic engineer, he would consider wasting Hetch Hetchy's energy potential the greatest evil.

City hall had other priorities. Preparation for the advent of public power was limited to work on Early Intake. And as planned, when the small powerhouse came online in 1918, its modest electrical output supplied the construction needs of the project. The California Power Administration, at the behest of H. G. Butler, the federal power administrator, ordered the small amount of excess power to be sold to the Sierra and San Francisco Power Company and PG&E, its lessee at the time, because of power shortages associated with the World War I economy. The companies bought the energy at a flat rate of one-half cent per kilowatt-hour, and then PG&E resold the power at much higher retail rates to consumers on its Tuolumne circuit. After the war the practice continued without challenge, even though the sale of Hetch Hetchy power to a private company was expressly prohibited by the Raker Act.

That was what the city really intended all along: to use Hetch Hetchy power for some municipal needs, sell the remainder to earn as much income as possible, and use that profit to subsidize the municipal budget. That was the city's definition of public power. Wasn't that a valid public purpose?

Yet if Hetch Hetchy could generate sufficient hydroelectricity to supply San Francisco's entire municipal and retail demand, at least for the foreseeable future, and so serve as the basis for a true public power system, why would the city not actively pursue that possibility, as it did a public water system? For the same reason the city would transfer a billion dollars' worth of "surplus" HHWP hydropower revenues to the general municipal fund from 1979 to 2000: money.

If San Francisco sold all Hetch Hetchy power through a public utility, the city would not make any profit, since the electricity would be sold at cost to consumers. Cheaper power might be a good deal for the public and businesses, but it could cost the city coffers, forcing city hall to find other sources of revenue, depending on how the city would use the hydropower profit. Economic theory and practical experience suggest that the local economy would benefit in the long term, although in the short term tax increases needed to replace the "lost" revenues might partially offset savings in monthly electric bills. And public power would put PG&E out of business in the Bay Area. In short, the complicated cost-benefit trade-offs between public power and the city's plan gave those with vested economic and political self-interests ample basis to plead their case in the guise of promoting the public interest.

As work subsequently began on the Mountain Tunnel and the Moccasin Powerhouse, which would yield significantly more power than Early Intake, questions about the disposal of hydroelectricity became more charged. Final decisions had to be made. How would San Francisco distribute the power? Would it purchase the PG&E grid or build its own? Was it serious about public power, as the Raker Act implied, or had the city simply acquiesced to the provisions as a political ploy to win approval of the water system?

San Francisco's position remained unchanged. In 1920 City engineer O'Shaughnessy reported, "Sound economic reasoning dictates that the Mountain or power generating division of the project be completed first, in order that the burden upon San Francisco's taxpayers of paying interest during construction may be reduced through receipts from power sales at the earliest possible moment." Mayor Rolph concurred, writing the same year in a printed statement issued to voters advocating the purchase of Spring Valley, "The city has gone ahead in good faith with the construction of the Mountain Division of the Hetch Hetchy project. It is expected it will be completed within three years. It will yield upwards of 66,000 electric horsepower, sufficient to pay interest and take care of all fixed operating and maintenance charges on that part of the project." Hetch Hetchy power was primarily intended to generate profit for the city to pay for the water bonds, not to create a public power system.

By the early 1920s questions regarding the fate of Hetch Hetchy power intensified as the project drew deeper and deeper into the original $45 million funding. Disagreements persisted over the purpose of the hydropower and the restrictions placed on it by Congress; some factions pushed for public power, others for limited municipal use and the sale of excess to private electric companies for profit. The press, the public, PG&E, city officials, and federal officials continued to perceive Hetch Hetchy power differently, while public and political support for the use of the original bonds to pay for development of hydropower components paled in comparison to the use of the funds for work on the water system. Water first, they felt; then power for municipal needs and profit. Voters had never given a clear mandate for public power, even though city hall had accepted the conditions imposed by the Raker Act.

And always behind the scenes PG&E lobbied to maintain its monopoly. From its viewpoint the city should develop as much Hetch Hetchy hydropower as possible *provided* the company retained control of its distribution. That way PG&E could profit from the power without having the expense of developing it—maximum return on minimum investment and risk, the perfect business plan. Despite the public power mandate in the Raker Act, perhaps everyone could benefit from a cozy arrangement with PG&E. The company would profit from the "wheeling" fee it would receive to transmit Hetch Hetchy power over its existing grid, while it could protect its monopoly. The city would profit from the sale of power to PG&E, save money on the power used by municipal functions, and avoid spending money to buy or build its own distribution grid. And the general public would benefit from lower taxes. After all, the cost for the city to acquire PG&E's grid and all the necessary auxiliary facilities, or to build its own system, could well equal the original cost for the entire water system. To cut costs somewhat, the city could build its own transmission line directly to municipal users and rely on PG&E to distribute the remainder of the power, leaving the sweetheart deal with PG&E largely intact; but this was hardly what Congress intended.

The expense of constructing a public power system was never a part of the original Phelan plan or the plan approved by the Garfield permit. It wasn't included in the water system San Franciscans overwhelmingly endorsed in 1910 together with the $45 million needed to build it. Nor were PG&E and Great Western corporate villains to nearly the extent that Spring Valley was; besides, the state railroad commission set electricity rates. And regardless of PG&E's political meddling, few voters understood the potential economic and service benefits of public power, which were very hard to calculate at the time. No wonder so many people balked at public power. Congress didn't have to pay for it, and it was easy for them to require it.

Yet San Francisco had formally accepted the terms of the Raker Act and knew the law's public power implications. In fact, the city played the hydropower potential of Hetch Hetchy as its trump card during the congressional debate. The legislative "contract" between the American people and San Francisco that sacrificed a rare part of a national park for the public good of the Bay Area was predicated on public water and public power. How could the city unilaterally abrogate that agreement? How has the broken promise persisted ever since?

CHAPTER 14

PG&E and the Politics of Public Power

July 1, 1925, was a day of eclipse for San Francisco; subtle, yet in hindsight nearly as earthshaking as April 18, 1906. An agreement signed that day between the city and PG&E cast the fate of Hetch Hetchy hydroelectricity, scuttling the promise of public power. The city has suffered the consequences ever since, perhaps costing electricity consumers a billion dollars or more in higher rates and years of poorer service. No smoking gun makes the case for the damage done by the agreement; it rarely does in such matters, but the circumstantial evidence is compelling, regardless of one's attitudes toward politics and corporate influence peddling.

However, the most insidious result might be the way the outcome has perpetuated the disease of governance based on economic self-interest and political expediency, gradually undermining public trust and a sense of civic responsibility, breeding apathy, and fostering a feeling of futility. Idealism and civic vision suffered in this sacrifice of municipal innocence. James Duval Phelan waged his crusade in the early 1900s to cleanse city hall of that debilitating disease of the public spirit. Other Progressive reformers carried the cause to cities all across America.

Bruce Brugmann has been telling the Bay Area this story for decades in articles in the *San Francisco Bay Guardian,* the independent weekly newspaper he publishes. The free paper looks like a magazine-format tabloid targeted to the Bay Area counterculture, with articles and ads tailored to the young, liberal wings of the political and social spectrums. The paper thrives catering to readers and covering issues largely overlooked by the dailies. It is not the sort of source one would usually rely on for probing investigative journalism into important issues. Yet in this case the activist-oriented *Bay Guardian* has scooped the more prominent, staid, and politically correct competitors for more than thirty years. "The greatest scandal in American urban history," Brugmann calls the story. Most Californians haven't listened to him, being quick to dismiss his message because of the brash tone and the alternative method of delivery. But they should listen.

Bruce Brugmann is a bear of a man, looming well over six feet tall with a massive frame and a full silver-white beard. When he recounts the history of the *Guardian*'s coverage of the public power story his restrained demeanor and quiet voice belie an underlying sense of anger, defiance, and indignation. "I'm for public power, and I'll tell you why. I come from a little town in Iowa called Rock Rapids, population 2,800, full of conservative German farmers and Republicans of the most conservative stripe. They've had public power for years and they love it. In the 1950s I could see that the town prospered more than nearby towns served by private power companies. One summer I worked for a Rural Electrification Administration crew and realized how much rural farmers benefited from electrification brought by FDR's programs. Private industry would not have provided it."

Brugmann then attended the University of Nebraska and gravitated toward the liberal, Progressive philosophy of George Norris. He began his journalism career at the *Lincoln Journal Star,* where his editor ghost-authored Norris's autobiography and the paper covered public power as a regular beat. Nebraska, Brugmann continues, "also has reliable, cheap, public power brought to you by the city or brought to you by the state." After a stint in the army working for *Stars and Stripes* and another with the *Milwaukee Journal Sentinel,* he migrated west to California in 1964 with the hope of starting a paper; the *Bay Guardian* was born in 1966.

"I went along fighting against the war in Vietnam and the normal causes of the time," he recounts, "when I received a message from Joe Neilands, a biochemistry professor at the University of California–Berkeley who was leading the successful campaign against PG&E's proposed Bodega Bay nuclear power plant just upwind from San Francisco. He told me there was a big scandal here involving the Raker Act and that he'd like to write a story about it for the *Guardian.*"

Professor Neilands learned of the scandal from Franck Havenner. Neilands recalled, "A few months before he died [in 1967], Franck Havenner sat up in his bed in a nursing home in San Francisco and told me of how the Pacific Gas & Electric Co. swindled San Francisco out of hundreds of millions of dollars of cheap hydroelectric power." Havenner would know; he served on the San Francisco Board of Supervisors from 1926 to 1936 and in the U.S. Congress from 1937 to 1941 and 1945 to 1953, with a stint on the California State Railroad Commission (now the California Public Utilities Commission) from 1941 to 1944 in between. He saw the scandal develop from several sides.

"The story was incredible," Neilands said. "PG&E and its political allies had defeated eight successive bond issues to establish a municipal electrical system in San Francisco and grant city residents and businesses the benefit of low-cost power produced by the city's Hetch Hetchy water system in the Sierras." As a result, Neilands later wrote, San Franciscans for decades had been paying PG&E through the nose for power, losing "about $30 million a year in profits [the city] would get from a public system." Havenner told his shocked confidant how in the beginning the Progressive advocates of public power had the support of some newspapers, "but in the end PG&E was able to buy them [the papers] all out with their newspaper ads." Neilands carefully researched Havenner's claims. The *Guardian* published the resulting exposé on March 27, 1969. The story found a kindred spirit and an enthusiastic advocate in Bruce Brugmann.

"So 1969 marked the start of the paper's campaign to bring public power to San Francisco and enforce the Raker Act," Brugmann states. "It's the greatest scandal in American history involving a city, in terms of money, tenure, and corruption at city hall. And that's why San Francisco is in such a mess. Power is an essential service and as such its provision should not be entrusted to the private sector. Just look at what recently happened in California with deregulation. You can't let market forces play with essential services." The dangers have been known from the outset. In 1905 *Arena* magazine summarized a series of scathing articles and editorials on the behavior of privately owned utilities, saying, "No influence in political, business or general life has proved so corrupting to government, so demoralizing to the press and other public opinion-forming organs, or so vicious in lowering the moral ideals and integrity of the people as private companies operating public utilities."

"Sacramento has a municipal utility district, Los Angeles has a public power authority, and thirty-three or so other cities throughout the state have public power," Brugmann said. "We went into the Yosemite National Park, dammed the beautiful Hetch Hetchy Valley, and drove John Muir off the cliff; we brought the water into San Francisco, but we never got the public power, even though we're the only city in the U.S. mandated to have public power because of the Raker Act. That was a condition of the grant, later upheld by the U.S. Supreme Court. Hetch Hetchy was supposed to be the Magna Carta of public power and public water. Why didn't we get the public power—our own Hetch Hetchy power that we paid hundreds of millions of dollars for by building dams, powerhouses, pipelines, and tunnels to provide it? The political power of PG&E, that's why.

"This is a political problem and a journalistic problem. You never read about this story in the old *San Francisco Examiner,* the old *San Francisco Chronicle,* or the new *Chronicle.* And since the local papers don't cover the story, it doesn't make the newswire or come to the attention of national papers like the *New York Times.*

"The local media has blacked out the story ever since William Randolph Hearst needed to get a batch of money from Herbert Fleishhacker, who ran the bank that handled much of PG&E's financing and was a board member of the transit and power trusts [Herbert's brother Mortimer was president of Great Western Power Company]. In the early days, when the *Chronicle* was already a staunch supporter of PG&E, William Randolph Hearst's *Call* and *Examiner* were strong proponents of municipal power, running big front-page stories rooted in populist, anti–big business belief. But by the mid-1920s, all Hearst's papers were promoting a position much friendlier to PG&E. Hearst would no longer stand in the way of a privatized water and electricity system.

"Franck Havenner thought that Hearst was paid off by PG&E after the utility started buying full-page ads in Hearst's papers. But there may be another reason why Hearst abandoned the Raker Act mandate. In the mid-1920s, overleveraged and desperate that no bank would lend him funds to keep his growing and nationwide empire afloat, Hearst turned to Herbert Fleishhacker, president of the London and Paris National Bank in San Francisco. Fleishhacker was one of the leading advocates in the push to privatize the city's water and electricity systems. Soon thereafter, Hearst was instructing his ranks to maintain 'pleasant relations' with Mr. Fleishhacker and to refrain from criticizing his enterprises.

"Part of the condition of the loan was that Hearst changes his position on Hetch Hetchy. His papers have been friendly to PG&E ever since. The Hearst media empire and the new *Chronicle* still maintain this position: no coverage of the Raker Act. It's an incredible media scandal that the local monopoly paper doesn't cover this issue. Monopoly supports monopoly here in San Francisco, and throughout the state. A big reason that we have public power in Sacramento is because of the McClatchy family, who own the *Sacramento Bee,* among other papers, and they've long been champions of public power.

"What are we to do about it? Public power has been taken off the agenda in California for decades. Labor took it off, coopted by big business. The newspapers took it off because they get a lot of advertising from PG&E. Culburt Olson was the last governor [1939–43] who advocated public power. The reason for this is that if you're a politician and you go against PG&E, they make sure you're not a politician for very long. We've watched this here in San Francisco. Politicians get elected, get to city hall, and then PG&E rolls them over and the scandal continues. When PG&E spits, city hall swims."

Colorful. Opinionated. Passionate. One senses that Bruce Brugmann needs this crusade against the great corporate-political-press combine in part because of a Don Quixote–like personality. It's who he is and how he has shaped his paper. And city hall knows Bruce Brugmann well, as do the political reporters and editors around the region; he's been in their faces for years. The crusade wears comfortably on him, like a well-worn overcoat. Yet even his critics know he serves a very important public role. Perhaps he overstates the collusion, but much of what he says rings true. His alternative paper is making a difference. Public power is once again becoming an issue in the Bay Area, attracting the attention of city hall, voters, and the daily papers. San Francisco at long last may be moving toward some form of a municipal utility district, finally undoing the decision of 1925 and the subsequent events that perpetuated it.

Several events in 1923 conspired to trigger that decision. First, fearful that the city would have no means to distribute Moccasin electricity when it came online—thus wasting the potential power and profit—the board of supervisors passed a resolution in July recommending that San Francisco either build its own distribution system or purchase an existing grid. A complementary resolution instructed the city engineer to develop cost estimates for both possibilities. Michael O'Shaughnessy's position covered the gamut; at times he asserted his commitment to public power, and at other times advocated the sale of power to the private utilities on the grounds that a city-owned system could not be completed until well after Moccasin was operational. Various cost estimates for the city to construct either a complete system or a partial system, and the revenues the city could expect from each, were bandied about by O'Shaughnessy and others, and squabbling continued over the legality of using existing bond monies for power purposes.

In an effort to settle some of the issues, Mayor Rolph empowered an advisory committee, including a former chief justice of the California Supreme Court, former mayor James Duval Phelan, and several other men of impeccable integrity. In October the committee unanimously declared that the Raker Act prohibited the city from selling Hetch Hetchy power to a private company and called upon the board of supervisors to pursue the purchase of an existing distribution system with the assistance of the state railroad commission. The board concurred and promptly charged the advisory committee to begin immediate negotiations with PG&E and Great Western.

It didn't take long for the negotiations to break down, so the advisory committee recommended the city initiate eminent domain proceedings against the companies. The issues featured prominently in the pending municipal elections in November. The board quickly passed a resolution directing the railroad commission to determine a fair purchase price, and committed itself to placing a bond issue before the voters to finance the acquisitions as soon as a price could be set following the pending election. However, two weeks after the election, the board inexplicably postponed the railroad commission's valuation. Accusations of political meddling by the power companies ran rampant. (The commission's valuation report was completed in 1929, but by then the city's plan to use eminent domain to purchase the power companies' assets in San Francisco had been dropped.)

Concurrent with these efforts, city hall adopted the strategy of funding the water and power components of the Hetch Hetchy project separately, even though separate bonds for power projects would be much less likely to win voter approval. Complete as much of the water system as possible with the original bond money, proponents thought, and let the final components of the power system, especially the long-distance transmission and local distribution lines, be funded separately and/or be subcontracted to PG&E. Presumably, city hall knew the implications of this approach: voters would likely approve the funding to finish the water system; how could they not? But they probably would not approve separate bonds for the power system, forcing the city into a cooperative agreement with PG&E. The board of supervisors authorized the city engineer to see how much PG&E would pay for the Moccasin output. O'Shaughnessy and the PG&E president agreed on an annual $2 million fee based on the former's desire that the fee cover the city's 5 percent interest payment on the $40 million in Hetch Hetchy bonds used so far. The $2 million annual fee also meant that PG&E would pay a half cent per kilowatt for the 400 million kilowatts O'Shaughnessy estimated the plant would generate.

Swirling about San Francisco's deliberations on how to dispose of the Moccasin hydropower were another set of negotiations between the monopoly and the Modesto and Turlock Irrigation Districts over disposal of hydropower about to come online from their new power plant at Don Pedro Reservoir. The districts' water and power needs had loomed just behind those of San Francisco since the Freeman plan enlarged the scope of the Hetch Hetchy project. Provision for the districts' water rights had figured prominently in the Raker Act, although the city had always fought to assert its wants and wishes over those of the districts.

Modesto and Turlock had long eyed the deep, narrow gorge on the Tuolumne River just downstream from Don Pedro Bar, along with the two canyons that branched out above, as a perfect dam and reservoir site to satisfy their storage need for irrigation water. The impoundment several miles below Moccasin Creek would inundate Don Pedro Bar, Red Mountain Bar, and Six Bit Gulch, once three of the richest placer mining areas in the world. But the gold had been harvested, leaving the landscape idle and the little mining towns nearby lifeless and abandoned. The districts moved ahead with plans for a dam and reservoir at Don Pedro in the 1910s based on their original water rights. However, they filed new rights specifically for the storage project when confronted with opposition from the California State Water Commission, prompted by San Francisco, which had been placed by the Raker Act in a position to potentially threaten the districts' water rights on the upper Tuolumne River, rights that had to be put to beneficial use or they could be forfeited. Turlock led the way, with Modesto finally joining the project in 1918. And as was the case for San Francisco and Hetch Hetchy, while the water part of the Don Pedro project was always clear to the districts, the power part was not.

In the 1910s demand for electricity in the districts came mostly from the needs of irrigation pumps and other agricultural uses. Few rural households were wired, and the small towns generated little retail demand. Electricity remained a luxury for most, not yet a necessity. And state law did not grant the districts the specific authority to generate hydropower for any uses other than those related to irrigation. However, a power plant that could generate far more electricity than those needs currently required could easily be developed at Don Pedro—power that could either be sold wholesale for profit, as San Francisco intended to do with its Hetch Hetchy power, or electricity that could be used as the cornerstone of a public power system to benefit local residents and businesses. This was, of course, the same debate being argued in San Francisco. But the districts, like many jurisdictions throughout the nation, would come to a different conclusion than the city. In 1919 the districts agreed to proceed with construction of the dam and reservoir, and the powerhouse, three days before the state law that enabled irrigation districts to develop power for nonagricultural uses took effect, over San Francisco's objection.

Work on the project commenced immediately. The 1,040-foot-long and 283-foot-high solid concrete gravity dam, the highest gravity dam in the world, would impound a 14-mile-long reservoir capable of holding more than 285,000 acre feet of water for irrigation and hydropower, with the products split between the districts based on their amount of acreage. Turlock, with 176,210 acres, would receive

68.46 percent of the output. Modesto, with 81,183 acres, would receive 31.54 percent. The official dedication was held in 1923, two years to the day since the official start and just two weeks after the reservoir had reached full pool. The stunning accomplishment triggered the same problem for Modesto that San Francisco confronted with its completion of Moccasin: what to do with the hydropower?

For those past two years Modesto had acrimoniously debated how to dispose of the pending hydropower, although the decision to include a powerhouse in the Don Pedro project had been made in 1919. (Turlock had taken the plunge into public power from the outset.) PG&E and its subsidiaries supplied power to the region and looked with hostility upon the possible competition from the districts. The monopoly fought vigorously to retain its dominance during negotiations with the districts over their long-term power supply and transmission needs, which had to interconnect with PG&E's regional grid. Despite the company's obstinacy, members of the Modesto district overwhelmingly supported public power, and they approved the necessary funding to construct Modesto's own distribution system. The districts began delivering power generated at Don Pedro to the public on May 20, 1923.

Over the coming years, Modesto and Turlock incrementally expanded their systems in competition with PG&E. Both public power systems proved to be more successful than originally envisioned, delivering significantly cheaper power and developing a customer base faster than did the private monopoly. Turlock purchased the company's assets in the district in 1931, having previously acquired the assets of the other private electricity provider. But the monopoly competed tenaciously in the Modesto district. This competition lasted a decade. Defeated, and no longer profitable because of its dwindling Modesto client base, PG&E finally sold its assets to the district in 1940, agreeing to provide wholesale supplemental power to Modesto as needed in the future. Twenty years of competition and litigation between the company and the district over the provision of power to retail consumers came to an end, concurrent with the Supreme Court ruling that San Francisco's power distribution agreement with PG&E was illegal. (That decision would again conjoin the city, the company, and the districts in the 1940s, when the city would seek an alternate market for its excess power in place of

PG&E and further cement the increasingly cooperative relationship between the parties begun in the mid-1930s.)

Meanwhile, in 1923, when administrators at the National Park Service heard of a possible deal between PG&E and the City of San Francisco, they wrote a letter to the secretary of the interior asking for an opinion about whether the Raker Act permitted the city to sell power to a private power company. In June the solicitor for the department responded: "I have indicated that in my opinion the law prohibits the sale of electric energy by the grantee for resale. The method of enforcing the Act is plainly stated." The Raker Act declares "That the grantee shall at all times comply with and observe on its part all the conditions specified in this Act, and in the event that the same are not reasonably complied with and carried out by the grantee, upon written request of the Secretary of the Interior, it is the duty of the Attorney General in the name of the United States to commence all necessary suits or proceedings . . . for the purpose of enforcing and carrying out the provisions of this Act."

Despite the legal grounds for federal intervention, the department's solicitor sought to avoid it. "I may add, however, that I would not recommend [that we] resort to that extremity at this time, but would make known to the grantee the views of this Department in the matter with a suggestion that an arrangement be made for the distribution of the surplus electric energy by a method which would not conflict with the law. . . . Instead of selling this power for resale and distribution, as has been done and further proposed, it occurs to me that it would be feasible for the parties to agree upon terms by which the grantee would have its power transmitted over the lines of the concern owning or controlling the existing distribution system." The solicitor must have been clairvoyant.

In early 1925, the original $45 million bond was nearly spent and Moccasin neared final completion, with power due to come online around June 1. Yet the electric transmission line needed to carry that current to San Francisco had not been completed, nor had a distribution grid in the city been acquired or constructed. The ninety-nine-mile-long Hetch Hetchy transmission line terminated about forty miles from the city—coincidentally only a few hundred yards from the PG&E Newark substation on the eastern shore of San Francisco Bay, where a new transbay high-voltage cable and transmission line from the substation to San Francisco had just been brought into service. The city claimed it had simply run out of funds to finish its own transmission line. The copper wire the city had purchased and stored in a warehouse to be used for the line was quietly sold for scrap several years later. Fortunately, the city line could connect into PG&E's regional grid at the Newark substation and the power could be transmitted over the company's lines virtually anywhere.

In April, desperate to make some use of Moccasin power, the board of supervisors instructed the mayor and the chairman of the finance and public utilities committee to negotiate a contract with PG&E to purchase or distribute the power until such time as the city could make permanent arrangements. The city's asking price for the power was $2 million per year, although at the prevailing rates PG&E could resell the power to municipal customers at more than four times that amount. (Had the city been able to distribute the power and receive its market value at the time, the net revenues could have been sufficient to finance the purchase of the entire PG&E grid in a relatively short time frame, after which the public's price for power could have been cut significantly.) The negotiations were hardly that; PG&E knew the city was in no position to dictate terms; time was running out. The deal was struck on July 1:

Whereas, the City has now completed the construction of the Moccasin power plant . . . , and has also completed the building of a transmission line to the vicinity of Newark in Alameda County . . . ; and

Whereas, the City has not yet constructed or acquired a transmission line from the point near Newark to the City limits, and has not yet constructed or acquired a distribution system for utilizing the power produced at Moccasin plant and delivering the same for general municipal uses and for sale to consumers of electric energy within the limits of the City and County; and

Whereas, pursuant to resolutions of its Board of Supervisors looking to the acquisition of a municipal owned electric distribution system, the City has commenced and there is now pending before the Railroad Commission of the State of California, proceedings for the determination by the Commission of the compensation to be paid by the City for the local distribution systems and certain steam plants now owned and operated by the Pacific Gas and Electric Company and the Great Western Power Company of California, respectively, when the same shall be taken over by the City under eminent domain proceedings, or otherwise;

Whereas, the City has not the funds available at the present time with which to purchase or construct a distribution system of its own and it will be necessary to submit a proposition to the people to vote bonds to provide money for that purpose, before a distribution system can be purchased or constructed, and the City cannot well determine whether to purchase one or both of the local distribution systems, or to construct a distribution system of its own until the Railroad Commission determines the amount of compensation to be paid by the City for the taking of either or both of said local distribution systems under the proceedings now pending before the Commission; and

Whereas, the City intends to complete its power transmission line from Newark to San Francisco and to acquire or construct a distribution system of its own; and

Whereas, the said Moccasin Power Plant is now in condition to operate at its full capacity of 70,000 kilowatts and unless some temporary arrangement is made between the City and County for the distribution to consumers of the electric energy which can be purchased at said plant during the period that must elapse before the City can acquire, own and operate a distribution system of its own, there will be a great waste of said potential energy and a great loss of potential revenue to the City and its taxpayers.

The contract was just what PG&E wanted. The company retained control of Hetch Hetchy power bought at a fixed wholesale rate from the city and resold it to the city at a flexible retail rate that could float with market fluctuations as permitted by the railroad commission. The city received $2 million per year in nontax-generated municipal revenues (while continuing to pay over $8 million annually in tax dollars for power used by city services). That was better than allowing the power to go to waste, but it was a far cry from the Raker Act's idea of "public power." And the contract continued the practice of selling Hetch Hetchy power to a private company that had started with the sale of excess electricity from Early Intake. The latter had been initially a special exception due to the world war; but the exigent circumstances were now the result of municipal negligence or malfeasance, not a war.

The public was not pleased. At the next election, they voted those supervisors who approved the contract and were running for reelection out of office. Yet local politics and public opinion toward public power were complicated. In 1924, voters had approved $10 million for additional work on the Hetch Hetchy water system and knew in the near future they'd again be asked to approve a major bond (of some $40 million) to purchase Spring Valley. By 1927 they feared the added expense of additional bonds for the power system, often confusing the tax implications of general obligation bonds with revenue bonds, which would be paid for by utility receipts. Public power and public water sounded wonderful in principle, but what was the cost to the taxpayer? City hall kept upping the ante in a seemingly endless series of bond requests. Meanwhile, few people agreed on the legal issues or the costs and benefits: not the factions in city hall, or the press, or the private companies, or the other government agencies, or the public.

Of course, PG&E exploited the confusion, using its influence in city hall and the press to promote its opposition to public power. The company also successfully marketed stock in the Bay Area, and then sent flyers to its 20,000 shareholders which decried public power due to the likely loss of corporate profits and the resulting decline in stock price. In November 1927 voters were asked to approve a $2 million bond to fund completion of a city transmission line from Newark into San Francisco, which would lessen the city's dependence on PG&E and be a necessary precursor to the creation of a public power distribution system. The company campaigned aggressively against the proposal, spending heavily for ads that misled voters into believing Congress could easily be convinced to remove the public power proviso in the Raker Act. San Franciscans failed to give the required two-thirds majority for the bond, with a vote of 52,216 for and 50,727 against. The following May, voters approved another $24 million in Hetch Hetchy water bonds and $41 million to finally purchase Spring Valley, ending the decades-long struggle to acquire the water monopoly.

Perhaps with that success, the public and politicians felt the promise of Hetch Hetchy had been realized, which further dampened interest in public power. In November 1928 voters rejected a general charter amendment for the issuance of revenue bonds to fund the acquisition, construction, or extension of a public (electric) utility; in August 1930, they voted down $44.6 million in bonds to acquire PG&E, $18.9 million to acquire Great Western, $3.5 million to build the transmission line from Newark to San Francisco, and $1 million to build a powerhouse at Red Mountain Bar. While voters would repeatedly approve bonds for the water system over the following decades, they would repeatedly reject bonds for the power system: in 1933 they rejected a $6.3 million bond for the Red Mountain Bar power plant; in 1935 they again rejected a general charter amendment for the issuance of revenue bonds to fund the acquisition, construction, or extension of a public (electric) utility; in 1937 they rejected a $50 million bond to acquire PG&E's local assets plus the construction of the Red Mountain Bar powerhouse; in 1939 they rejected a $55 million bond for the same purpose; and in 1941 they rejected a $66.5 million bond for the same again. Not until 1955 did they approve funds for a power purpose—$54 million to build two of the powerhouses originally proposed by Freeman. But they would never approve funds to acquire a local distribution grid.

On October 28, 1934, Harold L. Ickes, the new secretary of the interior, toasted the arrival of Hetch Hetchy water at the official ceremony near the Crystal Springs Reservoir. The celebration had been postponed due to conflicts in his schedule. Michael O'Shaughnessy had died during the delay. Eighty-nine workers had been killed while working on the project. The ceremony was aired on the radio coast to coast over the Columbia Broadcasting System. Ickes later wrote, "San Francisco also develops power from this water. . . . Unfortunately, private utilities have such a grip on San Francisco that it cannot actually sell its own power to users in San Francisco. I held there was a violation of the [Raker] Act. . . . The newspapers and most of the politicians have seen to it, by propaganda and other devious methods, that a method of complying with the Act has been defeated."

Senator George Norris recalled the situation in his autobiography, "Among other assignments which fell to me when I entered the

United States Senate in 1913 was one to the Public Lands Committee.

"It had before it the bitterly controversial issue of developing the water and power resources of the Hetch Hetchy watershed for the benefit of the people of the city and county of San Francisco.

"There could be, in my judgment, no better example of the slow and painful processes through which the American people ultimately in their wisdom may come into the full benefits of some of the great natural wealth which belongs to them.

"Now, thirty years later—three full decades—the powerfully intrenched private interest which prevented San Franciscans from enjoying what belongs to them still thwart the express will of the American Congress, the clear-cut mandates of the federal courts, and the Department of the Interior, under both conservative and liberal administrations. Strangely, these forces flaunt their defiance seemingly with the approval and support of the government of the city of San Francisco, and indirectly its people, for whom the projected was undertaken and to whom Congress granted rights with certain sound limitations."

The villain was as clear then to Senator Norris as it is now to Bruce Brugmann. "I underestimated the resourcefulness of the Pacific Gas and Electric Company," continued the Senator. "When I spoke so hopefully and so confidently (not only I but many others) it was incredible that a great utility could control the policies of city government in San Francisco, with all of the resources at its command could battle through the courts to defeat—only to stave off that defeat by delaying rear-guard actions, and then reappear in the halls of Congress itself to renew the fight, and at all times and under all circumstances continue to defeat the original purpose and spirit of Hetch Hetchy. But, it has done all this."

San Francisco's contract with PG&E and the company's political meddling outraged Harold Ickes, who led a campaign throughout his thirteen-year tenure as the secretary of the interior (1933–46) to remedy the travesties by trying to enforce the public power provisos in the Raker Act. His inability to do so defies reason. Irascible, at times tactless, and a stickler for details, his fastidious management style and constant crusade against corruption earned him the nickname "Honest Harold." Ickes seemed the perfect person to lead the fight to enforce the Raker Act.

A Republican lawyer from Chicago, he had fought the endemic corruption there for three decades with leading political and social reformers including Jane Addams, who was a close personal friend. Ickes was a staunch, lifelong Progressive and conservationist. He campaigned for Theodore Roosevelt's unsuccessful Bull Moose Progressive Republican Party in 1912, and for successive Progressive presidential candidates. However, by 1932 he no longer agreed with the policies of President Herbert Hoover (1929–33) and headed a committee of liberal Republicans who switched their support to the New Deal platform of Franklin D. Roosevelt (1933–45). In return, FDR appointed Ickes to be the secretary of the interior.

Secretary Ickes sought to redefine the department into the "Department of Conservation" by merging it with the U.S. Forest Service and other land management agencies, but failed, only able to add what would become the U.S. Fish and Wildlife Service to the department. Yet under his leadership the National Park System flourished, expanding in size from 8.2 million acres to more than 20 million acres. He advocated the establishment of a national wilderness system and national seashore program, both of which would occur after his tenure, and supported the multipurpose dam-building conservation programs conducted by the Bureau of Reclamation.

His leadership of the Public Works Administration from 1933 to 1939 marked his greatest accomplishment while secretary. The enormous $3.3 billion New Deal construction program built public buildings, bridges, dams, and housing developments, and made loans to states and municipalities for similar plans. Among the thousands of projects were the Triborough Bridge and the Lincoln Tunnel in New York City, the Grand Coulee Dam in Washington State, and the Key West Highway in Florida.

How could San Francisco dodge its legal obligations with Ickes on the case? He would wrestle with San Francisco to compel the city into compliance throughout his tenure, most of the time with Mayor Angelo J. Rossi (1931–44). But Rossi and San Francisco escaped every move Ickes made by craftily stalling when confronted with federal orders and timetables, relying on the same tactic it used so

successfully to avoid the withdrawal of the Garfield permit and ultimately gain congressional approval for Hetch Hetchy.

San Francisco city hall must have known that the federal government was loath to actually exercise its authority to take over the project. That was likely the last outcome the federal government sought,
and would have been a political and administrative nightmare.
Perhaps in some other place and time, the federal government could
successfully provide water or power to the public through some form
of quasipublic agency, such as the Tennessee Valley Authority or the
Bonneville Power Authority, but not in the 1930s and 1940s in San
Francisco; the local politics prevented it. In hindsight, one suspects
Mayor Rossi knew exactly what he was doing, and Secretary Ickes
was powerless to prevent him.

A proud Italian-American man, bald and stout, always impeccably
dressed in striped trousers and cutaway, Angelo Rossi was James
Rolph's hand-picked successor as mayor. A lifelong florist, Rossi
always wore a white-carnation boutonniere—Mayor Rolph always
wore a gardenia. When Rolph resigned to become governor, he
appointed his dapper protégé from the board of supervisors to succeed him, providing extraordinary continuity in city policy for the
project over their combined thirty-two years in office. During Rossi's
tenure the Golden Gate Bridge and the San Francisco–Oakland Bay
Bridge were built and Hetch Hetchy was completed, among other
major civic improvements. The city certainly had the ability to complete the public power system; it just never had the will to do so.

The clash between Ickes and Rossi had probably begun before
they toasted the completion of the Hetch Hetchy water system that
day in October 1934. In preparing for the visit, Ickes must have
learned of the three-year plan his predecessor and Mayor Rossi had
negotiated several years earlier, for San Francisco to create a public
power agency. The plan called for the board of supervisors to place
bond issues on the ballot to finance the agency. But voters rejected
the $68 million in bonds to purchase PG&E and Great Western and
build additional facilities in 1930, after a vigorous campaign in opposition to the proposals was mounted by the power companies. Given
the start of the Great Depression, the vociferous opposition of
PG&E, and the tepid support of the city administration for the

bonds—as well as the public's general confusion—the huge offering had no chance of approval. The city claimed it had tried to comply; even a small bond was rejected in 1933. What else could they do?

Ickes had also learned of the sweetheart deal for the handling of Moccasin power between the city and PG&E, and of the 1923 solicitor general's opinion in response to the National Park Service inquiry. He instructed the solicitor to reexamine the situation. In August 1934, Ickes concluded that the contract remained a clear violation of the Raker Act and urged San Francisco to remedy the situation by establishing a municipal power system as quickly as possible. Mayor Rossi acknowledged the instruction and referred the matter to the city's public utilities commission, and there the issue died. In 1935 the administration again gave little support to a charter amendment for public power, which lost decisively under an onslaught of propaganda from PG&E.

Ickes persisted, repeatedly warning San Francisco about complying with the law. The city responded by placing a self-financing revenue bond issue to purchase PG&E on the 1937 ballot, instead of general obligation bonds as had been offered before. It made no difference. The solicitor general concluded the issue failed due "to lack of support by the Mayor and his failure to campaign for it." (PG&E's campaign contributed as well.) Two days later Ickes cabled Mayor Rossi, giving him fifteen days to show how San Francisco was serious about complying with the Raker Act. When Rossi failed to respond, Secretary Ickes ordered the U.S. attorney general to file suit against the city. That got Rossi's attention. He immediately cabled Ickes and requested a delay in the legal action and a meeting in Washington to resolve the issue. Ickes responded that for two years he had "patiently tried to persuade San Francisco to obey the mandate in a law which it originally concurred in, but without success." There was no point in further discussion for Ickes; the city's motives were clear. "Apparently," the solicitor for the Department of the Interior commented to Ickes, "the Mayor was completely bewildered and disconcerted by the knowledge of the fact that conferences and delays would no longer be the regular order of things." Now the courts would compel compliance.

As expected, on April 11, 1938, the U.S. District Court for Northern California ruled that the sales agreement between San

Francisco and PG&E violated the Raker Act. However, hoping that the city would accept the court judgment and comply, Ickes didn't ask for a forfeiture ruling in which the Hetch Hetchy grant would revert to the federal government. In response, the judge issued an injunction forbidding the city from selling power to a private company, and then suspended enforcement for six months to enable the city to devise a plan for compliance that would be acceptable to the interior secretary. Ickes announced that he was "ready to consider any proposals officials of San Francisco might have to offer." Rossi's response was to appeal the court decision, vowing to fight the ruling all the way to the U.S. Supreme Court if need be, or "if worst comes to worst . . . the city should move for amendment by Congress of the Raker Act." There no longer could be any lingering doubt about the city's intentions for Hetch Hetchy hydroelectricity or the creation of a public power system.

The U.S. Ninth Circuit Court of Appeals reversed the district court's decision on September 13, 1939. The appeals court agreed with San Francisco's contention that the city had no choice but to use PG&E as its "agent" to distribute Moccasin power as long as local voters rejected the bond issues and charter amendments that were needed to acquire or build a public power system. Motives didn't matter; methods didn't matter. Only the results mattered. And the results were that voters repeatedly rejected the city's meager attempts to create a public power system. However, motives and methods *did* matter to Secretary Ickes, who requested the solicitor general to appeal the ruling to the U.S. Supreme Court.

Justice Hugo Black wrote the April 22, 1940, Supreme Court opinion on behalf of the eight-to-one majority. The Raker Act and congressional intent were unequivocal: there was to be public power with no transmission, transferral, or sale of any power permitted to any private entity for any reason. "The City has in fact followed a course of conduct which Congress, by Section 6, has forbidden," Justice Black wrote. "Mere words and ingenuity of contractual expression, whatever their effect between the parties, cannot by description make permissible a course of conduct forbidden by law." Motives and means also mattered to the Supreme Court. "When we look behind the word description of the arrangement between the City and the power company to what was actually done," Justice

Black continued, "we see that the City has—contrary to the terms of Section 6—abdicated its control over the sale and ultimate distribution of Hetch-Hetchy power. . . . The City is availing itself of valuable rights and privileges granted by the Government and yet persists in violating the very conditions upon which those benefits were granted."

The Court showed no sympathy to the city's arguments: "Congress clearly intended to require—as a condition of its grant— sale and distribution of Hetch-Hetchy power exclusively by San Francisco and municipal agencies directly to consumers in the belief that consumers would thus be afforded power at cheap rates in competition with private power companies, particularly Pacific Gas & Electric Company." However, the Court concluded, "the City does not itself distribute and sell the power directly to consumers; it has not provided competition with the private power company; and it has transferred the right to sell and distribute the power to a private company in violation of the express prohibition of Section 6 of the Act."

With thinly veiled irritation, the Court chastised the city's hypocrisy. "When the Raker Bill was before Congress, the City filed with the Public Lands Committee of the House a brief and argument in support of the Bill. Citing authorities, including this Court's opinions, and legislative precedents, the City submitted to Congress that as grantee it would be bound by and as grantor Congress was empowered to impose 'the conditions set forth in the Hetch-Hetchy bill.' After passage of the Bill the City accepted the grant by formal ordinance, assenting to all the conditions contained in the grant, constructed the required power and water facilities and up to date has utilized the rights, privileges and benefits granted by Congress. Now the City seeks to retain the benefits of the Act while attacking the constitutionality of one of its important conditions." The Supreme Court forcefully affirmed the decision of the district court and reinstated the injunction against the continued sale of power to PG&E.

What was the reaction in San Francisco? The *Chronicle* and the *Examiner* both excoriated the decision and lampooned Ickes and Congressman Franck Havenner for trying to impose public power on the city. The papers editorialized that the city's interests would be better served by the continued sale of power to PG&E; they asserted that public power would cost the city the millions of dollars it received annually from the PG&E contract. Only the *San Francisco News* supported the decision, pointing out that every other city with public power had found it very lucrative, and that the potential benefits from public power would dwarf the annual fee paid by PG&E. Nor did the obstinate civic and political leaders accept the Court's ruling; they enlisted Thomas Rolph, a local U.S. representative, to propose legislation in Congress to amend the Raker Act and remove the public power mandate, with the support of California senator Hiram Johnson. Hearings in the House Committee on Public Lands were eventually held on the proposed bill (77 H.R. 5964) in December 1941 and January 1942, but the bill failed in committee.

In the meantime, a month after the Supreme Court decision, a contingent from San Francisco met in Washington with Secretary Ickes to resolve the issue. The group included Mayor Rossi, the city attorney, the president of the board of supervisors, and the manager of the public utilities commission. Ickes told them that he intended to revoke the grant if the city didn't quickly come up with an acceptable plan for the disposal of Hetch Hetchy power. "You would be here on a much better footing," he stated, "if the record of delay, evasion and double-crossing hadn't been what it has been on the part of officials of San Francisco." The utilities manager responded that the city "has seen the handwriting on the wall," and that something could be worked out in time. "Yes," Ickes retorted, "all you want is time until I'm out of office. . . . I have always believed that a man can be fooled once, but a man is a damn fool who allows himself to be fooled a second time, and this isn't only the second time."

The contingent returned with plan in hand a month later. The city proposed to lease PG&E lines and distribution facilities, for a flat annual fee, and hire the company's local sales, service, and repair staffs. PG&E had already approved the lease in principle. Although not pleased, Ickes agreed to ask the district court to grant a temporary stay in the injunction to give the city several months to renegotiate several components of the deal with PG&E. If the negotiations didn't work out, Mayor Rossi promised to place a new bond issue to acquire PG&E's assets before the voters as soon as possible.

In April 1941 the city forwarded the renegotiated lease to Ickes for review and approval. Ickes sent the lease to the chairman of the

federal power commission, who responded, "It is clear that the proposed arrangement not only does not offer the city the advantages of
public distribution of Hetch Hetchy power, but may even have the
effect of freezing high rates." So the secretary rejected the plan and
called another meeting with city officials to try again to resolve the
differences. During the May meeting, Mayor Rossi admitted the plan
favored PG&E at the expense of the city, but justified it as the best
deal the city could get from the monopoly. He then asked Ickes to
request the district court to grant another extension of the stay in
order for the city to place another bond issue before the voters in
November. Ickes acquiesced, *provided* city hall and civic leaders
actively campaigned in favor of the bonds.

Word of the deal between Ickes and the mayor raised the ire of the
papers and civic groups like the Chamber of Commerce and the
Downtown Association, who decried it as tantamount to extortion
and a gag order designed to suppress public debate. In response,
they joined PG&E in an aggressive campaign against the bonds.
Several weeks before the vote, the front page of the *Chronicle* her-
alded a sweeping reduction in local electricity rates by PG&E. The
bond issue failed.

Secretary Ickes then informed Mayor Rossi that he now had no
alternative but to begin proceedings to revoke the Hetch Hetchy
grant. No more delays would be approved; no more excuses would
be accepted. Time had finally run out for the city. Time had finally
run out for the nation, too. Several weeks later the Hetch Hetchy
public power issue in San Francisco was swept aside as bombs fell on
Pearl Harbor in the early-morning hours of December 7, 1941.

As it had for the small amount of Early Intake power during
World War I, the federal government purchased the power from the
Moccasin plant during World War II and diverted it to an aluminum-
smelting facility built near Modesto. When the facility shut down in
June 1944 and the district court injunction was about to be reinstated,
San Francisco did what it had done so many times before: it requested
a delay so it could make arrangements for the disposal of the power.
And once again the tactic worked, despite angry comments about it
from the district court. In August the new mayor, Roger Lapham
(1944–48), submitted a scheme in which PG&E would transmit about
200 million kilowatt-hours a year of Hetch Hetchy power from its

Newark substation to municipal facilities in San Francisco in return for the free use of the remaining Hetch Hetchy hydropower, which was thought to be roughly 300 million kilowatt-hours a year. Undersecretary Abe Fortas rejected the plan while Secretary Ickes was on vacation. Although increasingly frustrated with the city, the district court granted it one final chance to propose an acceptable plan.

On it went: Lapham wrote Ickes with a draft scheme in December based on negotiations between the city, the monopoly, and the irrigation districts. He now proposed that the city pay PG&E an annual wheeling fee to transmit enough Hetch Hetchy power from Newark to San Francisco to satisfy municipal needs. Excess power would be sold to the Modesto and Turlock Irrigation Districts as permitted in the Raker Act, instead of to PG&E. Modesto had been buying substantial amounts of supplemental power from PG&E for several years, and so the proposed arrangement would sharply reduce the cost of that power. In contrast, Turlock's share of Don Pedro power exceeded the district's need, so it had been wholesaling excess to PG&E for years. In the mid-1930s Modesto had offered to buy any surplus Hetch Hetchy power from San Francisco. The city refused. Lapham's latest scheme also enabled the districts to sell to PG&E any Hetch Hetchy power that remained after their needs were met, to avoid the excess power from going to waste.

Secretary Ickes was initially noncommittal on the scheme, reminding the mayor that the final plan was due by year's end and that the Department of the Interior would "not participate in any evasion of the law, however complex and ingenious." He warned Lapham, "I hope that your leadership will not, this time, have to waste time, energy and newsprint in the fruitless pastime of beating the devil around the PG&E bush."

In January 1945, Ickes rejected the latest Lapham scheme, writing, "The proposed agreements do not carry out the intent of the Congress in the Raker Act, which was designed to bring City-owned power, over the City's transmission and distribution system, directly to the citizens of San Francisco." The many plans proposed by San Francisco were in effect simply subtle variations on the basic idea of placing the power under the control of PG&E, which was a fundamental violation of the Raker Act, regardless of the contractual nuances between the city and the monopoly.

For several more months, plans and promises and warnings flew back and forth between San Francisco and Washington. Negotiations between all the parties and the district court continued. The nagging problem posed by Turlock's power glut and past practice of selling excess to PG&E was resolved by permitting the district to continue to sell excess power to the company when it received Hetch Hetchy power, but only up to the same amount of excess Don Pedro power it had sold the company in 1944. (Turlock's power needs would soon exceed the power supply it obtained from Don Pedro, ending the sale of excess power to PG&E.) Beyond the resolution of that problem, nothing of substance changed in the city's proposed arrangement with PG&E.

Ickes finally conceded in June, perhaps out of frustration and a sense of futility as his tenure was about to end, or perhaps out of a recognition that the circumstances had changed. The district court concurred. Grudgingly Ickes accepted the city's proposal for a four-year contract with the company, while asserting that the agreement still violated the Raker Act. With the usual caveat that during the contract term the city would find an acceptable way to permanently dispose of the power and that the Department of the Interior would oppose continuation of the agreement if they hadn't done so after that time, the deal was done. Twenty years in the making, it still dodged the intent of Congress and the courts. In 1945, San Francisco began the sale of excess Hetch Hetchy hydropower to the Turlock and Modesto Irrigation Districts, in place of PG&E, for which the city continued to earn a profit, and PG&E retained control of the city's retail market. While the districts had displaced PG&E and developed public power in their service areas, San Francisco had not.

Eventually circumstances had changed in San Francisco's favor, just as city hall had hoped all along. The politics in Washington had changed, and public opinion had changed nationwide. The New Deal and the Progressive Era were over. Ickes had departed. The postwar economy was beginning, and it desperately needed electricity to power expansion. A new conservative agenda was rapidly replacing the populist, liberal idealism of the past. And the proponents of that new agenda simply didn't care that San Francisco continued to violate the Raker Act and the Supreme Court ruling.

CHAPTER 15

Restoring the Promise

W hile electricity consumption surged nationwide during the postwar economic boom, generation capacity lagged in some regions. This spurred development of the untapped Hetch Hetchy potential that Freeman had designed into the system. Since the completion of Moccasin Powerhouse in 1925, few improvements had been made in the system's power generation or transmission capacities. Inexpensive power was readily available from PG&E and other private suppliers, so the profit potential for the city from the development of additional Hetch Hetchy generation capacity did not warrant the effort. By the mid-1950s the economics and politics of power were changing. San Francisco's municipal needs were growing rapidly, as were the demands of the Turlock and Modesto Irrigation Districts. The price of power was also increasing, and political pressure was rising to make full use of Hetch Hetchy's hydroelectricity potential. These forces justified the construction of the two additional powerhouses Freeman proposed in the plan. Completion of a massive dam on Cherry Creek in 1956 to provide water storage for irrigation and power generation set the stage for Holm Powerhouse to come online in 1960, at which time Early Intake went offline. Completion of the Canyon Tunnel in 1965 enabled Kirkwood Powerhouse to replace Early Intake in 1967. Two years later, when the new powerhouse at Moccasin came online, followed by a small low-head generating plant just downstream in 1986, Hetch Hetchy's maximum hydroelectric potential had finally been fully tapped. But the promise of public power had not.

Since 1945, the city and PG&E have renegotiated their distribution agreement on several occasions. Each long-term contract has been more complex than its predecessor, but each also has retained many of the basic tenets first proposed by Mayor Lapham in December 1944. Today the city has an "interconnection agreement" with PG&E through 2015, allowing the City and County of San

Francisco (CCSF) to transmit or wheel up to 200 megawatts of
Hetch Hetchy hydropower over PG&E lines to municipal consumers. (Peak demand of municipal load is approximately 130
megawatts.) The primary consumers of this municipal load power
include the airport, the water and clean water enterprises, the municipal railway, and other city departments.

This municipal load power is delivered over CCSF lines to the
PG&E Newark substation, where it enters into the utility's overall
system and in theory is transmitted to CCSF users within the city
limits and in selected locations on the peninsula over PG&E lines.
(In fact, the power delivered to CCSF customers may have been
generated at any power plant contributing current to the Newark
network.) For this service, CCSF pays PG&E an annual wheeling
fee, typically $15 million to $18 million, based on the amount and
voltage of power taken by the CCSF customers. Other fees associated with the transmission may also apply, including those for firm
transmission services and demand. On the other hand, the CCSF
collects an annual franchise fee from PG&E of several million dollars, as regulated by the California State Public Utilities Commission, for the utililty's use of the public right of way.

The amount of power generated by the four Hetch Hetchy
hydropower plants can fluctuate daily and seasonally. Similarly, the
power demands of its consumers vary, creating a relationship called
the "load shape." Matching power generation to the load shape challenges system management, especially since HHWP hydropower
generation is typically dictated by the requirements for the delivery
of water to its consumers, and the flow of water varies dramatically
during the year. The contractual provisions for the handling of
power excesses and shortages are extremely complex and intertwined with regionwide electricity supply and demand. And the various parties involved often have very different perceptions and
concerns.

Until the late 1980s the amount of power generated exceeded
municipal needs for most of the year, with all the excess power purchased by the irrigation districts at the prevailing rate and transmitted over HHWP lines directly to the districts, in accordance with the
Raker Act and existing contracts. To maximize the value of this
excess, during the Feinstein mayoral administration in the mid-1980s

the CCSF sought to "firm" the power sold to the districts by guaranteeing that power in amount and time. The districts would pay a premium for the certainty of supply, because that certainty better enabled them to efficiently manage their systems. At times when HHWP generated insufficient power to meet both the municipal needs and the amount guaranteed the districts, the CCSF could go to the spot market, like any other wholesale buyer, and purchase the supplemental power needed to satisfy the shortfall, for less than the contract price to the districts. So in 1987 the CCSF and the districts signed a thirty-year contract that firmed the city's power obligations to the districts. Throughout the 1990s CCSF profited handsomely, with revenues of several hundred million dollars.

Around 2000 the situation changed dramatically. The wholesale price of power on the spot market spiked well above the $35 per megawatt-hour price for firm power CCSF had guaranteed the districts. Hence, when HHWP generation was unable to meet total demand—primarily because of insufficient water flow from the reservoirs during the latter part of the year and during drought conditions—CCSF was purchasing spot power at an average cost of around $150 per megawatt-hour to meet its obligations to the districts, losing tens of millions of dollars in the process.

To hedge its losses, in May 2001 CCSF signed a five-year contract with another power company to buy a set amount of supplemental power for about $75 per megawatt-hour whether or not the power was actually needed. Shortly thereafter the spot price of power dropped back to the pre-spike levels of the 1990s, leaving CCSF locked into a costly $173.5 million contract with the supplemental supplier.

In August 2001, CCSF filed a lawsuit in San Francisco Superior Court to void its firm-power contracts with the districts. The litigants are now arguing over a range of issues arising not only from the 1987 contract but also from the Raker Act and the historical water and power relationships of the districts to the city. Old animosities, fundamentally differing perceptions of rights, and perhaps even distrust lie just below the surface.

During spring runoff, when inflows to the reservoirs exceed storage capacity and consumer demands, CCSF enjoys another opportunity. Rather than simply permitting this unused flow to continue down the Tuolumne River, additional power beyond the needs of the CCSF and the irrigation districts can be generated as the water is "spilled" back into the river. CCSF can sell this "dump" power on the open market to other public entities, yielding about $5 million annually, although CCSF pays PG&E a transmission fee for the delivery of the dump power to purchasers other than the irrigation districts.

The total cost to generate Hetch Hetchy power, including overhead, is currently about $17 per megawatt-hour. This compares favorably with the market rate for wholesale power, which recently has fluctuated between $20 and $50 per megawatt-hour.

To cover the cost of generating Hetch Hetchy power and the costs associated with purchasing additional power over the course of a fiscal year, CCSF internally charges itself different rates for different departments. For example, general fund or nonrevenue-generating departments are charged an electrical rate of $37.5 per megawatt-hour, a lower rate than they would be charged by an investor-owned utility like PG&E. For enterprise or revenue-generating departments, a retail rate equivalent to that approved by the California Public Utilities Commission, or the same as would be paid to PG&E for like service, is applied. The aggregate of the internal city charges typically balance or exceed what it needs to cover all costs associated with meeting its own obligations and needs.

San Francisco city hall believes these arrangements comply with both the letter of the law and the Supreme Court decision. It argues that since 1945 no SFPUC contract with PG&E has violated the Raker Act. As Patricia E. Martel, general manager of SFPUC, explained, "Those who claim the City has been in constant violation of the Raker Act believe the City is obligated to serve residents and businesses within San Francisco with Hetch Hetchy power. They are wrong. The Raker Act allows and encourages the City to serve Hetch Hetchy power to its residents, and it is the official City policy to do so some day, but the Raker Act does not require the City to do so. The City's power contracts comply with Section 6 of the Raker Act. The Department of the Interior has reviewed and approved every power contract that the City has entered since 1945, including the current contract with PG&E."

Does the SFPUC-PG&E contract in fact comply, or is Martel's statement simply political rhetoric? Ultimately only the courts can decide whether the current contract violates the Raker Act and the Supreme Court ruling. Unfortunately, from the late 1940s until the present, despite repeated reports and rulings that the questionable relationship between the city and PG&E continued, few people in San Francisco city hall or Washington have been willing to question that relationship, and fewer still in positions of power have been willing to act on such allegations.

In 1955 few people listened or responded when Representative Clair Engle, a powerful, ambitious, and flamboyant Democrat from California who chaired the House Committee on Interior and Insular Affairs, presented his committee with compelling evidence obtained from the federal power commission, and from damning cross-examination of witnesses, that the Modesto and Turlock Irrigation Districts had been reselling more than 10 percent of the Hetch Hetchy power they received to PG&E, in direct violation of the Raker Act and the 1945 agreement with Secretary Ickes. The districts denied the allegation. Engle was a longtime antagonist of PG&E and a supporter of public water and power projects.

The committee hearings resulted from a bill Engle had proposed (H.R. 2388) on behalf of his district to enable Tuolumne County to build a power plant on the site just below Early Intake that the Raker Act had allocated to the City of San Francisco. Boosters in Tuolumne County, eager to promote economic growth and development there, had targeted the site for their purposes and enlisted Engle's support, hoping he would champion their cause in Congress by sponsoring the legislation needed to transfer the development rights from San Francisco to Tuolumne County. The county claimed that the city had forfeited its claim to the site due to the forty-year delay in developing it and because of the ongoing violations of the Raker Act in municipal disposal of hydropower. The contentious hearings continued the acrimonious political fight begun between the mountain county, San Francisco, PG&E, and the irrigation districts, as soon as county officials announced their plan several years earlier. The bill died when San Francisco voters overwhelming approved the $54 million funding for the Holm and Kirkwood power plants, but the debate had helped prompt the city to develop the plants in order to safeguard these sources of income.

Nor did many people listen or respond in 1973 when a San

Francisco grand jury concluded that the contract between the city and PG&E was of "questionable legality" especially with regard to the wheeling agreement. The grand jury had been convened to investigate possible Raker Act violations in those contracts. It recommended that the city acquire its own electricity distribution system and purchase whatever PG&E assets were needed to conform to the spirit and letter of the law. In response, the board of supervisors held a hearing the next year to discuss the authorization of a feasibility study for the acquisition of PG&E's assets, as recommended by the grand jury. The eight-hour meeting featured extensive testimony from PG&E, which claimed the value of its local assets was $600 million, despite the fact that the existing tax rolls valued them at only $300 million. Key public power advocates were not invited to the hearing, and not one board member supported funding the feasibility study. As had been the case for nearly fifty years—from the late 1940s to the late 1990s—the public power intentions of the Raker Act were again ignored in the corridors of political power and public office.

However, the public did try to keep the issue alive. In 1972–73, at the behest of the San Francisco Neighborhood Legal Assistance Foundation, a group of volunteer CPAs called San Francisco Accountants for the Public Interest studied the economic implications of public power in San Francisco. Relying on publicly available data (since PG&E would not cooperate), they concluded the city could "profit" by $15 million to $22 million annually if it acquired PG&E's distribution system and created a true public power system. That cost savings could then double after the bonds used to finance the acquisition were paid off. Like the grand jury, which was running its investigation around the same time, the accountants urged the city to conduct an independent feasibility study for the purchase of PG&E's assets. PG&E vehemently disagreed with their findings. Curiously, the San Francisco Accountants for the Public Interest were not invited to the hearing held by the board of supervisors.

In 1974, neighborhood activist Charles Starbuck had had enough of what he perceived to be evasion behavior and collusion on the part of city hall and PG&E. He filed suit in federal court alleging that the city was in violation of the Raker Act. If the city attorney wouldn't do it and the U.S. attorney general wouldn't do it, as charged in the act, then he would do it as a private citizen. Mr. Starbuck claimed he and all other electricity consumers in San Francisco had been injured by the years of paying higher rates and receiving poorer service than they would have had the city obeyed the law and established public power. He argued the wheeling agreement was illegal according to Section 6 of the act and that PG&E directly benefited from that violation. And he asserted that the act intended Hetch Hetchy power to compete with power provided by PG&E, not to be complicit with it.

His complaint was never heard on the merits. In 1977 the federal court of appeals threw the case out, concluding, as had the district court, that the plaintiffs lacked standing to bring the suit. Only the San Francisco city attorney, the U.S. attorney general, groups specifically named in the law—such as the Modesto and Turlock Irrigation Districts—or those with a demonstrable benefit from the law, such as other municipalities, could bring suit (as had, for instance, the City of Palo Alto). An important factor in the court's decision was its conclusion that the plaintiffs failed to show that electricity rates would decline if their complaint was affirmed. The court no longer was willing to assume public power automatically meant lower rates in this specific instance; because of this, if the court granted the plaintiffs relief, it might be contradicting a key intention of the Raker Act— that is, to provide the public with electric power as inexpensively as possible. The court wrote,

In 1913, Congress anticipated that San Francisco would shortly build its own transmission lines and that direct service to consumers would provide consumers with abundant power more cheaply than that supplied by private utilities. The congressional assumptions might have come true had the taxpayers seen it Congress' way in the decades that followed the Raker Act. But the taxpayers repeatedly refused to approve the bond issues that would have supplied the revenue to build the transmission facilities. In the meantime, energy shortages, inflation and escalating costs of rights of way, of construction, and of the debt service have obliterated Congress' rosy vision of San Francisco's energy future. Even if we could reasonably assume that Bay Area taxpayers would now be willing to assume the debt burden to build these facilities, we cannot infer that energy delivered over those newly constructed lines would be cheaper than energy deliv-

ered over PG&E's lines. The rate structure for direct delivery would
necessarily reflect the enormous costs involved in building the system. If any inference would be permissible, it would be that the cost
of energy to the consumers would be more, not less, than that available under the present wheeling arrangements. In short, the dominant cheaper energy purpose of the Raker Act would be defeated,
rather than fulfilled, if appellants were to be given the remedy they
seek.

Ironically, while the public power mandate in the Raker Act had
been affirmed several times in the courts, and while the courts had
recognized that the city had been in violation of that mandate for
decades, circumstances may well have arisen over those many years
to render the mandate no longer practical—no matter what the
motives were for the violations, and no matter what the means were
for them, only the outcome mattered. In effect, allowing the city to
violate the law might constitute the better fulfillment of the law's
most basic intent for cheap electricity than actually enforcing the
law's public power proviso—the ultimate realization of San
Francisco city hall's delaying tactic.

Yet how could the court conclude that public power was no longer
cost-effective, given the San Francisco accountants' calculation and
abundant data from public power cities nationwide? Potential plaintiffs would now carry the burden of proof for the economic advantages of public power in San Francisco, necessitating a detailed, and
expensive, independent feasibility study.

In 1978 the board of supervisors again considered a resolution to
municipalize PG&E. The company claimed that that would cost perhaps a billion dollars, although the board of equalization calculated
the cost to be less than half that amount. The factions also squabbled
over the likely cost of a feasibility study for the buyout, the necessary
first step toward public power. After a heated hearing, packed with
PG&E supporters, the board voted eight to three against that first
step. One supervisor commented, "We lost because of political pressure. There's never been a more dramatic case of big corporate interest on one side of an issue and the interest of the public on the other."

A citizen group called San Franciscans for Public Power continued the fight in 1982, placing Proposition K on the ballot, which

required the city to conduct the long-sought feasibility study. As it had in response to every previous challenge to its monopoly, PG&E again mounted an aggressive campaign against the initiative, mobilizing shareholders and asserting its influence in city hall and the media. Opponents of the proposition received 93 percent of their large campaign war chest from PG&E. Mayor Dianne Feinstein opposed the initiative. The daily papers opposed the initiative. PG&E again claimed the cost would be prohibitive, based on suspect data. Proponents challenged in court some of the outrageous figures published in the voters guide, but the judge ruled the figures acceptable. At a press conference outside company headquarters, Assemblyman Art Agnos denounced the monolith's blatant attempt to buy San Francisco's vote. In the end, the initiative failed.

Another decade passed, and little changed on the surface. By the mid-1990s PG&E and the city had renegotiated their contract, and public power proponents cried foul over its terms and the backroom politics that led to them. The transfer of the Presidio from the U.S. Army to the National Park Service, and the potential supply of the new park's power from a public source—Hetch Hetchy—presented another threat to the PG&E monopoly and triggered a heated controversy ultimately decided in the company's favor. And an investigation into the small franchise fee paid the city by PG&E for the right to deliver Hetch Hetchy power over the public right of way, versus the generous wheeling fee it collected from the city for transmitting that power, led to a policy by the board of supervisors that the franchise fee be raised over several years, to up to eight times the historical rate, to bring it closer to national norms. When PG&E balked at paying the fee increase, city hall blinked; the higher fee was contested and the payment ignored.

Throughout, Bruce Brugmann and the *San Francisco Bay Guardian* have continued their crusade to enforce the Raker Act and create a public power authority in San Francisco. "PG&E has always fought like hell to stop the public from controlling any basic utility asset; they want to keep those assets under private control," he asserts. "They'll tolerate no footholds; each potentially weakens their control of electric power. That's why they fought so hard to privatize the Presidio." He believes that the California Public Utilities Commission has never been able to control PG&E; the monopoly is too powerful and has too much money. "Despite being regulated by the state PUC, PG&E is not like other private companies," he explains. "General Motors, for example, is set up to compete against other automakers. As a monopoly, PG&E has no competition, and they fight like hell to keep it that way. So they have the arrogance and inefficiency and overexpense of that dominance, and they don't have to answer to anybody." Ultimately, he believes, "PG&E is to blame for the city's violation of the Raker Act and the absence of public power here; *it's* the villain, not the public officials. Politicians can't resist the pressure the company can exert. It has money and influence and continuity. Politicians need money and support to get elected, and they come and go. But PG&E is always there."

Have the daily papers been complicit in this by purposely blacking out the story, or have they simply ignored it because the story just isn't of interest? Chuck Finnie, the investigative reporter and now editor on local politics and legal matters for the *San Francisco Chronicle,* and the coauthor of the exposé on the Hetch Hetchy water and power systems, agrees with some of Bruce Brugmann's beliefs about the Hetch Hetchy story, but attributes the lack of coverage of the story in the major dailies to different reasons. In his experience at the *Examiner* and the *Chronicle* covering this and other similar stories about local political issues, he hasn't seen overt censorship. "Reporters find stories and pitch story ideas to the editor," he explained, "and I've never been told that I can't do a story that I was interested in doing. I believe the lack of attention to the Hetch Hetchy story, as I look back through the clips, simply comes from the reporters' lack of interest in the story whose beat might naturally bring them to cover the SFPUC.

"It wasn't until the energy crisis in California in the late 1990s that daily newspapers started paying attention to whether or not our light switches really work, where the power comes from, and how the market is organized. Coverage of deregulation of the power industry in 1996 was mostly focused on heavy nuts-and-bolts and policy issues—not very sexy. Coverage, or the lack thereof, was the same for the Hetch Hetchy water issues. No conspiracy, just a focus mostly on other, sexier, social issues that seem to more directly affect people. Now we're beginning to wake up to the issue of potable water both locally and globally. I come at the water and power issues from a municipal finance perspective since I spend a lot of time covering money and politics. On the money side, it's a fascinating story: what San Francisco has done with Hetch Hetchy and how the system's use has been diverted from what was clearly intended."

Yet the conservative political status quo on public power that has been in place for the past fifty years, since the end of the Progressive Era, is giving way to a more liberal and populist political climate. Public power has recently reappeared on San Francisco's political agenda, together with rising concerns over the security of the water system. In 1994–95 the board of supervisors, composed of several new liberal members, approved legislation that required the city to conduct a preliminary feasibility study of public power. City hall fought the proposal, but the board mustered the votes to override the mayor's veto. The gloves had finally been removed in the political fight for public power: the mandate also established that any city official who blocked implementation would be guilty of misconduct and subject to removal from office. The first feasibility study was completed by a consultant in 1996, under suspect contracting circumstances that triggered more heated accusations of political meddling. The report concluded that public power probably would not be worth the effort. Advocates claimed the report was purposely slanted in favor of privatization and PG&E. Calls on the board for a more complete feasibility study were squelched as the balance of power shifted after retirements due to term limits and new elections. However, Pandora's box had been pried open by the advocates. By the late 1990s, public power was again on the front page.

P. J. Johnston, former mayor Willie Brown's press secretary, explained it this way: "PG&E certainly has had a lot of influence through the years by virtue of its size as an employer and taxpayer, but that went out the window with the blackouts, their bankruptcy, and the other power crises of the past few years, and their cavalier attitudes. Now it's politically expedient to dump on them. At some point in this city, people believe a corporate utility becomes too big, unpopular, and unresponsive to the public consumer. The recent energy crisis has shown that the profit motive is a real problem when it comes to a lifeline resource. You can live without cable TV, even phone service, but you need power and water. The crisis showed the Bay Area and the state that it's problematic when the large corporate utility, with its responsibilities not only to customers but to share-holders, to its parent company, and to distant investors, has to gener-ate profits. Beyond the power outages, people reacted more to the sense that PG&E was acting on behalf of its corporate needs than public responsibilities."

Public power advocates led a successful petition drive in 2000 to place an initiative for a municipal utility district on the November ballot. City hall fought the initiative, causing it to be postponed until the 2001 election. Proposition F called for the SFPUC to be replaced by a new municipal water and power agency, governed by an elected board, with a goal to provide public power to San Francisco. Another proposition went even further: Proposition I called for the formation of a regional municipal utility district that would manage a broad range of utilities beyond water and electricity. As it had always done, PG&E waged war against the propositions, presumably to protect its profitable business in the Bay Area. (In fact, for years these profits offset other corporate losses.)

Proposition F lost by just 500 or so votes, less than a half a percent of the total. The more sweeping Proposition I lost by several thou-sand votes. Buoyed by the close call, advocates tried again the next year, placing Proposition D on the November 2002 ballot. The ballot also contained Proposition A—the $1.6 billion bond issue to fund the repair and improvement of the Hetch Hetchy water system and a revenue bond oversight committee, thus commingling the politics of Hetch Hetchy water and power issues. Water won, again. Proposition D, the proposed charter amendment to make the SFPUC the primary provider of electricity to San Francisco resi-dents and businesses lost, again.

What does it all mean? Larry Weis, general manager of the Turlock Irrigation District, views Hetch Hetchy from a much differ-ent perspective than that of the City of San Francisco. History, self-interest, and civic pride color the city's perspective. Like the suburban wholesale water customers, the Turlock and Modesto Irrigation Districts also see the project through those same tints, but their resulting views from the Central Valley differ with the view from San Francisco as much as the differences in lifestyles and land-scapes between the two vantage points. Since the project's inception, the districts have been integral participants. Weis thinks San

Francisco just hasn't fully recognized that fact. From his outsider's perspective, he believes opportunities abound for cooperation between the city and the irrigation districts—opportunities for greater efficiency and equity in the development of both water and power—if the city can look past its narrow focus. Sadly, he senses that the days when visionary municipal leaders could mobilize the public and private sectors behind great infrastructure projects may be past. He feels that, too often, projects now move along propelled by bureaucratic momentum rather than enlightened leadership. "There're three issues with Hetch Hetchy: water, power, and money," Weis says. "And what's the most important of the three?" he asks rhetorically. "Money," he answers.

Tom Ammiano, president of the Board of Supervisors for the City and County of San Francisco, has an insider's perspective. He thinks the city has been very possessive of the Hetchy Hetchy system over the years, and perhaps rightly so, since one of the primary reasons for the project was to enable the city to have a water supply independent of private companies or other municipalities. Consequently, he believes the transfer of excess hydropower revenues from HHWP to the general municipal fund was appropriate. "I think it's fine to use some of that money for city projects, that's the whole point of it, that you would have that extra money," he said. "But there has also been some injudicious transferring of funds while the infrastructure was not attended to." He helped place the public power initiatives before the voters in 2001 and again in 2002, while he also led efforts to pass Proposition A in 2002 to fund long-neglected system repairs and improvements. Among the city hall insiders, Ammiano has been particularly sensitive to the way Hetch Hetchy management affects both the city internally and the other external stakeholders.

And always behind the scenes he's sensed the presence of PG&E—at least until recently. "I think the Raker Act has been violated," he stated, "and I think a lot of it has to do with the money PG&E has spread around. The company has been the thousand-pound gorilla all along. Their influence might have started small, but the company certainly soon came to see the benefits of controlling transmission and the potential for profit-making. PG&E preceded many people to the city. Those recent arrivals might have had water and public power as concerns, but not as prominent as their concerns for civil rights, feminist and gay issues, and antiwar campaigns. This enabled PG&E to take root and infiltrate public opinion in the sense that they could spread their influence by selling stock, serving as an employer, and other means. For many people, PG&E was a way to make money and pay the rent. The company was very patriarchal, creating a built-in sense of loyalty and allegiance." When the company voiced a position on an issue, the public listened.

Ammiano senses conflicting tendencies in San Francisco politics as portrayed in the city's historical handling of Hetch Hetchy. The split between the populist tendencies seen in social and environmental activism, and the political interests of big business and powerful political bosses, might not be schizophrenic, but it's certainly bipolar, he says. "And it seems to me that papers like the *Chronicle* have been dissuaded from covering the Hetch Hetchy story. They've never come out for public power or even supported a feasibility study for it because they have downtown interests too. Occasionally they'd give some coverage of the issues, but rarely, and in general only with a paucity of analysis. The movement for public power was ridiculed and trivialized by some papers in past years. However, they're getting better now."

Chuck Finnie at the *Chronicle* sees it this way: "In passing the Raker Act Congress clearly envisioned the delivery of cheap, clean hydroelectricity to San Franciscans, but it did not explicitly require the city to do so. It did not say that power *had* to be sold to San Franciscans; instead, it prohibited the sale of Hetch Hetchy hydropower to any private company. In 1940 the Supreme Court ruled the city was selling power directly to PG&E for resale, in direct violation of the act. What's the difference now in how SFPUC disposes of its power? Instead of selling power to PG&E, it sells power to the Modesto and Turlock Irrigation Districts, public power utilities who then sell the power to their consumers. The city essentially swapped out the irrigation districts for PG&E, instead of making that power available to its residents. What the city is doing is not illegal, but it certainly is not what Congress intended.

"From the beginning there was a vested powerful interest held by PG&E to stop development of public power, which would require the city to pass bonds to finance construction or purchase of power plants and transmission lines. Was there collusion between city officials and PG&E to maintain the status quo and the company's monopoly? We don't know because we weren't there to talk with the participants or watch them. But it wouldn't surprise me if there was. Yet sometimes people simply come from the same economic position and so naturally share the same political agenda. They have the same predispositions. They might own PG&E stock, play golf and socialize together, and share a similar worldview. Collusion—no; they just agree. The city and PG&E formed an alliance in 1942 when they joined to lobby Congress to change the law. Why did they do that? Maybe it was because they were colluding. Or maybe it was because they were advocates for public power but couldn't get the voters to go along, perhaps because they were only making a halfhearted effort. Or maybe the change just fit both their agendas. It's hard to tell.

"There's no question that PG&E has never wanted competition in the city from public power. After the Raker Act passed, San Francisco built power plants and transmission lines but never completed the lines into the city, and it started selling off to PG&E excess power for profit after the municipal and irrigation districts' needs were met. That relationship served PG&E very well. Not only was the company getting power from Hetch Hetchy at wholesale that it could resell at retail rates, but the monopoly was avoiding competition. After the interior department sued and the Supreme Court upheld Harold Ickes's position, San Francisco continued to treat Hetch Hetchy as a cash cow for city government. It left San Francisco's retail electricity market to PG&E, which definitely benefited the company. The share of the company's overall revenues that come from that market is substantial. PG&E no longer got excess Hetch Hetchy power, but they kept the lucrative retail market. That's what they wanted to preserve. In short, residents and businesses in San Francisco today are probably paying substantially more for electricity from PG&E than they would have had the city developed a public power system around the Hetch Hetchy foundation. Hetch Hetchy can't supply all the city's power needs, but it was quite an asset around which they could have built a public power system. On the other hand, some people point out that the city makes money selling excess power to the irrigation districts and on the franchise fee it charges PG&E for the monopoly, and the city collects business taxes from the company; so the arrangement is a financial winner for San Francisco. Legal? Yeah. What the Raker Act intended? No.

"Once the promise was made by the City of San Francisco, even one on the scale as that embodied in the act, there's still a heck of a lot of work to do to ensure that promise is kept. On the water side, the promise was kept in the sense that the city built the aqueduct, but the city has certainly not been managing the water system very well. On the power side, the city never delivered on the promise. It turned the power side into a cash cow for city government. It left the city market to PG&E, and it did the bare bones to comply with the act. The downside of that broken promise is seen in the electricity rates paid by the public."

To Bruce Brugmann and other believers in public power, the cause has gained ground. "The walls are closing in on PG&E. Mayor Willie Brown hired a veteran public power administrator from Sacramento to be the city's principal energy planner. The board of supervisors voted eight to three to place the charter amendment to create public power on the 2002 ballot. The *Guardian* led the cause, while the dailies remained silent, at least until the last moment. But it's no longer possible for a city official to come out publicly and say he's for PG&E, even someone who has been a strong supporter all along. Those days are gone. We now win votes on council eight to three, when we used get beat nine to two or ten to one. That's the wave of the future. It's inevitable now: we *will* have public power." Only the timing and the vehicle to achieve it, and the details of its form, remain uncertain.

Perhaps a century after the city made a promise to the American people for public power, to gain congressional support for the damming of Hetch Hetchy, the promise will finally be fully realized. And with that realization, perhaps the San Francisco Public Utilities Commission will be reorganized in a way to more efficiently and effectively manage the dynamic nature of a utility, placing more responsibility in the hands of technical staff and less in the hands of politically appointed commissioners with little technical expertise. We can only hope for this, given how poorly politics has mixed with the provision of public water and power in San Francisco.

CHAPTER 16

Old Issues; A New Dream

Priest's Grade looms over Moccasin like an ocean swell about to break. The landscape atop the grade differs dramatically from that below. Above the 1,800-foot rise, the rolling terrain of the foothill woodlands feels cooler than the parched mosaic of chaparral, grasslands, and scrubby forests below. Grazing dominates the lower elevation, with derelict gold mines littered about. This was the landscape of the Mother Lode, a place of production and extraction; its scars are still healing in the relentless summer sun. Many of the tiny mining towns have long since disappeared, abandoned when the gold ran out. Those that survive, like Mariposa, Bear Valley, and Coulterville, have found new purposes. Above the rise, small towns like Big Oak Flat and Groveland, which lie on the way to the mountains, have always been places mostly for support, first for the gold rush, now for tourism to Yosemite National Park, with a short period of prosperity due to the construction of Hetch Hetchy in between. The High Sierra stands in the distance. Yosemite beckons. The rise forms a boundary between the two distinct worlds, a threshold like Altamont Pass.

The grade takes its name from Mrs. Margaret Priest, the charming Scottish-American proprietor of a popular hotel at the top for tourists en route to Yosemite in the late 1800s. She and her first husband, Alexander Kirkwood, added the hotel onto a miner's store in 1855 just as Yosemite's wonders began to attract attention. Kirkwood's Hotel, or Station, earned a national reputation for offering a welcomed respite to those making the arduous trek to the mountains. After Alexander died in 1870, Margaret married a handsome Kentuckian named William Priest, and they continued the hotel's traditional excellence. Old Priest Station Inn still serves as a beloved way station for pilgrims.

When Kirkwood's opened, only a primitive trail made the daunting ascent up the rise. Most travelers had to hike up the two-mile Old

Priest's Grade because horses struggled with the rocky climb. In 1870 the trail was converted into a crude wagon road. Most people still walked up the grade; a team of horses had difficulty pulling even an empty stage. Fortunately, a spring and a small shady spot offered relief halfway up, with a shanty nearby containing tools and ropes for emergency repairs. Everyone stopped—well-to-do tourists, circuit-riding preachers, Miwok Indians laden with dusty deer meat often teeming with flies, dirty miners perhaps carrying a heavy pack and a buckskin bag of gold dust, and an occasional highwayman who preyed on unwary passersby.

The wagon road was eventually paved for automobiles, which continued to stop at the spring for water and repairs. The current route on Highway 120, built in 1915 and widened since, takes eight miles of tight, twisting turns etched into the steep hillside to make the ascent up New Priest's Grade, on the opposite side of Grizzly Gulch from the old road. The much shorter and steeper old road remains, daring those with reliable cars and a sense of adventure to try the historic climb.

Private landowners and entrepreneurs like the Priests who provided public access to and accommodation in Yosemite would dominate the valley's future. Unlike most national parks, which were undeveloped and unclaimed parts of the public domain when they were created, much of Yosemite Valley was not. This legacy continues to shape our expectations of the park and the way the government manages it. And it also affected the fate of Hetch Hetchy.

Two attitudes resulting from the valley's legacy of private exploitation made the sacrifice of Hetch Hetchy more acceptable than might have been the case had Yosemite remained pristine. The amount of attention paid to the Yosemite Valley, while the remainder of the park was largely overlooked, made it easier for people to approve the dam and reservoir. Their concerns centered squarely on Yosemite: save Yosemite; sacrifice its little-seen sibling, Hetch Hetchy.

And if Yosemite was nearly sacred to Americans and had roads, hotels, and other human uses, then how could one oppose a shimmering reservoir for San Francisco's water supply in Hetch Hetchy, together with a hotel and a scenic road for tourists? Development and recreational use in Yosemite made it easier to accept the Hetch Hetchy plan, because people dating back to the original inhabitants had always modified the valley landscape to better meet their needs. Yosemite was not a virgin landscape untouched by human hands. To the contrary, the valley had long been used by people, and since the arrival of white prospectors and settlers about a decade before it became a public park, a place subject to private claim and exploitation.

Big Oak Flat lies about a mile east of Priest's Grade, less than thirty miles from the entrance to Yosemite. The fabled park draws me forward, as it has millions of visitors past and present, although I still can't see the High Sierra. The approach ascends gradually, lacking the drama of an approach to a range that erupts from the surrounding plain. I can see in my mind's eye the famed view from Inspiration Point as I drive toward the mountains—the view looking down the length of the valley at the chiseled silhouette of Half Dome in the distance, framed by Bridalveil Fall and Glacier Point on the right and El Capitan on the left. I recall Greeley, Olmsted, and Muir's awestruck descriptions on first seeing the valley. Will Yosemite work the same magic on me, or has familiarity immunized me to its wonder?

Route 120 races through the flat now, approximating the path of the original Big Oak Flat Road that linked the place with mining towns below the grade. It's a pretty spot, still retaining some of the landscape character from which the name derived. During the gold rush a hodgepodge of miners' tents and flimsy wooden structures lined the crude road as it wound through a small canyon before emerging into a clearing with a mammoth oak standing as the focal point. Today the roadsides have the casual, chaotic look of sporadic development strung for miles, common to towns with a linear form. Few vacation homes and little tourist-oriented development clutter the scenery here as they do along the entrance roads to some national parks. The flat retains a sense of the past and an "off the beaten path" feel even though it's a major way to Yosemite.

For generations the local Miwok Indians annually burned the flat to maintain a grassy parklike landscape with giant oaks scattered about from which they harvested acorns. The openness made hunting easier. Fires favored the grasses by suppressing the growth of forest and understory species intolerant of the heat. And the periodic burns prevented the buildup of sufficient combustible biomass to fuel a fire hot enough to damage the oaks. But miners replaced that disturbance regime with grazing, just as they displaced the native people.

Small, muscular, with dark-tanned skin, James Savage was one of the first to come, arriving on the flat in autumn 1848, where his rapid rise to local fame and fortune began. "He has I believe 33 wives among the mountain females of California," a soldier who served under his command in the Mariposa Battalion would recall several years later, "5 or 6 only however of which are now living with him. They are from the ages of 10 to 22 & are generally sprightly young squaws, they are dressed neatly, their white chemise with low neck & short sleeves, to which is appended either a red or blue skirt, they are mostly low in stature & not unhandsome [and] they always look clean and sew neatly." The Miwoks were amazed that Savage would trade them food, blankets, tin cups, and clothes for the dust gathered mostly by women from the two- to twenty-foot-deep gold-bearing gravel deposits in nearby streams. It didn't last long. Word of the wealth brought six thousand miners to "Savage's Diggings" in a year, forcing the founder to flee with his harem and workers to more remote sites.

The cluster of tents, ramshackle shacks, and stone buildings was quickly renamed after the beloved oak, twenty-eight feet in circumference, which residents enacted an ordinance to protect. But the "Big Oak" would die an ignominious death. Greedy miners are rumored to have dug away most of the soil around its roots under the stealth of night in 1863 to pan for gold; they also dug under the road in their frantic search. A fire subsequently left only a charred hulk standing. In 1869 the top of the tree fell off, leaving only the lower trunk. That soon fell over too and lay in place for thirty years, so massive that even a person on horseback could not see over it. No one had the heart to remove it. The town simply grew up around the mascot. Finally a cold camper accidentally set fire to the corpse in 1900. Since its founding, Big Oak Flat has suffered from repeated cycles of boom and bust, never able to retain the prosperity brought by those who have passed through.

I drive on. The flat dissipates, more than it ends, and Groveland fades in a mile or so to the east, the boundary between the two towns indistinguishable. It's about ten o'clock when I arrive at the Hotel Charlotte in the center of Groveland. After a long day that began on the East Coast, with a flight across the country and a three-hour drive inland from the San Francisco airport, I'm ready for a beer and a shower before sleep. The two-story, wood-frame structure resembles a hotel from a Western movie set. Built in 1918, the ten-room bed & breakfast is listed on the National Register of Historic Places. On pleasant summer evenings like tonight guests join the proprietors sitting on the second-floor porch overhanging the sidewalk. The infamous hanging that gave the town its original name, Garrote, occurred from an oak that stood in the alley along the hotel's flank. The tree was cut down and the stump shaved level to the ground when motorized vehicles replaced pack trains in the early 1900s. I drive over its site to reach the parking lot behind the building.

Diagonally across the street the large iron doors of the Iron Door Saloon stand open. Like the hotel, the saloon is a throwback to the town's mining and pioneer days, complete with a long ornate wood bar, a tin ceiling, and a treasure of historical memorabilia accumulated over the years, including bullet holes in the walls and old pictures of John Muir and Hetch Hetchy. Perhaps the ale is no longer brewed locally, but tourism hasn't dampened the local flavor of the saloon. Did Muir, Manson, or O'Shaughnessy have a nightcap here?

I'm off again at dawn for the forty-five-minute drive through Stanislaus National Forest to the park entrance, where there's still no hint of the wonders to come. The wide road winds gracefully through the sugar pine, ponderosa pine, and incense-cedar woodlands, gradually gaining elevation from 3,000 feet to about 4,800 feet at the park entrance. Along the way, private drives pull off and lead to in-holdings, some posing the same management complications for the national forest adjacent Yosemite as the private holdings posed within the park. Even after the park's boundary revision in 1905 a significant number of in-holdings remained. Choice sugar pine stands owned by private timber companies presented the greatest problem. Until 1930, the Park Service exchanged parcels at its boundary, mostly with the Forest Service. Since 1930, when the government purchased over 15,000 acres of private land in Yosemite— half with money donated by John D. Rockefeller Jr. and the rest from a fund provided by Congress for such acquisitions—the Park Service has primarily sought to buy the in-holdings.

And during the 1930s the government also sought to protect the scenery along the Big Oak Flat Road by purchasing in-holdings in Stanislaus National Forest or by negotiating management agreements between the Forest Service, the Park Service, the state, and the owners of these properties. Thousands of acres were acquired and agreements reached on others for the use of selective cutting and careful removal of timber. Today little evidence of logging or grazing detracts from my scenic drive to the park.

Route 120 continues along the approximate path of the Big Oak Flat Road, reaching the park entrance with little fanfare. The road splits to make room for a small booth between the inbound and out-bound lanes. A modest visitor center and parking lot sit to the side, less conspicuous than most turnpike rest stops or welcome centers at state borders. The wooden booth is stained in the ubiquitous dark brown color of Park Service buildings. Rangers greet you, usually seasonal hires during the summer, dressed in the standard uniform of warm gray shirt, dark green pant, and round, flat-brimmed campaign hat, the style a legacy of the U.S. Cavalry's management of the national parks. (The original uniform was designed in 1913–14 by the Department of the Interior's first general superintendent of parks.)

The War Department had assumed primary responsibility for the parks in 1886 when the cavalry entered Yellowstone to control vandalism and poaching. That worked as an emergency remedy, but as Yosemite and other parks were created in the 1890s, the need became apparent for an army of managers trained specifically for the job, modeled after the corps Pinchot was recruiting for the Forest Service in 1905. As he formed a well-run and well-funded bureaucracy, the national parks remained in administrative and political limbo. The lack of coordinated management among the individual parks became problematic. Efforts to remedy the situation began in 1900 when Iowa congressman John Lacey unsuccessfully introduced legislation to "establish and administer national parks." But congressional interest focused on other conservation programs.

A decade later the issue had ripened. In 1910 Secretary of the Interior Ballinger, bowing to intense lobbying led by J. Horace McFarland and the American Civic Association, proposed the creation of a Bureau of National Parks. President Taft approved, stating in December during his second annual message to Congress, "Our national parks have become so extensive and involve so much detail of action in their control that it seems to me there ought to be legislation creating a bureau for their care and control." The resulting bill again failed passage. Other bills followed, written jointly by McFarland, Frederick Law Olmsted Jr. (who had assumed the mantle from his father), the Sierra Club, and others.

Resistance remained widespread in Washington. The U.S. Forest Service feared that a rash of new national parks would be cut from forest lands. Pinchot felt it would threaten the Forest Service's favored position. Although no longer in government, he retained tremendous influence and sought to protect the power and prestige of the bureaucracy he fathered. And some critics simply felt another full-fledged agency was unwarranted. In response, proponents changed the name of the proposed agency to the National Park Service, reducing its status to be coequal with the U.S. Forest Service.

The change had little effect. The Forest Service still fought for control of national monuments and parks created from its lands, undermining the goal of unifying all of them in a single system. Pinchot continued to press for a park system managed for multiple resource use, not primarily for scenery and recreation as the preservationists proposed. Hetch Hetchy overtones reverberated in the background. And in the aftermath of the first conference on national parks held at Yellowstone in September 1911, political cynics questioned the motives of the proponents because of their intimate relationship with the railroads. The conference attracted seventy participants, including Department of the Interior staff, park superintendents and custodians, and other government officials, as well as representatives of the railroads, park concessionaires, and a few leaders of the park movement, most notably McFarland. Attendees discussed how to foster tourism to the parks and how to better manage them.

The railroads had been the first to realize the potential profits from tourism to the western parks and quickly became their strongest commercial advocates as a means of creating rail traffic. By the early 1900s some national parks were nearly synonymous with their "sponsoring" railroad that offered access, built grand resort lodges, and promoted visitation with colorful advertising campaigns.

Luxurious railroad posters of the parks became icons. Secretary of the Interior Fisher opened the Yellowstone conference praising the "enlightened selfishness" of the railroads and felt they deserved "grateful recognition" for their support—what was good for the goose was good for the gander. The railroads' marketing tapped into the nation's western mythos, the preservationist rhetoric about the value of scenery, and the rising public interest in outdoor recreation to help form an image of the parks as public playgrounds in places of great natural beauty—pure Americana.

The combination of these forces and the inherent practicality of a unified park system gradually overwhelmed political resistance. In 1913 President Wilson and Secretary of the Interior Lane recognized the administrative confusion affecting the national parks and monuments, supporting the centralization of responsibility that was split at the time between the Departments of Agriculture, Interior, and War. Civilian "rangers" employed by Interior were replacing cavalry troops in Yosemite and other parks. Horace Albright, an assistant in Lane's office and later the successor to Stephen Mather as director of the National Park Service, wrote that Lane possibly "felt embarrassment at the role he played, shortly after taking office in 1913, in putting through the Hetch Hetchy Act." As he was strongly opposed to the Hetch Hetchy plan, Albright continued, "one of the most heartbreaking tasks I had to perform when I first started my job was signing the Secretary's name to hundreds, I suppose even thousands, of answers to letters that came in protesting the dam."

Over the next two years Secretary Lane gradually assumed greater responsibility for the parks, appointing a deputy specifically to handle the growing duties. When the position became vacant in 1915, he hired a wealthy forty-seven-year-old Sierra Club member named Stephen Mather to fill the post. Mather had made a fortune in mining and distributing borax, his company known by the famous "Twenty Mule Team Borax" slogan. Lane knew of Mather and his familiarity with the national parks, and so asked the mountaineering buff to write him a letter outlining their condition. Mather wrote of his outrage at the violation of the Yosemite and Sequoia National Parks that he witnessed during a Sierra Club High Trip in 1914. "Dear Steve," Lane responded, "if you don't like the way the national parks are being run, come on down to Washington and run them yourself." He did. For the next fourteen years Mather would shape the fledgling National Park Service with the same effectiveness that Pinchot had shaped the Forest Service.

Mather promptly set to work lobbying the various government stakeholders to build consensus for a single bureaucracy to govern a park system. He also coordinated his political efforts in Washington with a coalition of outdoor groups across the country, including the American Civic Association, the Sierra Club, and the General Federation of Women's Clubs. The groups jointly mounted a media campaign in support of the plan. Lessons learned and connections made during the Hetch Hetchy debate paved the way.

Some members of Congress became convinced during the debate that a national park system was needed to avoid such debacles in the future. Bills to that effect were proposed every year in Congress from 1911 to 1915, sponsored most prominently by Utah senator Reed Smoot and California representative John Raker, who had introduced the bill to dam Hetch Hetchy. None of the bills made it out of committee. However, in the aftermath of Hetch Hetchy, other members had second thoughts on the outcome and began to look favorably on the creation of a park system.

By 1916 the proponents were meeting on a regular basis in Washington to coordinate their efforts, often at the F Street home of California congressman William Kent. Other regular attendees included Mather or his assistant Albright, Olmsted Jr., McFarland, and Gilbert Grosvenor, editor of *National Geographic.* Ironically, Kent had been a star witness during the 1913 Hetch Hetchy hearings *for* the project, even though he was an admirer of John Muir and advocate of preservation causes. In 1908 Kent had donated the land for Muir Woods National Monument to the nation, so his testimony in support of the project was particularly damning to the opponents. The controversy apparently convinced him—as it had Secretary Lane and Representative Raker—that a clearer congressional mandate and administrative structure were needed for the parks.

The F Street group selected Kent to introduce their lead bill, instead of Raker, who had introduced bills in 1912 and 1913, because Raker had developed political baggage with several key members of Congress. Olmsted Jr. contributed pivotal language to the draft, drawing on the Yosemite plan prepared by his father a generation before. *National Geographic* and the *Saturday Evening Post* ran feature articles in support. A colorful buckram-bound collection of pamphlets about the national parks, called *National Parks Portfolio* and funded personally by Mather and seventeen western railroad companies, was sent to every member of Congress. The women's clubs developed a mailing list for it and additional materials to 275,000 likely supporters.

The campaign worked. On August 25, 1916, President Wilson signed the Organic Act, which established the National Park Service, to "promote and regulate the use of the Federal areas known as national parks, monuments and reservations . . . by such means and measures . . . [as necessary] to conserve the scenery and natural and historic objects and the wild life therein and to provide for the enjoyment of the same in such manner and by such means as will leave them unimpaired for the enjoyment of future generations." Congress had finally determined that the parks were for scenery and outdoor recreation as Muir and the preservationists had argued, not for multiple resource use as Pinchot and the conservationists sought. The administration of the sixteen existing national parks and the twenty-one national monuments, and all that would follow, had finally been brought together under the jurisdiction of a single agency specifically created for the task. Some good had come out of the Hetch Hetchy "damn dam-damnation," after all.

The Big Oak Flat Road continues a gradual, winding ascent once inside the park, reaching an elevation of about 6,000 feet near Crane Flat and the junction with Tioga Road, which follows the path of the Mono Indian Trail eastward to Tuolumne Meadows and then over the crest of the Sierra. White pine, sugar pine, and red fir mix with the ponderosa pine, incense-cedar, and emerging sugar pine in the area, last logged in the 1920s. Whitethorn ceanothus and greenleaf manzanita comprise the sparse understory, with young shade-tolerant incense-cedar and white fir. The forest would have looked more open to visitors in Muir's day, nearly a century of fire suppression since enabling the gradual proliferation of shade-tolerant species beneath the canopy.

The native mixed conifer forest was well adapted to the low-intensity fires that recurred on average about every ten years. Fire crews now gather fallen limbs and combustible debris into five-foot-high piles scattered every hundred feet or so to be burned in the winter when snow pack prevents the fire from spreading. In other places the material is removed or prescribed burns are used to mimic the natural disturbance regime, sometimes too late. As the entrance road winds along the shoulder of a low mountain, just before beginning the descent into Yosemite Valley, it passes through the charred landscape left by the 1990 A-Rock fire that burned the hillside and the meadow around the small village of Foresta below. The burned area looks menacing and emaciated to me as I drive by, despite the rebirth underway.

A mile or so further, the road rounds a bend, and there it is, at last: Yosemite Valley. It looms in the distance, spellbinding, even just seen out the windshield of a moving car. Words cannot capture the sublime spectacle. What was the impact for someone slowly approaching on foot or horseback as the view was gradually revealed? I'm no less in awe than was Greeley, Olmsted, or Muir, even though I've seen pictures of the place and read their descriptions. It's hard to keep the car on the road.

Why is the view so mesmerizing, like gazing across the Grand Canyon? What makes it so compelling and unlike the scenery of other parks? Perhaps it is the unique juxtaposition of the raw, overpowering wildness seen in the sheer rock faces that form the towering canyon walls and the dramatic waterfalls, in contrast to the garden-like, even pastoral valley floor. Where else can one feel so dwarfed by the forces of nature and yet soothed by its luxurious abundance? Albert Bierstadt interpreted this rare combination in his paintings of Yosemite, romanticizing and infusing them with moral meanings. Perhaps Ansel Adams captured it more purely with his camera.

Tomorrow I begin a five-day hike from the valley up to Tuolumne Meadows, and then down the wild Grand Canyon of the Tuolumne River to the upper reach of Hetch Hetchy Reservoir, where I'll climb out of the deep canyon to reach "civilization" at White Wolf Campground. After the hike I'll boat the reservoir. I want to understand the landscape context of the dam and reservoir as best I can. What was lost? What might have been, as Muir had planned for perhaps the most scenic trail in the world? Scenery and recreation sat at the core of the controversy. How do Yosemite and Hetch Hetchy look now, and what form of recreation do they host? Like some participants in the debate, I've come to see for myself to better understand the issues. First I'll explore Yosemite Valley, after checking into my tent cabin at Curry Village.

David and Jennie Curry opened Camp Curry (now Curry Village) in 1899 to provide a half-price alternative to the hotels in Yosemite Valley. For $2 a night campers could rent one of seven sleeping tents and eat meals in a larger tent that contained the kitchen and dining room. "A good bed and clean napkin with every meal," the advertisements stated. The novel tent-camp idea flourished. By season's end the campground contained twenty-five tents circled around a central fire ring for group activities. In the hundred years since, Camp Curry has become synonymous with Yosemite, as much a part of the park as its natural features. Today the village contains 427 tent cabins plus 183 wood cabins and 18 standard motel rooms nestled in the trees beneath Glacier Point, in addition to a cavernous cafeteria and restaurant, an outdoor patio with food service, an amphitheater, a general store, a camping store, a pool, bathroom-shower facilities for guests, and large parking lots. The Spartan tent cabins have changed little over the years. About the size of a one-car garage, each sits on a wood floor raised several steps above the ground and is built of canvas stretched over a wood frame in the shape of a cabin. Inside are several metal cots, a small dresser with mirror, and a single light bulb dangling overhead. The $2 fee is long gone; my tent cabin cost over $70.

Concessionaires like the Currys have been central to the Yosemite story since the first white residents in the valley built homes and hotels in the 1850s. By the time the state reserve was established in 1864, a small community thrived there, much of which catered to tourists. Had the valley been vacant when the state reserve was established, perhaps the park might have had less tourist-oriented development. Once the development was established, however, it created an expectation that continues to this day—the Yosemite Valley welcomes tourists for family-friendly recreation, providing hotel accommodations, dining, and programmed outdoor activities. I suspect this level of development exceeds the level envisioned by Olmsted or Muir. Both men wanted the public to visit the park and benefit from its wonder, but both also believed the provision for that use should not dramatically affect the scenery. Unfortunately, it has. Yet vegetation management practices that Olmsted and Muir probably would have supported have also changed the scenery. At times these practices have sought to maintain the pastoral quality that Olmsted admired, and at other times they have suppressed the natural fire-disturbance regime, which both Olmsted and Muir misunderstood.

The symbiotic relationship between the park and the private entrepreneurs who provided tourist accommodations continued after the state acquired their property claims in the 1870s. It simply made more sense for the state to permit them to remain in operation by granting them a concession than it did for the state to run the facilities itself. And the prevailing perception of the park as a place for public recreation precluded the removal of most facilities and the return of the valley closer to its condition prior to white settlement, more in line with the limited development envisioned by Olmsted and Muir.

Tourist facilities flourished, run by concessionaires based on short-term leases negotiated with the park. Massive wooden hotels like Stoneman House, the Sentinel, and the Glacier Point Hotel, as well as smaller facilities, came and went as spectacular fires consumed some and competition consumed others. Stores, artist studios, saloons and bars, a billiard hall, a barbershop, a bakery, an open-air pavilion for dances, lectures, and movies, a woodworking shop, a stable, and a chapel were among the other facilities in the bosom of nature. Visitors loved it. Yosemite had become a recreational wonderland, a theme park for nature of a different sort than some preservationists preferred.

In 1901 Camp Curry contained a large, permanent dining room, a rustic office, and nearly seventy-five sleeping tents on wooden platforms. A sewer system, restrooms, and a bathhouse were added the next year. Guests were entertained in the evening with nightly campfires, concluding with a spectacular "firefall," in which a bonfire was set ablaze on Glacier Point and then pushed over the precipice, creating a glittering cascade of embers slowly drifting downward while a single violin serenaded the enthralled onlookers. Tunnels large enough for a carriage to drive through were cut into immense sequoias in nearby groves. Just as Muir thought, "Thousands of tired, nerve-shaken, over-civilized people" were learning that going to the mountains was going home—but because it offered all the comforts of home, not because they were experiencing the wilds of the backcountry, as he intended.

The recreation orientation of the valley changed little after it was added to the national park in 1906. The arrival of cars soon made Yosemite even more popular and convenient, especially for people from the Bay Area and the Los Angeles basin who could now reach the valley for weekend visits and, later, day trips. Improved access and the development of Hetch Hetchy induced San Franciscans to think of Yosemite as their private playground. In 1925, with work on the vast water and power project progressing, the National Park Service forced the two remaining concessionaires to merge so that a single company would handle all guest accommodations under a long-term lease. The Yosemite Park and Curry Company resulted, which continues today under corporate ownership and a new name.

I catch the free shuttle at the Curry Village bus stop to tour the valley, now home to a modest-size city, albeit with a relaxed pace of life in a breathtaking natural setting. I stop at Yosemite Village, the heart, to get my wilderness permit and bear canister at the Wilderness Center. The village contains the "municipal" offices (the park headquarters and the Wilderness Center), a museum, a medical clinic, an official U.S. post office with its own zip code (95389), various stores and restaurants, the grand Ahwahnee hotel, the Ansel Adams gallery, and even an auto repair service. Other facilities scattered about the valley include the Yosemite Lodge (a motel), the Happy Isles Nature Center, the Sierra Club's LeConte Memorial Lodge, a stables, four large campgrounds with drive-in sites, several walk-in campgrounds, a bike-rental shop, giant day-use parking lots, and the Curry Village complex. The local elementary school is used as long as there are enough students to fill it; high school students are bussed outside the park. Less noticeable are housing complexes for seasonal and resident staff, and various maintenance and management facilities. Seven thousand vehicles and twenty-five thousand people enter the park daily during the summer season, the vast majority headed to the valley. Half the visitors come from California.

Few people (2 percent) venture beyond a paved path into the wilderness overnight.

The valley pulses with activity beneath the canyon walls: hikers, bikers, horseback riders, rafters, rock climbers, sightseers, and picnickers, with cars and RVs coming and going. Tourist services in the park are not inexpensive, although compared to an amusement park admission remains a bargain, at $20 per car for a week or $40 for an annual pass (weddings cost $150, excluding the park admission fee). A room for two at the Ahwahnee starts at nearly $400 per night; a room at Yosemite Lodge begins at about $140. Of course, groceries and souvenirs can be expensive, too. Many visitors have household incomes above the state or national average. But for those people who camp or come in an RV, the visit can be very affordable compared to other forms of vacation. Drive-in campsites cost $18 per night; walk-in sites $5; and the entertainment provided by nature or park programs is free. There's plenty to see and do for individuals or families, and with a rigorous day hike you can reach some of the most scenic spots on the planet and see some of its oldest and largest living things. It's an amazing place for many reasons.

What does all this mean? Who should the park cater to and what types of accommodations and conveniences should be provided for them? To me the valley still looks and feels "natural," despite the amount of development it holds; there is nothing gaudy or obtrusive, no bright neon, blaring music, or hubbub. Of course, the place is not untouched by human hands, whether those of the Indians or those of the current caretakers.

But "natural" is not an absolute; rather it exists on a continuum with an amorphous boundary between natural and unnatural based on one's expectations, knowledge of place, and environmental values, instead of a sharp line defined by a universal standard. Can natural scenery be preserved in a place like Yosemite while simultaneously providing recreation opportunities for a broad cross-section of the public as required by the acts that created the park and the National Park Service? Is this compromise between permitting recreational use and the preservation of undisturbed nature still desirable, or have our concept of a national park and our sense of its purpose changed? Regardless, I think the National Park Service has done a sensitive job in the Yosemite Valley in the design and placement of facilities given the history, politics, and public preferences it inherited, and then fostered with development programs.

One of these programs was Mission 66, a ten-year project begun in 1956 with the goal of making the parks more visitor friendly by improving access and upgrading and expanding facilities in time for the agency's fiftieth anniversary. Although it triggered a national debate, particularly concerning Yosemite and the rebuilding of Tioga Road into the park, Mission 66 proved to be the right idea at the right time, practically and politically. With a surging national economy fueled by pent-up consumer demand, a postwar baby boom, an explosion in highway construction, including the beginning of the interstate system, and a park system suffering from years of neglect, the program proved a huge success. "See the USA in your Chevrolet," Dinah Shore sang to millions of growing families eager to see the sights during summer vacation. "Yogi Bear" and "Jellystone Park" became Saturday-morning staples. The public loved the Mission 66 improvements and the national parks, which they continued to consider as "natural," even in developed areas like the Yosemite Valley.

By and large we still love the improvements and the parks, which we still perceive as natural. However, in the 1970s concerns that the accommodation of tourists had gone too far in places like the Yosemite Valley began to change park policy to better balance recreational use and ecological-based preservation. The park's 1980 general management plan called for a reduction in some tourist facilities in the valley, while restoring altered ecosystems and enhancing the visitor's "nature" experience throughout the park.

Nevertheless, most Americans believe that the national parks should welcome all people, not just those who are able to backpack in the wilderness. Most of us believe everyone should have a reasonable opportunity to enjoy the natural wonders of Yosemite regardless of age, income, or physical ability. Does that mean the park must accommodate RVs in the valley and those people who need assistance to stay in the backcountry?

The Hetch Hetchy debate raises fundamental questions like these. I wonder whether the public supported the valley's preservation because they really wanted it left untouched and open only for sightseeing, keeping it wild with just primitive trails within, or because they wanted it developed for outdoor recreation as the Yosemite Valley had been and remains to this day. If O'Shaughnessy Dam were removed and the Hetch Hetchy Valley eventually restored to its original splendor, as some people propose, should it be used the same way the Yosemite Valley is used today, or should we treat Hetch Hetchy differently?

The National Park Service continues to manage Yosemite based on goals established in the park's 1980 general management plan and updated in 2000 by the Yosemite Valley plan. These set five priorities: reclaim the park's priceless natural beauty by reducing the amounts of administrative function, commercial service, and visual intrusion, especially in the valley; markedly reduce traffic congestion by relocating parking areas and staff housing to the perimeter of the park, and by the use of shuttle buses; allow natural processes to prevail by reestablishing native plant communities and respecting natural disturbance regimes; reduce crowding by setting limits on visitation and facilities to levels consistent with the environment's carrying capacity, visitor expectations, and the visitor experience; and promote visitor understanding and enjoyment through enhanced interpretive programming and effective, high-quality educational facilities, while balancing development and use in such a way to preserve nature's wonders and keep them from being overshadowed by the intrusions of the human environment.

Few land management problems pose more complicated challenges than those faced by the National Park Service working to balance the often conflicting values of the many stakeholders. As the Hetch Hetchy controversy uncovered, most people had an opinion about the park; many were passionate. Yet politics and economics dictated the outcome more than the philosophical and environmental issues.

I begin my backpacking trip early the next morning from the trailhead at Happy Isles, elevation 4,035 feet. It's been ten years since I last did this. The decade has worn on me and my equipment. Time hasn't been good to my knees or to the waterproofing on the tent, poncho, and pack during storage in the basement. Thankfully, the forecast is clear and it rarely rains here at this time of year. (Famous last words.) The familiar uneasiness felt on past backpacking trips

puts me on edge as I begin the steep ascent up the paved trail to
Vernal Fall (5,044 feet). It's not fear or anxiety, but rather a recognition that for the next five days I'll be without the support system I
take for granted in everyday life. I love the backcountry. I love the
physical and psychological challenges it poses and its raw, natural
beauty. I relish drinking directly out of a stream and gazing into a
milky Milky Way that lights an otherwise truly black night sky. I
revel in the quiet and solitude. But I'm not comfortable there. I don't
go frequently enough for that.

The Mist Trail is already crowded with people headed toward the
fall. Few people carry packs, even small daypacks. For most tourists,
taking a hike like this half-day loop is as far from the valley floor as
they'll go. The more adventurous might take a full-day hike to the top
of Glacier Point, Yosemite Falls, or Half Dome, or take the shuttle to
Tuolumne Meadows and hike down the river canyon to see one or
two of its nearest cascades. Most people on this trail, however, turn
back at the famous stairs that climb up the 320-foot-high vertical face
of the fall like a fire escape. Those who reach the top can walk within
feet of the brink, blocked by a railing, and look back down at the valley a thousand feet below. Some risk their lives to play in Emerald
Pool just upstream.

Another rugged climb comes a half mile beyond. I've taken the
shorter but more difficult trail that skirts Nevada Fall to the north; it
was a bad decision, as that trail has dozens of tight switchbacks going
straight up a talus slope formed from rockfalls to 6,000 feet. At the
top the trail assumes a gentle slope as it passes through a stand of
mixed conifers. The path is soft underfoot between the burnt orange
trunks and fibrous bark of the stately incense-cedars. Short trails
branch off to Half Dome and the Little Yosemite Valley Campground, the most popular wilderness campground in the park.

I continue on, the trail less well traveled after the junctures. I'm
gradually ascending along Sunrise Creek, a tributary to the Merced
River that arises in a broad meadow beneath Tresidder, Echo, and
Cathedral Peaks. I'll make camp there tonight. Turning northward
and away from the Merced, the trail becomes steeper and harder to
follow as it climbs moraines beneath the south buttress of the Clouds
Rest eminence. No grand panoramas visible in this stretch through
the closed canopy. I lose the path for a mile or so climbing through a

lodgepole pine forest cluttered with giant granite boulders and fallen snags on the tortuous southern face of Sunrise Mountain. Wilderness can be a bother at times. Nature tends to be messy, not tidy like human-dominated landscapes. Most wild places are inconvenient for our purposes. That's a big reason we change them—to make them better suited to our wants and wishes.

I relax a bit once I reacquire the trail. It's noon now; I rest and eat lunch in a small clearing along the mountain's eastern slope, at 9,750 feet the high point for the day. I've not seen another hiker for several hours. The sky is crystal clear and deep blue, the brilliant sunshine reflecting off the smooth rocks, boring into my body. From here the trail descends several hundred feet along the mountain's flank to Long Meadow. I reach Sunrise High Sierra Camp by mid-afternoon, my T-shirt caked with dry sweat and granite dust; my body exhausted; but my spirit satisfied with the fifteen-mile hike and the mile of elevation gain. I wish I weren't so goal oriented. Wilderness should be experienced on its own terms, without an itinerary, an agenda, or a watch. But I have a hard time leaving the accoutrements of civilization behind.

Sunrise sits on a rocky bench fifty feet above the meadow, facing east toward the Cathedral Range. Run by the park concessionaire, the camp has nine tent cabins similar to those in Curry Village and a dining tent where the thirty-four guests get meals; the cost is about $125 per night. Tents have dormitory-style steel-frame cots with mattresses, pillows, woolen blankets or comforters, and are reserved well in advance. The camp also provides restrooms and showers with hot water and soap. Guests pack in their own sheets and towels, along with their clothes, on the half-day hike from the nearest road at Tuolumne Meadows.

Perhaps the chain of five High Sierra camps in Yosemite represents an appropriate compromise between preserving the park untouched and providing wilderness recreation for a wider range of people than those who can backpack. I pitch my tent next to Sunrise camp, cook dinner on a small backpacker's stove fueled with white gas, and watch the alpine glow on the surrounding peaks as the sun sets. I am too tired to move.

I'm on the trail at eight the next morning, stiff from the climb yesterday and chilled in the brisk air. The sun hasn't been over the distant peaks long enough to dry the dew off the tent, but I'm anxious to get underway. Today will be easier. Once over Cathedral Pass, several miles from here, I'll hike downhill to Tuolumne Meadows and then beyond to the Glen Aulin High Sierra Camp, at 7,800 feet near the top of Tuolumne Canyon.

After an hour of easy walking, the trail leaves Long Meadow, wrapping around Columbia Finger with a few gentle switchbacks that emerge onto a promontory of polished granite dotted with boulders left by the glaciers that carved the valleys below. Cairns point the way across the rock face as the trail rises to a high point along the shoulder of Tresidder Peak. Stunning panoramas of the distant Clark Range open to the south and east. The trail parallels a long, open swale leading up to the pass. Humpback-rock outcrops smoothed by glacial action rise just above the turf. At mid-season, the swale becomes a floral wonderland. Beyond the pass the trail fills with day hikers who have come up from Tuolumne Meadows to explore the lakes at the base of Cathedral Peak, its sharp, jagged spires reflected in the glassy surface of the shallow upper lake. Campsites are few, but the four-mile-long, thousand-foot descent through a lodgepole and mountain hemlock forest to Tuolumne Meadows is not difficult.

I cross Tioga Road and the meadow, flooded with tourists, without stopping. It's hard to imagine how the place could be dammed, as some Hetch Hetchy proponents also advocated. To the east and south high peaks like Mt. Dana (13,057 feet) encircle the broad meadow, forming the headwaters of the Tuolumne River and San Francisco's water supply. The river meanders to the northwest across the plain, with no dam site apparent. In several miles it begins the plunge down the canyon to Hetch Hetchy. Ninety percent of the watershed sits above 6,000 feet with little human use other than that here and at Glen Aulin Camp seven miles beyond.

Similar to Sunrise, Glen Aulin has eight cabins for thirty-two guests, but it has no showers. The circle of tent cabins and the dining tent sit at the base of White Cascade and Tuolumne Fall, where the river pours a hundred feet into a pool bordered by a sandy beach. It's early afternoon, hot, and I'm tired, so I soak my feet in the icy water before pitching my tent in a camping area for backpackers just behind the tent cabins. A new high-tech latrine stands nearby on a ten-foot-high rock promontory. The press had fun chiding the Park

Service for the "two-seat wonder" with a several-hundred-thousand-dollar price tag. I laughed too, until I saw the sensitive location beside San Francisco's water supply, miles from the nearest road, requiring building materials to be carried in by mule or helicopter.

For years the city has voluntarily funded Park Service projects to protect the water quality in the Tuolumne drainage, since the work is vital to the city's interests. The amount of the annual cash contribution—of late $1 million to $3 million—is determined by the San Francisco Public Utilities Commission after they receive a project list prepared by the Park Service staff. The contribution usually covers only part of the requested budget. Projects typically include policing the dam and reservoir, patrolling and maintaining trails, restoring damaged sites near streams, and building various sanitation and wastewater projects like the latrine.

In addition, the Raker Act requires the city to pay the federal government an annual fee "to be applied to the building and maintenance of roads and trails and other improvements in the Yosemite National Park and other national parks in the State of California," as determined by the secretary of the interior. Payments began in 1918, were set initially at $15,000 a year for ten years, increased to $20,000 annually for the next ten years, and went to $30,000 thereafter, to remain there unless Congress acts to change the amount. To date it hasn't, leaving the fee San Francisco pays for the use of the park as a reservoir and water source at $82.19 per day, just as it was nearly seventy years ago. What a bargain. Proposals to increase the fee to some higher amount more inline with market value, if such a figure can be determined, have failed, although the current administration just tried again, proposing an increase to $8 million. That equals about $3.33 per year for each water consumer, or about $19 per acre for the use of the watershed compared to the current rate of seven cents per acre. The reaction of city officials and Democrats from California, including Senator Feinstein, was predictable and emphatic: No way. Congressional Republicans, even some from California, were supportive, but no action was taken.

I'm on the trail again at about nine the following morning, after sharing breakfast with another camper who lost his food when a small bear made off with his canister last night. Bears have become bold around humans, from years of people feeding them and from successful scavenging for food in cars, campsites, and trash cans. To break the bears of the behavior, people throughout the park are now required to store their food and place their trash in bear-proof lockers or containers. Backpackers must carry an approved four-gallon canister that bears cannot open. You cache your food in the canister and at night simply leave it out in the open away from your tent. Since the bear can't open the canister, it leaves the plastic keg alone and moves on. This camper had left his canister in the ten-foot gap between our tents, so we both heard the bear pawing at the temptation overnight. Unfortunately, the camper discovered the next morning that he hadn't locked the lid.

The trail splits just after leaving Glen Aulin. The popular Pacific Crest trail heads off to the north, and the Tuolumne trail descends westward into the upper reach of the canyon. Almost all backpackers head north. I join the day hikers headed to the waterfalls. The intimidating canyon stretches out before me with a dramatic view that looks five miles down its length and drop of several thousand feet. I'll make camp somewhere down there this afternoon. Steep switchbacks drop over a series of rocky cliffs, like giant stair steps, each several hundred feet high, and each forming a thundering cascade or fall: California Falls, LeConte Falls, and Waterwheel Falls. Day hikers scurry carefully around the gushing shoots and swirling pools. The sun bakes us, reflecting off the rock polished by flowing water. The glare is blinding. Trail crews are at work repairing the switchbacks.

The forest gradually changes as I descend deeper and deeper into the canyon, from lodgepole pine and red fir, mixed with some Jeffrey pine and junipers, to white fir, sugar pine, incense-cedar, and Jeffrey pine, and then to incense-cedar, black oak, and gold-cup oak. (John Muir's idol—Alexander von Humboldt—formulated a famous theory to explain the way elevation, microclimate, and site conditions stratify plant communities.) The canyon also begins to change in cross-section due to subtle differences in the rock structure, becoming more V-shaped than the common U-shape of glaciated valleys. As the canyon approaches the heart of Hetch Hetchy it will become U-shaped again. Evidence of Yosemite's glacial and geological history is everywhere once one learns to see it.

I camp on a small trailside ledge overlooking the river, opposite

Ten Lakes Canyon, a two-thousand-foot-high cleft cut by Ten Lakes Creek. Swarming mosquitoes are the only drawback to the shady spot. I'm not using repellant or sunscreen, which might wash off into the river. For relief I bathe in a frigid pool using organic, nontoxic soap, and then lie in the sun on a smooth rock slab with the river rushing around me. I drink my fill and top off my water bottles. It's a spectacular spot: quiet despite the wind and constant roar of the water, and sublime as the setting sun highlights the different colors in the canyon walls. The scenery differs from that in the high country. No panoramas here; the canyon has closed down, becoming so narrow and steep-walled that it's almost claustrophobic. The only views are up the vertical sides; trees and slight turns in the trail block views down the canyon. I've not seen a soul since passing the last cascade at noon. For the first time I feel as though I'm really in the wilderness.

Why is that? What is wilderness? Is it the absence of a human presence either in person or effect? I believe wilderness is subjective, like the meaning of "natural," so there is no single definition—what the Indians considered a nurturing home was often perceived by the pioneers who replaced them as a threatening wilderness. Perception of both conditions—natural and wilderness—depends on one's point of view.

The laws creating the national parks and the Park Service said nothing about the preservation of wilderness. Ironically, that idea arose in the Forest Service in the 1920s with Arthur Carhart, a landscape architect, and Aldo Leopold, a forester schooled in the Pinchot philosophy. Leopold led the push in the agency to designate such areas, soon joined by another young forester named Robert Marshall, resulting in a handful being created by administrative authority over the following decades.

Yet because the areas lacked a legislative basis, their status and use were subject to administrative change. With the stroke of a pen they could be declassified and opened for resource development. This constant threat and the desire to preserve additional wilderness areas led Marshall, Leopold, and others to form the Wilderness Society in 1935 to champion the cause and lobby the government for a national wilderness system. In the 1950s Howard Zahniser would lead the battle, following the tragic deaths of thirty-eight-year-old

Marshall in 1939 and sixty-one-year-old Leopold in 1948. Zahniser eventually won. When Congress passed the Wilderness Act of 1964 (78 Stat. 890), it formally defined such places and gave them a permanent legislative basis. But Zahniser didn't live to see the final victory. He died four months before President Lyndon Johnson signed the act Zahniser had shepherded through eighteen congressional hearings and sixty-six rewrites during eight years of lobbying. The act states,

> A wilderness, in contrast with those areas where man and his own works dominate the landscape, is hereby recognized as an area where the earth and its community of life are untrammeled by man, where man himself is a visitor who does not remain. An area of wilderness is further defined to mean in this Act an area of undeveloped Federal land retaining its primeval character and influence, without permanent improvements or human habitation, which is protected and managed so as to preserve its natural conditions and which (1) generally appears to have been affected primarily by the forces of nature, with the imprint of man's work substantially unnoticeable; (2) has outstanding opportunities for solitude or a primitive and unconfined type of recreation; (3) has at least five thousand acres of land or is of sufficient size as to make practicable its preservation and use in an unimpaired condition; and (4) may also contain ecological, geological, or other features of scientific, educational, scenic, or historical value.

All federal land, whether in a national forest, a national park, or other jurisdiction, is subject to wilderness designation; and if designated by Congress, the original jurisdiction administers the wilderness area consistent with the rules set forth in the act. Today the National Wilderness Preservation System contains over 105 million acres (4.67 percent of the nation's land area) in 662 tracts located in 44 states, although Alaska contains 54 percent of the total acreage. The southern portion of the Yosemite wilderness is a part of a 2.25-million-acre complex, the second largest in the contiguous United States. Muir and Olmsted would be pleased that over 90 percent of Yosemite National Park is designated as wilderness. Perhaps the wilderness system better reflects what they really envisioned for the national parks. No doubt they would also like to see the intensity of development in Yosemite Valley reduced. Regardless, the National Wilderness Preservation System and the National Park Service represent a uniquely American philosophical, political, and environmental gesture to the world. No other nation in the temperate latitudes could or would designate so much of itself as forever wild or set so much of itself aside for the preservation and enjoyment of natural scenery.

Can "wilderness" be restored to an altered landscape? The Wilderness Society believes it can. Once signs of human influence have been removed and natural systems predominate, a place can be considered for wilderness designation—including Hetch Hetchy.

The weather is again gorgeous on day four: low humidity and brisk morning temperatures in the 40s, warming to the 80s when the afternoon sun finally reaches the canyon floor. The hike continues in the tight confine: no falls or cascades, and few distant views up or down the length. The walls rise higher and higher as I descend, although the rim remains at about eight thousand feet. The trail still challenges, with dozens of steep switchbacks climbing up and down several rocky knobs, one of which is five hundred feet high.

I cross a sixty-foot-high bridge over Rodgers Creek and pass along the lip of Muir Gorge, overlooking the river as it churns among mammoth boulders below. Beyond, the trail is easier going, traversing a nearly level, shady stretch with burned snags, the result of careless campers. I stop for the day at Pate Valley, a flat of several acres, the first since Tuolumne Meadows twenty miles up the canyon. The river flows peacefully over a gravelly bed through the center. I'm only a half-dozen miles now from the headwater of Hetch Hetchy Reservoir. Tomorrow I will climb out of the canyon to the White Wolf Campground, 11 miles away and 4,000 feet higher, and then will conclude my story at its source.

Since the Hetch Hetchy project, no significant dam has been built in a national park. But it almost happened, and this triggered a similar controversy. In the 1940s, the Bureau of Reclamation planned a ten-dam, billion-dollar project on the Colorado River for flood control, irrigation, recreation, and hydropower—many of the same purposes served by Hetch Hetchy. The vast Colorado River Storage Project called for a dam at Echo Park in Dinosaur National

Monument. The spectacular steep-walled canyon at the confluence of the Yampa and Green Rivers in northwest Colorado had been named in 1869 by John Wesley Powell during his famous expedition to the Colorado Plateau. When the secretary of the interior approved the dam in 1950, "in the interest of the greatest public good," the fight was on.

The national parks and wild areas were again under attack by those seeking to exploit their resources to feed the postwar economic boom. Loggers eyed the thick Douglas fir stands in Olympic National Park. Dams were pending in both Glacier and Grand Canyon National Parks. And Los Angeles longed to tap the water resources in Kings Canyon National Park. As it did for Hetch Hetchy, the need for congressional authorization triggered a heated national debate over the proposed Echo Park dam. The institutional memory of the earlier debacle remained fresh. Senator Hubert H. Humphrey reminded his colleagues, "where once there was the beautiful Hetch Hetchy Valley . . . there is now the stark, drab reservoir of O'Shaughnessy Dam." This time the opponents would win, having learned important lessons from their prior defeat.

Howard Zahniser and David Brower led the way, like Robert Underwood Johnson and John Muir before them: Zahniser, the politically savvy head of the Wilderness Society; and Brower, the firebrand executive director of the Sierra Club. The rhetoric, arguments, and tactics used by both sides were similar to those used with Hetch Hetchy. However, this time the opponents were better funded, better organized, and thoroughly professional. They not only challenged the proposal on emotional, philosophical, and aesthetic criteria, as had the Hetch Hetchy opponents, but they also countered the government's technical arguments with equally credible quantitative data. And by this time the public and Congress were more comfortable with the concept of wilderness and familiar with the value of its preservation. Still, the fight was hotly contested and the outcome in doubt until Congress approved the Colorado River Storage project in 1956, with the caveat that "no dam or reservoir constructed under authorization of the Act shall be within any National Park or Monument."

Brower noted that in controversies involving the preservation of wilderness, victory is not possible; rather, one can only win a stay of execution for the wild place because people hell-bent on exploiting natural resources will always lie in wait. Fortunately, with so little wilderness left, public opinion now places the burden of proof on those who would develop the wilderness to show why development is necessary, and that's a tough case to make, as the government was recently reminded by its latest attempt to permit oil drilling in the Arctic National Wildlife Refuge.

Attitudes toward dams and water projects in general continue to change. Efforts are now under way to reopen the floodgates and restore the natural flow of some rivers, like the Colorado River, perhaps even to tear down the dam. What was a symbol of American ingenuity and technical prowess a generation ago has become to some people one of our most offensive environmental blunders. Few things make them bristle more than dams. The concrete megaliths seem so permanent and unyielding, emphatically asserting our defiance of nature. And their impacts are so devastating to the river and adjacent land above and below the impoundment. Once, the huge dams and the great water projects of the Bureau of Reclamation and the U.S. Army Corps of Engineers meant progress and sound resource conservation, especially in the West: flood control, irrigation, hydroelectricity, and recreation—just like Hetch Hetchy. Now the cost-benefit calculus often comes to a different conclusion.

My luck with the weather runs out the next day as I begin the steep climb out of the canyon. The trail starts the ascent several miles upriver from Hetch Hetchy Reservoir and several hundred feet above its full pool elevation at about 3,800 feet, before the water body comes into view. What I have seen all morning are black clouds building over it as a storm approaches up the canyon. It reaches me as I start the rocky climb. With a worthless poncho and no cover from the deluge on the canyon wall, I keep going, straining from the exertion and soaked from the rain. Several better-prepared hikers pass me on the way. I haven't climbed very high before I can see the reservoir snaking off until it bends around Kolana Rock and disappears about seven miles in the distance. Slogging back and forth up the switchbacks, I focus on the water body that floods the valley floor below me, where the canyon widened to once form a garden landscape like the Yosemite Valley.

Hetch Hetchy Reservoir looks like dozens I've seen before. There

are no roads or trails around this one; no hotel or cabins; and no
boats. Nor could there be, to protect the water purity—a prime reason for damming the river in the valley instead of someplace outside
the park. Completely isolated, the reservoir rests in a rocky canyon
surrounded by rugged, arid-looking mountains; there is no sign of
people, other than the reservoir itself, and no hint of what was
flooded. The best sense of that loss comes from touring the Yosemite
Valley. Historical black-and-white photographs of Hetch Hetchy
before the dam was built confirm that the valley was in fact very similar in character to its sibling, corroborating the firsthand accounts.

Is the reservoir beautiful? I don't think so. It's certainly dramatic
because of its setting. But its desolation doesn't have the stark beauty
of the arid canyons of Lake Powell. I can think of lakes that are more
scenic. The argument that the reservoir improved the beautiful
scenery over that of the valley floor was vacuous. And the Grand
Canyon of the Tuolumne River, upriver from the reservoir, is spectacular. Tragically, this grand canyon lost its climax when the valley
was flooded.

The O'Shaughnessy Dam and the Hetch Hetchy Reservoir were
a mistake. They were unnecessary and justified on spurious, self-
serving reasons. Although the Hetch Hetchy project was a tremendous technological feat, it was not warranted on aesthetic, economic,
philosophical, or public policy criteria. Even the political justifications were inappropriate. San Francisco could have and should have
obtained its water elsewhere. The project would never be approved
today, and it should not have been approved in 1913, even recognizing the complicated history and context of the time.

From senior management to seasonal rangers, National Park
Service staff see it as a scab in the park and dream of its removal. But
the agency has no official position on the proposal. Congress makes
its mandate, which since 1913 has been to manage the park with a
reservoir in its midst.

Neither does the SFPUC have a position on Hetch Hetchy and its
possible removal and restoration. It too implements the policies and
priorities set by its governing bodies—the board of commissioners
and the city administration. The proposal has little political support
from them; there is too much vested economic interest and civic
pride at stake. Perception of Hetch Hetchy as the rightful property of

the city remains commonplace. Public opinion in the Bay Area is harder to judge. People are torn between the sense of loss and the personal gain: unfortunate, yes; remove it, probably not.

Mainstream environmental groups support the plan but won't fight for it. Practicality, not the inflamed idealism of the past, dominates their modus operandi now. They fight the battles they can win and obtain the greatest benefit from. Highly trained professionals have replaced most of the hot-blooded tree huggers, perhaps for good reason. The passion and commitment remain, only the method to achieve goals has changed.

What does the American public think? I suspect we would support the removal and restoration, just as we opposed the damming originally. Would you?

Ultimately the decision rests in Washington. Have the politics of environment and economics changed over the past hundred years to the extent that Congress would support a bill now to undo what it did in 1913? Who would lobby for the bill and who would oppose it? What would the arguments be, pro and con? Would Congress listen to public opinion this time, or would economic interests and politics again dictate the outcome? There seems to be little doubt that a "win-win" option for the removal and restoration is technically feasible, and even relatively easy compared to the challenges posed by the construction of the project. Nor is the cost more than a red herring. Congress routinely spends billions on other projects with less lasting and worldwide significance. Rather, the real issue is politics; it is as simple and complicated as that.

I've finally reached the canyon rim. Mercifully, the terrain levels and the trail ducks beneath a tree canopy. But the storm has passed. The sky becomes a brilliant blue again. The three-mile walk to White Wolf over a spongy forest floor goes quickly. I have a car parked at the campground for the forty-five-minute drive to O'Shaughnessy Dam.

Tioga Road takes me to Crane Flat, where I turn onto Big Oak Flat Road and exit the park. A mile beyond the entrance booth, Evergreen Road branches off toward the City of San Francisco's Camp Mather, and Hetch Hetchy. Pastures, fences, and in-holdings give this portion of Stanislaus National Forest a much different look than the scenic forest along Big Oak Flat Road, suggestive of the difference in management philosophy and practice between the National Parks and National Forests. This is Pinchot's landscape, a place of multiple uses.

Halfway to the reservoir, the road comes to a junction around which Camp Mather has grown like a small village, the site of a former Miwok settlement. The camp originated when the city built a saw mill, a railhead, and a support facility here during the construction of its dam. The Yosemite Park and Curry Company also built tourist accommodations in it for people visiting the park or the massive construction project. When the dam was completed, the city transformed the facilities into a summer camp for residents. Today Camp Mather offers cabins, tent sites, meals, and a wide variety of outdoor activities and programs for hundreds of guests each summer. And like Yosemite, the camp has become a tradition for Bay Area families, reinforcing the sense of Yosemite as their personal playground.

The logging, grazing, and recreational development stops at the Hetch Hetchy entrance to the park. A big sign next to the small ranger booth announces, "Yosemite National Park Hetch Hetchy Area, DAY USE HOURS: 7 A.M.–9 P.M., Gate Locked at Night, NO VEHICLES OVER 25 FEET." The ranger hands out a pamphlet from the San Francisco Public Utilities Commission extolling the benefits of the dam and reservoir together with the standard Park Service material on the park.

The rugged landscape looks dry with sparse forest cover, in contrast to the more lush approach to Yosemite. O'Shaughnessy Dam and the Hetch Hetchy Reservoir come into view from miles away. The vast scale deceives. The dam looks so tiny in the distance, a plug dwarfed by the embracing canyon walls. From this perspective the place feels desolate, not welcoming like its nearby sibling. And from here the proposal to remove the 312-foot-high, 900-foot-long dam doesn't seem so outrageous.

Secretary Hodel initially suggested it in 1987. The resulting concept study released the next year by the Bureau of Reclamation, the agency created to construct dams, asked, "Could the City of San Francisco receive a comparable water and power supply from other sources? Could the Hetch Hetchy Valley be restored as part of the living heritage of our National Park system? In a world of diminishing natural resources, what is the highest use of the valley? These questions are worth asking." The dam builders concluded that the proposal might actually be feasible and a detailed study was warranted.

Since the late 1990s, when the Sierra Club and Restore Hetch Hetchy took up the cause, support for a full-scale feasibility study has grown. Editorials in favor of a study have appeared in major papers coast to coast and in many Bay Area papers. If it took the City of San Francisco over a decade to gain approval to build the project, then a target date for approval of a plan to remove the dam and restore the valley on the centennial of the Raker Act, in 2013, seems appropriate.

Evidence of the plan's feasibility also mounts. The most comprehensive study to date, "Paradise Regained: Solutions for Restoring Yosemite's Hetch Hetchy Valley," released in 2004 by Environmental Defense, concludes, "practical, proven water storage, conveyance and treatment alternatives can provide San Francisco a healthy, reliable and secure supply of water that is adequate for current and future needs . . . [and] hydropower lost as a result of restoring the valley can be replaced without contributing to air pollution or global warming." Although the study did not analyze all possible alternatives, those it did analyze "demonstrate that workable solutions for restoring Hetch Hetchy Valley exist." The study estimated the cost at $1 billion to $2 billion, and projected that a century would be needed for reasonably full restoration of the valley.

The political will in support of a feasibility study continues to build. On November 11, 2004, California governor Arnold Schwarzenegger's secretary of resources took the historic step of directing state agencies to undertake a comprehensive study of the costs and benefits of restoring the valley. "California, its governor and its citizens, are committed to economically feasible restoration of ecosystems and preservation of open space," announced the secretary. "This commitment translates into an interest in reasonable proposals for expanding our trust resources. Specifically, I have asked the Department of Water Resources (DWR) to review the growing body of studies and analyses that have been prepared over the last 20 years including Environmental Defense and U.C. Davis efforts, and summarize the range of conclusions and considerations in this work.

Additionally, DWR will consider the larger water supply impacts. Clearly, one of the foremost challenges posed by the proposal stems from the fact that California, faced with significant water demands, needs a net increase in water storage capacity, not a decrease. Any plan to remove or modify the existing water storage system would need to be balanced by a viable alternative plan to, at a minimum, replace the water supply now provided by the Hetch Hetchy reservoir." The secretary also instructed his Department of Parks and Recreation to "work with the National Park Service to identify accepted economic approaches to estimate a parkland value for a restored Hetch Hetchy Valley. Consideration of factors such as what relief, if any, might a Hetch Hetchy restoration offer to the heavy visitation pressure on Yosemite Valley may add value for this review."

I park in the small, dam-side lot overlooking the spillway. A little-used campground sits behind me, hidden from view by a ring of rocky mounds. I still have no accurate sense of scale to the place. The gap between the canyon walls is so small at the base, I feel as though I could touch both sides by stretching out my arms. No wonder engineers like Grunsky, Manson, O'Shaughnessy, and Freeman were in awe of the site.

It's eerie being here, after studying the Hetch Hetchy story for so long. Fragments flash through my mind as I walk a hundred yards to the boat launch where a dam keeper and the Park Service liaison to SFPUC-HHWP wait to give me the tour. For the past three days I drank directly from the free-flowing Tuolumne River. It's hard to believe that people in the Bay Area a world away in time and place drink the same water. Deserted dams like this one give me an uneasy feeling, as does an empty cathedral or city street. So much work goes into building a dam, which results in so much environmental change, and then we seemingly walk away, leaving it like a discarded relic for others to find.

I climb aboard the open-hull skiff. The boat's gentle swaying motion makes me queasy. We're off. This is the only craft on the reservoir. Access is strictly limited to protect the water quality: no boating; no swimming. My two-hour tour took a year to arrange with the cooperation of Patricia Martel, the general manager of the SFPUC. I can't grasp that a wondrous valley like the one I toured five days ago once existed three hundred feet below, now buried in a form of suspended animation beneath these 117 billion gallons of water. All I sense is the shimmering water surface, as if nothing else ever existed. The scale of the place remains incomprehensible, exaggerated here versus the Yosemite Valley by the absence of trees or other surface elements on the placid water. The canyon walls stand fully exposed. They don't look several thousand feet high, nor does the reservoir seem eight miles long.

Martel had intended to conduct the tour, but had to cancel at the last moment to meet with city officials, who had spent the night in the agency's rustic lodge overlooking the reservoir. Roughly the size of a comfortable suburban home, the lodge was built about the time the dam was constructed and is one of the few remaining structures from the period. I've heard stories from several SFPUC staff of lavish parties in the lodge hosted by the agency over the years for people important to its mission, mostly Bay Area politicians and business and civic leaders. While the "wining and dining" may have moderated in recent years, the lodge remains for the private use of the SFPUC leadership. Not even the National Park Service has open access.

Back on land, I walk out on the dam, water lapping just below the railing on one side, the raw canyon floor over three hundred feet below the railing on the other side. The walkway across the top is open for tourists and the occasional hiker. No vehicles, no bicycles, no pets permitted. It's quiet and still. Kolana Rock dominates the reservoir's southern wall. Tueeulala Falls and Wapama Falls on the northern wall frame the view. What would John Muir and Gifford Pinchot say if they were here?

If I could bring a person to one place, one landscape, and tell them the story of that place in order for them to understand as much as possible about our relationship to nature, our environmental values, and our politics, I would bring them here, to O'Shaughnessy Dam, and I would tell them the Hetch Hetchy story. It highlights three phases in the evolution of American environmental values and politics.

The first phase began with the colonization of the New World and the unrestrained exploitation of its resources to promote economic growth and development as settlement raced westward across the continent. During this phase, the stump, the plow, the pasture, and the fence were the signs of progress. We waged an imperialistic war on the indigenous people and the landscape they inhabited. We came with a vision of what might be, based on our European heritage, but not the sensitivity to adapt that vision to the existing conditions. Brute strength and technology made it possible for us to impose our will on a land that seemed limitless in extent, fertility, and plentitude. We prospered at the expense of others.

By the end of the 1800s, however, we began for the first time to encounter the limits and constraints imposed by nature. Wilderness only existed in isolated pockets as settlement had transformed most of the continent. The 1890 U.S. census could no longer draw a line demarcating the frontier boundary on the map. Mounting concerns about potential shortages in some resources, like forests and water, gave birth to the conservation and preservation movements. People began to question the prevailing assumption that environmental exploitation was always good. Anxieties arose over the rapid pace of change and the profound shifts in American life as we moved from farm to city. In 1800 more than 90 percent of Americans lived on the farm. By 1900 most lived in an urban area. Modernity required adjustments. Hetch Hetchy marked the beginning of this second phase as clearly as any other event.

We're asking more probing questions now about our use of the land than the utilitarian, economic questions of the past century. We're beginning to apply self-restraint not just because of the limits and threats posed by nature, but because we choose not to exploit our resources. We're beginning to understand that the costs to our collective aesthetic, philosophical, and moral values, and to our environmental souls, is at times simply too great. In fact, we're undoing the damage done to some landscapes by prior generations. Hetch Hetchy could again be the milestone, marking the real beginning of phase three. What would be more symbolic of our newfound wisdom than the removal of this dam and the restoration of the valley it flooded for the entire world to see?

Tear it down! Tear down this damn dam-damnation and restore the Hetch Hetchy Valley. Heal this self-inflicted wound in Yosemite National Park and our national heart and soul. We can do it. We have the technology. We have the money. All that stops us is the will. We know all the reasons not to: cost, politics, and public priorities; practical, commonplace reasons that we've clung to for generations in defense against such dreams. Yet those who envisioned Hetch Hetchy a century ago set aside that reasoning to achieve what they believed was a great public good, regardless of whether you think they were misguided. The questions and issues raised by Hetch Hetchy will never change. Perhaps our values have, however, so different answers might be possible.

We're beginning to more fully recognize what George Perkins Marsh wrote in *Man and Nature:* that environmental health directly affects human well-being, for which income and consumption are only partial measures. Other voices have made the same point: John Muir, Aldo Leopold, and Rachel Carson, among many others. Technology has temporarily enabled us to overlook that intimate relationship. We must reformulate the public debate on issues related to landscape change, from one of environmental quality versus economic prosperity to one of how best to realize individual and collective well-being.

It's time to undo the past and make a profound statement about our present priorities and place on this planet—not because it's cost-effective (although it might be), but because it is the right thing to do. We need such symbolic acts to serve as beacons for the future. Why not make that statement here and now? A century ago we drew the line defining progress across the narrow mouth of the Hetch Hetchy Valley. We were less mature in our environmental thinking then. Let us now remove that dam and erase that line as we redefine progress and voluntarily limit our economic-based exploitation of nature for a higher concept of the greater good.

SOURCE NOTES

Background research for the historical content relied on both original source documents and secondhand materials. Information regarding the contemporary components of the story was drawn primarily from newspaper articles, government reports, and personal interviews. Interviews were tape recorded by permission and quotes from them edited as needed to improve style, sequence, and clarity. Interviewees who were quoted were given drafts of the corresponding manuscript for review and approval.

Four sources of material were particularly important. Pat Martel and the staff at the San Francisco Public Utilities Commission responded to my many questions with cooperation and good will. Ron Good at Restore Hetch Hetchy generously shared with me his materials on the current and historical aspects of the Hetch Hetchy debate. I relied heavily on the *San Francisco Chronicle*'s coverage of recent events and benefited significantly from Chuck Finnie's insights. And Bruce Brugmann, founder, publisher, and editor of the *San Francisco Bay Guardian,* opened his extensive files on the public power controversy to me.

Preface

The literature on and by John Muir is extensive. I've relied throughout the text most heavily on general biographies by Stephen Fox, *The American Conservation Movement: John Muir and His Legacy* (Madison: University of Wisconsin Press, 1985); Frederick Turner, *John Muir: Rediscovering America* (Cambridge: Perseus Publishing, 1985); and Linnie Marsh Wolfe, *Son of Wilderness: The Life of John Muir* (New York: Knopf, 1945). John Warfield Simpson's *Yearning for the Land: A Search for the Importance of Place* (New York: Pantheon, 2002) and Millie Stanley's *The Heart of John Muir's World: Wisconsin, Family, and Wilderness Discovery* (Madison: Prairie Oak Press, 1995) provide insight into his boyhood landscapes and life. Additional insight on Muir was drawn from William Frederic Badè, *The Life and Letters of John Muir,* 2 vols. (Boston: Houghton Mifflin, 1924); Michael P. Cohen, *The Pathless Way: John Muir and American Wilderness* (Madison: University of Wisconsin Press, 1984); Richard F. Fleck, *Henry Thoreau and John Muir among the Indians* (Hamden, Conn.: Archon Books, 1985); Steven J. Holmes, *The Young John Muir: An Environmental Biography* (Madison: University of Wisconsin Press, 1999); Holway R. Jones, *John Muir and the Sierra Club: The Battle for Yosemite* (San Francisco: Sierra Club, 1965); and Thurman Wilkins, *John Muir: The Apostle of Nature* (Norman: University of Oklahoma Press, 1995). Of Muir's actual writings, his *Story of My Boyhood and Youth, A Thousand Mile Walk to the Gulf,* and *My First Summer in the Sierra,* reprinted in Graham White, ed., *John Muir: The Wilderness Journeys* (Edinburgh: Canongate Books, 1996), were most useful. See as well

Linnie Marsh Wolfe, ed., *John of the Mountains: The Unpublished Journals of John Muir* (Madison: University of Wisconsin Press, 1979).

General background on Gifford Pinchot was drawn from his autobiography, *Breaking New Ground* (New York: Harcourt, Brace and Company, 1947); and Char Miller, "The Greening of Gifford Pinchot," *Environmental History Review* 16(3) (1992), and *Gifford Pinchot and the Making of Modern Environmentalism* (Washington: Island Press/Shearwater Books, 2001).

1 • *The Struggle for the Valley*

The history of Yosemite National Park was drawn from Lafayette H. Bunnell, *Discovery of the Yosemite and the Indian War of 1851, Which Led to That Event* (Yosemite National Park, Calif.: Yosemite Association, 1990); Linda Wedel Greene, *Yosemite: The Park and Its Resources: A History of the Discovery, Management, and Physical Development of Yosemite National Park* (U.S. Department of the Interior, National Park Service: September 1987), available online at www.nps.gov/yose/nature/ exhibits.htm; Hank Johnson, *The Yosemite Grant, 1864–1906: A Pictorial History* (Yosemite National Park, Calif.: Yosemite Association, 1996); Irene D. Paden and Margaret E. Schlichtmann, *The Big Oak Flat Road: An Account of Freighting from Stockton to Yosemite Valley* (San Francisco, Calif.: n.p., 1955); Alfred Runte, *Yosemite: The Embattled Wilderness* (Lincoln: University of Nebraska Press, 1990); and Carl Parcher Russell, *One Hundred Years in Yosemite: The Story of a Great Park and Its Friends*, omnibus ed. (Yosemite National Park, Calif.: Yosemite Association, 1992). See also Hans Huth, "Yosemite: The Story of an Idea," *Sierra Club Bulletin* 33(3) (March 1948): 47–78; Francois Emile Matthes, *Sketch of Yosemite National Park and an Account of the Origin of the Yosemite and Hetch Hetchy Valleys (by F. E. Matthes)* (U.S. Department of the Interior, office of the secretary, 1912); "Yosemite Grant": Act of June 30, 1864, ch. 184, 13 Stat. 325; and U.S. Congress, 1863–1864 *Congressional Globe*, 38th Congress, 1st Session, 2300–01 (1864).

For explanations of Yosemite place names, see Peter Browning, *Yosemite Place Names: The Historic Background of Geographic Names in Yosemite National Park* (Lafayette, Calif.: Great West Books, 1988); and Erwin Gustav Gudde, *California Place Names: The Origin and Etymology of Current Geographical Names*, 4th ed., ed. William Bright (Berkeley: University of California Press, 1998).

Background on John Charles Frémont can be found in Tom Chaffin, *Pathfinder: John Charles Frémont and the Course of American Empire* (New York: Hill & Wang, 2002).

Horace Greeley's account of his visit to Yosemite and the Mariposa Big Tree Grove was obtained from Horace Greeley, *An Overland Journey from New York to San Francisco in the Summer of 1859* (Lincoln: University of Nebraska Press, 1999).

Additional background on George Perkins Marsh can be found in David Lowenthal, *George Perkins Marsh: Versatile Vermonter* (New York: Columbia University Press, 1958); and George Perkins Marsh, *Man and Nature*, ed. David Lowenthal (Cambridge: Harvard University Press and Belknap Press, 1965).

For a sampling of the vast scholarship on American land laws and distribution policies, see Daniel J. Boorstin, *The Americans: The National Experience* (New York:

Vintage, 1965); Marion Clawson, *America's Land and Its Uses* (Baltimore: Johns Hopkins University Press, for Resources for the Future, 1972) and *The Federal Lands Revisited* (Baltimore: Johns Hopkins University Press, for Resources for the Future, 1983); Michael P. Conzen, ed., *The Making of the American Landscape* (Boston: Unwin Hyman, 1990); John Brinckerhoff Jackson, *Landscapes: Selected Writings of J. B. Jackson,* ed. Ervin H. Zube (Amherst: University of Massachusetts Press, 1970); Hildegard Binder Johnson, *Order Upon the Land: The U.S. Rectangular Land Survey and the Upper Mississippi Country* (New York: Oxford University Press, 1976); D. W. Meinig, *The Shaping of America: A Geographical Perspective on 500 Years of History,* vol. 1: *Atlantic America, 1492–1800* (New Haven: Yale University Press, 1986) and vol. 2: *Continental America, 1800–1867* (New Haven: Yale University Press, 1993); John Opie, *The Law of the Land: Two Hundred Years of American Farmland Policy* (Lincoln: University of Nebraska Press, 1994); Joseph M. Petulla, *American Environmental History* (San Francisco: Boyd and Fraser, 1977); John R. Stilgoe, *Common Landscape of America, 1580–1845* (New Haven: Yale University Press, 1982); Norman J. W. Thrower, *Original Land Survey and Land Subdivision: A Comparative Study of the Form and Effect of Contrasting Cadastral Surveys* (Chicago: Rand McNally and Co., 1966); Donald Worster, *The Wealth of Nature: Environmental History and the Ecological Imagination* (New York: Oxford University Press, 1993); and Dyan Zaslowsky and T. H. Watkins, *These American Lands: Parks, Wilderness, and the Public Lands,* rev. and exp. ed. (Washington, D.C.: Island Press, 1994). For an overview of the State of California's land policies during the 1800s, see Paul W. Gates, *Land and Law in California: Essays on Land Policies* (Ames: Iowa State University Press, 1991).

For general background on public values that underpinned the political movement to preserve park land, see Fox, *The American Conservation Movement;* Samuel P. Hays, *Conservation and the Gospel of Efficiency: The Progressive Conservation Movement, 1890–1920* (Cambridge: Harvard University Press, 1959); Hans Huth, *Nature and the American: Three Centuries of Changing Attitudes* (Berkeley: University of California Press, 1957); John Ise, *Our National Parks* (New York: Arno Press, 1979); Roderick Frazier Nash, *Wilderness and the American Mind,* 4th ed. (New Haven: Yale University Press, 2001) and *American Environmentalism: Readings in Conservation History,* 3rd ed. (New York: McGraw-Hill, 1990); Max Oelschlaeger, *The Idea of Wilderness: From Prehistory to the Age of Ecology* (New Haven: Yale University Press, 1991); Alfred Runte, *National Parks: The American Experience,* 3rd ed. (Lincoln: University of Nebraska Press, 1997); and Peter J. Schmitt, *Back to Nature: The Arcadian Myth in Urban America* (Baltimore: Johns Hopkins University Press, 1990).

2 • *Olmstead, Muir, and the State Reserve*

Material on Frederick Law Olmsted was drawn from Laura Wood Roper, *FLO: A Biography of Frederick Law Olmsted* (Baltimore: Johns Hopkins University Press, 1983); Witold Rybczynski, *A Clearing in the Distance: Frederick Law Olmsted and America in the Nineteenth Century* (New York: Scribner, 1999); and John Warfield Simpson, *Visions of Paradise: Glimpses of Our Landscape's Legacy* (Berkeley:

University of California Press, 1999). Olmsted's plan for the Yosemite reservation was reprinted as "The Yosemite Valley and the Mariposa Big Trees: A Preliminary Report, 1865," *Landscape Architecture* 43(1) (1952).

Additional background on the development of American aesthetic values and preferences for romantic images of "wild" nature can be found in William H. Truettner, ed., *The West as America: Reinterpreting Images of the Frontier, 1820–1920* (Washington, D.C.: Smithsonian Institution Press, 1991). See also Kenneth Clark, *Landscape into Art*, rev. ed. (New York: HarperCollins, 1979); Gina Crandell, *Nature Pictorialized: "The View" in Landscape History* (Baltimore: Johns Hopkins University Press, 1993); Kenneth T. Jackson, *Crabgrass Frontier: The Suburbanization of the United States* (New York: Oxford University Press, 1985); Leo Marx, *The Machine in the Garden: Technology and the Pastoral Ideal in America* (New York: Oxford University Press, 1964); and Henry Nash Smith, *Virgin Land: The American West as Symbol and Myth.*

The discussion of the reservation's management from 1864 to 1890 and the resolution of land claims derived from the sources on its general history listed in chapter 1.

Background on the events leading up to the creation of Yosemite National Park in 1890 and on Muir's role was drawn from Jones, *John Muir and the Sierra Club: The Battle for Yosemite*; Runte, *Yosemite: The Embattled Wilderness*; Turner, *John Muir: Rediscovering America*; and Wolfe, *Son of the Wilderness: The Life of John Muir.* For further background on Muir, see the references listed in the Preface. Quotes from Muir were obtained primarily from his *Story of My Boyhood and Youth, A Thousand Mile Walk to the Gulf*, and *My First Summer in the Sierra*, reprinted in *John Muir: The Wilderness Journeys.*

An overview of the development of geographical and scientific thought in the nineteenth century, including the role of Alexander von Humboldt, can be found in Preston E. James and Geoffrey J. Martin, *All Possible Worlds: A History of Geographical Ideas*, 2nd ed. (New York: John Wiley and Sons, 1981); Charles Van Doren, *A History of Knowledge: Past, Present and Future* (New York: Ballantine Books, 1991); and Donald Worster, *Nature's Economy: A History of Ecological Ideas* (New York: Cambridge University Press, 1977) and *The Wealth of Nature: Environmental History and the Ecological Imagination.*

3 • *Pinchot, the Park, and the Conservation Movement*

The overview of the conservation movement was obtained from Fox, *The American Conservation Movement: John Muir and His Legacy*; Hays, *Conservation and the Gospel of Efficiency: The Progressive Conservation Movement, 1890–1920*; Nash, *Wilderness and the American Mind* and *American Environmentalism: Readings in Conservation History*; and Petulla, *American Environmental History.* See also the sources on John Muir and the history of Yosemite National Park listed previously. Additional insight into the founding of the Sierra Club can be obtained from Michael P. Cohen, *The History of the Sierra Club, 1892–1970* (San Francisco: Sierra Club Books, 1988).

Material on the founding of Yellowstone National Park was obtained from Simpson, *Visions of Paradise: Glimpses of Our Landscape's Legacy.* For overviews of

Yellowstone's history and role in the national park movement, see Ise, *Our National Parks,* and Runte, *National Parks: The American Experience.*

Quotes from John Muir's articles in *Century* were obtained from "The Treasures of the Yosemite," *Century* 40(4) (August 1890); and "Features of the Proposed Yosemite National Park," *Century* 40(5) (September 1890).

See also "Yosemite National Park Act": California Forest Reservation Act, ch. 1263, 26 Stat. 650 (1890) and the *Congressional Record* for the 51st Congress, 1st session, for the floor proceedings and debates.

The biographical sketch of Gifford Pinchot was derived from Simpson, *Visions of Paradise: Glimpses of Our Landscape's Legacy;* see also Miller, *Gifford Pinchot and the Making of Modern Environmentalism* and "The Greening of Gifford Pinchot"; and Pinchot, *Breaking New Ground.*

4 · *Theodore Roosevelt; The Park's Revision*

Background on Roosevelt's visit to Yellowstone and Yosemite was drawn from Edmund Morris, *Theodore Rex* (New York: Random House, 2001); and Theodore Roosevelt, *Theodore Roosevelt: An Autobiography* (New York: Charles Scribner's Sons, 1924). For details on John Muir's response to the president's visit to Yosemite, see Fox, *The American Conservation Movement;* Turner, *Rediscovering America;* and Wolfe, *Son of the Wilderness.*

Background on American attitudes toward wilderness and modernity was drawn primarily from Nash, *Wilderness and the American Mind;* see also Huth, *Nature and the American: Three Centuries of Changing Attitudes.* Kenneth T. Jackson provides an excellent overview of the historical and social forces leading to the development and spread of suburbia and the transformation of urban America in *Crabgrass Frontier: The Suburbanization of the United States* (New York: Oxford University Press, 1985). Peter J. Schmitt provides additional insight in *Back to Nature: The Arcadian Myth in Urban America.*

For background on Frances Griffith Newlands and the politics leading to the passage of the act that bears his name, the Newlands Reclamation Act (32 Stat. 388), see Brechin, *Imperial San Francisco: Urban Power, Earthly Ruin* (Berkeley: University of California Press, 1999). See also Jessica Teisch, "William Hammond Hall: City Water and Progressive-Era Reform in San Francisco," in Clark Davis and David Igler, eds., *The Human Tradition in California* (Wilmington, Del.: Scholarly Resources, 2002). General background on the development of national irrigation and flood control policy within the context of the Progressive movement can be found in Hays, *Conservation and the Gospel of Efficiency: The Progressive Conservation Movement, 1890–1920.*

Material on the revision of Yosemite National Park's boundary was obtained primarily from Jones, *John Muir and the Sierra Club: The Battle for Yosemite;* and Runte, *Yosemite: The Embattled Wilderness.* See also "Yosemite National Park Boundary Act of 1905": Act of Feb. 7, 1905, P.L. No. 58-49, 33 Stat. 702; 39 *Congressional Record* 406-07, 58th Congress, 3rd session, part 1, December 19, 1904; and 39 *Congressional Record* 889, 58th Congress, 3rd session, part 1, January 14, 1905.

Background on John Wesley Powell was obtained from Wallace Stegner, *Beyond the Hundredth Meridian: John Wesley Powell and the Second Opening of the West* (Lincoln: University of Nebraska Press, 1982). See also John Wesley Powell, *Report on the Lands of the Arid Region of the United States, with a More Detailed Account of the Lands of Utah,* Wallace Stegner, ed. (Cambridge: Harvard University Press, 1962).

Description of the recession of the state reserve to the federal government was drawn from Johnston, *The Yosemite Grant, 1864–1906: A Pictorial History;* Jones, *John Muir and the Sierra Club: The Battle for Yosemite;* and Runte, *Yosemite: The Embattled Wilderness.* See also "Acceptance of the Yosemite Grant Recession": 34 Stat. 831, June 11, 1906 (59th Congress, 1st session, H.J.R. 118, Public Resolution 27).

5 · *Spring Valley and the Boomtown Politics of Water*

The portrayal of San Francisco's early growth and corresponding search for adequate water, including the Spring Valley Water Company story, was obtained primarily from Brechin, *Imperial San Francisco: Urban Power, Earthly Ruin;* Warren D. Hanson, *San Francisco Water and Power: A History of the Municipal Water Department and Hetch Hetchy System* (San Francisco: City and County of San Francisco, 1994); Norris Hundley, *The Great Thirst: Californians and Water, 1770s–1990s* (Berkeley: University of California Press, 1992); and Ray W. Taylor, *Hetch Hetchy: The Story of San Francisco's Struggle to Provide a Water Supply for Her Future Needs* (San Francisco: Richard J. Orozco, 1926). See also Philip J. Ethington, *The Public City: The Political Construction of Urban Life in San Francisco, 1850–1900* (Berkeley: University of California Press, 2001); Marc Reisner, *A Dangerous Place* (Vancouver: Greystone Books, 2003); and James P. Walsh and Timothy J. O'Keefe, *Legacy of a Native Son: James Duval Phelan & Villa Montalvo* (Los Gatos, Calif.: Forbes Mill Press, 1993).

Additional material on Frederick Law Olmsted was found in Roper, *FLO: A Biography of Frederick Law Olmsted;* and Rybczynski, *A Clearing in the Distance.* For further details on Olmsted's plan for Golden Gate Park, see Olmsted, Vaux & Co., *Preliminary Report in Regard to a Plan of Public Pleasure Grounds for the City of San Francisco* (New York: Wm. C. Bryant, 1866).

Details on Colonel George Mendell's report were obtained from *Report on the Various Projects for the Water Supply of San Francisco, Cal. made to The Mayor, The Auditor, and the District Attorney, constituting the Board of Water Commissioners by G. H. Mendell, engineer of the Water Commission* (San Francisco: Spaulding and Barto, 1877).

Background on William Chapman Ralston and his role with the Spring Valley Water Company, Golden Gate Park, and the Palace Hotel was found in David Lavender, *Nothing Seemed Impossible: William C. Ralston and Early San Francisco* (Palo Alto: American West Publishing Company, 1975); and George D. Lyman, *Ralston's Ring: California Plunders the Comstock Lode* (New York: Charles Scribner's Sons, 1937); in addition to sources cited above.

Material on James Duval Phelan was drawn primarily from Walsh and O'Keefe, *Legacy of a Native Son: James Duval Phelan & Villa Montalvo*. Additional sources on Phelan included Brechin, *Imperial San Francisco: Urban Power, Earthly Ruin*; Hanson, *San Francisco Water and Power: A History of the Municipal Water Department and Hetch Hetchy System*; and Taylor, *Hetch Hetchy: The Story of San Francisco's Struggle to Provide a Water Supply for Her Future Needs.*

Background on Daniel Burnham, the City Beautiful movement, and the Columbian Exposition was obtained from George B. Tobey, *A History of Landscape Architecture: The Relationship of People to Environment* (New York: American Elsevier Publishing Company, 1973). See also Peter Geoffrey Hall, *Cities of Tomorrow: An Intellectual History of Urban Planning and Design in the Twentieth Century*, 3rd rev. ed. (Malden, Mass.: Blackwell Publishers, 2002); and William H. Wilson, *The City Beautiful Movement* (Baltimore: Johns Hopkins University Press, 1989).

Portrayal of San Francisco as an imperial city and its reliance on imperialistic behavior toward surrounding landscapes has several sources, in particular Brechin, *Imperial San Francisco*. For access into the vast literature on the imperialistic aspects of water development in the western United States, see, among others, Hundley, *The Great Thirst: Californians and Water, 1770s–1990s*; Marc Reisner, *Cadillac Desert: The American West and Its Disappearing Water* (New York: Viking, 1986); and Donald Worster, *Rivers of Empire: Water, Aridity, and the Growth of the American West* (New York: Oxford University Press, 1992). Chester Hartman provides a glimpse into another form of corporate-municipal imperialism, as seen in the post–World War II development boom in metropolitan San Francisco, in *City for Sale: The Transformation of San Francisco*, rev. ed. (Berkeley: University of California Press, 2002).

Background on Frederick Law Olmsted was drawn from Roper, *FLO: A Biography of Frederick Law Olmsted*; and Rybczynski, *A Clearing in the Distance: Frederick Law Olmsted and America in the Nineteenth Century.*

The U.S. Geological Survey reports on Hetch Hetchy were found in *Twelfth Annual Report of the United States Geological Survey to the Secretary of the Interior, 1890–'91, by J. W. Powell, Director*, Part II—Irrigation (Washington, D.C.: U.S. Government Printing Office, 1891); and *Twenty-first Annual Report of the United States Geological Survey to the Secretary of the Interior, 1899–1900, Charles D. Walcott, Director*, Part IV—Hydrography (Washington, D.C.: U.S. Government Printing Office, 1901).

Additional sources on the sequence of steps taken by Phelan, Grunsky, and the city of San Francisco leading to Secretary Hitchcock's rejection of their permit application include Dwight H. Barnes, *The Greening of Paradise Valley: The First 100 Years (1887–1987) of the Modesto Irrigation District* (Modesto, Calif.: Modesto Irrigation District, 1987); Alan M. Paterson, *Land, Water and Power: A History of the Turlock Irrigation District 1887–1987* (Glendale, Calif.: The Arthur H. Clark Company, 1987); San Francisco Board of Supervisors, *Reports on the Water Supply of San Francisco, California, 1900 to 1908, Inclusive* (San Francisco: Board of

Supervisors, 1908); and the "Right-of-Way Act of 1901": Act of Feb. 15, 1901, ch. 372, 31 Stat. 790 (repealed 1976).

7 · *The Private Debate over Hetch Hetchy*

Sources of material about the experience of James Duval Phelan and Enrico Caruso during the April 1906 earthquake are those listed in chapter 6 for Phelan. Additional insight on the San Francisco earthquake was obtained from Reisner, *A Dangerous Place: California's Unsettling Fate.*

For more information on Abraham Ruef and the associated political scandal, see Walton Bean, *Boss Ruef's San Francisco: The Story of the Union Labor Party, Big Business, and the Graft Prosecution* (Berkeley: University of California Press, 1952); and Lately Thomas, *A Debonair Scoundrel: An Episode in the Moral History of San Francisco* (New York: Holt, Rinehart, and Winston, 1962). For additional insight on the Progressive Era reforms in San Francisco, see Teisch, "William Hammond Hall: City Water and Progressive-Era Reform in San Francisco."

Additional sources on the city's efforts to obtain permission to proceed with the project from the secretary of the interior include the "Garfield permit," found in George J. Hesselman, ed., *Decisions of the Department of the Interior and the General Land Office in Cases Relating to the Public Lands,* vol. 36, July 1, 1907–June 30, 1908 (Washington, D.C.: U.S. Government Printing Office, 1908); Elmo R. Richardson, "The Struggle for the Valley: California's Hetch Hetchy Controversy, 1905–1913," *California Historical Society Quarterly* 38(3) (September 1959): 249–258; San Francisco Board of Supervisors, *Reports on the Water Supply of San Francisco, California, 1900 to 1908, Inclusive;* and Taylor, *Hetch Hetchy: The Story of San Francisco's Struggle to Provide a Water Supply for Her Future Needs.*

8 · *A National Cause Célèbre*

The account of the political maneuverings and public debate from the Garfield permit until passage of the Raker Act was drawn from Kendrick A. Clements, "Politics and the Park: San Francisco's Fight for Hetch Hetchy, 1908–1913," *Pacific Historical Review* 48 (May 1979): 185–215; Fox, *The American Conservation Movement: John Muir and His Legacy;* Brian E. Gray, "The Battle for Hetch Hetchy Goes to Congress," *Hastings West-Northwest Journal of Environmental Law and Policy* 6(2 and 3) (Winter/Spring, 2000): 199–238; Ise, *Our National Parks;* Jones, *John Muir and the Sierra Club: The Battle for Yosemite;* Michael Maurice O'Shaughnessy, *Hetch Hetchy: Its Origin and History* (San Francisco: n.p., 1934); Nash, *Wilderness and the American Mind;* Elmo R. Richardson, "The Struggle for the Valley: California's Hetch Hetchy Controversy, 1905–1913"; San Francisco Board of Supervisors, *Reports on the Water Supply of San Francisco, California, 1900 to 1908, Inclusive;* Ray W. Taylor, *Hetch Hetchy: The Story of San Francisco's Struggle to Provide a Water Supply for Her Future Needs;* Frederick Turner, *Rediscovering America;* and Linnie Marsh Wolfe, *Son of the Wilderness.*

For the 1908–09 congressional hearings, committee reports, and floor debates, see "San Francisco and the Hetch Hetchy Reservoir: Hearing on H.J. Res. 184

Before the House Committee on Public Lands," 60th Congress, 2nd Session, December 16, 1908; "San Francisco and the Hetch Hetchy Reservoir: Hearing on H.J. Res. 223 Before the House Committee on Public Lands," 60th Congress, 2nd Session, January 9, 12, 20, and 21, 1909; "Report of the House Committee on Public Lands, February 8, 1909, Granting Use of the Hetch Hetchy Valley to the City of San Francisco," 60th Congress, 2nd Session, House Report No. 2085, to accompany H.J. Res. 223; "Hetch Hetchy Reservoir Site: Hearing on S. 123 Before the Senate Committee on Public Lands," 60th Congress, 2nd Session, February 10 and 12, 1909.

Both the Sierra Club and Restore Hetch Hetchy maintain Web sites that contain numerous excerpts and reprints related to the public debate obtained from newspaper and magazine articles and books. See www.sierraclub.org/ca/hetch-hetchy/ and www.hetchhetchy.org/, respectively. And the American Memory: Evolution of the Conservation Movement, 1850–1920 database of the Library of Congress contains many documents related to the debate; these can be accessed online at www.memory.loc.gov.

Background on John Ripley Freeman was obtained from Vannevar Bush, "Biographical Memoir of John Ripley Freeman, 1855–1932," in *Biographical Memoirs*, vol. 27 (Washington, D.C.: National Academy of Sciences, 1937). The Freeman report was obtained from John Ripley Freeman, "On the Proposed Use of a Portion of the Hetch Hetchy, Eleanor, and Cherry Valleys Within and Near to the Boundaries of the Stanislaus U.S. National Forest Reserve and the Yosemite National Park as Reservoirs for Impounding Tuolumne River Flood Waters and Appurtenant Works for the Water Supply of San Francisco, California, and Neighboring Cities" (San Francisco: Board of Supervisors, 1912). See also John Ripley Freeman, *The Hetch Hetchy Water Supply for San Francisco* (San Francisco: Rincon Press, 1912).

9 · *The Political Outcome*

Additional sources on the controversy include the "Fisher decision," found in George J. Hesselman, ed., *Decisions of the Department of the Interior and the General Land Office in Cases Relating to the Public Lands*, vol. 41, May 1, 1912–March 15, 1913 (Washington, D.C.: U.S. Government Printing Office, 1913); United States Army Corps of Engineers, *Hetch Hetchy Valley, Report of Advisory Board of Army Engineers to the Secretary of the Interior on Investigations Relative to Sources of Water Supply for San Francisco and Bay Communities, February 19, 1913* (Washington, D.C.: U.S. Government Printing Office, 1913); the "Raker Act," P. L. No. 63-41, 38 Stat. 242 (1913); Michael Maurice O'Shaughnessy, *Hetch Hetchy: Its Origin and History*.

For the 1913 Congressional Proceedings, see: "Hetch Hetchy Dam Site: Hearings on H.R. 6281 Before the House Committee on Public Lands," 63rd Congress, 1st Session, June 25 and July 7, 1913; "Hetch Hetchy Grant to San Francisco," House Report No. 41, to accompany H.R. 7207, Committee on Public Lands, 63rd Congress, 1st Session, August 5, 1913; "Hetch Hetchy Reservoir Site: Hearing on H.R. 7207 Before the Senate Committee on Public Lands," 63rd Congress, 1st Session, September 24, 1913; and "Hetch Hetchy Grant to San

Francisco," Senate Report No. 113, to accompany H. R. 7207, Committee on Public Lands, 63rd Congress, 1st Session, September 25, 1913. See as well the *Congressional Record,* 63rd Congress, 1st Session, Volume 50; and 63rd Congress, 2nd Session, Volume 51.

The conservation policies of the Progressive Era, the Ballinger-Pinchot affair, and the 1912 presidential election have been the subject of numerous histories. See for example Samuel P. Hays, *Conservation and the Gospel of Efficiency: The Progressive Conservation Movement, 1890–1920;* Alpheus Thomas Mason, *Bureaucracy Convicts Itself: The Ballinger-Pinchot Controversy of 1910* (New York: Viking, 1941); James L. Penick, *Progressive Politics and Conservation: The Ballinger-Pinchot Affair* (Chicago: University of Chicago Press, 1968); and Elmo R. Richardson, *The Politics of Conservation: Crusades and Controversies, 1897–1913,* University of California Press Publication in History vol. 70 (Berkeley: University of California, 1962).

Additional material on William Bourn II can be found in Ferol Egan, *Last Bonanza Kings: The Bourns of San Francisco* (Reno: University of Nevada Press, 1998); and Richard Peterson, *The Bonanza Kings: The Social Origins and Business Behavior of Western Mining Entrepreneurs, 1870–1900* (Norman: University of Oklahoma Press, 1991).

10 · *Competing Claims for Water*

Material from Margaret Bruce, the director of environmental programs for the Silicon Valley Manufacturing Group, was obtained via e-mail correspondence in June 2002; Stan Ketchum, principal planner for the City of San Jose, was interviewed via telephone in October 2002; and material from Ann Draper, the planning director for Santa Clara County, was obtained via e-mail correspondence in June 2002 and July 2004.

Discussion of the bottling of Hetch Hetchy water was based on articles appearing in the *San Francisco Chronicle* (Patrick Hoge, "S.F. to Sell Bottled Hetch Hetchy Water, Sierra Product Said to be Purer than Tap," March 14, 2003; Ilene Lelchuk, "Bottled Hetch Hetchy Arrives with a Splash, Tapping Reservoir, S.F. Hopes for Profit," March 25, 2003); the *Los Angeles Times* (*Times* editorial staff, "New Life for Hetch Hetchy," March 22, 2003); the *Sacramento Bee* (*Bee* editorial staff, "Editorial: Yosemite in a Bottle, Sale Should Pay for Hetch Hetchy Study," March 18, 2003); *Contra Costa Times* (Mike Taugher, "Move Over, Evian, Hetch Hetchy's Got Cachet," March 26, 2003); and the *New York Times* (Dean E. Murphy, "City by the Bay Becomes a Bottler, to Loud Attack," March 26, 2003).

Portrayal of Secretary of the Interior Donald Hodel's proposal to remove the dam, and the reaction to his proposal, was obtained from a telephone interview with Mike McCloskey conducted in July 2002; additional information was drawn from Secretary Hodel, "Yosemite and Hetch Hetchy," *Commonwealth* (January 1988); and from Carl Pope, "Undamming Hetch Hetchy," *Sierra* (November/December 1987). See also the concept study produced in response to Secretary Hodel's initiative, "Hetch Hetchy: A Survey of Water & Power Replacement Concepts" (Sacramento, Calif.: Bureau of Reclamation, Mid-Pacific Region, February 1988).

Material on Restore Hetch Hetchy was obtained from its executive director, Ron Good, in numerous e-mails and several interviews in 2002–03.

Insight on the Sierra Club position was obtained from Bruce Hamilton, conservation director, during an interview in 2002, and from a telephone interview with the club's president, Jennifer Ferenstein, in 2002.

Additional opinions on the environmental community's response to the proposal to remove the dam and restore the valley, and to the effort to find funding for the study of that proposal, came from telephone interviews in 2002 with Mike Finley, executive director of the Turner Foundation, and Bill Meadows, president of the Wilderness Society.

Regional newspapers in the San Francisco Bay Area and newspapers nationwide have repeatedly covered these proposals. For example, recent articles have appeared in the *Contra Costa Times* (Mike Taugher, "Rethinking Hetch Hetchy Reservoir: Some Thirst for Pristine Yosemite, Some for Water," October 26, 2002); the *Fresno Bee* (Mark Grossi, "Activists Target Yosemite Reservoir," October 9, 2000); the *Los Angeles Times* (editorial, "Another Yosemite, Maybe," August 17, 2002; and John M. Glionna, "Dam Dispute Looses a Flood of Emotions," August 11, 2002); the *New York Times* (editorial, "Bring Back Hetch Hetchy," October 19, 2002; and Dean E. Murphy, "An Effort to Undo an Old Reservoir in Yosemite," October 15, 2002); the *San Francisco Chronicle* (see most notably a special report by Susan Sward, Chuck Finnie, and Staff Writers, September 15–20, 2002); the *San Francisco Examiner* (David Kiefer, "A Dry Hetch Hetchy," January 9, 2003; and Eric Brazil, "Quest to Restore Hetch Hetchy Revived," October 12, 2000); the *Sacramento Bee* (editorial, "Hetchy Hypocrisy," August 13, 2002; and Tom Philp, "Water: Bring Back Hetch Hetchy?," April 21, 2002); and the *Stockton Record* (Francis P. Garland, "Activists Push for Rebirth, Hetch Hetchy Valley Focus of Restoration," October 20, 2002).

Data on the Altamont Pass wind farm was obtained from "Staff Report: Wind Performance Report Summary, 2000–2001," California Energy Commission, publication #P500-02-034F, December 2002. For general data on electrical usage in the state, see the California Energy Commission Web site at www.energy.ca.gov.

The historical sketch of the San Joaquin Valley—"Paradise Valley"—and the origins of the Modesto and Turlock Irrigation Districts and their role in the Hetch Hetchy controversy were derived primarily from Barnes, *The Greening of Paradise Valley: The First 100 Years (1887–1987) of the Modesto Irrigation District;* and Paterson, *Land, Water and Power: A History of the Turlock Irrigation District 1887–1987.* See also Taylor, *Hetch Hetchy.* For additional background on John Charles Frémont, see Tom Chaffin, *Pathfinder: John Charles Frémont and the Course of American Empire.*

For additional insight on nineteenth-century American perceptions of the West, see Simpson, *Visions of Paradise,* and Henry Nash Smith's classic, *Virgin Land: The American West as Symbol and Myth* (Cambridge: Harvard University Press, 1970).

11 · *Mismanaging the Dream*

Description of the leak in the HHWP San Joaquin pipeline was obtained from correspondence in 2004 with Matthew Gass, engineering manager of Hetch

Hetchy Water and Power. See also Phillip Matier and Andrew Ross, "Pipe Break Cuts Hetch Hetchy Supply in Half, Rupture near Modesto Creates Ripple Effect across Bay Area," *San Francisco Chronicle*, November 13, 2002; Phillip Matier and Andrew Ross, "Alarm Bell for Hetch Hetchy, Tiny Pin Nearly Brings System to Its Knees," *San Francisco Chronicle*, November 14, 2002; and Chuck Finnie, Susan Sward, and Staff Writers, "Water Leak a Symbol for Hetch Hetchy, S.F. Siphons Off Cash to General Fund," *San Francisco Chronicle*, November 15, 2002. Interviews in 2002–03 with HHWP engineering staff provided additional insight.

Descriptions of the maintenance and management issues related to the SFPUC and HHWP were found in California State Auditor, "San Francisco Public Utilities Commission: Its Slow Pace for Assessing Weaknesses in Its Water Delivery System and for Completing Capital Projects Increases the Risk of Service Disruptions and Water Shortages," Report #99124, February 2000; California Policy Research Center, "Water Governance in the San Francisco Bay Area: Challenges and Opportunities," CPRC Brief, vol. 13 (3), August 2001; Bay Area Economic Forum, "Hetch Hetchy Water and the Bay Area Economy," October 2002; and a *San Francisco Chronicle* Special Report by Susan Sward, Chuck Finnie, and Staff Writers, September 15–20, 2002.

Background on the maintenance and political issues was also obtained from interviews in 2002–03 with Patricia Martel, general manager, SFPUC, Eric Sandler, director of financial planning, and input from other central office staff, and the staff of Hetch Hetchy Water and Power in Moccasin. In San Francisco city hall: P. J. Johnston, press secretary to Mayor Willie Brown; and Tom Ammiano, president of the board of supervisors. At the *San Francisco Chronicle:* Chuck Finnie. At the Bay Area Water Supply and Conservation Agency: Art Jensen, general manager.

Additional published materials that shed light on these issues included the Annual Report for the Public Utilities Commission of the City and County of San Francisco and the annual accounting statement for Hetch Hetchy Water and Power; the SFPUC master bond indenture for the water enterprise; "Best Practices for Financing Large Capital Improvement Projects at Municipal Utilities in the State of California," prepared for Tom Ammiano, president of the board of supervisors, by the board budget analyst, June 10, 2002; "Report to the San Francisco Board of Supervisors: Management Audit of the San Francisco Water Department," prepared in 1994 by the budget analyst for the board; the San Francisco city charter for 1935, 1994, 1996, and 2002; and *City of Palo Alto v. City and County of San Francisco*, 548 F.2d 1374 (1977).

Additional background on the California state legislature's thinking that led to A.B. 1823, A.B. 2058, and S.B. 1870 was obtained from interviews in 2003 with California state senator Jackie Speier and her legislative aide, Mike Paiba, former assemblyman Lou Papan, and his former legislative aide Nick Louizos. See also "Hetch Hetchy Water: Governing a Vital Regional Resource," a policy overview of the Hetch Hetchy Water System by Assemblyman Louis J. Papan, 19th Assembly District.

12 • *Constructing the Engineering Marvel*

The construction sequence for the HHWP system was obtained from Hanson, *San Francisco Water and Power: A History of the Municipal Water Department and Hetch Hetchy System,* and Taylor, *Hetch Hetchy: The Story of San Francisco's Struggle to Provide a Water Supply for Her Future Needs.* See also O'Shaughnessy, *Hetch Hetchy: Its Origin and History.*

13 • *The Raker Act's Ignored Mandate*

General background on the issues related to the distribution and sale of Hetch Hetchy hydropower—the public power debate—was obtained from the *San Francisco Bay Guardian,* which first called public attention to the issue when it published an article written by University of California–Berkeley professor Joe Neilands titled "How PG&E Robs S.F. of Cheap Power" on March 27, 1969. The *Bay Guardian* maintains an extensive file of background materials and articles it has published on the issue, both online at www.SFBG.com and in paper copy at its office. See also the *San Francisco Chronicle* Special Report by Sward, Finnie, and Staff Writers, September 15–20, 2002; and the U.S. Supreme Court decision for *U.S. v. City and County of San Francisco,* 310 U.S. 16 (1940). Additional historical background was found in Hanson, *San Francisco Water and Power: A History of the Municipal Water Department and Hetch Hetchy System;* O'Shaughnessy, *Hetch Hetchy: Its Origin and History;* and Taylor, *Hetch Hetchy: The Story of San Francisco's Struggle to Provide a Water Supply for Her Future Needs.*

Interviews in 2002–03 with various SFPUC staff, including Patricia Martel, general manager, and Eric Sandler, director of financial planning, provided the agency's perspective on the issues. Larry Weis, general manager of TID Water and Power, provided additional insights.

The discussion of the public power issues intertwines with the legislative history of the Raker Act. See for example: Clements, "Politics and the Park: San Francisco's Fight for Hetch Hetchy, 1908–1913"; Gray, "The Battle for Hetch Hetchy Goes to Congress"; Judson King, *The Conservation Fight: From Theodore Roosevelt to the Tennessee Valley Authority* (Washington, D.C.: Public Affairs Press, 1959); and Nash, *Wilderness and the American Mind.*

Testimony before the congressional hearings and committee reports on Hetch Hetchy in 1908–09 and 1913 shed light into the controversy. Similarly, statements made in the House and Senate during the floor debates and proceedings provided critical sources of insight in congressional intent. See sources listed in chapters 8 and 9. Facsimiles of congressional reports, debates, and bills related to Hetch Hetchy and Yosemite, and various materials on associated conservation topics, can be accessed online in the American Memory: Evolution of the Conservation Movement, 1850–1920 database of the Library of Congress at www.memory.loc.gov.

Background on the role of the Pacific Gas and Electric Company was obtained from Paul Kontos, "The Case Against Investor-Owned Utilities and the Need for

Municipal Power Systems," unpub. Doc. Diss., Golden Gate University, 2001. See also Florence Riley Monroy, "Water and Power in San Francisco since 1900: A Study in Municipal Government," unpub. Master's thesis, University of California–Berkeley, 1944; Charles M. Coleman, *P.G. and E. of California: The Centennial Story of Pacific Gas and Electric Company, 1852–1952* (New York: McGraw-Hill, 1952); and George W. Norris, *Fighting Liberal: The Autobiography of George W. Norris* (New York: Collier Books, 1961).

For further background on the period and some key players, see Hays, *Conservation and the Gospel of Efficiency: The Progressive Conservation Movement, 1890–1920;* Egan, *Last Bonanza Kings: The Bourns of San Francisco;* David Nasaw, *The Life of William Randolph Hearst* (Boston: Houghton Mifflin, 2000); Curt Gentry, *Frame-Up: The Incredible Case of Tom Mooney and Warren Billings* (New York: W. W. Norton, 1967); and Carl D. Thompson, *Confessions of the Power Trust* (New York: E. P. Dutton and Co., 1932).

14 • *PG&E and the Politics of Public Power*

In addition to the sources on the public power controversy cited above, interviews in 2002–03 with Bruce Brugmann, publisher and editor of the *San Francisco Bay Guardian;* Chuck Finnie, reporter and political editor at the *San Francisco Chronicle;* Tom Ammiano, president of the board of supervisors for the City and County of San Francisco; P. J. Johnston, press secretary to Mayor Willie Brown; Patricia Martel, general manager of the San Francisco Public Utilities Commission; and Larry Weis, general manager/CEO of the Turlock Irrigation District provided important insights into the current politics of the public power debate.

The quotes from Bruce Brugmann were drawn from a radio interview hosted by the Commonwealth Club of California aired on May 22, 2001, edited and combined with supplemental statements inserted from other interviews and editorials published by the *San Francisco Bay Guardian.* For background on the Hearst-PG&E relationship, see Nasaw, *The Life of William Randolph Hearst.*

Background on the Modesto and Turlock Irrigation Districts was obtained from Barnes, *The Greening of Paradise Valley: The First 100 Years (1887–1987) of the Modesto Irrigation District;* and Paterson, *Land, Water and Power: A History of the Turlock Irrigation District 1887–1987.*

Harold Ickes wrote extensively. For background on him, see *The New Democracy* (New York: W. W. Norton and Company, 1934); *Back to Work: The Story of PWA* (New York: Macmillan, 1935); *Fightin Oil* (New York: A. A. Knopf, 1943); *The Autobiography of a Curmudgeon* (New York: Reynal and Hitchcock, 1943); and *The Secret Diary of Harold L. Ickes* (New York: Simon and Schuster, 1953–54).

The chronology of events leading up to and after the U.S. Supreme Court case concerning San Francisco's violation of the Raker Act was drawn primarily from material obtained from the files and archives of the *San Francisco Bay Guardian* and from Kontos, "The Case Against Investor-Owned Utilities and the Need for Municipal Power Systems." See also Monroy, "Water and Power in San Francisco since 1900: A Study in Municipal Government."

The U.S. Congress House Committee on Public Lands hearings on San

Francisco's amendment to the Raker Act proposed in H.R. 5964 of the 77th Congress, held December 11, 1941, and January 15–17, 19–24, 26, and 27, 1942, provide an excellent overview of the entire Hetch Hetchy controversy to that date, in addition to great detail on the public power aspects, its local politics, and the role of PG&E.

15 • *Restoring the Promise*

Primary sources were those listed for chapters 13 and 14, in particular the files of the *San Francisco Bay Guardian.* For background on the Starbuck controversy and court ruling, see *Charles Starbuck v. City and County of San Francisco,* 556 F.2d 450 (1977). Stephen P. Sayles provides an excellent discussion of the issues related to power development by the irrigation districts and San Francisco in the 1950s in "Hetch Hetchy Reversed: A Rural-Urban Struggle for Power," *California History* 64(4) (Fall 1985), 254–63, 311. Eric Sandler, director of financial planning, and Marla Jurosek, acting manger of power operations, at SFPUC provided details on SFPUC's current power contracts and disposal arrangements, with input from Larry Weis, general manager of TID Water and Power.

16 • *Old Issues; A New Dream*

Historical background on Big Oak Flat, Groveland, and the drive from Priest's Grade to Yosemite was drawn from Paden and Schlichtmann, *The Big Oak Flat Road: An Account of Freighting from Stockton to Yosemite Valley.*

Background on the founding of the National Park Service was obtained from Horace M. Albright, *The Birth of the National Park Service: The Founding Years, 1913–33* (Salt Lake City: Howe Brothers, 1985); and Runte, *National Parks: The American Experience.* See also Russell, *One Hundred Years in Yosemite: The Story of a Great Park and Its Friends;* and the "National Park Service Organic Act": P.L. No. 64-235, 39 Stat. 535 (1916). The biographies of John Muir and Frederick Law Olmsted contain background on their roles in the origins of Yosemite National Park and the National Park Service.

Sources used for the park's more recent history included Ise, *Our National Parks;* Johnston, *The Yosemite Grant, 1864–1906: A Pictorial History;* Runte, *Yosemite: The Embattled Wilderness;* Conrad Wirth, *Parks, Politics, and the People* (Norman: University of Oklahoma Press, 1980); and the National Park Service, *General Management Plan for Yosemite National Park* (1980) and *Yosemite Valley Plan* (2000). These and other planning documents for the park can be accessed online at www.nps.gov/yose/. Visitor data were obtained from the study *Yosemite Area Regional Transportation Strategy* (YARTS) prepared by Nelson/Nygaard Consulting Associates in 1998; "Yosemite National Park Visitor Use Study," prepared by the park staff in 1999; and the October 2004 "Monthly Public Use Report" for the park.

Description of Yosemite's trails and its biophysical history was obtained from Jeffrey P. Schaffer, *Yosemite National Park: A Natural-History Guide to Yosemite and Its Trails,* 3rd ed. (Berkeley: Wilderness Press, 1992). Descriptions of general plant communities in the Sierra region and the park were found in John Sawyer and Todd Keeler-Wolf, *A Manual of California Vegetation* (Sacramento: California Native Plant Society Press, 1995), and in *Yosemite Valley Plan.* The description of my hike from the Yosemite Valley to Tuolumne Meadows, and then down the Grand Canyon of the Tuolumne River, exiting the canyon at the head of Hetch Hetchy Reservoir to White Wolf, was described in reverse order for literary effect: the actual hike began at White Wolf and ended at Yosemite Valley, followed by the boat tour of Hetch Hetchy Reservoir and an overnight stay at Curry Village.

For additional background on the Wilderness Act of 1964 and the Echo Park Dam controversy, see Nash, *Wilderness and the American Mind.*

Studies that examine the feasibility of removing O'Shaughnessy Dam and restoring the Hetch Hetchy Valley include Bureau of Reclamation, Mid-Pacific Region, "Hetch Hetchy: A Survey of Water & Power Replacement Concepts"; Sarah E. Null, "Re-Assembling Hetch Hetchy: Water Supply Implications of Removing O'Shaughnessy Dam," Master's thesis, University of California-Davis, December 2003; and Spreck Rosekrans, Nancy E. Ryan, Ann H. Hayden, Thomas J. Graff, and John M. Balbus, *Paradise Regained: Solutions for Restoring Yosemite's Hetch Hetchy Valley* (San Francisco: Environmental Defense, 2004). The Environmental Defense study has been reported by the press nationwide; see for example the series of thirteen articles and editorials on the issue published by the *Sacramento Bee* from August 22 through September 20, 2004. In addition, the Sierra Club, Restore Hetch Hetchy, and Environmental Defense maintain Web sites devoted to the issue; these are www.sierraclub.org/ca/hetchhetchy, www.hetch hetchy.org, and www.environmentaldefense.org/hetchhetchy, respectively.

The discussion of the contemporary environmental movement, the proposal to remove O'Shaughnessy Dam and restore the Hetch Hetchy Valley, and the response to that proposal benefited from interviews with or input from various stakeholders. In the Sierra Club these were Mike McCloskey, chairman emeritus; Jen Ferenstein, president; and Bruce Hamilton, director of conservation. In the National Park Service: John Reynolds, regional director. At Yosemite National Park: Mike Tollefson, superintendent; his predecessor, Dave Mihalic; Scott Gediman, chief of media & external relations; Martha Lee, YNP liaison to HHWP; and her predecessor, Mary Kline. At Restore Hetch Hetchy: Ron Good, executive director. At Environmental Defense: Spreck Rosekrans. At the Turner Foundation: Mike Finley, executive director. And at the Wilderness Society: Bill Meadows, president.

ACKNOWLEDGMENTS

Thanks to the many officials in public and private organizations who found time in their hectic schedules to chat with me about the complexities of the Hetch Hetchy issue (the titles listed are as of the time of our primary communication): Patricia Martel, general manager, Public Utilities Commission of the City and County of San Francisco, Paula Kehoe, her administrative assistant, Eric Sandler, director of financial planning, Marla Jurosek, acting manager of power operations, and the staff of the Hetch Hetchy Water and Power division (HHWP) in Moccasin, including Alexis Halstead, superintendent of operations, Matthew Gass, engineering manager, Bob Wood, senior engineer, and Khalaf Hirmina, senior electrical engineer; in San Francisco city hall: P. J. Johnston, press secretary to Mayor Willie Brown; Tom Ammiano, president of the board of supervisors; and Tom Owen and Mark Blake, deputy city attorneys; California state senator Jackie Speier and her legislative aide, Mike Paiba, former state assemblyman Lou Papan, and Nick Louizos, his former legislative assistant; in the national office of the Sierra Club: Mike McCloskey, chairman emeritus, Jen Ferenstein, president, and Bruce Hamilton, director of conservation; in the National Park Service: John Reynolds, regional director; at Yosemite National Park: Mike Tollefson, superintendent, and his predecessor, Dave Mihalic, Scott Gediman, chief of media and external relations, Martha Lee, YNP liaison to HHWP and her predecessor, Mary Kline; at Restore Hetch Hetchy: Ron Good, executive director; at Environmental Defense: Spreck Rosekrans; at the Turner Foundation: Mike Finley, executive director; at the Wilderness Society: Bill Meadows, president; at the *San Francisco Bay Guardian:* Bruce Brugmann, editor and publisher; at the *Fresno Bee:* Mark Grossi; at the *San Francisco Chronicle:* Chuck Finnie; at the Santa Clara County Planning Department: Ann Draper, director; at the City of San Jose Department of Planning, Building and Code Enforcement: Stan Ketchum; at the Silicon Valley Manufacturers Group: Margaret Bruce, director of environmental programs; at the Turlock Irrigation District: Larry Weis, general manager/CEO; at the Bay Area Water Supply and Conservation Agency: Art Jensen, general manager; at the California Municipal Utilities Association: Jerry Jordon, executive director; at the California Energy Commission: Andrea Gough; at the U.S. Department of the Interior Bureau of Reclamation: Barry Wirth, regional public affairs officer for the upper Colorado region, and Bob Walsh, external affairs officer for the lower Colorado region; at the Western Area Power Administration: Clayton Palmer, environmental and resource planning manager for the Colorado River Storage Project.

Thanks as well to friends who shared with me their intimate knowledge of the specific aspects of the general controversy, including Brian Gray, Doug Jones, Rod Nash, Joe Neilands, Bob Righter, and Rich Simpson. Harold Gibbs, my hiking partner in Yosemite, shared with me many insights about the region and its management, as well as good companionship.

Katherine Hall at the Moritz Law Library of The Ohio State University, Wendy Owens at the Wallace Stegner Environmental Center and Mitzi Kanbara and Tom Carey at the San Francisco History Center of the San Francisco Public Library, and Theresa Salazar at the Bancroft Collection of Western Americana in the Bancroft Library of the University of California–Berkeley and Paul King in the Institute of Governmental Studies Library at the University of California–Berkeley all assisted my research.

A number of people have lent portions of the manuscript their sharp editorial eyes, including Bruce Brugmann, Matthew Gass, Ron Good, Art Jensen, Ray McDevitt, Rod Nash, Joe Neilands, Alan Paterson, Jim Snyder, Tony Walker, Larry Weis, Don Worster, and David Yaffe. Thanks to each of them for their insights and cooperation. Of course any remaining errors in fact or interpretation are mine alone.

Lastly, my thanks begin and end with Jane Garrett, my editor, and the production staff at Pantheon Books.

J. W. S.
Columbus, Ohio
November 2004

INDEX

About the Author

John Warfield Simpson received a B.S. in landscape architecture from the Ohio State University, an M.L.A. from Harvard University's Graduate School of Design, and an M.A. from Duke University's School of Forestry and Environmental Studies. Since 1983 he has taught at Ohio State, where he is currently professor of landscape architecture and natural resources. In 2001 he was visiting research fellow at Heriot-Watt University in Edinburgh, Scotland. He is the author of Visions of Paradise: Glimpses of Our Landscape's Legacy *(1999) and* Yearning for the Land: A Search for the Importance of Place *(2002). He lives with his wife and children in Upper Arlington, Ohio.*

A Note on the Type

This book was typeset in a digitized version of Engravers' Old Style 205. A transitional typeface based on French copperplate lettering and on the Cochin letterform, it was originally designed in the eighteenth century. Later adapted by Sol Hess, it was revised by Matthew Carter for Bitstream.

Composed by North Market Street Graphics,
Lancaster, Pennsylvania

Printed and bound by Berryville Graphics,
Berryville, Virginia

Maps by David Lindroth

Designed by Iris Weinstein